W9-CXO-912

Legal Office: Concepts and Procedures

Robert Cummins, J.D.
Chairperson, Legal Studies
Southern College
Orlando, Florida

Barbara Tietsort, Consulting Editor
University of Cincinnati
Raymond Walters College
Cincinnati, Ohio

JOIN US ON THE INTERNET
WWW: http://www.thomson.com
EMAIL: findit@kiosk.thomson.com   A service of I(T)P®

South-Western Educational Publishing
an International Thomson Publishing company I(T)P®

Cincinnati • Albany, NY • Belmont, CA • Bonn • Boston • Detroit • Johannesburg • London • Madrid
Melbourne • Mexico City • New York • Paris • Singapore • Tokyo • Toronto • Washington

Managing Editor: Karen Schmohe
Project Manager: Inell Bolls
Production Coordinator: Jane Congdon
Art Coordinator: Ann Small
Marketing Manager: Al S. Roane

ISBN: 0-538-715316

4 5 6 7 8 9 10 DH 09 08 07 06 05 04 03

Printed in the United States of America

Library of Congress Cataloging-in-Publication Data

Cummins, Robert R.
      Legal office : concepts and procedures / Robert R. Cummins.
            p.   cm.
      Includes index.
      ISBN 0-538-71531-6
      1. Legal assistants--United States--Handbooks, manuals, etc.
I. Title.
KF319.C84 1996
340' .02373--dc21   96-39575

                                                CIP

Preface

So great moreover is the regard of the law for private property, that it will not authorize the least violation of it; no, not even for the general good of the whole community.

Sir William Blackstone, *Commentaries on the Law of England (1783)*

The field of study for the legal office assistant, often called legal secretary, has long required a textbook–workbook devoted to the basic concepts of law as they pertain to the tasks required of the legal office assistant. This textbook–workbook is an attempt to provide the legal office assistant with the fundamental concepts of American jurisprudence in a clear and concise manner, allowing the legal office assistant to better support the legal office team. Therefore, I have chosen what I felt to be the essential areas of law and provided an introduction to the basic principles of that field. Each chapter provides fundamental concepts of the law, followed by an analysis of the basic documents supporting that area. The documents are presented with the perspective of content on a paragraph-by-paragraph basis.

Although no single text can attempt to provide coverage of each principle of law for each state, I have attempted to present the basic principles of law and related documents from the standpoint of general American jurisprudence. The legal office assistant student is encouraged at each juncture to consult the substantive and procedural law of the particular state, because there are differences to be found in both form and content. Also, at no point do I intend to suggest that the documents presented are anything more than a *suggested* manner of preparation. In addition to the specific requirements dictated by local court rule, state statute, and case law, the individual client will have definite needs and constraints that compel a deviation from any single general structure. It is the task of the legal office assistant to tailor the general format of the document to the specific needs of the individual client in conformity with state law. This textbook–workbook is designed to teach the legal office assistant student that process.

ORGANIZATION

I have organized this textbook–workbook into three parts to provide the legal office assistant student with a logical frame of reference in the study of the basic concepts of the law. Part 1 provides an analysis of the legal office environment as it relates to the legal office assistant. Chapter 1 takes a close look at the legal office assistant profession, while chapters 2 through 4 review the legal office from the standpoint of its communication needs, record-keeping requirements, and its accounting system.

Part 2 provides the legal office assistant student with an analysis of the court system and the procedures involved in practice before those courts. Chapters 5 and 6 provide a look at the federal and state court systems. Chapter 7 looks at the discovery process, while chapters 8 and 9 present an analysis of appellate procedure and legal research.

Part 3 offers the legal office assistant student an analysis of the fundamental principles of law, involving specific areas of practice. Chapters 10 through 17 provide the legal office assistant student with the substance of the law of domestic relations, torts, criminal law, wills and trusts, contracts, business organizations, real estate, and bankruptcy. Each chapter provides the fundamental concepts of law, along with the legal documents used in each area.

Each chapter provides an epigram related to the content of the chapter. The quotes are designed to elevate the student's thought and orient attention to the subject. The objectives stated for each chapter are my concept of what the legal office assistant student will be able to accomplish after a careful consideration of the content of the text. The text presents the substance of the area concerned, followed by the documents related to that area. The chapter provides marginal notes highlighting the terms used at that point in the text. The purpose here is twofold: the first is to offer a convenient reference for the meaning of each term, and the second is to emphasize the importance of terminology for the legal office assistant. I am of the opinion that if the legal office assistant student can master the terminology of the law, then the concepts of the law are more easily assimilated. Following the summary of each chapter are review questions designed to give the legal office assistant student a convenient review of the materials.

The computer activity at the end of each chapter is a section that I hope will occasionally amuse the legal office assistant student, as well as provide practical, hands-on experience in the preparation of legal documents. Many of these scenarios are taken from factual settings found in actual case law. Each activity involves the retrieval of a sample document or exercise from the student template diskette furnished with the book. The student template is formatted for WordPerfect 6.1 and can easily be converted to Microsoft Word, allowing retrieval through the operating systems and programs used in most colleges. The student is then instructed to key changes to the document, print a hard copy for the instructor, and save the changes on the diskette.

For the legal office assistant, this textbook–workbook will provide a fundamental knowledge of the basic principles of American jurisprudence, along with an opportunity to perform "hands-on" tasks that will be required in the legal office setting. The student will receive invaluable experience to reinforce the concepts discussed in each chapter. Documents and exercises developed on the student template diskette will form the nucleus of a "forms library" for use in the legal office.

ACKNOWLEDGMENTS

This book is the product of the efforts of many individuals, without whose contribution the completion would not have been possible. The love, encouragement, and technical support provided by my wife, Margaret Ann Cummins, allowed me to enjoy this project from inception to completion. It is to her that I offer my most heartfelt gratitude.

I am especially grateful to South-Western Publishing Company for offering me the opportunity to put this effort into print. The efforts of my editors, Dr. Inell Bolls and Barbara Tietsort, have provided the support and vision to make this textbook–workbook a reality. I would also like to acknowledge the following reviewers for their contribution: Mary Gronefeld, PLS, and Julie Settimio, PLS.

Table of Contents

Part 1
Legal Office Environment

Part 2
Court System

Part 3
Substantive Law

Chapter 14
Law of Contracts

Chapter 15
Law of Business Organizations

Chapter 16
Law of Real Estate

Chapter 17
Law of Bankruptcy

Part 1
Legal Office Environment

Chapter 1
Legal Office
Assistant
Profession

Chapter 2
Legal Office
Communication

Chapter 3
Legal Office
Records

Chapter 4
Legal Office
Accounting

1

Chapter 1

Legal Office Assistant Profession

Objectives

After completing this chapter, you will be able to:

1. Describe the general organization of a legal office.

2. Identify the various positions held by individuals in the legal office.

3. Compare the types of legal offices.

4. Understand the Code of Professional Responsibility.

5. Discuss the unauthorized practice of law.

6. Explain the concept of professionalism in a legal office assistant.

7. Describe the attorney/client privilege.

8. Understand the importance of the avoidance of conflict of interest.

9. Outline the concept of legal malpractice.

10. Identify the various organizations available for the legal office assistant.

The goal of a professional legal office is to provide advice and counsel to clients regarding their legal problems. The legal office assistant will find the practice of law to be diverse in nature. There will also be a wide variation in the type and size of the legal office itself. The choice of a career in the field of law as a legal office assistant can provide you with personal and professional challenges.

LEGAL OFFICE ORGANIZATION

Legal offices are diverse in both size and the nature of the law that is practiced. The legal office may be a private law firm consisting of a sole practitioner, a private law partnership made up of several

2

attorneys, or a professional corporation. The legal office also may exist as a legal department of a large corporation or municipal body.

PROFESSIONAL DESIGNATIONS

The typical legal office consists of similar basic professional designations, regardless of its size or the nature of its practice. The basic designations are attorney, office administrator, and legal office assistant. Larger offices might include additional personnel such as receptionists, law clerks, paralegals, bookkeepers, and investigators. Illustration 1-1 provides the structural outline of a typical legal office setting.

Attorney. An **attorney** is an individual authorized to practice law in a state. In a legal office, one or more attorneys are available to provide legal services for clients, render advice on legal matters, and represent clients before tribunals, courts, and administrative agencies. Attorneys are known by the term *lawyer, counselor, barrister, advocate, practitioner,* or *legal advisor.*

To become an attorney, an individual must have completed four years of undergraduate study, preferably with a major emphasis on a pre-law program, receiving a baccalaureate degree. Additionally, the person must earn a Juris Doctor from an accredited law school, which takes three years. Once the graduate has received a law degree, application can be made for admission to the bar in the state selected for practice. Upon successful completion of the bar examination, the individual will then be admitted to practice in that state. Each state has its own set of rules and regulations regarding who may sit for the bar examination. Those rules typically require not only a law degree, but also that the individual seeking admission be of a high moral and ethical character and not have a criminal record. Many law school graduates sit for the bar examination in more than one state to increase their ability to find employment, as well as to broaden the level of service that can be offered to the client.

An attorney in a legal office other than a sole practitioner may be a **partner** or **shareholder.** A partner/attorney, or a shareholder/attorney, is an attorney that has an ownership interest in the legal office, shares in the profits and losses of the firm, and has a management role. The attorney is considered a *partner* if the form of ownership of the legal office is a partnership form of business organization. The attorney is considered a *shareholder* if the form of ownership of the office is a corporation organized under the professional corporation statutes of the state in which the firm is located.

The legal office may also employ non-owner attorneys known as **associate attorneys.** The associate attorney is an employee of the firm and has no real management role other

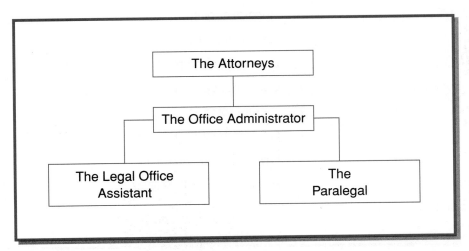

Illustration 1-1
Organization of the Legal Office

attorney

partner
shareholder

associate attorneys

than some duties delegated by a partner. An associate does not share in the profits and losses of the firm, nor in the day-to-day decision-making process. Associates can be considered as candidates for partnership or shareholder status after serving a substantial apprenticeship and proving a definite value to the future of the firm.

administrator

Legal Office Administrator. The office **administrator** is responsible for the general administration of the office, including human resources management, accounting, payroll, budget concerns, and marketing. The administrator may be one of the managing partners of the firm, but usually is a person with a degree in business, finance, or management. Many administrators have obtained a degree in law office management. The role of the legal office administrator is to relieve the day-to-day management load from attorneys, allowing them to concentrate on servicing the needs of their clients. Legal office administrators now have the option of membership in the Association of Legal Administrators, ALA. The term *office manager* is also frequently applied to the position, although usually with smaller firms.

legal office assistant

Legal Office Assistant. The term **legal office assistant** is applied to the professional employee of a legal office who provides assistance and support to the attorney. In many legal offices, the legal office assistant is referred to as the legal secretary. However, to refer to a legal office assistant as a *secretary* brings to mind an image of one who only keys forms and makes coffee. In the modern legal office, the legal office assistant is a highly skilled professional with the specialized abilities listed in Illustration 1-2 to assist the attorney and the client.

Although this list of duties and skills appears extensive, the legal office assistant is trained to handle these and related responsibilities. Many legal office assistants have received formal educational training with an institution offering a curriculum designed specifically for the "legal" office assistant, culminating in a degree. A highly skilled legal office assistant must also possess a command of English grammar, spelling, and punctuation, as well as the basics of mathematics. In addition, a legal office assistant receives training in accounting, legal terminology, and the basic principles of the substantive law. Keyboarding skills are essential—a speed of seventy words per minute (70 wpm), along with a knowledge of several different word processing and spreadsheet software programs, is required.

• Reception for client and office guests	• Recordkeeping
• Telephone responsibilities	• Accounting and payroll
• Mail sorting and handling	• Duplication and photocopying
• Keyboarding, word processing	• Correspondence preparation
• Computer operations	• Proofreading
• Transcription	• Office supply maintenance
• Filing and cataloging	• Law library maintenance
• Document preparation	• Personnel responsibilities
• Docket and calendar maintenance	

Illustration 1-2
The Legal Office Assistant Skills

Depending on the size of the office, the legal office assistant may work for more than one attorney. In a small office, the legal office assistant may be assigned to two or three attorneys, while in a larger firm, each attorney will be assigned a legal office assistant.

TYPES OF LEGAL OFFICES

The nature of the legal office assistant's position is determined to a certain extent by the type of legal office. Although the size of the legal office determines the actual duties and responsibilities expected of the legal office assistant, the type of legal office will dictate the nature of the work.

Government Legal Offices. Many federal, state, and municipal offices and agencies have a legal department that services that particular organization. The government legal department may employ one or more attorneys to provide the legal representation required. The legal office assistant is an essential element, providing the necessary technical skills to support those attorneys, regardless of whether the department is local, state, or national. The government legal office may be responsible for handling various legal matters such as tax law, property law, environmental law, labor relations law, workers' compensation law, condemnation, contract law, or criminal law.

The court system at each level also requires the skills of the legal office assistant. Local, state, and federal courts employ legal office assistants to support government attorneys and judges in their respective capacities.

Corporate Legal Offices. Most large corporations maintain their own legal department. The corporate legal department is concerned solely with those legal matters that directly affect the corporation itself. It is a legal office with only one client: the corporation. Typical corporations that maintain in-house legal offices may include:

- banks
- insurance companies
- large multimillion-dollar companies
- large manufacturers
- hospitals

The corporate legal department is generally structured in an organizational manner similar to the typical legal office, with one or more attorneys serving as both managers and counselors. It is staffed with an administrator, paralegals, and legal office assistants. The duties of the corporate legal office assistant consist primarily of document preparation, correspondence, and record maintenance. The corporate legal department does not bill the corporation for its legal services. Each of the employees assigned to that department is paid a salary, like any corporate employee.

The corporate legal office handles a wide range of legal matters that directly concern the corporation, including:

- taxation
- labor relations
- contracts
- real estate
- environmental concerns
- securities and exchange filings
- general civil litigation

Since the corporate legal department is usually too small to handle all of the corporate legal matters, the department will frequently retain outside private counsel to handle those matters.

Private Legal Offices. The vast majority of attorneys practice law in a private legal office. A private legal office is a business run for profit engaged in the practice of law to provide legal services to a variety of clients. Depending on the number of attorneys, the private legal office may take the form of a sole practitioner, partnership, or professional corporation. A firm would be considered small with one to ten attorneys. A medium-size firm would have ten to fifty or sixty attorneys, and a large firm would have attorneys numbering from sixty to several hundred.

The **sole practitioner** is the most commonly seen type of private legal office; almost half of the attorneys in the United States engage in this type of law practice.

The sole practitioner has a private legal office in which one individual owns all of the assets of the business, and is its sole licensed attorney. This type of private legal office usually handles a wide variety of legal matters in the form of a general practice. The office is structured to keep overhead to a minimum. Thus, the office may consist only of the attorney and his legal office assistant, with each sharing the multiple tasks required to run a law practice. Frequently seen is the situation where a number of sole practitioners share office facilities, receptionist, library, and even legal office assistant to maintain control over expenses.

The **partnership** is a form of private legal office where two or more attorneys own all of the assets of the law firm, yet is organized as a partnership rather than a corporation under the laws of the state in which it practices.

The business organization is covered by a contractual agreement called a partnership agreement. Partnership agreements and the form of ownership will be discussed in greater detail in chapter 15, "Law of Business Organizations." The advantage of the partnership over the sole practitioner is that there is more than one professional to share the burdens of the firm in terms of management, finance, and the provision of legal services to its clients. Also, the partnership is able to offer a wider variety of legal services to its clients by being able to have various partners specialize in different fields of law. The legal office assistant's role in the partnership would consist of the traditional tasks outlined previously, depending on the type of law practiced by the attorney to whom the assistant was assigned.

Professional Corporations. Most states have statutory provisions allowing for the incorporation of a business by individuals offering personal services in a discipline that is licensed by the state. Attorneys fall within that category, and may incorporate under a state charter referred to as a **professional corporation.** The benefit to the private legal office organized as a professional corporation is usually financial, and is related to certain tax advantages that may befall its owners. In addition, the attorneys/owners are not responsible for the liabilities of the corporation. The owners of the professional corporation are the attorneys who might be considered *partners* in another form of ownership. These "partners" own all of the stock of the corporation, elect a board of directors, and maintain a corporate form of government. This will be discussed in greater detail in chapter 15. In addition to attorneys/owners in the professional corporation legal office, the firm usually hires associate attorneys. These are lawyers who do not have an ownership interest in the business and are hired solely as employees. This form of private legal office is structured much the same as the typical legal office, although it may become more departmentalized, depending on its size.

Plaintiff/Defense Legal Offices. Private legal offices can be categorized by their orientation toward the type of client represented. Some offices choose to represent the **plaintiff** in a legal action. The plaintiff is the party to a lawsuit that commences the

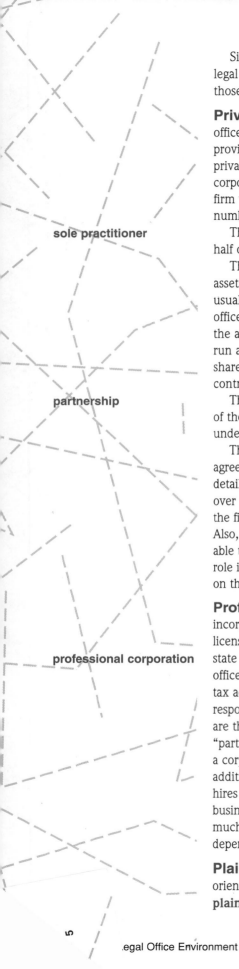

sole practitioner

partnership

professional corporation

action. There are other law firms that are traditionally defense-oriented; that is, they represent the **defendant.** The defendant in a lawsuit is the party against whom an action has been brought.

Since the plaintiff-oriented legal office represents the party originating the action, many of these cases are retained on a **contingency fee** basis, whereby no attorney fee is paid unless there has been a recovery in the case. On the other hand, the defense-oriented firms generally represent the insurance company insuring the risk of the defendant. Those legal offices bill the insurance companies on an hourly basis. From the standpoint of the legal office assistant, the duties involved in the plaintiff-oriented firm will differ from the defense-oriented firm, particularly with the amount of client contact involved. The legal office assistant in the plaintiff-oriented firm will have much more day-to-day contact with the individual plaintiff for information gathering and investigation than will his or her counterpart in the defense-oriented legal office.

ETHICS

A consideration of the issue of legal ethics is important to the legal office assistant. The legal office's clients, and the community in general, must have confidence in the quality of the legal representation offered by the firm. An unethical act on the part of a legal office assistant reflects upon the entire office, and may subject the attorney to official sanction or a lawsuit for legal malpractice. Thus, not only is the reputation, pride, and quality of the office at question, but the legal office may also suffer actual harm from an unethical act.

ETHICAL STANDARD

Ethics is the term that refers to an individual's compliance with a professional standard of conduct and behavior. The **ethical standard** is an established set of rules defining acceptable conduct and motives. When an ethical standard is applied to the law, it is referred to as professional responsibility. Each individual professional practitioner must act responsibly in his or her dealings with clients, the public, and the court system. Ethical standards govern not only the behavior of the attorney, but also determine acceptable conduct and behavior for employees of the legal office.

Legal Ethics. Usages and customs among members of the legal profession, involving their moral and professional duties toward one another, toward clients, and toward courts, are judged by a code of legal ethics—the branch of moral science that addresses the duties a member of the legal profession owes to the public, to the courts, to professional colleagues, and to his clients.

The concept of an ethical standard for attorneys and their employees reflects the belief that the law is tied to a sense of morality and equity. Professionals within the legal system cannot consistently claim to espouse fairness and justice for their clients on the one hand, and conduct themselves irresponsibly on the other.

CODE OF PROFESSIONAL RESPONSIBILITY

American jurisprudence has long supported the idea of a standard of conduct for its licensed professionals, the attorneys. The **American Bar Association (ABA),** a voluntary association of attorneys to improve legal services, adopted the first collection of ethical standards for its attorneys in 1908, titled the *Canon of Professional Ethics.* In 1969 those canons were revised into the *Model Code of Professional Responsibility,* which was then updated to the current ***Model Rules of Professional Responsibility.***

Most states have adopted the *Model Rules* as the basic format for their own code of ethics to be applied to the conduct of attorneys. Strictly speaking, the rules for attorneys

defendant

contingency fee

ethics
ethical standard

American Bar
Association (ABA)

*Model Rules of
Professional
Responsibility*

are not applicable directly to the legal office assistant or any other nonlawyer employee of the legal office. But, the rules do make the attorney responsible for the ethical conduct of his employees. Therefore, if a legal office assistant were to commit an act of unethical conduct, the attorney would be held accountable. Most commonly, the rules of conduct for attorneys require the following:

A practitioner should assist in maintaining the integrity and competence of the legal profession.

A practitioner should assist the legal profession in fulfilling its duty to make counsel available.

A practitioner should assist in preventing the unauthorized practice of law.

A practitioner should preserve the confidences and secrets of clients.

A practitioner should exercise independent professional judgment on behalf of a client.

A practitioner should represent a client competently.

A practitioner should represent a client zealously within the bounds of the law.

A practitioner should assist in improving the legal system.

A practitioner should avoid even the appearance of professional impropriety.

The American Bar Association *Model Rules of Professional Responsibility* provide specifically for the responsibility of the attorney for the conduct of his or her nonlawyer employees, as set forth in Rule 5.3 (Illustration 1-3).

With respect to a nonlawyer employed or retained by or associated with a lawyer:

(A) A partner in a law office shall make reasonable efforts to ensure that the firm has in effect measures giving reasonable assurance that the person's conduct is compatible with the professional obligations of the lawyer.

(B) A lawyer having direct supervisory authority over the nonlawyer shall make reasonable efforts to ensure that the person's conduct is compatible with the professional obligations of the lawyer.

(C) A lawyer shall be responsible for conduct of such a person that would be a violation of Rules of Professional Conduct if engaged in by a lawyer if:

(1) the lawyer orders or, with the knowledge of the specific conduct, ratifies the conduct involved; or

(2) the lawyer is a partner in the law office in which the person is employed, or has direct supervisory authority over the person, and knows of the conduct at a time when its consequences can be avoided or mitigated but fails to take reasonable remedial action.

Illustration 1-3
Rule 5.3: Responsibilities regarding Nonlawyer Assistants   *Model Rules of Professional Responsibility*

Although neither the American Bar Association rules, nor the rules of conduct of individual states, apply to legal office assistants, there have been efforts to create a code of conduct for the assistant. The **National Association of Legal Secretaries (NALS)** has adopted its own *Code of Ethics and Professional Responsibility,* which binds its members to the standards of conduct required of attorneys.

To ensure the integrity and high standards of the legal office assistant profession, NALS has included the following canons in its code:

- Canon 1. Members of this association shall maintain a high degree of competency and integrity through continuing education to better assist the legal profession in fulfilling its duty to provide quality legal services to the public.

- Canon 2. Members of this association shall maintain a high standard of ethical conduct and shall contribute to the integrity of this association and the legal profession.

- Canon 3. Members of this association shall avoid a conflict of interest pertaining to a client matter.

- Canon 4. Members of this association shall preserve and protect the confidences and privileged communications of a client.

- Canon 5. Members of this association shall exercise care in using independent professional judgment and in determining the extent to which a client may be assisted without the presence of a lawyer and shall not act in matters involving professional legal judgment.

- Canon 6. Members of this association shall not solicit legal business on behalf of a lawyer.

- Canon 7. Members of this association, unless permitted by law, shall not perform paralegal functions except under the direct supervision of a lawyer and shall not advertise or contract with members of the general public for the performance of paralegal functions.

- Canon 8. Members of this association shall not perform any of the duties restricted to lawyers or do things that lawyers themselves may not do and shall assist in preventing the unauthorized practice of law.

- Canon 9. Members of this association not licensed to practice law shall not engage in the practice of law as defined by statutes or court decisions.

- Canon 10. Members of this association shall do all other things incidental, necessary, or expedient to enhance professional responsibility and participation in the administration of justice and public service in cooperation with the legal profession.

NALS uses a modified version of its code in the form of a pledge at every meeting, workshop, and conference (see Illustration 1-4). The legal office assistant must be ever mindful that these standards of conduct are purely voluntary, as opposed to those established for the attorney. The ethical standards for attorneys and legal office assistants are designed to ensure the integrity of the profession and to maintain high standards of conduct for its professionals. The adherence to these principles by the legal office assistant will avoid official sanction and professional liability for the attorney.

National Association of Legal Secretaries (NALS)

Every member shall:

ENCOURAGE respect for the law and the administration of justice;

OBSERVE rules governing privileged communications and confidential information;

PROMOTE and exemplify high standards of loyalty, cooperation, and courtesy;

PERFORM all duties of the profession with integrity and competence;

PURSUE a high order of professional attainment.

Illustration 1-4
Code of the National Association of Legal Secretaries *National Association of Legal Secretaries*

PROFESSIONALISM AND CONFIDENTIALITY

professional

A **professional** is someone who is employed in a capacity requiring a high level of training and competence. Professionalism refers to the practice of that high level of training and competence that is expected of the legal office assistant. Although that expectation comes from the legal office, the court system, and the public, it is the client that embodies the greatest trust that his or her interests will be handled in a professional and ethical manner.

PRINCIPLE OF CONFIDENTIALITY

For the client of the legal office to feel that his or her affairs will be handled in a professional manner, he or she must be assured that the firm can be entrusted with that client's affairs, and must be confident that those matters will remain private. That assurance is called **confidentiality.** The client must be made to feel that confidentiality applies not only to communications with the attorney, but also with the nonlawyer staff, which would include the legal office assistant as his or her agent.

confidentiality

The purpose of the principle of confidentiality is to ensure that a client can consult with an attorney without any concern that those communications will be passed on to others, causing some future harm. No client wants private matters aired publicly, or to have them come back to haunt at a later date. Without the security of confidentiality, the client would be reluctant to reveal all of the facts pertaining to his or her case, thus compromising the ability of the attorney to provide effective representation. The principle of confidentiality provides that security.

ATTORNEY–CLIENT PRIVILEGE

Closely related to the principle of confidentiality is an ethical legal standard that has been in existence for centuries, termed the **attorney–client privilege.** It prohibits the disclosure of any confidential communications from the client by an attorney or any person in the office. Preeminent legal scholar Professor Wigmore states:

attorney–client privilege

> (1) Where legal advice of any kind is sought (2) from a professional adviser in his capacity as such, (3) the communications relating to that purpose, (4) made in confidence (5) by the client, (6) are at his instance permanently protected (7) from disclosure by himself or by the legal advisor, (8) except the protection be waived. 8 J. Wigmore, *Evidence* § 2292 (McNaughton rev. ed. 1961).

The attorney–client privilege goes one step further than the principle of confidentiality. Although confidentiality prevents disclosure on an ethical basis, the attorney–client privilege prohibits the nonvoluntary disclosure of confidential communications by the court or any person in an official capacity. No attorney, or employee, may be forced to disclose confidential information. If questioned in court or by the authorities, a refusal to answer is required unless the client has waived the privilege and permitted the disclosure.

The privilege has been embodied in a rule of evidence whereby no privileged communication may be allowed into evidence in court without waiver of the privilege by the client. Thus, if a party to a lawsuit seeks to introduce into evidence some information that was disclosed in confidence, the court will refuse to allow its introduction or any interrogation into the disclosure.

This rule of evidence has been a cornerstone of American jurisprudence for centuries, although the principle is not without exception. The concept of attorney–client privilege has recently received consideration by the United States Supreme Court in the case of *United States v. Zolin* (491 U.S. 554, 109 S.Ct. 2619, 105 L.Ed.2d 469 [1989]), where the court addressed the time-honored principle while recognizing that it is not absolute. In the *Zolin* case, the court was faced with the consideration of the production of sealed documents in the form of tapes by the Internal Revenue Service. The respondents claimed that the tapes were given to their attorney in good faith and that the attorney–client privilege barred their disclosure. The IRS argued that the tapes fell within the "crime-fraud" exception to the privilege in that they were communications in furtherance of future illegal conduct. In holding that the IRS could not gain production of the tapes through the crime-fraud exception to the attorney–client privilege rule, the Court affirmed the validity of the privilege in furtherance of our adversarial form of jurisprudence (see Illustration 1-5).

Questions of privilege that arise in the course of the adjudication of federal rights are "governed by the principles of the common law as they may be interpreted by the courts of the United States in the light of reason and experience (Fed. Rule Evid. 501). We have recognized the attorney–client privilege under federal law, as the "oldest of the privileges for confidential communications known to the common law." . . . Although the underlying rationale for the privilege has changed over time, see 8 J. Wigmore, *Evidence* § 2290 (McNaughton rev. 1961), courts long have viewed its central concern as one "to encourage . . . full and frank communication between attorneys and their clients and thereby promote broader public interests in the observance of law and administration of justice." . . . That purpose, of course, requires that clients be free to "make full disclosure to their attorneys" of past wrongdoings . . . in order that the client may obtain "the aid of persons having knowledge of the law and skilled in its practice." . . .

The attorney–client privilege is not without its costs. . . . "(S)ince the privilege has the effect of withholding relevant information from the factfinder, it applies only where necessary to achieve its purpose." . . . The attorney–client privilege must necessarily protect the confidences of wrongdoers but the reason for that protection—the centrality of open client and attorney communication to the proper functioning of our adversary system of justice—"ceas(es) to operate at a certain point, namely, where the desired advice refers not to prior wrongdoing, but . . . to future wrongdoing." . . . It is the purpose of the crime-fraud exception to the attorney–client privilege to assure that the "seal of secrecy," . . . between lawyer and client does not extend to communications "made for the purpose of getting advice for the commission of a fraud" or crime.

Illustration 1-5
United States v. Zolin   491 U.S. 554, 109 S.Ct. 2619, 105 L.Ed.2d 469 (1989)

work product

A related concept is that of **work product**. The rules of procedure in federal courts, and in virtually all state courts, protect from disclosure any notes, papers, and memorandum of the attorney in preparation for litigation. An attorney, and the persons in the office, must be allowed to record their private strategies, research, investigation, and ideas to prepare for proper representation of a client without fear of disclosure. Thus, the legal office assistant may prepare a memorandum to the attorney regarding the client without concern over the discovery of that information and its disclosure in open court.

CONCEPT OF CONFLICT OF INTEREST

conflict of interest

The concept of **conflict of interest** is an ethical concern that must be adhered to by the attorney and the employees. A conflict of interest occurs where an attorney or the legal office staff have competing professional loyalties that would prevent the firm from acting in that client's best interest. A conflict of interest arises under any of the following conditions:

- An attorney, or any employee of the legal office, simultaneously represents two clients with opposing interests.

- An attorney, or any employee of the legal office, previously represented a client with opposing interests.

- An attorney, or any employee of the legal office, has a personal interest that opposes that of the client.

- An attorney, or any employee of the legal office, has a business interest that opposes that of the client.

Therefore, a conflict of interest exists whenever the situation arises whereby the attorney, or the legal office assistant, has an interest that would interfere with the loyal representation of the interests of the client. Clients of a legal office are entitled to have their interests placed above those of the attorney and the office staff.

LEGAL MALPRACTICE

legal malpractice

An attorney is accountable for his or her actions, and the actions and conduct of the legal office staff, when there has been a **legal malpractice.** Legal malpractice occurs where the lawyer, or a member of the staff, fails to exercise the requisite level of skill and prudence due the client. The failure to adequately protect a client's interests can take many forms. Some of the most common types of malpractice are the following:

- failure to file an action within the time allowed

- failure to know the law

- inadequate investigation of the facts

- clerical error

- conflict of interest

- violation of the attorney–client privilege

- failure to properly calendar an action

- failure to follow a client's instructions

- lack of client consent for a particular act

Regardless of the type of malpractice, the attorney and the legal office face liability in the form of a financial recovery by the client for the damage that results from a malpractice. Most firms carry some form of malpractice insurance to cover such failures, yet the legal office that commits malpractice will suffer greatly from its damaged reputation, and, ultimately, in professional standing.

UNAUTHORIZED PRACTICE OF LAW

Legal office assistants are not permitted to engage in any activity that can be interpreted as practicing law, an area strictly reserved for the attorneys. Such behavior is referred to as the **unauthorized practice of law.** The legal office assistant engaging in such an activity might be guilty of a crime. Every state has a statutory prohibition against the "practice of law" by nonlawyers, rendering such action a criminal offense. For example, the state of Florida's statutory prohibition against the unauthorized practice of law is typical of that found in most states, making the conduct criminal in nature (see Illustration 1-6).

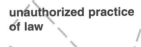

unauthorized practice of law

The purpose behind the law is to prevent incompetence in the legal representation of the client. Although the American Bar Association has not directly defined what constitutes the unauthorized "practice of law," its *Model Rules of Professional Conduct* do prohibit attorneys from assisting nonlawyers in the practice of law. Rule 5.5 spells out this prohibition:

> A lawyer shall not . . .
> (b) assist a person who is not a member of the bar in performance of an activity that constitutes the unauthorized practice of law.

Although there is no definitive interpretation of the "unauthorized practice of law," it is generally considered to be the furnishing of advice on the law as it applies to a particular case or situation. Through judicial interpretation, the courts have held that certain criteria are to be used to resolve the question:

- The activity is one that is traditionally performed by an attorney.

- The activity is commonly understood to be one performed by an attorney.

- The activity involves a personal relationship between the attorney and the client.

- The activity is one in which the public interest is best served by requiring that it be performed by attorneys.

You can avoid any sense of impropriety when it comes to the question of the unauthorized practice of law by following a few simple guidelines:

- Always identify yourself as a legal office assistant.

- Never quote a fee to a client without authorization from an attorney.

- Always have your work supervised by an attorney.

Any person not licensed or otherwise authorized by the Supreme Court of Florida who shall practice law or assume or hold himself out to the public as qualified to practice in this state, or who willfully pretends to be, or willfully takes or uses any name, title, addition, or description implying that he is qualified, or recognized by law as qualified, to act as a lawyer in this state, and any person entitled to practice who shall violate any provisions of this chapter shall be guilty of a misdemeanor of the first degree, punishable as provided . . .

Illustration 1-6
Florida Statutes Annotated   *Florida Statutes Annotated § 454.23*

- Never mail out anything that has not been authorized by an attorney.
- Never tell a client what legal strategy to use.
- Never agree to accept or decline a case without authorization from an attorney.

The legal office assistant will be protected from the unauthorized practice of law by following these few simple guidelines. It is the province of the attorney to provide the advice on the law and to develop a legal strategy. It is the job of the legal office assistant to aid in the implementation of that strategy.

PROFESSIONAL ORGANIZATIONS FOR LEGAL OFFICE ASSISTANTS

There are a number of national, state, and local professional organizations for the legal office assistant. These organizations provide the legal office assistant with continuing education and professional growth opportunities through interaction with other assistants and through the presentation of seminars, workshops, and lectures.

The largest professional organization for the legal office assistant is the National Association of Legal Secretaries, NALS, founded in 1929. The organization was developed to encourage professional growth through educational programs and the promotion of ethical standards. Members include legal office assistants, legal secretaries, office administrators, and employees of public institutions. NALS offers the following to its members:

- texts and handbooks for professional use
- manuals to assist the legal office in developing procedures and systems
- training courses and independent study for certification examination
- educational conferences and seminars

Members may also join a number of specialty divisions within the organization, depending on the nature of the area of legal practice in which they are engaged.

NALS provides for professional certification through an examination process. There are two levels of certification available, the **Accredited Legal Secretary (ALS),** and the **Certified Professional Legal Secretary (PLS).** The ALS certification is obtained by successfully completing a one-day examination covering such topics as written communications comprehension and application, office administration, legal terminology, accounting, ethics, human relations, and applied office procedures. This designation is designed for the apprentice-level legal office assistant.

The PLS certification is achieved by an individual possessing a mastery of professional skills, a working knowledge of procedural law, ability to draft correspondence and legal documents, and ability to interact with attorneys, courts, and clients. A two-day examination is required, covering seven areas of testing:

- written communication skills and knowledge
- ethics
- legal secretarial procedures
- accounting
- legal terminology, techniques, and procedures
- judgment
- legal secretarial skills

Accredited Legal Secretary (ALS)

Certified Professional Legal Secretary (PLS)

For membership information, contact:

National Association of Legal Secretaries
2250 East 73d Street, Suite 550
Tulsa, OK 74136-6864
(918) 493-3540

Another organization, Professional Secretaries International, PSI, also offers a certification program for its members. The Certified Professional Secretary (CPS) designation is achieved by successfully completing a two-day examination covering business law, economics and management, accounting, office administration, and office technology.

Regardless of the organization, the interaction between professional legal office assistants results in a higher level of professionalism. The legal office assistant profession will continue to grow and change with the technological changes occurring in the field of law through contact with these professional organizations.

SUMMARY

The profession chosen by the legal office assistant is one that demands a high degree of technical skill and professional integrity. The legal office is an organization designed for the effective representation of the interests of its clients, regardless of the type of legal office or the nature of the area of practice. The professionals that make up the legal office team—the attorneys, the administrators, the paralegals, and the legal office assistants—all have a role that is integral to that representation. In reality, no one professional is more important than the other. The legal office cannot function without each of its elements in place and operating at an optimum level. The attorney cannot effectively represent the client without the support of the legal office assistant, just as that assistant cannot function without the supervision of the attorney.

The client of the legal office has the right to expect each of the professionals in that office to perform the activities in a manner that conforms with the ethical and legal standards imposed upon the profession by the state legislature. The client has the right to expect the legal office assistant to comply with the established ethical standards; respect confidentiality; not violate the rule of attorney–client privilege; avoid any conflict of interest; not commit any form of legal malpractice; and not engage in the unauthorized practice of law. It is through strict adherence to such long-standing ethical principles, continually reinforced through professional association, that the legal office assistant can be a professional.

Chapter Activities

Review Questions

1. List the professional legal office designations in the typical legal office.

2. Describe the various types of legal offices.

3. Discuss the forms of ownership that can be applied to a private legal office.

4. What is an ethical standard as it applies to the legal office assistant?

5. Summarize the relevance of the ABA *Model Rules of Professional Responsibility* to the legal office assistant.

6. What is the rationale behind the principle of confidentiality?

7. Discuss how the attorney–client privilege affects the legal office assistant.

8. What is the principle of work product as concerns the legal office assistant?

9. How do the principles of legal malpractice affect the conduct of the legal assistant?

10. Discuss the guidelines that the legal office assistant should follow to avoid the unauthorized practice of law.

Computer Activity

You are a recent graduate of your college's legal office assistant program and have been hired by two new attorneys who are just setting up their own legal office. The attorneys, Hiram Bask and Renate Glow, have formed a professional corporation (P.C.) for the practice of law in your state, called Bask & Glow, P.C. They have hired Ms. Virginia Reel as their paralegal and intend to have a general practice, representing individual clients in the areas of domestic relations, wills, and bankruptcy.

The attorneys are concerned about the responsibilities of the employees of the firm; they want to avoid any breach of an ethical standard and to prevent a legal malpractice. They are of the opinion that an organizational chart of the firm would provide a clear picture of the responsibilities of each person in the legal office.

A. From the student template retrieve act1.doc. This document is an organizational chart to be completed with the identification of the appropriate individuals represented in this scenario. Beneath the designation for legal office assistant, prepare a list of responsibilities that will fall onto you. Refer to the chapter for examples.

B. Save this information on the template as orgchart.doc.

C. Print one copy for your instructor. Make sure your name appears for identification purposes.

Chapter 2

Legal Office Communication

The information highway is moving forward at a high rate of speed. New equipment, methods, and programs are being developed almost daily.

Eugene Bartlett,
Cable Communications

Objectives

After completing this chapter, you will be able to:

1. Understand the role of the computer in the legal office communications.

2. Describe the various components of the computer hardware.

3. Compare the various types of computer software available for the legal office.

4. Summarize the nature and use of the equipment necessary for the legal office communications.

5. Profile proper communication with the client.

6. Explain the "seven canons of client communication" for the legal office assistant.

7. Demonstrate proper telephone etiquette.

8. Understand the role of the written communication in the legal office.

The business of any legal office is the processing and communication of information essential to the office, the court, other attorneys, and the general public. The modern legal office environment depends on the efficient and accurate communication of that information. The legal office assistant must facilitate communication of information, both internally and outside the legal office, at every level through the use of equipment, personal contact, and written communication.

17

LEGAL OFFICE EQUIPMENT

Equipment used to process and communicate information within the legal office is changing rapidly, reflecting growth in modern technology. Information processing begins with the computer, used by virtually every legal office in the United States. It is supported by additional equipment such as copy machines, dictation equipment, typewriters, postage machines, telephones, facsimile machines, and on-line information services.

computer

COMPUTER

No single piece of equipment has done more to revolutionize and facilitate communication in the modern legal office than the computer. The computer is used for information storage, word processing, litigation support, accounting, recordkeeping, and multitask jobs. The information system that constitutes the computer is made up of two elements: (1) its hardware components and (2) its software programs. The legal office assistant is a key factor in that information system, because it will not function without human interaction.

Hardware. A **computer** is an electronic device to accept and store data, execute a program of instructions, and report the results. It is an integral part of the legal office information system, and can consist of anything from a single computer to a large system based on a mainframe unit.

hardware

The physical devices of a computer are known as **hardware,** and consist of four basic components:

- central processing unit (CPU)
- monitor
- keyboard
- printer

These four physical pieces of equipment function in harmony as a system to process and deliver information through the operation of the hardware by the legal office assistant, as shown in Illustration 2-1.

central processing unit (CPU)

A **central processing unit (CPU)** is the main information processing component of the computer. It receives input data through the keyboard, stores the data electronically, organizes it, and delivers it through output devices such as the monitor and the printer.

microprocessor chip

The "brain" of the CPU is its **microprocessor chip,** which is made up of silicon electronic circuitry that performs the mathematical functions of the computer to process information.

data
memory

Information is stored in the computer in the form of **data.** Data are stored in the computer's **memory,** which is made up of more silicon electronic circuitry to hold information in electronically arranged clusters.

hard drive

The memory of the CPU is referred to as its **hard drive,** which is nothing more than a name for the data storage function of the unit. Hard drives are measured by the amount of data that can be stored electronically, referred to as **megabytes.**

megabytes

floppy disk

All computers have the capacity to store and process data on another storage facility called the **floppy disk.** The floppy disk (also called a diskette) is a plastic storage diskette

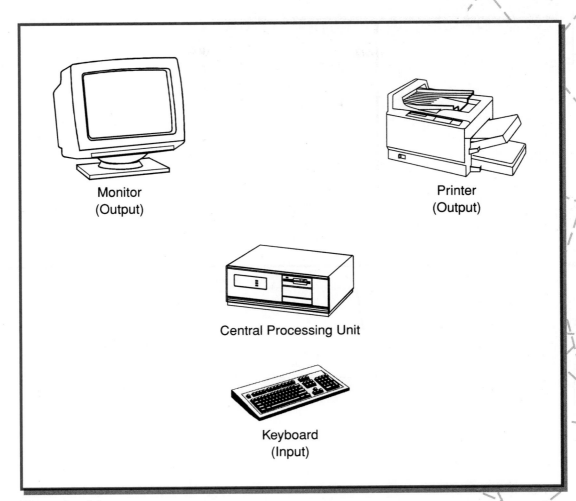

Monitor
(Output)

Printer
(Output)

Central Processing Unit

Keyboard
(Input)

Illustration 2-1
Computer Hardware Components

used in all computers for saving information in the form of data or software programs. The CPU can write information to the floppy disk or it can read information from the floppy disk. A floppy disk is 3½ inches square, and can hold approximately 1.4 megabytes of information, or about 1,400 pages of text. See Illustration 2-2.

Computer systems for the legal office come in a variety of sizes and configurations, based on speed and capacity. The largest of the computer systems is the **mainframe computer**, which is an immensely powerful computer capable of processing a huge volume of information. Mainframes are used by large legal offices such as government facilities, or a few of the nation's largest of law firms. The legal office assistant communicates through the use of a **terminal**, which consists of a monitor and a keyboard but has no internal computing capability. See Illustration 2-3.

Closely related to the mainframe computer is the **minicomputer**. It has significantly less memory and capacity, yet can still process a large volume of information. Minicomputers are used for data processing on a large volume, such as would be required in a law firm of a hundred or more attorneys. Both the mainframe and the minicomputers require full-time operators.

The **microcomputer** is the smallest category of computer, known as a "PC," ranging in size from portable laptop models to standing floor models. The microcomputer is popular with most legal offices and is the equipment with which most legal office

mainframe computer

terminal

minicomputer

microcomputer

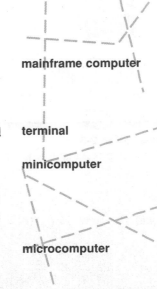

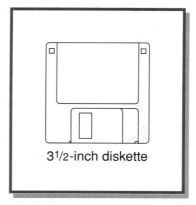

Illustration 2-2
Sample Floppy Diskette

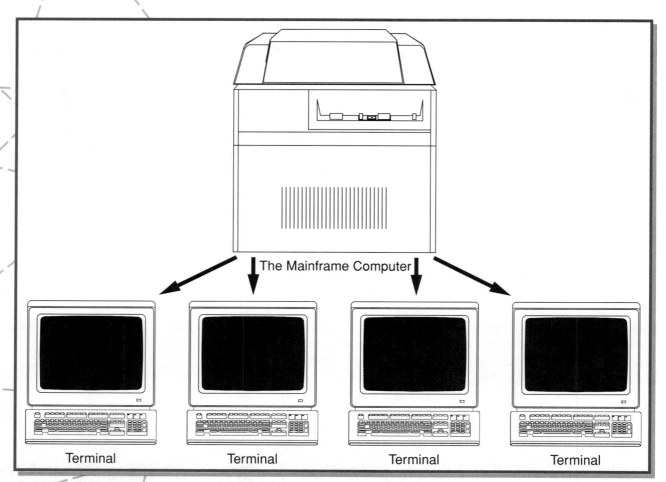

The Mainframe Computer

Terminal   Terminal   Terminal   Terminal

Illustration 2-3
The Setup of a Mainframe Computer System

assistants will find themselves familiar. It is an end-user system in that it is not dependent on a mainframe for processing information. It may be linked to other microcomputers in the office through a **local area network (LAN)**. A LAN is a system to link independent microcomputers to share data, software, and peripheral devices such as printers through a common computer server, as shown in Illustration 2-4.

Information in the form of data is entered into the computer through the use of input peripheral devices. The most essential device is the **keyboard**, which is a platform with

local area network (LAN)

keyboard

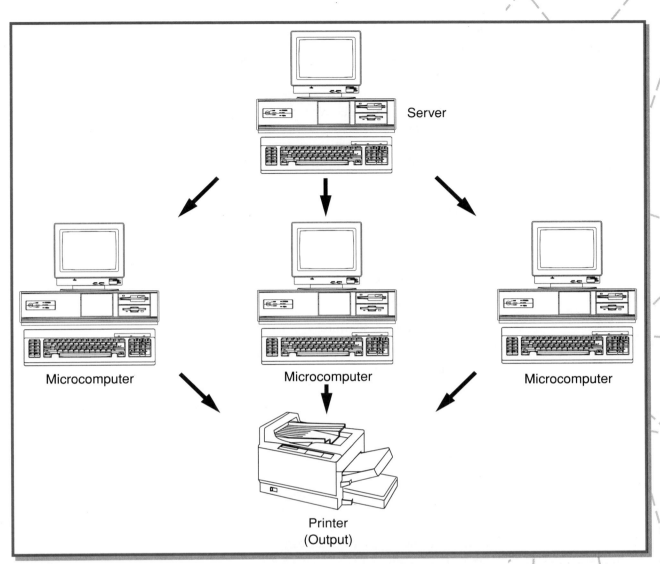

Illustration 2-4
A Local Area Network (LAN)

keys similar to a typewriter, along with alphanumeric keys, function keys, and cursor moving keys. Another input device is the **mouse,** which is a pointing device used to move the cursor around the screen of the monitor to perform various functions.

The information generated by the computer is provided by output devices such as the **monitor** and the **printer.** A monitor is similar to a television screen for the display of information. A printer is used to produce the information onto paper, known as a *hard copy.*

Software. The hardware of the computer is of no value without a set of instructions directing it to perform tasks. That set of instructions comes in the form of **software,** or what is known as a *computer program.* The legal office assistant must be familiar with the two basic types of software:

- operating system software

- application software

Operating system software is the computer program that instructs the computer hardware on how to communicate within itself. There are several different types of

mouse

monitor
printer

software

operating system software

operating system programs from which to choose, depending upon the size of the computer. Large mainframe computers may use an operating system such as UNIX or OS/2. Microcomputers usually use an IBM-compatible operating system such as MS-DOS or Windows 95. **MS-DOS,** Microsoft Disk Operating System manufactured by Microsoft Corporation, has been the most widely used operating system for microcomputers, but is rapidly being replaced by the Windows operating environment.

It is known as a single-user, single-tasking system using a system of programmed commands to perform such jobs as copying files and formatting disks. MS-DOS is a text-based operating system, while Microsoft **Windows** is a graphical operating system using icons, dialog boxes, and a mouse to communicate with the hardware and perform operations.

Application software consists of a computer program that directs the information processing tasks required by the operator. Applications are generally categorized as:

- word processing software
- spreadsheet software
- database software
- communication software

Word Processing Software. Software is used to create documents by keying letters, numbers, symbols, and graphics into the computer. It then allows the user to edit and format the text created before printing. On a daily basis, the legal office assistant will become most familiar with word processing software. The most widely used word processing software programs in legal offices are WordPerfect, manufactured by Novell, Inc., and Microsoft Word, manufactured by Microsoft Corporation. Many other applications are available for word processing and related tasks, such as desktop publishing and presentation graphics.

Spreadsheet Software. Software that allows a user to display numbers and financial information for financial management is called spreadsheet software. It is used by many legal offices for budgets, payroll, cash management, and other financial calculations. Many spreadsheet applications are designed exclusively for the legal office accounting needs. Timeslips, manufactured by Timeslips Corporation, and Verdict, manufactured by Micro Craft, Inc., are two legal timekeeping and billing software programs used by many legal offices.

Database Software. Software that is designed to store large amounts of information such as names, addresses, and zip codes, and that allows the user to categorize the information by search and sorting, is called database software. A typical use for the legal office might be a database of names and addresses of clients and local attorneys with whom there is regular correspondence. The WordPerfect and Microsoft Word programs both offer a database capability.

Communication software is designed to allow the legal office to communicate electronically over telecommunication lines. Such systems as electronic mail, voice mail, and facsimile machines can greatly reduce the amount of paperwork for the legal office assistant, along with providing rapid communication of information.

COPY MACHINE

The copy machine, or photocopier, is the most common piece of office equipment in the legal office today. Multiple copies of documents are routinely required for the office files, courts, opposing counsel, clients, and others. Copy machines come in many different shapes and sizes, depending on their capabilities. The following features vary among copiers:

- pages per minute copied

- automatic document feed

- sorter and stapler

- duplexing or two-sided copies

- multiple paper-size capacity

- enlargement and reduction

The cost of a copy machine for the legal office is related to its features and the volume of copying to be done. It is not uncommon for a legal office assistant to produce tens of thousands of copies annually.

TYPEWRITER

Utilization of the typewriter has declined with the increased application of the computer in the legal office. A computer can perform most of the tasks of the typewriter more rapidly and with greater flexibility. However, there is still a place for the typewriter with the legal office assistant. Many areas of the law require the use of preprinted forms for courts, bureaus, and agencies. These forms cannot easily be completed using a computer. Thus, the information required must be supplied manually, through the use of the typewriter. In addition, odd size envelopes and labels are easier to complete with a typewriter. The modern typewriter has many of the same features as a computer when it comes to word processing, such as spell-checking, boldface, italics, assorted fonts, and memory. The legal office assistant will find familiarity with the typewriter to be a helpful skill.

DICTATION EQUIPMENT

Dictation equipment is used for the oral creation of a letter or legal document to be later transcribed into "hard copy" by the legal office assistant through the use of a computer or typewriter. Some hand-held equipment uses microcassettes, while desktop machines may use the standard cassette. Although dictation may be more cumbersome than other forms of document production because it involves several stages of development, it does have the advantages of portability and can be accomplished by the attorney while the legal office assistant is engaged in other tasks.

POSTAGE MACHINE

The practice of law requires a substantial reliance on the U.S. Postal Service. The postage machine automatically applies the proper amount of postage required for mailing. The proper postage may be applied either directly to the envelope or to a label, which is then affixed to a larger envelope. The postage machine may either be owned or rented by the legal office. Regardless of the form of ownership, the upper portion of the machine must be taken to the post office for billing purposes. The use of the postage machine has declined somewhat with the rise in use of alternative postal and package services, such as UPS and RPS discussed in chapter 3, as well as the use of electronic transmission of documents.

TELECOMMUNICATIONS EQUIPMENT

Telecommunications is a term applied to the sending of any information by voice, data, or image signal over long distances through communication technology. The legal office assistant can no longer be content to rely solely on a basic knowledge of how to place and take a call. Office automation for the legal office consists of the telephone, voice mail, facsimile machines, modem communication, and electronic mail.

telecommunications

Telephone Equipment. A telephone system is a key component of any legal office communication equipment scheme. It is through the use of the telephone that attorneys and office staff communicate with clients, attorneys, courts, agencies, and each other. The system utilized by the legal office will vary greatly, depending on the size of the office. A sole practitioner may need only a simple system with two to four lines and extensions, while a large legal office will require a **Private Branch Exchange (PBX)**.

The features offered with the larger systems can include the following:

- *Hold*—the user may stay connected to the caller without maintaining direct contact.

- *Speaker*—the user may talk on the phone without lifting the receiver.

- *Speed-dialing*—preprogrammed numbers frequently called can be dialed with the use of one button.

- *Discriminating ring*—the ring pattern varies with outside calls or inside extension calls.

- *Call transfer*—an incoming call can be transferred to another extension.

- *Call pickup*—to continue a conversation at another location, the call can be "parked" at one location and picked up at another.

- *Conference calls*—multiple lines can be connected for a telephone conference.

- *Camp-on-call*—the operator can "beep" the user to advise of another incoming call.

- *Automatic call-back*—if a call is placed to a busy number, it can be called back when the line is free merely by lifting the handset.

- *Call forwarding*—a call can be diverted to another number or extension after a pre-set number of rings.

- *Intercom paging*—individuals can be paged within the office.

- *Account coding*—a call can be logged to a client billing code automatically.

- *Liquid crystal display (lcd)*—the feature allows the user to display the amount of time of a call for billing purposes, as well as the number of the incoming call.

In addition to the features offered by an office system, telecommunications carriers offer a wide variety of services. A common feature for the legal office is to maintain a **Wide Area Telecommunications Service (WATS)** to reduce the cost of long-distance calling. Local carriers offer the WATS line as a flat monthly rate for a line that can be used as often as needed. The WATS line can be used solely for outgoing calls, referred to as an outward line, or it may also be used for inward lines. It is through inward lines that larger legal offices can be accessed through an 800-number.

Local telecommunications carriers offer other services that can also benefit the smaller office and do not require the use of an expensive PBX system. The services may include:

- *Call waiting*—a tone will signal an incoming call while the user is on a current call. The current call can be placed on hold to access the new incoming call.

Private Branch Exchange (PBX)

Wide Area Telecommunications Service (WATS)

- *Call forwarding*—local and long distance calls can be transferred to another number.

- *Three-way calling*—a third party can be added to a local or long distance conversation for conference calling.

- *Speed dialing*—frequently called numbers are input into the phone's memory so they can be accessed with a one- or two-digit number.

As an alternative to the services provided by the local telecommunications carriers that serve major metropolitan areas, communication services are also available from large national and international carriers, such as MCI Telecommunications, Southern Pacific Communication (SPRINT), United States Transmission Systems, Western Union (MICRO), and others.

Voice Mail. Closely related to the computerized telecommunications of many legal offices is a system that stores and delivers voice messages, called **voice mail**. In voice mail, a telephone call is forwarded to a person's voice "mailbox" automatically when that person is unavailable. The caller may then leave a message to be retrieved at a later time. The advantage of voice mail is the fact that it can operate when the office is not open. This computerized system does not require the use of an operator or legal office assistant to operate, and allows the assistant to be otherwise productive.

Facsimile Machine. The **facsimile machine (fax)** is used for the transmission of text and graphic images for their reconstruction and duplication at a receiving location. The equipment operates through the use of a specialty fax machine at one location that employs a high-speed modem. A document is inserted into the machine and is transmitted over a telephone line to a similar machine at a different phone number at the rate of one to four pages per minute. Many personal computers in the legal office contain the modem hardware and facsimile circuitry to allow the transmission of a document directly from the computer over the telecommunication lines to a fax machine or another computer comparably equipped. Thus, the fax-equipped personal computer employed by the legal office assistant can now serve as a printer for a computer located many miles away. Depending on the rules of the local judiciary, documents may be filed with the court by fax, as long as the documents are of limited length.

Modem and Information Services. Through the use of a **modem,** the telecommunication capability of the computer is virtually unlimited. The modem is an electronic peripheral device for a computer that allows the computer to exchange information with another computer over telecommunication lines. It is through the use of a computer's modem that the legal office assistant may access any of the legal information services that are available by subscription to the legal office. Those services include on-line legal research and legal news for attorneys such as:

- WESTLAW

- LEXIS/NEXIS

- ABA/NET

In addition to the legal research and news services, the Internet information superhighway may be accessed through the use of the modem by subscribing to one of the major on-line providers such as America Online, Prodigy, CompuServe, Reuters, or Dow-Jones. Local Internet access servers are also available for the legal office, depending on the nature of its practice. The information superhighway will become an increasingly important tool for the legal office in the years to come.

voice mail

facsimile machine (fax)

modem

electronic mail (E-mail)

Electronic Mail. Electronic mail (E-mail) in the legal office can be employed to defeat that perennial gremlin of information float known as "telephone tag." E-mail lets an individual send an electronic message anywhere within the office or to another computer in another legal office. The message is stored in the receiver's computer for retrieval at that person's convenience. E-mail reduces paper flow and information lag, offering a tremendous reduction in time/cost to the legal office. The legal office assistant will find an increase in efficiency through the use of E-mail. It is available commercially through the Internet providers such as CompuServe or Prodigy.

INTERACTION WITH THE CLIENT

An effective relationship with its clients is one of the major factors in the success of any legal office. Thus, communicating in a positive and effective manner with the client is of the utmost importance to the legal office assistant. The skills required to maintain a good client relationship are based on the ability of the assistant to effectively exchange information and ideas with others. The communication of information and ideas occurs through personal client relationships, use of the telephone, and written communication.

SEVEN CANONS OF CLIENT COMMUNICATION

Generally speaking, the foundation of the legal office's relationship with its clients is good, sound communication. Good client communication allows the legal office to provide effective legal representation. The role of the legal office assistant can be significant in the communication with the client, and can "make or break" an effective client relationship.

communication

Communication with the client consists of the exchange of information and ideas relative to the case. The following seven canons of client communication are essential for the legal office assistant to maintain the development of good client relationships.

Canon 1. Be Professional. The professional legal office assistant is mindful of client confidentiality and privacy. Adherence to the *Canons of Professional Responsibility* will form the basis of professionalism. But professionalism also requires that the legal office assistant use tact and courtesy to communicate effectively with the client. Rude behavior by the legal office assistant is not to be tolerated. An attitude of cooperation must be maintained at all times, along with empathy for the needs of the individual client.

Canon 2. Be Timely. Promptness and timeliness in responding to the needs of the client are of paramount importance to the legal office assistant. Every client of a legal office has the right to be considered the most important person that the office is handling. No single complaint is heard more frequently than that the client's interests were not met promptly. Telephone calls must be returned in a timely fashion, correspondence must be answered and sent promptly, and promises to act must be kept. Such concern to the immediate needs of the client will foster effective client communication.

Canon 3. Treat Each Client As Your Own. If the legal office assistant can remember to treat each and every client of the office as important to the well-being of the firm, then the client will be justified in the feeling of importance to the legal office. The client must not be kept waiting in the lobby or on the telephone beyond what is considered normal courtesy. The client must never be made to feel that the assistant, or anyone else in the office, has more important things to do. An attitude of treating each client as being responsible for the livelihood of the office will foster effective client communication.

Canon 4. Avoid Legalese. Any attempt to appear more knowledgeable than the client on matters of the law concerning the client's case will create a barrier to communication. No client wants to be "talked down to." The client is well aware that it is the legal expertise of the particular office that formed the basis for its selection. To adopt an attitude of superiority will serve only to intimidate the client and reduce the ability to communicate effectively.

Therefore, the legal office assistant should at all times remember to communicate with the client at the client's level of understanding. Complicated matters of the law should be left to the attorneys to explain. Using legal jargon can only serve to cause confusion and create a communication gulf because the client will not be familiar with the terminology.

Canon 5. Send Status Reports. Each client is entitled to be informed of the status of the case. Periodic reporting to the client of the progress being made, or an explanation for any delay, will help maintain effective client communication. You should develop a procedure to furnish the client with copies of all relevant documents, pleadings, memos, and letters concerning the case. The client has retained the legal office for more than the achievement of a result. The client must be made a part of the "process" in achieving that result.

Canon 6. Be Prepared. In all dealings with the client, the legal office assistant must have a current knowledge of the status of the client's case. Nothing can be more disconcerting to a client than to be made to feel that no one knows what is going on. You should be well organized before contacting a client and should have anticipated the client's concerns and questions. A few moments spent in preparation for some contact with the client will produce efficient and professional communication. Preparation includes the review of the client's file, the making of a list of matters to be reviewed, and consultation with the attorney assigned to the matter.

Canon 7. Listen! Good communication is based on good listening skills. Effective client communication requires that the legal office assistant master the skill of listening. The client has information that is essential to the handling of the case. The legal office assistant can be more effective in fostering good client relationships by learning how to listen patiently before asking any questions or attempting to convey any information. To assist the listening process, you should learn to repeat the client's name in conversation, and to make frequent eye contact. Responses to any questions from the client should be answered directly and as completely as possible.

TELEPHONE ETIQUETTE

The telephone is the most frequently used communication device in the legal office. It is incumbent upon the legal office assistant to be aware of the proper etiquette in using the telephone for communication with clients, other attorneys, the courts, and the general public. **Etiquette** is the term that applies to the form and manners considered essential in a professional setting.

etiquette

When using the telephone, be mindful of form and manners throughout the telephone process. The stages of the telephone process consist of:

- developing a proper telephone personality
- planning the call
- placing the call
- listening
- answering the call
- screening the call
- transferring the call
- taking messages
- placing the call on hold
- ending the call

In each phase of the telephone process, professional form and manners must be maintained by the legal office assistant, as shown in this photo.

Developing a Proper Telephone Personality. It is through the telephone that the legal office assistant can create an image of professionalism. Since the caller cannot "see" the assistant, it is imperative that a positive impression be made through energy and enthusiasm. A standard greeting delivered in a natural and pleasant manner with clear enunciation will avoid a negative impression. If possible, use the caller's name as soon as an identification has been made, thus avoiding having to ask for it to be repeated. "Please," "thank you," and "you're welcome" are powerful phrases that will convey a friendly and professional manner.

Planning the Call. Before each telephone call is placed, the legal office assistant should carefully plan the message as if it were to be in writing. Notes should be made of relevant information, and necessary documents should be at hand. In planning the call, it is best to make the call at a time that is convenient for the recipient in order to avoid wasted time and effort by merely leaving a message. Planning creates a professional image and shows consideration for the person being called.

Placing the Call. The placement of the call begins with the correct telephone number and extension, if necessary. Record the number in case the individual is busy on the first attempt. When the recipient answers, identify yourself in a professional manner. Do not assume that the recipient will recognize a voice. If a great deal of information is to be exchanged, it is considerate to inquire if the individual has time for the conversation, and, if not, suggest an alternative. If the legal office assistant is placing the call on behalf of an attorney or supervisor, it is considerate to be sure that the attorney or supervisor is available at that time.

Listening. As in face-to-face conversation, the legal office assistant will appear professional through the development of good listening skills. Concentration on the other person will avoid having to have information repeated. The telephone conversation should be approached just as though the conversation was face-to-face. You should avoid trying to perform other tasks while engaged in a telephone conversation.

Answering the Call. The professional legal office assistant should demonstrate efficiency by answering the call promptly and courteously on the first or second ring. No caller likes to be kept waiting, and is unaware that the assistant may be busy with other matters at the time the call is placed. When the call is answered, the assistant should cease the task being performed at the time, and devote full attention to the call. An attempt to do two or three things simultaneously appears inconsiderate and unprofessional. The caller will realize if he or she does not have the full attention of the assistant, particularly if work or conversations in the background can be overheard.

Screening the Call. Screening calls for an attorney or supervisor is one of the most delicate tasks of the legal office assistant. The caller should be made to feel important, but should be told that the timing is not good for the attorney. An offer to be of personal assistance is the most effective means of screening the call and yet assuring delivery of the information. If the caller will not accept assistance, and is insistent on speaking with the attorney, then advising that the individual is unavailable at the moment and taking a message is appropriate. The caller's name should have been secured at the initial greeting in order to avoid the embarrassing situation where the caller is told that the attorney is not available only after the caller is identified. A professional and courteous manner to screen calls when the attorney is in the office but is unavailable to speak to that individual is to use a phrase such as: "Mr. Wilson is not available at the moment. May I help you?"

If the attorney or supervisor for whom the calls are being screened is not in the office, one of the following phrases might be appropriate:

- "Mr. Wilson is not expected until later in the morning. May I help you?"

- "Mr. Wilson will be out of the office until Monday morning. May someone else help you, or may I take a message?"

The circumstance of being caught in an embarrassing untruth can directly affect the reputation of the office and the professionalism of the legal office assistant. Most callers will soon be aware when they are being deceived, and such action will reflect unfavorably on the office. The legal office assistant can be polite, yet firm, in stating that the attorney is unavailable and that assistance or the leaving of a message is available. Such a response will never serve to embarrass the office or the assistant.

Transferring the Call. Routine telephone matters should be handled by the legal office assistant. If assistance cannot be provided, then the call can be referred to the attorney or supervisor. The transfer of the call should be completed with the permission of the caller. If the caller does not wish to be transferred, then you should suggest that the call be placed at a later time.

Taking Messages. The situation will arise frequently where the legal office assistant cannot provide the necessary assistance, and a message must be taken. Most offices have preprinted message pads detailing the date and time of the call, the caller, the person being called, message text, and a selection as to what response the message requires. Some callers will wish to call back, while some may wish to have the attorney call back when available. It is the responsibility of the legal office assistant to ascertain how the caller desires the message handled.

Placing the Call on Hold. Various reasons may occur to place the caller on hold while a call is being transferred or information is being sought. It is the responsibility of the legal office assistant to secure the caller's permission to be placed on hold temporarily. A lengthy period of time on hold will cause the caller to become impatient and irritated, and can be avoided by using phrases such as:

- "I am sorry to keep you waiting. Mr. Wilson should only be a few more minutes. Would you like to continue to hold, or may I take a message?"

- "Thank you for waiting. I can transfer your call now."

- "I appreciate your patience. I have the information that you need."

The legal office assistant that leaves the caller on hold for less than thirty seconds will appear efficient and professional to the caller, leaving a favorable impression of the office.

Ending the Call. The legal office assistant should always terminate the call with a courteous closing and a gentle replacing of the handset. Colloquial phrases such as "Thanks," "Caio," or "Bye-Bye" do not sound professional. The phrase, "Have a nice day," is overused and should be avoided. An acceptable closing would be:

- "Thank you for calling, Mr. Jones. Good-bye."

- "You're welcome, Mr. Jones. Good-bye."

Telephone calls occur multiple times throughout the business day of the legal office assistant. They require a high skill level to convey courtesy and professionalism to the caller, creating a favorable impression of the office and the assistant.

WRITTEN COMMUNICATION

Traditionally, the law has relied on the written word as the best expression of intention. No other form of expression in the legal office is more critical than written communication. It is important that the legal office assistant appreciate the significance of the written communication to express ideas clearly and persuasively.

WRITING PRINCIPLES

The fundamental rule of writing for the legal office assistant is to direct the communication as though talking directly to the recipient. The writer should avoid colloquialism, slang, and jargon, as well as appearing too mechanical and stiff. Professional written communication for the legal office assistant should express the proper (1) tone, (2) conciseness, (3) grammar, and (4) accuracy. Always proofread your work.

tone

Tone. The **tone** of the written communication is the attitude of the writer as expressed through the written word. The legal office assistant should ensure that the tone of the communication is courteous and personal, and that it expresses a concern for the interests of the recipient. Tone reflects the ability of the writer to anticipate the viewpoint of the reader and to select phraseology to address that view.

Negative words and phrases have no place in the written communication if it is intended to be courteous and professional. The following suggestions will illustrate how the same message can be conveyed without negativity.

Negative: The deadline is June 30.
Positive: You have until June 30 to respond.

Negative: You have failed to pay as per the agreement.
Positive: Please forward your draft to comply with the agreement.

Negative: Mr. Wilson will be unavailable for depositions in the month of August.
Positive: Mr. Wilson will be available for depositions after September 1.

There are a number of phrases used in written communication that contribute to an archaic tone in the writing. You can create a more natural tone by avoiding phrases like those that appear in the following list:

acknowledge receipt thereof	in reference to
attached hereto	inasmuch
await your reply	permit me to
duly recorded	take the liberty to
enclose herewith	thank you in advance
for your information	the undersigned
in accordance with your request	upon receipt thereof
in lieu of	with reference to

Tone is also conveyed in the *voice* of the sentence. If the subject of the sentence is acting, then the sentence uses **active voice.** If the subject of the sentence is acted upon, then the sentence uses **passive voice.** Sentences written in the active voice have more impact than those written in passive voice because they state information quickly and forcefully. The following examples of active voice versus passive voice show the direct impact of the former:

Passive: The deposition was taken by Mr. Wilson on Tuesday.
Active: Mr. Wilson took the deposition on Tuesday.

Passive: The agreement was mailed to you on Friday.
Active: Mr. Wilson mailed the agreement on Friday.

The voice used in the legal office written communication can make the writer appear to be more professional by seeming to be more actively involved in the process, rather than merely present.

Conciseness. Conciseness refers to the expression of the message in as few words as possible. A writing that is too wordy wastes both the writer's and the reader's time, and is often unclear as to its message. If the writer has used terms redundantly, confusion may occur. If the writer has been too brief, the reader will not be informed. A communication that is concise appears to be clear and efficient, creating the impression of a writing that is courteous and professional.

Grammar. The legal office assistant must have a good foundation in the principles of sound grammatical correctness. Nothing can detract from a written communication, and appear more unprofessional, more surely than grammatical errors. Numerous references are available for the legal office assistant to resolve grammatical questions as they arise, and should be kept at hand. Ensuring accuracy in such grammatical concerns as pronoun usage, subject–verb agreement, tense, modifiers, and parallelism is the responsibility of the legal office assistant. The attorney should not be relied upon as the final arbiter of grammatical usage.

Proofreading. The final responsibility for the accuracy and appearance of any written communication rests with the legal office assistant. Proofreading should include an emphasis on the content of the document, as well as a check for spelling errors, grammatical usage, punctuation, and accuracy of dates and address. Proofreading is best accomplished by reading the written communication from the standpoint of the recipient.

WRITER'S TOOLS

A number of tools can assist the legal office assistant in the creation of a professional writing. The software used for word processing in most legal offices will include a spell checker and a grammar checker. Available in book form, as well as in the form of software, are the traditional writer's tools; dictionary, thesaurus, and style manual.

Spell Check. Computer software programs provide a tool for the checking of the proper spelling of words. The feature searches the document, or parts of the document, for misspelled words, duplicate words, and irregular capitalization. The tool searches from a database of its own main dictionary containing thousands of words, and also searches from a supplemental dictionary that is designed by the writer by adding words and phrases during a spell-check session.

Grammar Check. Another feature for the aid of the legal office assistant contained in the software used by most legal offices is the grammar-checking tool. Grammar-check

active voice
passive voice

conciseness

proofreads documents, or parts of documents, for style errors. The feature can be customized for the writer's preferential style of writing.

Dictionary. The dictionary is available in both software and book form for the legal office assistant. It should be kept within reach at all times and referred to for usage, definition, and spelling whenever necessary. It is an invaluable tool to ensure professional writings in the legal office setting.

Thesaurus. The thesaurus is a tool for the legal office assistant to search for words that are synonyms or antonyms of words. It is available with the software used by most legal offices, and is also found in book form for handy reference. The thesaurus is a useful tool to search for alternative words to avoid redundancy in a legal writing.

Style Manual. The style manual is a handbook of grammar and usage that performs a function similar to the grammar-check feature of computer software. It is available commercially as a book, or is provided by the larger legal offices to the legal office assistant as a guide to the preferred form and usage for the office. The manual should be kept within easy reach for reference when developing any writing.

It is through the written communication that the image of a legal office is presented. The legal office assistant plays a significant role in the development of every writing of the legal office by exhibiting professionalism, accuracy, and courtesy in the written documents of the legal office.

Desk Reference Manual. Many legal office assistants find it essential to have a desk reference manual available as a handy tool. *How 7: A Handbook for Office Workers,* South-Western Publishing Co., is a good general reference tool for office assistants. Also, several commercially available legal office reference manuals for attorneys, paralegals, and legal office assistants might be of periodic benefit.

SUMMARY

The art of communicating fosters the reputation of the legal office, maintains effective client relationships, and creates an image of professionalism for the legal office assistant. Communication is accomplished through the use of legal office equipment, such as the computer, copy machine, typewriter, dictation machine, postage machine, and the telecommunications equipment. The equipment serves to facilitate good communication in an efficient manner, ensuring client respect as well as maintaining productivity. Interaction with the client in a courteous and professional manner in person, by telephone, or in writing requires the use of the basic canons of communication. Ultimately, it is through the written communication that the legal office finds its highest expression. From the standpoint of the client, the courts, the legal community, and the general public, it is through the written word that the practice of law derives its value. The role of the legal office assistant is vital in every phase of the communication process with the client and with the public.

Chapter Activities

Review Questions

1. Describe the fundamental business of any legal office.

2. What is considered to be the basic use of equipment in the legal office?

3. List and discuss the four components of the computer hardware.

4. Describe the difference between operating software and application software.

5. What are the primary applications for use in the legal office?

6. What are the principle features of the copy machine available to the legal office assistant?

7. Why is a typewriter necessary in the modern computerized legal office setting?

8. Discuss the role of telecommunications in the legal office.

9. List the main components of the telecommunications equipment for the legal office.

10. List and discuss the importance of the seven canons of communication.

11. Describe the basic stages with which to be concerned in the telephone etiquette process.

12. What is the primary rule for the legal office assistant when screening telephone calls?

13. What are the principles of written communication that the legal office assistant should express?

14. Which of the writer's principle tools are available to the legal office assistant?

Computer Activity

Attorneys Ernest Flick and Frances Twitch, legendary local anachronisms and practicing corporate lawyers, have recently experienced a decline in their clientele. The law firm of Flick & Twitch, P.C., was organized in October 1956, and has remained virtually unchanged since that time. Flick & Twitch have decided that with the arrival of the millennium, change is in order. In a bold move, they have resolved to replace the IBM Selectric III typewriter, the rotary dial telephone (in black), the mimeograph machine, and the stamp sponge. The attorneys have also decided that there needs to be an improvement in client communications through the use of the telephone.

A. From the student template retrieve act2.doc. Prepare appropriate responses to the typical telephone scenarios by keying your response. Refer to the chapter for examples.

B. Save your work on the template as phone.doc.

C. Print one copy for your instructor. Make sure your name appears for identification purposes.

Chapter 3

Legal Office Records

I long to accomplish a great and noble task, but it is my chief duty to accomplish humble tasks as though they were great and noble. The world is moved along, not only by the mighty shoves of its heroes, but also by the aggregate of the tiny pushes of each honest worker.

Helen Keller
(1880–1968)

Objectives

After completing this chapter, you will be able to:

1. Understand the importance of a filing system in the legal office.

2. Describe the methods of filing in the legal office.

3. Summarize the equipment used for a filing system.

4. Outline the process for handling incoming mail.

5. Summarize the classes of outgoing mail.

6. Describe the services offered by public and private postal services.

7. Understand the need for a docket control system.

8. Define the types of docket control systems.

9. Explain the importance of a law library for the legal office.

10. Classify the functions of the legal office assistant regarding the law library.

Information is the basic product of the legal office. The organization, storage, and retrieval of information is critical to the smooth operation of the office. The failure to handle information in an organized and efficient manner can adversely affect a client's case and the reputation of the office. The legal office assistant works with the organizing, storing, and retrieving of the legal office's information on a daily basis.

FILING

Maintaining the records of the legal office and its clients is an important function of the legal office assistant. The records, files, documents, papers, reports, and related material provide the information necessary for the operation of the legal office and the disposition of a client's case. This chapter will illustrate the importance of records management to the operation of the legal office.

FILING SYSTEM

The management of the documents and records of the legal office is the responsibility of the legal office assistant. The records and documents necessary to the operation of the legal office include correspondence, legal documents, pleadings, investigative reports, photographs, physical evidence, and financial records relative to a client's case. The items to be managed may be in the form of paper, tapes, diskettes, film, or property. Regardless of the nature of the information or its form, it must be organized, stored, and retrieved efficiently. The process of the organization, storage, management, preservation, retrieval, and disposal of information in a legal office is referred to as the **filing system.**

A good filing system must be:

- *secure*—the system must prevent unauthorized access and protect from damage by fire.

- *accurate*—files must be complete, intact, and contain all material relevant to the case.

- *simple*—the system must be easily learned and conveniently accessed by all legal office staff.

- *custodial*—files must be maintained for each client as long as is appropriate.

An effective system must meet these requirements regardless of the method used to store and index the material. Meeting these standards will ensure the most efficient function of the legal office.

FILING METHODS

There are different ways to effectively file information in the legal office. A law firm might use one or a variation of one of the following methods: (1) alphabetic; (2) numeric; or (3) alpha-numeric. Regardless of the system to be employed, the legal office must determine whether the system will be centralized or decentralized, and must furnish a master index.

Rules of Indexing. The well-organized legal office will develop a system using one of the various methods of filing. Regardless of the system adopted, there must be some conformity to the basic rules of **indexing.** Indexing is the process of determining where the information is to be stored. **Coding** is a guide to facilitate referencing information using a letter, number, color, or other symbol to mark items for filing.

Although there may be some variation between legal offices for filing rules, a consistent set of rules is provided by the Association of Records Managers and Administrators, Inc. (ARMA). A knowledge of the rules of indexing will assist the legal office assistant in locating material within the system. The rules provide an order for indexing names using a key unit followed by second, third, and fourth units, depending on the name. Material is filed by the first unit, followed by the second unit, and so forth. The basic rules are provided in Illustration 3-1. Application of the basic rules of indexing will allow anyone in the legal office to locate and replace files and other information for efficient future access.

Alphabetic Filing System. The **alphabetic filing system** uses the last name of the individual client, or the name of the business, for organization. This is the most common system. It is used in the vast majority of legal offices that do not have a large number of cases. Where there is a large number of cases, alphabetizing files can lead to

filing system

indexing
coding

alphabetic filing system

Rule 1: Personal Names. Personal names are indexed in the following order:

- last name
- first name or initial
- middle name or initial
- professional title

Examples:

NAME	KEY UNIT	UNIT 2	UNIT 3	UNIT 4
James Wilson	Wilson	James		
James R. Wilson	Wilson	James	R.	
J. Reginald Wilson	Wilson	J.	Reginald	
Dr. James R. Wilson	Wilson	James	R.	Dr.

Rule 2: Business Names. The name of a business is indexed in the manner in which the company refers to itself. An acronym is indexed as a single name. Business names starting with a number come before those indexed alphabetically. Disregard the ordinals st, nd, and th.

Examples:

NAME	KEY UNIT	UNIT 2	UNIT 3	UNIT 4
1st Union Bank	1	Union	Bank	
2nd St. Pest Control	2	St.	Pest	Control
First Union Bank	First	Union	Bank	
Second St. Pest Control	Second	St.	Pest	Control

Rule 3: Hyphenated Names. Personal and business names that are separated by a hyphen are considered to be one name for indexing purposes and should be filed by the first unit.

Examples:

NAME	KEY UNIT	UNIT 2	UNIT 3	UNIT 4
Susan Rift-Bilge	Rift-Bilge	Susan		
Wilson-Smith Co.	Wilson-Smith	Co.		

Rule 4: Compound Names. Names that are separated by a space are considered separate for indexing purposes.

Examples:

NAME	KEY UNIT	UNIT 2	UNIT 3	UNIT 4
Office Warehouse	Office	Warehouse		
Yore Market	Yore	Market		
This Olde House	This	Olde	House	

Illustration 3-1
The Rules of Indexing

Rule 5: Articles in Names. If the name of a business begins with The the article is placed at the end of the name.

Examples:

NAME	KEY UNIT	UNIT 2	UNIT 3	UNIT 4
The Bread Basket	Bread	Basket	The	
The Legal Suppliers	Legal	Suppliers	The	

Rule 6: Identical Names. Where identical names occur, the names should be indexed by address. Addresses should appear in the following order: (1) city, (2) state, (3) street name, and (4) house or building number.

NAME	KEY UNIT	UNIT 2	UNIT 3	UNIT 4
Jane Wayne 10 West Ln. Ocala, FL	Wayne	Jane	Ocala	FL
Jane Wayne 230 Barn Dr. Yeller, TX	Wayne	Jane	Yeller	TX

Illustration 3-1
The Rules of Indexing (continued)

confusion, due to the similarity and repetition of names. Where practicable, the alphabetic system is preferable because the legal office assistant will not have to rely on memory of a file number to locate the material. See Illustration 3-2 for examples.

Numeric Filing System. The **numeric filing system** is organized by the use of a separate file number for each case. The numeric system assigns and records a new number for each case as it is taken in and opened by the office, resulting in the files being arranged chronologically. Some offices may preface the file number with a number representing the year in which the file was opened or referencing the type of legal matter involved. For instance, if an office assigns the last two numerals of the year in which a file is opened as the first two numbers of the file number, it might appear: "95-111." If all personal injury cases were assigned a numerical code of "10," then a personal injury case may be designated: "10-111." If all files assigned to a particular attorney received the same first two numbers, the file might appear: "4-111." The system must be uniform and as simple as possible for convenience and efficiency. See Illustration 3-3.

numeric filing system

Alpha-Numeric Filing System. The **alpha-numeric filing system** combines the features of the alphabetic system and the numeric system as the basis of its organization. This system uses a letter or a series of letters of the alphabet, followed by a series of numbers, to designate a particular legal matter. Typically, the letters are related to a certain type of legal matter or a particular attorney, with the sequential number representing the chronological opening of the case. For instance, if a legal office practiced probate law and real estate law, the probate matters might begin with the designation "PB" and the real estate matters "RE." A probate file would then appear: "PB-111." This system solves a

alpha-numeric filing system

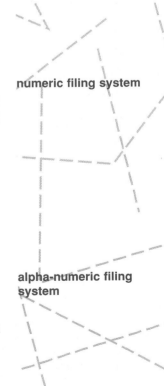

NAME	KEY UNIT	UNIT 2	UNIT 3	UNIT 4
Andrews, Stephen	Andrews	Stephen		
Barnes, Daniel	Barnes	Daniel		
Carpenter, Jean	Carpenter	Jean		
Dillard, Susan	Dillard	Susan		

Illustration 3-2
Alphabetic Filing System

BY YEAR

NAME	KEY UNIT	UNIT 2	UNIT 3	UNIT 4
96-222	96	222		
97-101	97	101		
97-301	97	301		
98-400	98	400		

BY TYPE OF CASE

NAME	KEY UNIT	UNIT 2	UNIT 3	UNIT 4
10-222 (personal injury)	10	222		
20-555 (probate)	20	555		
40-18 (commercial)	40	18		

BY ATTORNEY

NAME	KEY UNIT	UNIT 2	UNIT 3	UNIT 4
1-456 (Smith)	1	456		
2-789 (Wilson)	2	789		
5-123 (Clark)	5	123		

Illustration 3-3
Numeric Filing System

common problem with the pure numeric system where long file numbers are difficult to remember. Shorter file numbers preceded by an alphabetic code are more easily remembered for frequent access. See Illustration 3-4.

centralized filing system

Centralized/Decentralized Filing System. A **centralized filing system** is a system that stores all of the files of the office in one file room or storage area. It is used where the filing system is more complex, or when the office might experience a high employee turnover rate. Larger legal offices with complex filing procedures and centralized control over the security of the files may be best served with the centralized system. A

decentralized filing system

decentralized filing system allows files to be kept in various locations throughout the

NAME	KEY UNIT	UNIT 2	UNIT 3	UNIT 4
PB-111 (probate)	PB	111		
PB-222 (probate)	PB	222		
RE-111 (real estate)	RE	111		
RE-222 (real estate)	RE	222		

Illustration 3-4
Alpha-Numeric Filing System

legal office. With this system the files are kept by the legal office assistant adjacent to the attorney to whom those files are assigned for convenience purposes. The benefits and drawbacks of each system depend on such factors as the size of the office, the number of individuals working on the files, the complexity of the filing system, and the preference of management. A large office may prefer a centralized system, because of the large number of employees handling each file. The small legal office with an attorney and legal office assistant working on the files lends itself to decentralized filing. A larger office with a team approach to handling files, where several attorneys, paralegals, and legal office assistants handle the files, may prefer the decentralized system.

Master File Index. It is essential that any filing system, whether it is alphabetic, numeric, alpha-numeric, centralized, or decentralized, maintain a central index called a **master file index.** The master file index must be cross-referenced between a numeric system and an alphabetic system. This allows for the file and client to be accessed by either name or number. This index can also be used to control open versus closed files and to check against a conflict of interest. Cross-referencing must be completed for both client and opposing party to avoid any conflict. Software is available to provide a master file index, cross-referencing, and the avoidance of conflicts (see Illustration 3-5).

master file index

FILE OPENING PROCEDURE

When the office retains a new client, or when a new matter is commenced for an existing client, a new file must be opened. The legal office should have a formal procedure for opening each new file, based on a standardized form. Numerous types of file opening forms can be used. The ideal form should contain the following:

- file number
- date opened/closed
- identification of client by name, address, telephone numbers, Social Security number
- type of case
- statute of limitations or other critical date(s)
- attorney(s) responsible
- fee information
- referral source

The form in Illustration 3-6 is an example of a form used by a plaintiff's personal injury law firm for opening new client files.

LAST NAME	FIRST NAME	ADVERSE PARTY	TYPE OF CASE	FILE NO.	ATTORNEY
Antique Auto			Commercial	50-333	Decline
Wilson	Fred	Wilson, Susan	Divorce	30-111	Cline

Illustration 3-5
Master File Index

CHANCELLOR, RIDDELL & KNIGHT, P.C.

FILE OPENING FORM

Date: _____   File No. _____

Client: _____
      (Last)   (First)   (Middle)

Telephone: _____

Social Security Number: _____

Address: _____

Dependents: _____

Employer: _____

_____

Defendant: _____

_____

Insurance Company: _____

Nature of Case: _____

Statute of Limitation: _____

Referral Source: _____

Fee Agreement: _____

Attorney: _____

Illustration 3-6
File Opening Form

A well-organized file may contain color-coded subsections for:

Correspondence	Miscellaneous
Discovery	Pleadings
Documents	Records
Evidence	Research
Investigation	Summaries
Memorandum	

Illustration 3-7
File Subsections

The format used by the legal office for the file itself is a matter of individual preference. The format is determined by the needs of the office, type of filing system used, and the nature of the practice. For instance, an estate planning file might have separate subsections for each category of information in the file, which would differ significantly from a litigation file. The various subsections may also be color-coded for easy reference. Illustration 3-7 provides a list of some typical subsections for file folders.

The means of fastening the material in the file folder varies from office to office. Some legal offices prefer metal fasteners to avoid loose documents in the folder. However, client documents that are originals should not have holes punched or be fastened in a manner that may mutilate the document. These documents should be stored separately in the file.

CONFLICT OF INTEREST

Closely related to the file opening procedure is the safeguard provided by a conflict of interest check. When a new matter is opened, the legal office assistant must ensure that the office has not represented any other party involved in that matter. The master file index can serve this function by maintaining a list of all clients represented by the legal office in the past. Database software, such as ISA Files and Conflict System from Prentice Hall, can meet the master file index needs of the office and fulfill the conflict of interest check. The check will ensure the loyal representation of the client without risk of malpractice.

FILE CLOSING PROCEDURE

Once a legal matter has been terminated and representation of the client on that particular matter is over, the legal office assistant will be required to "close" the file to save office space. The process of retiring a file includes several steps, depending on the preference of the legal office:

1. Review the contents.

2. Remove extraneous material, such as duplicate copies or research notes.

3. Purge the file of any duplicate copies or other unnecessary material.

4. Return original documents to the client (if requested).

5. Physically package the file for removal to an in-house or outside storage facility.

6. Prepare a closed file form.

The closed file form is used to track the location of closed files for future reference. A closed file should be assigned a closed file number that differs from the open file number recorded on the master file index. For example, file number 10-111 could be closed as 98-111, reflecting the year and file number for closing.

Other file storage methods are available to the legal office for closed files, as an alternative to the physical retention of the material. One alternative would be a process referred to as **micrographics.** Micrographics is a photographic process for duplicating file material for storage on film. It can take the form of microfiche, ultrafiche, or microfilm rolls.

Another alternative to physical storage is provided through the computerized storage media. Computer diskettes can be used to store large volumes of information that have been digitally reduced to data through the use of a **scanner.**

A scanner is a computer hardware peripheral device that "reads" documents, photographs, or other written material, reducing the image to electronic data. The material in a file to be closed can be "scanned" by the legal office assistant and stored on diskette for later retrieval as necessary. The diskettes used for storage can range from the 3½-inch floppy diskette to the large-capacity **compact laser disc (CD-ROM).**

A CD-ROM disk is a highly durable optical disk containing large volumes of information that have been recorded through the use of laser technology. While a 3½-inch diskette is limited in the number of pages of copy that it can retain, the CD-ROM can hold more than 500,000 pages of text as well as photographs, data, and sound.

Once files have remained closed for a substantial period of time, the manager of the legal office may elect to destroy them. Care must be taken in the destruction of files to prevent the loss of original documents that still have legal effect. Although neither federal nor state law prescribes a file retention period, the individual preference of the law firm will determine the destruction policy.

FILING EQUIPMENT

Equipment used for file management can vary significantly between legal offices. The individual preference of the managing partners, size of the firm, nature of the practice, and the budget are all factors that will control the equipment needs. Selection of the appropriate equipment should take into consideration the following factors:

- available space
- frequency of access
- volume of information
- organization of material
- length of time open
- skill of personnel
- centralized versus decentralized

Equipment should be attractive, durable, and fireproof, regardless of the form taken. The legal office assistant may find the office using various types of filing equipment, including:

- *vertical files*—upright metal or wood filing cabinets from two to five drawers in height
- *lateral files*—similar to vertical files, with the exception that the files are stored sideways or perpendicular to the drawer
- *open shelf files*—resembling book shelves, the file folders are placed on open shelves, usually with color coded tabs for identification

micrographics

scanner

compact laser disc (CD-ROM)

The individual preference of the legal office management will determine the type of equipment.

In addition to becoming familiar with the cabinet equipment required for filing, the legal office assistant must also be acquainted with the filing supplies. Filing supplies include:

- *file folder*—folders used for information storage, varying in size, weight, tabs, and color

- *file guides*—dividers for file drawers providing sections for identification

- *labels*—identification tabs for ease of recognition

- *out cards*—a card identifying the current location of the file

As an alternative to the physical storage of files containing the information related to a client's case, the legal office may select electronic filing. Electronic filing procedures are similar to physical filing, with the exception that the equipment consists of a computer, diskettes, and CD-ROMs. Electronic filing has the advantage of space and ease of retrievability over the physical storage of files, but does not have the convenience of a readily available hard copy.

MAIL

Legal office mail-handling procedures are of particular importance to the legal office assistant. The volume of mail generated in this electronic age presents the necessity for organization and efficiency. The cost of handling incoming and outgoing mail from a time/labor standpoint can result in the loss of thousands of dollars to the legal office, costs that must be passed along to the client. The legal office assistant can save the office significant costs through the expeditious handling of the mail. The primary duties of the legal office assistant include the processing of incoming and outgoing mail.

INCOMING MAIL

The legal office assistant must develop a procedure for the handling of the incoming mail. The first step in the procedure is to open the mail when it arrives. The mail might contain urgent matters that require immediate attention, along with routine matters that can pile up if not handled. A system for processing the incoming mail should involve four steps:

1. Sort the mail.

2. Open the mail.

3. Prioritize the mail.

4. Process the mail.

The performance of these four functions routinely and efficiently will reduce the cost of mail handling and avoid mistakes. Some legal offices require the additional somewhat cumbersome and time-consuming step of recording all incoming mail in a register or on a list.

Sorting the Mail. Once the legal office assistant has received the mail, it must be sorted by individual recipient. Once that preliminary sort has been accomplished, a more detailed sorting of the mail should be completed. The mail sort should then include a classification similar to the following:

- *immediate attention*—includes notices of hearing, pleadings, certified mail, confidential correspondence

- *routine correspondence*—includes routine letters, interoffice memorandum, invoices

- *reading materials*—includes periodicals, circulars, advertisements, library material
- *packages*—includes voluminous records, transcripts

Opening the Mail. The legal office assistant can be efficient at opening the mail if preparations have been made. The procedure should include:

- having a letter opener, time and date stamp, routing slips, stapler, and paper clips available
- arranging envelopes facing the same direction, tapping the envelopes so that the letters are at the same end of each envelope to avoid being cut accidentally, and slitting the top of the envelope with the letter opener
- removing the material and stacking it face up
- paper clipping enclosures in the envelope to the cover letter
- attaching dated envelopes to the letters for materials where a deadline is of significance
- time and date stamping all correspondence and pleadings for a record of its receipt

The mail-opening procedure can be accomplished in a few moments if the preparations have been made and the mail has been sorted properly.

Prioritizing the Mail. To prioritize the mail, the legal office assistant must first read the mail to determine its importance. Significant information could be highlighted with a colored marker to enable the recipient to scan letters at the attorney's option. Explanatory notes attached to the correspondence or pleadings will help the recipient respond efficiently.

Processing the Mail. Once the mail has been read and annotated, you can then route it to the proper recipient for review and handling. The routing is accomplished through routing slips in larger offices and is merely placed in a convenient location for the attorney in a smaller office. The recipient should have a designated area for incoming mail if no mail box is available.

OUTGOING MAIL

The legal office assistant is the individual in the legal office responsible for the preparation of outgoing mail. The procedure for the preparation of outgoing mail should be streamlined and efficient, so as to guarantee efficiency and accuracy.

Preparation of the Mail. The following procedures should be followed in preparing the outgoing mail:

- Letters should be dated, addressed, and properly signed.
- Letters should be error-free, and the paper should not be wrinkled, mutilated, or torn.
- "Enclosure(s)" should be placed below the signature of any correspondence enclosing additional material.
- Copies of all correspondence and enclosed materials should be made for the appropriate file.
- Envelopes should be of sufficient size and properly addressed.
- Letters should be properly folded in thirds to accommodate the envelope.

- Proper postage should be affixed by hand or postage meter, depending on the classification of the mail.

- The envelope should be sealed once its contents have been verified.

The legal office assistant who has developed a procedure for preparing the mail will avoid costly errors due to faulty mail handling.

Classes of Mail. You can make a significant contribution to the cost effectiveness of the legal office through an understanding of the various classes of mail available. Applying only the correct amount of postage to particular materials can result in cost savings to the legal office. Domestic mail in the United States is sent by air, regardless of the classification. Information is available from the U.S. Post Office in a publication titled *Domestic Mail Manual* available from:

Superintendent of Documents
U.S. Government Printing Office
Washington, D.C. 20402-9371

The classifications determine the speed in which the mail is handled by the U.S. Post Office. The mail is classified as follows:

- *First-class mail* is the quickest way to send mail that weighs less than twelve ounces and is sealed. It cannot exceed certain size restrictions without incurring additional cost.

- *Priority mail* is for items weighing between twelve ounces and seventy pounds. Larger envelopes will receive first class treatment if sent by priority mail and stamped accordingly.

- *Second-class mail* is used for magazines, periodicals, and newspapers that are not sealed.

- *Third-class mail,* referred to as "advertising mail," is for bulk mailings and printed materials weighing less than 16 ounces.

- *Fourth-class mail* is generally considered as "parcel post." Fourth-class mail is for materials weighing between one and seventy pounds.

- *Express mail* is the fastest and most efficient means of delivery, although more costly. Delivery is guaranteed for the next afternoon, and it is insured at no additional cost.

Special Postal Services. In addition to the regular services of the post office, the U.S. Post Office offers the following special services to provide convenience and security of delivery:

- *Registered mail* is the most secure way to send first-class and Priority mail because it is closely controlled by the post office and is insured for the value of its contents. It is the best way to send anything of value through the mail.

- *Insured mail:* first-class, third-class, and fourth-class mail may be insured up to the value of the contents through this service.

- *Certified mail* requires proof of delivery by the post office. This service allows the delivery of first-class mail to be recorded and traced. A signed receipt is demanded of the recipient upon delivery.

- *Collect on delivery (COD)* is available for packages where the recipient has agreed to pay the postage upon receipt.

- *Special delivery* services are available for perishable items or those that need to be delivered on a holiday or a Sunday.

- *Special handling* allows for the special handling of delicate or fragile material sent third or fourth class.

Alternative Delivery Services. Private companies can offer the legal office assistant an alternative to the U.S. Postal system. These companies offer convenient and cost-effective shipping for packages and documents, but it is worth the effort to investigate each for cost comparisons and pick-up and delivery schedules.

Courier services such as Emery Air Freight Corporation, Federal Express Corporation, Purolator Courier, Railway Package Express (RPS), and United Parcel Service (UPS) offer delivery by truck, rail, and air to locations worldwide. Because costs may vary depending on package size and delivery location, the legal office assistant should investigate the charges before a commitment is made.

Electronic Mail Services. Electronic mail (E-mail) is the transmission and storing of text messages on a computer for convenient reference at a later time by the recipient. E-mail is an increasingly important fact of life for the legal office assistant because of the convenience and speed offered by the services.

E-mail can be sent within the legal office to another computer through the office's LAN, if available, providing a convenient means of transmitting interoffice memorandum. It can also be sent to computers outside the legal office via telecommunications equipment and one of the many Internet providers. Passwords are used to protect an individual's own computer from access by anyone outside the legal office. One of the many advantages of E-mail is that the same information can be sent to multiple sources at the same time.

The facsimile machine (fax) discussed in chapter 2 is another form of electronic mail service. Operating similar to a long-distance copy machine, the fax machine allows an exact duplicate of a document to be forwarded to a remote location electronically, through telecommunications equipment. The fax machine is a cost-effective means of transmitting information quickly when the recipient does not require a formal document or letter.

Telex machines are a form of electronic teletypewriter used to electronically transmit messages over telephone lines. Larger law firms with a national or global practice, along with Western Union, have a Telex service available.

Voice mail is a type of electronic mail service, not to be confused with E-mail. Voice mail, also discussed in chapter 2, is the electronic storage of a voice message for later access by the intended recipient. It differs from E-mail, which stores a text message in electronic form. Both types of electronic service have the advantage of speed and cost-effectiveness.

DOCKET CONTROL SYSTEM

The legal office assistant plays an important role in the operation of an active legal practice, which is always burdened with critical dates. The practice of law involves schedules, appointments, court hearing dates, deposition dates, trial dates, deadlines, statutes of limitation, and other dates requiring tracking. The legal office assistant must see that these dates are recorded properly and acted upon at the appropriate time.

NATURE OF A DOCKET CONTROL SYSTEM

A **docket control system** is a scheduling system to track important dates. It consists of a system for recording the dates and events critical to the proper representation of the clients of the legal office. The system may be either manual or computerized, or a combination of both, and may be centralized or decentralized. The system is known by many different names, depending on the preference of the legal office. It can be called a *diary,* a *calendar,* a *tickler,* a *follow-up,* a *record,* a *register,* an *agenda,* or a *program.* The

telex machines

docket control system

purpose of the docket control system is to allow the legal office to professionally represent its clients. A missed deadline, court date, appointment, or other important date can mean the loss of the client and a lawsuit for legal malpractice. The legal office assistant is the individual in the legal office who has the primary responsibility for maintaining the docket control system. The legal office assistant must record the information, monitor the deadlines, and respond at the appropriate time.

The nature of the information tracked on the docket control system will vary with the nature of the practice of the legal office. Litigation firms require an accurate control over court and deposition dates, while commercial law practices track appointments, deadlines, and expiration dates. The following items are typically recorded by the legal office assistant on the docket control system:

- statutes of limitation
- court hearing dates
- deposition dates
- due dates for pleadings
- due dates for briefs
- closing dates
- deadlines
- meeting dates
- office appointments
- review dates
- expiration dates
- renewal dates

Because the attorneys are busy with many matters at any one time, it is the responsibility of the legal office assistant to monitor the docket control system. Appointments with clients, witnesses, co-counsel, office meetings, and out-of-office meetings must be entered into the docket. Deadlines, reminders, and review dates are all entered to keep the office on a professional level and to avoid a loss for its clients. It is critical for the legal office assistant to enter items into the system immediately upon receipt of any notification. To anticipate the need for an entry, the legal office assistant must be familiar with the local court rules controlling times and deadlines for filings. It is also important that office policy be followed regarding the time for review of documents, estates, and other time-sensitive matters.

MANUAL DOCKET CONTROL SYSTEM

The legal office assistant will be faced with many different types of docket control systems. The systems will vary, depending on the size of the legal office, the nature of the practice, and the preference of the managing partners.

A manual docket control system is seen most frequently in small and medium-size legal offices. A manual system may be nothing more than a calendar for a sole practitioner, to a more sophisticated card system for the medium-size legal office. A calendar entry system will be adequate for a small office where a single central calendar contains all of the entries for the entire office, including appointments, court dates, depositions, and any other relevant entries. This system allows the attorney and the legal office assistant to view the docket at a glance to avoid conflicts. Difficulty may arise when the attorney requires the calendar while away from the office and the legal office assistant has entries to be made. The delay of entry can cause confusion and conflict, as well as being time-consuming. See Illustration 3-8.

HART & LUNGE, P.A.
DAILY DOCKET CALENDAR
FEBRUARY 29, 1999

TIME/ATTORNEY	CLIENT/FILE NO.	EVENT
9:00 LVH	Klein 11-412	Appointment with client
10:00 LVH	Klein 11-412	Deposition in office
1:00 LVH	Fault - new	Appointment with client Workers' compensation
3:15 LVH	Harris 20-129	Motion to dismiss Circuit court

Illustration 3-8
A Sample Docket Calendar

WHEAT & GRAINGER, P.C.   FILE NO.

Case: Attorney:

Date: Event:

Illustration 3-9
A Sample Tickler Card

A card system uses a card similar to an index card to track deadlines and appearance dates. This is known as a *tickler system,* and works well for reminders, follow-ups, and review dates. It requires the completion of the card for each event to be entered into the system, a daily review of the applicable cards, the retrieval of the card, and the performance of the task. It is the responsibility of the legal office assistant to maintain the cards, review the dates, and retrieve the tasks on a timely basis. Illustration 3-9 provides an example of a *tickler card* used for tracking court hearing dates.

The card system has limitations if cards are misplaced or if the system is not monitored daily. In addition, the system may require daily, weekly, monthly, and annual reports that must be manually prepared. This can be very time-consuming for the legal office assistant, but may be required in order to secure malpractice insurance. Any manual system will only be as reliable as the individuals operating the system.

COMPUTERIZED DOCKET CONTROL SYSTEM

Computerized docket control systems for the legal office are available with a wide range of features, as well as cost. Datebook, Daymaker, and Docket Time are examples of docket control software. The level of sophistication of the system will vary, depending on the size of the firm, budgetary concerns, and the nature of the practice. All of the computerized docket control software have similar features, such as:

- data entry screen
- annual calendars
- repeating entries
- conflict warnings
- centralization
- reporting
- case summaries
- priorities

The benefits from computerized docket control are significant for the legal office assistant. Entries can be performed at one workstation simultaneous with another. The reporting features and the daily reviews allow a clear picture of items. The system is less prone to error and adds to the professionalism of the legal office.

LAW LIBRARY

The law library is an essential tool to the practicing attorney, providing the resources to allow the attorney to properly advise the client. It is also one of the most costly acquisitions of the legal office, requiring an ongoing annual expense. It is frequently the job of the legal office assistant to assume the role of law librarian in addition to the other duties required of the position. To manage the library properly, the legal office assistant must be familiar with its contents, understand what is necessary to maintain it, and take advantage of new technological advances in legal research.

LAW LIBRARY CONTENTS

The law library is a significant expense for any legal office, regardless of its size. The nature of the contents of the library is dictated by the type of law practiced as well as the amount of money to be invested. A good basic law library should include certain basic multivolume resources:

- **case law**—case law reporters for both federal and state courts that come in large, multivolume sets that can be purchased either new or used; also available on CD-ROM
- **statutory law**—large multivolume sets containing the legislative enactments of a state
- **citators**—multivolume sets of books that provide subsequent history of cases and statutes
- **digests**—a multivolume set of books providing a topical reference to case law

case law

statutory law

citators

digests

encyclopedia

periodicals

treatises

- **encyclopedia**—a general multivolume set providing a research tool for a fundamental understanding of the law

- **periodicals**—numerous periodicals available for any area of practice, enabling the practicing attorney to remain current on changes in the law

- **treatises**—single-volume works on a specific area of the law

LAW LIBRARY MAINTENANCE

Maintenance of the law library is a task that is frequently assigned to a particular legal office assistant who serves as the law librarian. The duties require the legal office assistant to:

- order new materials as needed

- route new material where appropriate

- catalog the contents of the law library

- track circulation of the materials

- purge the library of outdated material

- file new material updating the existing volumes

- install pocket supplements

Law library maintenance is a task that requires constant attention. Periodicals, pocket parts, and supplemental material arrive on a frequent basis and must be attended to immediately in order for the collection to be current. Most legal offices will have standardized the library procedures to streamline its function, maintain a lid on costs, and ensure its validity as a current resource. The legal office assistant can contribute to the efficiency of the library through attentiveness and suggestions for improvement.

ADVANCE TECHNOLOGY FOR THE LAW LIBRARY

The use of computer-assisted legal research can greatly improve the efficiency of the legal office. Two prominent legal information services are available: WESTLAW and LEXIS/NEXIS. These consist of large databases containing federal and state case law and statutory law. Research is conducted through the use of a computer that has a dedicated terminal or through a personal computer that is "logged on" to the services. The advantage of computer-assisted legal research is in its speed and accuracy. It is continually updated with the latest changes, allowing the attorney access to the most recent law.

The major publishers of law materials offer state and federal case law reporters, statutory law, and administrative reports on CD-ROM. It is less expensive than the acquisition and purchase of an entire set, the older volumes of which may receive very little use. The collection is periodically updated to keep the library current, providing efficient access through the attorney's individual computer.

SUMMARY

The practice of law is essentially a function of the presentation of information in the representation of a client. The legal office assistant has a key role in the information process of the legal office. The organization of that information, its storage, the ease of its location, and the retrieval of the material are primary functions of the legal office assistant. The filing system of the legal office is designed to facilitate those functions in an orderly and efficient manner to effectively represent the interests of the client. An inefficient filing system can result in lost time, lost information, and ultimately in lost clients. It is the legal office assistant that makes the filing system work to the advantage of the entire legal office.

Information is the basic product of the legal office, and mail serves as the principal means of conveying that information. In the process of conveyance, it is again the legal office assistant that performs an integral role. The legal office assistant is the individual responsible for handling the mail at each step in the process of receipt, processing, delivery, and response.

A critical element in the function of any legal office is the quality of its docket control system. Without any system, chaos would soon result, with attendant loss of clients and exposure to legal malpractice. No legal office can function without some measure of calendar and docket control. The legal office assistant maintains the docket control system, makes the entries, coordinates the information, anticipates the needs of the client, and takes the appropriate action.

The law library is to the legal office as the tool box is to the tradesperson. The resources contained in the law library form the basis of the expertise offered by the practicing attorney. It is through those resources that the legal office can support the client's interests, render accurate advice, and remain current on recent developments in the ever-changing legal landscape. The legal office assistant, functioning as law librarian, provides the necessary support to the legal office to maintain that resource base. The legal assistant as law librarian has an essential role in the viability of the legal office.

Chapter Activities

Review Questions

1. Define a filing system.

2. Discuss the goals of the legal office assistant in the development of a filing system.

3. List the basic rules of indexing.

4. List and discuss the basic types of filing systems.

5. Describe the basic steps in the file closing procedure.

6. List and discuss the four basic steps performed by the legal office assistant in the handling of incoming mail.

7. What basic procedures are to be followed by the legal office assistant in processing outgoing mail?

8. Summarize the classes of mail to be used by the legal office assistant to handle outgoing mail.

9. What is E-mail?

10. What are the items to be recorded by the legal office assistant in an effective docket control system?

11. List the basic elements of a good law library collection.

12. Discuss the principal duties of the legal office assistant regarding the law library.

Computer Activity

The Association of Legal Office Helpers and Assistants (ALOHA) has just held its annual convention on the Kona Coast of Hawaii. The partners in your law firm, Rusty Prime and Wayne Decline, sent you to the ALOHA convention in an effort to improve efficiency in their estate-planning practice. While Prime & Decline, P.C., enjoy a good reputation in the community, like most law offices the systems in place predate the advent of the electric typewriter. The docket control system consists of a wall calendar from Decline's wife's gardening club. The filing system is based on the Greek alphabet, a throw-back to Prime's glorious days as a running back for Slippery Rock State. The law library contains the original textbooks used by the partners during their formative law-school days, which they have never seen the need to update. The mail is retrieved on an almost-daily basis by Decline on his way home from the office, and is brought in to the office the following day, most of the time.

A. From the student template retrieve act3.doc. The document is used for file opening. From the information in this scenario, prepare the form for the office's newest client, Wilson Pettibone, IV. He is having a will prepared.

Mr. Pettibone resides at 10 Flowers Lane in your city, phone number is 555-2121, and has a Social Security number of 304-98-3984. His wife's name is Ismelda, and there are no children. He is self-employed as a house painter. Refer to the chapter for examples.

B. Save this information on the template as opener.doc.

C. Print one copy for your instructor. Make sure your name appears for identification purposes.

Chapter 4

Legal Office Accounting

Objectives

After completing this chapter, you will be able to:

1. Discuss the basic principles of accounting.
2. Describe the distinction between a cash basis and an accrual basis system.
3. Distinguish between a journal and a ledger.
4. Understand the income statement and the balance sheet.
5. Describe the legal office payroll.
6. Summarize the types of legal fee agreements.
7. Explain the systems for legal office timekeeping and billing.
8. Discuss the legal office checking account.
9. Discuss the legal office client trust account.
10. Understand the ethics of the client trust account.

GENERAL ACCOUNTING PRINCIPLES

Just as in every type of business, the legal office must maintain accurate and detailed financial records. Some of these are required by law, while other types of financial records are mandated by the nature of the business of the legal office. The legal office assistant plays an important role in the maintenance of the financial records of the legal office, and must therefore be familiar with the basic principles of accounting.

BASIC PRINCIPLES OF ACCOUNTING

Every type of legal office, including the government, private, and corporate office, requires proper accounting. If the legal office does not have a designated bookkeeper, the maintenance and analysis of financial records, or **accounting,** might be a significant portion of the daily responsibilities of the legal office assistant.

The records must be maintained to:

- report income and expenses for income tax purposes
- report earnings for attorneys and legal office staff
- manage cash flow
- account for fees and expenses to clients
- manage client funds in trust

To properly maintain the financial records of the legal office, the legal office assistant must be familiar with the basic principles of accounting: cash versus accrual systems, debits and credits, journals, ledgers, income statements, and balance sheets.

Cash versus Accrual System. There are two fundamental bookkeeping systems used for accounting in the legal office. Accounting for income and expenses as they are actually received or paid is referred to as accounting on a **cash basis.** Legal fees may be earned in one particular accounting period but not actually paid for until another. In cash basis accounting, the legal fees are accounted for in the period actually received. The same would hold true for an expense item. The recording of the payment of any expense item does not occur at the time an invoice is received, but at the time actual payment is made. The cash-basis bookkeeping system is widely used by small to medium-sized legal offices because it involves a simpler set of accounting books and records.

The **accrual basis** bookkeeping system records legal fees as revenue when they are earned, not actually paid, and expenses at the time incurred, not when an invoice is actually paid. This system of bookkeeping requires the maintenance of a record of monies to be received at a later date, called an **accounts receivable** record. In addition, the system also requires the maintenance of a record of obligations to be paid, called an **accounts payable** record.

The accrual basis system involves the use of a more sophisticated set of books and records and is generally used by the larger legal offices. The advantage of the accrual system is that revenues and expenses can be compared on a period-by-period basis to illustrate a profit or loss situation. The legal office is then able to make financial decisions on the basis of an accrual system, as opposed to the cash basis system.

Debit and Credit. A key element in accounting systems is the proper use of debits and credits. Entries in accounts are made manually on the left or right side of what is known as the **T account.** The T account is a graphical means of displaying the entries to an account and its current status. For instance, in Illustration 4-1, the cash account, the left side of the "T" is considered the **debit** side of the account.

A *debit* is the term used for entries made on the left side of an account. For an account that is considered an **asset** (an item of value owned by the legal office) entries made on the left side are called *debit entries.* Any *increase* to an asset account is a debit to the account and should be entered on the left side. If the account is a **liability** account (an account representing the debts or obligations of the legal office), then debit entries to the left side record *decreases* in the account. Illustration 4-1 reflects a cash account, which would be considered an asset account. Debit entries (a) appear on the left side of the "T" and are considered to be increases to the asset.

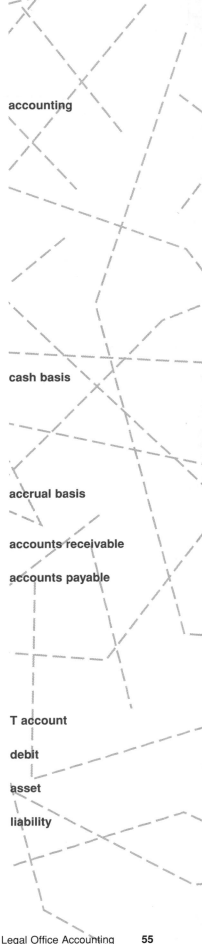

accounting

cash basis

accrual basis

accounts receivable

accounts payable

T account

debit

asset

liability

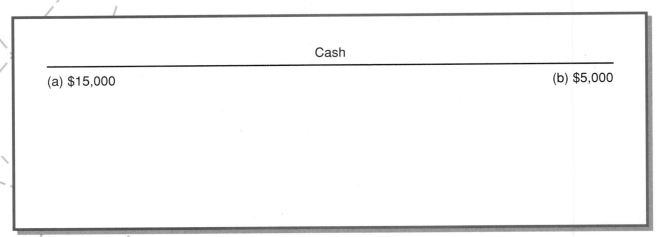

Cash

(a) $15,000   (b) $5,000

Illustration 4-1
A Sample T Account

credit

A **credit** is the term used for entries made to the right side of the account. Credit entries made to the right side of an asset account are considered *decreases* in the account. Illustration 4-1 shows a credit entry to the cash account (b) reflecting a decrease in the amount of cash in the account. Credit entries made to the right side of a liability account are considered to be *increases* in the account.

revenue

When the legal office receives income from legal fees, the office has received what is called **revenue.** An increase recorded in a revenue account is a credit entry on the right side of the account. A decrease in the revenue account is recorded as a debit entry on the left side.

expense

Where the legal office has incurred an **expense** (the cost of any goods and services used to produce revenue) the expenses may be recorded in an expense account. Decreases in the expense account are debit entries made on the right side, and increases in expenses are credit entries made on the left side of the account. Illustration 4-2 provides a guide for debiting and crediting accounts.

journal

Journal. The **journal** is a daily chronological record of all transactions made by the legal office. The journal records the following information:

- the date of the transaction
- the title of the account to be charged
- a description of the transaction
- a posting reference
- the amount

A simple journal will have columns for each element of the transaction to be recorded, as in Illustration 4-3.

The *date* column is headed with the year only. Each transaction is dated with the month and day. The *description* column contains a reference to the file number and/or name, along with the check number if monies are paid out and the reason for the expense or nature of receipt. The *posting reference* column is for entries to be made at the time of transferring the information to another account at a later time. No entries are made in this column at the time of the transaction. These amounts should be entered in both dollars and cents.

A more sophisticated journal system for a larger legal office would include more columns in the journal, reflecting greater detail surrounding the nature of each

Asset Accounts	
Debit	Credit
Enter the original amount on this side. Enter increases on this side.	Enter decreases on this side.

Liability Accounts	
Debit	Credit
Enter decreases on this side.	Enter the original amount on this side. Enter increases on this side.

Revenue Accounts	
Debit	Credit
Enter decreases in revenue on this side.	Enter the original amount on this side. Enter increases on this side.

Expense Accounts	
Debit	Credit
Enter the original amount on this side. Enter increases in expenses on this side.	Enter decreases in expenses on this side.

Owner's Equity Accounts	
Debit	Credit
Enter decreases in expenses on this side.	Enter increases in expenses on this side.

Illustration 4-2
Guide for Debits and Credits

Date 1999	Name of Account	Post Ref	Debit	Credit
1/4	94-101 Smith - check #1099 Medical records			$104.98
1/5	94-227 Wilson retainer		$1500.00	

Illustration 4-3
A Simple Journal

transaction and its effect on the legal office accounts. For instance, a sophisticated journal might include the following columns:

- Cash—Bank Account, Debit
- Cash—Bank Account, Credit
- Client Trust Bank Account, Debit
- Client Trust Bank Account, Credit
- Accounts Receivable, Debit
- Accounts Receivable, Credit
- Accounts Payable, Debit
- Accounts Payable, Credit
- Legal Fees Billed, Debit
- Legal Fees Billed, Credit
- General Ledger, Debit
- General Ledger, Credit

This journal system presents the legal office with more detail regarding each entry and its effect on the bank accounts of the office. The legal office assistant may find that a modification of the more detailed system is required to suit the individual needs of a particular legal office.

A few simple rules for journal entries will aid the legal office assistant and prevent errors:

1. Debit cash received to the bank account in which it is deposited.
2. Credit cash received to its corresponding account.
3. Credit bank account withdrawals to the account from which they are drawn.
4. Debit cash payments to the corresponding account related to the bank withdrawal.
5. Debit an account receivable when a bill for legal services is sent.
6. Credit an account receivable when a payment is made for legal services.

The legal office assistant must always remember that for each journal entry debit, there should be a corresponding credit in another account, and for each journal credit, there should be a corresponding debit to another account. This is referred to as **double-entry bookkeeping.**

The double-entry bookkeeping principle simply means that every transaction has an effect on two separate accounts. If there is a credit to one account, then there must be a debit to another account. For instance, if the legal office billed Mr. Harley Haughtier $1,000 for legal fees on the fifteenth of the month, a journal entry would be made crediting the *Legal Fees Billed* account, and a corresponding entry would debit the *Accounts Receivable* account. The legal office assistant would be required to make a double entry; two separate entries in the amount of $1,000 would be made in the journal to the appropriate accounts.

Ledger. Although the journal presents a chronological record of each transaction, the information must also be recorded in an account that summarizes the status of a category. The summary of the accounts is called a **ledger.** The legal office will have a general ledger containing all of the collective information of the office, and it will also have subsidiary ledgers for each account (such as each account receivable, account payable, and client trust fund). The process of recording information from the journal to each ledger is known as **posting.** It is the responsibility of the legal office assistant assigned the bookkeeping tasks to post the journal entries to their respective ledgers at the end of each day. Posting involves recording the following information in the ledger:

- the date of the transaction
- the amount of the transaction
- debit/credit
- balance
- the journal page on which is found the entry

The journal page contains a column reflecting *Posting Reference,* in which the account number should be made at the time of posting. This ensures posting to the proper account.

Legal Office Income and Expenses. The **income** of the legal office, or its revenue, comes from the generation of fees for providing professional services. Occasionally, income refers to something of value other than money received in exchange for legal services. For instance, a client may satisfy a fee obligation to the legal office by tendering title to property or stock. The **gross income** of the legal office is the amount of revenue received in a given time period before there has been any deduction for expenses.

The expenses of the legal office can be separated into those expenses that are the cost of doing business and those expenses that are the costs involved in the preparation and handling of the client's case. Client expenses include such items as:

- filing fees
- copying costs
- service of process fees
- records fees

Office expenses are the costs involved in the administration of the legal office and are referred to as **overhead**. Such expenses may include:

double-entry bookkeeping

ledger

posting

income

gross income

overhead

- employee salaries
- employee benefits
- rent
- utilities
- equipment

profit

A large portion of the gross income of the legal office is spent on overhead. To maintain a position of **profit,** that is, the administration of the legal office within its gross income, control must be exercised over expenses.

income statement

The accounting tool used to reflect the profit or loss from the operation of the legal office is the **income statement.** The income statement is a detailed financial statement that shows the revenue, expenses, and net income or loss of the legal office over a specific period of time. Illustration 4-4 shows an example of an income statement used by a legal office to make its financial decisions.

The income statement can reflect the revenue and expenses for any specific period the office deems necessary. It can be completed by the legal office assistant assigned the task on a monthly basis. The size of the firm often controls the length of the period preferred.

balance sheet

Balance Sheet. A financial statement reflecting the legal office's assets, liabilities, and the owner's equity is called a **balance sheet.** It is of value to the legal office because it shows the status of the business at a given point in time. The balance sheet is usually prepared at the end of an accounting period, such as the end of the calendar year. Illustration 4-5 is an example of a balance sheet showing the firm's assets, liabilities, and the partner's **equity.**

equity

Equity is the value expressed in dollars and cents of the owner's interest in the business. The balance sheet will always show that the assets of the business equal its liabilities plus the owner's equity.

TRIAL & ERROR, P.C.
Attorneys at Law

INCOME STATEMENT
For the Month Ended March 30, 1999

Income		
Professional Services Rendered		$6,980.00
Expenses		
Rent	$1,000.00	
Payroll	1,500.00	
Telephone	246.00	
Insurance	310.00	
Total Expenses		3,056.00
NET INCOME		$3,924.00

Illustration 4-4
A Sample Income Statement

TRIAL & ERROR, P.C.
Attorneys at Law

BALANCE SHEET
As of December 31, 1999

Assets		Liabilities		
Cash in Bank	$9,563.33	FICA	$189.20	
Client Trust Acct.	2,525.00	Other Withholding	345.00	
Furniture and Equipment	6,941.25	Total Liabilities		$534.20
Library	8,500.00			
Accounts Receivable	1,108.20	**Owner's Equity**		
Prepayments	2,000.00	Capital	$30,000.00	
		Net Income	103.58	
		Total Stockholder's Equity		30,103.58
		TOTAL LIABILITIES AND		
TOTAL ASSETS	$30,637.78	OWNER'S EQUITY		$30,637.78

Illustration 4-5
A Sample Balance Sheet

LEGAL OFFICE PAYROLL

The production of the payroll for the legal office is a complicated task. In small and medium-sized law firms, the payroll may be completed internally. It can be done either manually or with the use of one of the many excellent computer software programs available. Larger legal offices use the services of an independent payroll auditing service. In either case, the payroll involves the deduction of certain items from the employee's salary. Deductions may include:

- federal withholding taxes

- Medicare withholding

- state withholding taxes

- municipal withholding taxes

- FICA

- health insurance premium

- retirement plan contributions

The amounts withheld by the legal office for certain benefits depend upon the benefit structure of the legal office. For example, the benefits might be borne totally by the legal office without deduction from the employee's salary.

Illustration 4-6 shows an example of a simple payroll register kept manually in a small legal office. The employee's name is followed by the number of allowances claimed for federal income tax purposes and the marital status. The number of hours worked may vary between employees, and the office may also pay overtime. If so, then the payroll register must also include a column for the overtime hours in addition to regular hours. The standard deductions are shown, but could include state income tax, insurance, retirement contributions, or any other category.

PAYROLL REGISTER

NAME	NO. OF ALLOW	MAR. STAT	HOURS WORK	PAY RATE	EARNINGS	FICA	MEDICARE W/HOLD	FED W/HOLD	NET PAY
Jean Green	2	M	40	8.00	320.00	26.50	8.87	30.20	254.43
Fred Redd	1	S	36	7.50	270.00	19.85	7.54	21.70	220.91
					46.35	16.41	51.90	475.34	
				590.00					

Illustration 4-6
A Sample Payroll Register

The legal office has the obligation of paying the taxes withheld to the proper agency, risking severe penalties for nonpayment. The Internal Revenue Service publishes a booklet titled *Circular E—Employer's Tax Guide.* The booklet provides the legal office assistant with the necessary information to produce the payroll and provide for the payment of withholding taxes. The booklet is updated periodically to keep pace with the tax laws.

COMPUTERIZED ACCOUNTING SYSTEM

Small and medium-sized legal offices may typically use a manual system of accounting. The manual systems involve checkbooks, ledger sheets, and reporting forms to track the office's financial matters. The manual system is labor-intensive for the legal office assistant, requiring the manual entry of an item in multiple journals, ledgers, and accounts.

Computer software is available for any size legal office to meet its accounting system needs. Systems may offer a variety of features, including:

- printing checks
- providing periodic reports and statements
- preparing graphs
- balancing accounts
- calculating payroll
- on-line banking
- budgeting

The advantages of computerized accounting systems include labor-saving characteristics, as well as reporting capabilities.

✴ LEGAL FEE AGREEMENTS

The attorney–client relationship is a matter of contract. The attorney promises to render legal services in exchange for a set fee for those services. The legal office will have established policies related to the office's fees for legal services based on consideration of its overhead. Rule 1.5a of the ABA *Model Rules of Professional Conduct* clearly states that an attorney's fee "shall be reasonable." The rule then provides the following eight criteria by which the profession judges fees to be reasonable:

- time and labor required, the novelty and difficulty of the questions involved, and the skill requisite to perform the legal service properly
- the likelihood, if apparent to the client, that the acceptance of the particular employment will preclude other employment by the lawyer
- the fee customarily charged in the locality for similar legal services
- the amount involved and the results obtained
- time limitations imposed by the client or by the circumstances
- nature and length of the professional relationship with the client
- experience, reputation, and ability of the lawyer or lawyers performing the services
- whether the fee is fixed or contingent

The structure of the legal fee agreed upon by the client and the attorney may take one of several different forms. The attorney fee can be an hourly rate fee, a contingency fee, a flat fee, a retainer fee, or a prepaid legal service. The legal office should also have an agreement with the client regarding the costs involved in rendering the legal services.

HOURLY RATE FEE

hourly rate fee

The **hourly rate fee** is an agreed upon rate at which the legal services are billed on an hourly basis to the client. In its simplest form, if the attorney and the client agree that the services will be billed at an hourly rate of $100, and the attorney spends eleven hours working on the matter, then the client would receive a bill for attorney fees in the amount of $1,100. The agreement can be more sophisticated when the hourly rate varies, depending on which attorney works on the matter. The hourly rate may vary between work done by a partner and work done by an associate attorney. The hourly rate may also vary as to the nature of the service rendered. For instance, a set hourly rate may apply to court appearances and depositions, while a lower rate may apply to legal research, correspondence, and telephone matters. The fee agreement should specifically address each of the various hourly rates and set forth the circumstances under which they apply.

CONTINGENCY FEE

contingency fee

A **contingency fee** is an attorney fee agreement whereby the attorney agrees to accept a fee based on a successful outcome. In such cases, the attorney is entitled to a percentage of the total amount recovered. If there is no recovery, then the attorney is not entitled to any fee but is entitled to a reimbursement for costs. The contingency fee is seen most frequently in cases where the attorney is representing the plaintiff in a negligence case, workers' compensation case, civil rights matter, or medical malpractice claim. The underlying purpose behind the contingency fee is that those individual plaintiffs who have a legitimate case have an opportunity to be represented by an attorney. Legal representation would be denied to all but wealthy individuals if the contingency fee structure were not available.

FLAT FEE

flat fee

A **flat fee** is an attorney fee for legal services billed as a fixed amount for a particular service. A legal office may set a flat fee for handling the preparation of simple wills, handling an uncontested divorce, or filing a bankruptcy. For instance, a legal office may offer to file a simple bankruptcy for individuals seeking protection from creditors for a flat fee of $250. The agreement is based on the theory that some legal matters are routine and involve few surprises for the attorney, justifying the assignment of a fixed fee for the service.

RETAINER FEE

retainer fee

A **retainer fee** is money paid by the client to the attorney for legal services already performed or to be performed in the future. There is a distinction between an *earned retainer* and an *unearned retainer.* The earned retainer fee occurs where the legal office has already earned the money in exchange for a legal service and is entitled to deposit the funds in the legal office general account. The unearned retainer is similar to a down payment for legal services to be rendered in the future. Until the services are rendered and the money is earned, the funds belong to the client and must be placed in the client's trust account, not the general account of the legal office. Ethical rules are very strict and specific on the use of unearned retainer fees, and local rules should be consulted.

PREPAID LEGAL SERVICE FEE

prepaid legal service fee

Another type of legal fee arrangement that is becoming more prevalent is the **prepaid legal service fee.** The prepaid legal service fee is a plan that has been purchased by the individual client, an employer, or the client's labor union, to provide legal services as a fringe benefit. The fees for certain enumerated services may either be free or at a greatly reduced rate.

AGREEMENT ON COSTS

To provide legal services on behalf of a client, the legal office will incur certain costs and expenses on the behalf of the client. The legal office is entitled to be reimbursed for those costs and expenses from the client. In a case involving extensive litigation over a period of years, the costs and expenses incurred by the legal office can be significant. It is the responsibility of the legal office assistant to maintain accurate records of the costs incurred, and prepare the statement with each periodic bill. The procedure for tracking costs and expenses will vary greatly between legal offices. Typical matters for which costs are incurred are:

- filing fees
- record costs
- court reporter fees
- expert witness fees
- travel expenses
- photocopying
- postage
- long-distance telephone charges
- WESTLAW or LEXIS/NEXIS costs for legal research

In some jurisdictions, the court may have to approve the costs allowed in a given matter. Local court rules should be consulted.

LEGAL OFFICE TIMEKEEPING

The careful recording of the time spent working for a client is the source of the legal office revenue. For the legal office to bill a client on an hourly rate fee, the office must be able to track the amount of time spent on behalf of the client. The legal office assistant is an integral part of the client billing process through the timekeeping practice.

TIMEKEEPING PRACTICE

Timekeeping is the term applied to the tracking of time spent in the delivery of legal services on behalf of a client. It is the responsibility of each person in the legal office to record *any* time spent on behalf of the client. You will be required to make an annotation for each task performed for each client. The recording of the amount of time spent on each matter is done on a **timesheet,** a written record of all time spent by a legal office staff employee in the representation of a client's interests.

The legal office will have a standardized timesheet to be used by each person in the office engaged in the process of legal service. The timesheet should include the following information:

- date
- client
- file number

timekeeping

timesheet

- service rendered
- attorney/legal office assistant
- time spent

The actual entry of the information on the timesheet should be done at the time that the service is performed while it is still fresh in mind. It is a common mistake to make time entries long after a task has been completed. Failure to promptly record timesheet information can result in lost revenue for the legal office because of forgotten items or poor recollection. Illustration 4-7 presents a simple manual timesheet to be used for billing purposes.

TRIAL & ERROR, P.C.
ATTORNEYS AT LAW

TIMESHEET

Date	Client	File No.	Name	Service	Time

Illustration 4-7
A Sample Timesheet

The notation of the service rendered on behalf of the client takes on a shorthand of its own in each legal office. You should be familiar with the abbreviations peculiar to the individual office for making brief entries. A typical code in a legal office may resemble Illustration 4-8 abbreviations.

The manner of recording the actual amount of time spent is a matter of individual office preference. It is common for a legal office to break each billable hour into tenths of an hour so that each billable time entry would be in six-minute multiples. Illustration 4-9 reflects the billable entries for billing in tenths.

Other legal offices may break the hour into sixths or quarters for entry purposes. The smaller the increment, the more accurately the entry will reflect the actual time spent on behalf of the client.

In most legal offices, the attorney responsible for a case is the ultimate authority regarding the time spent on a file. The attorney is the individual that should review each timesheet for a file for any adjustments that may be due. The standardized manual time sheets are then turned into the individual responsible for billing. Each entry is then transferred to the client's billing sheet for tabulation. Some manual sheets are adhesive, and each separate entry can be removed and pasted to the client's record.

COMPUTERIZED TIMEKEEPING SYSTEM

Computer software is now available for timekeeping and billing purposes. The benefits include accuracy, timesaving, ease of reporting, and cash-flow analysis. The client benefits from receiving a billing that is professional in appearance and accurate in

```
CA  = court appearance      R  = research
CW = conference with        T  = travel
LF  = letter from           TF = to/from
MT = memo to                TT = telephone call
P   = preparation
```

Illustration 4-8
Sample Timesheet Codes

0–6 minutes	.1 hour		31–36 minutes	.6
7–12 minutes	.2		37–42 minutes	.7
13–18 minutes	.3		43–48 minutes	.8
19–24 minutes	.4		49–54 minutes	.9
25–30 minutes	.5		55–60 minutes	1.0 hours

Illustration 4-9
Billing in Tenths

content. Most legal offices, even small offices, have gone to computerized billing due to the timesaving benefits and its reasonable cost.

With computerized billing, the legal office assistant must still make entries on a time slip for later recording on the computer on a periodic basis. The program then tracks the time spent and services rendered until time for billing.

LEGAL OFFICE CHECKING ACCOUNT

Every legal office maintains one or more checking accounts at a commercial bank. The office requires a general checking account to pay for its general office expenses, obligations, and expenses incurred on behalf of its clients. The office may also maintain a separate checking account for the office payroll, created by the transfer of funds from the general account in the amount of the payroll on a periodic basis. The office may also maintain a client trust account for the purpose of retention of client monies.

CHECKS

check

A **check** is a written order to a bank to pay the person named an amount stated and to charge the maker's account. The legal office that writes the check and whose account is charged is known as the *drawer* of the check. The person to whom the check is written is known as the *payee.* The bank upon which the check is drawn is known as the *drawee.* A check is sometimes called a *draft.*

A legal office may have one or more persons entitled to be a signer of its checks. Some offices even require the signature of two individuals to make the check valid. It is rare that someone other than a managing partner is a signatory on the office checks although occasionally, the authority is given to the legal office assistant.

The actual type of check used by the legal office will vary, depending on individual preference. The checkbook may have check stubs, a checkbook register, carbon copies, or some combination of these. The legal office assistant assigned the responsibility of the checkbook must become familiar with the recording required for tracking checks drawn on the account.

ENDORSEMENT

endorsement

The payee of a check must sign the back of the check to be able to cash or deposit the check. The signature on the check by the payee is known as an **endorsement** of the check.

The endorsement of a check is made on the reverse side in the space(s) provided. If the payee's name is incorrect, the incorrect name should be signed first and the correct payee's name underneath. Checks made out to the legal office are frequently endorsed with a rubber stamp that includes the account number of the office, along with some other restriction on the use of the check, such as "For Deposit Only."

Several types of endorsements can be applied to the check:

- *endorsement in blank*—contains only the signature of the payee, making the check payable to anyone presenting the check, although banks usually require some identification

- *restrictive endorsement*—restricts the use of the check to the restriction stated on the back of the check; e.g., "For Deposit Only"

- *special endorsement*—used to make the check payable to another person; i.e., "Pay to the Order of John Smith"

- *qualified endorsement*—used where the endorser warrants no legal responsibility for payment if there are insufficient funds in the account; e.g., "Without Recourse"

TYPES OF CHECKS

There are several specialized types of checks to which the legal office assistant may be exposed. Other than the typical check in the form of a written order to the bank to pay a certain amount to the payee, the banking system also supports the use of the certified check, the cashier's check, and the bank draft.

Certified Check. A **certified check** is a check drawn on the maker's account and certified on its face by the bank that sufficient funds have been set aside to honor the check when presented.

To obtain certification, the check is presented to a teller at the bank, who then verifies that sufficient funds are available, stamps "Certified" or "Accepted" on the face of the check, and then sets those funds aside until the check is presented for payment. Once that procedure has been accomplished, the bank becomes the party liable for payment of the amount of the check, since the drawer's account has already been credited.

Cashier's Check. A **cashier's check** is a check drawn on a bank's own account. The procedure involves the payment of the amount of the check to the account of the bank, plus a service charge, in exchange for the issuance of the check to a named payee by the bank. The bank is then responsible for the ultimate payment.

Bank Draft. A **bank draft** is a type of check issued by a bank upon its funds located in another bank, usually in another city. The purpose is to allow the payee to travel to another state or city and be able to present a local check for payment.

BANK STATEMENTS

As with an individual's personal checking account, the legal office's bank furnishes a monthly bank statement containing a listing of all transactions for the past month. In addition to returning the canceled checks, the statement will include:

- name and account number
- beginning balance
- deposits
- checks presented for payment
- closing balance

The bank statement will not have any reference to those checks that have been issued and that are still outstanding, or deposits made and not yet recorded by the bank. To obtain a current balance for the checking account, the legal office assistant must **reconcile** the bank statement. Reconciling the bank statement is a process of ensuring that the bank's records for an account agree with the legal office's records. The procedure to reconcile the statement is as follows:

1. Compare deposits recorded on the statement with the office records.

2. Add outstanding deposits to the current balance reflected on the statement.

3. Compare canceled checks with the office records to determine if any are still outstanding.

4. Deduct outstanding checks from the current balance reflected on the statement.

5. Deduct any bank service charges from the office records as a journal entry and debit to an expense account.

certified check

cashier's check

bank draft

reconcile

Once this procedure has been performed, the balance on the office records should conform to that of the bank records. Errors found after careful review should be reported immediately to the bank.

CLIENT TRUST ACCOUNT

client trust account

As mentioned, most legal offices have more than one checking account. In addition to the general office account and the payroll account, the legal office usually maintains a **client trust account.** The client trust account is a separate bank account maintained by the legal office for unearned client funds. This account must be entirely separate from the office's general account. Such accounts are also known as a *trust account* or an *escrow account.*

commingling

Ethical concerns dictate the need for the client trust account. The rules of ethics strictly prohibit the **commingling** of client funds with those of the legal office. Commingling is the mixing of unearned client funds with the funds of the legal office. It is a common problem for legal offices and has been the source of many malpractice claims and state bar reprimands or suspensions. Rule 1.15 of the ABA *Model Rules of Professional Conduct* says:

> (a) A lawyer shall hold property of client or third persons that is in a lawyer's possession in connection with a representation separate from the lawyer's own property. Funds shall be kept in a separate account.

The *Rules* also require that the attorney keep records of the trust account for a period of five years after the termination of representation. Client trust account funds cannot be used to pay any legal office expenses. It is a violation of ethical rules for a legal office to "borrow" money from the client trust account. The money must be delivered to the client promptly upon completion of the representation.

The legal office uses the client trust account for a number of purposes. For instance, if the office has received an unearned retainer for legal fees, the unearned portion must remain in the client trust account. Also, if the legal office has received any monies on behalf of a client—such as a settlement of a case—those monies must be deposited in the client trust account until there is a distribution of funds.

SUMMARY

The stock and trade of the legal office is time. Time is the commodity, when combined with expertise, for which the legal office receives its revenue. The basic principles of accounting are employed by the legal office, as with any other business, to account for its revenue, expenses, fees, costs, and other financial records.

The legal office assistant will be called upon to play an active role in the legal office accounting system. That role may be as limited as merely making an occasional time entry on a timesheet, or it may involve the actual maintenance of the office books. Whatever the role, the legal office assistant must be familiar with the basic principles of accounting as they may apply to the legal office. In addition, there must be a full understanding of how the legal office earns its revenue: an hourly rate fee, a contingency fee, a flat fee, a prepaid fee, or a retainer fee. The client's funds and costs are also an important part of legal office accounting for the legal office assistant. The client trust account and the firm's costs expended on behalf of the client must be carefully monitored, as they often form a common basis for complaint.

The legal office assistant that is familiar with the accounting and bookkeeping requirements of the legal office contributes to its efficiency and professionalism. The attorneys often find themselves busy with the handling of client matters, requiring the delegation of the financial record responsibilities to the legal office assistant. That capability frees the attorney to concentrate on providing legal services and enhancing firm revenue.

Chapter Activities

Review Questions

1. What is the importance of a knowledge of the basic principles of accounting to the legal office assistant?

2. What is the distinction between a cash basis accounting system and an accrual basis system?

3. What is the function of the journal in the legal office accounting?

4. What are the basic rules regarding debits and credits?

5. What is the purpose of a balance sheet for the legal office?

6. What are the benefits of a computerized accounting system for the legal office?

7. What are the basic types of legal fees charged by the legal office?

8. What is the role of the legal office assistant in the timekeeping for the legal office?

9. What are the various types of endorsements used on checks?

10. What is the importance of the client trust account?

Computer Activity

Like many new law firms, the offices of Barge & Charge, P.C., were suffering from severe growing pains associated with an active law practice. They found themselves in the position of having to practice law all of the time and had no time to run their business. Fortunately, all of their cases were handled on a contingency fee basis, due to the nature of their practice. There were no timesheets to be concerned with, nor were there any outstanding fees to be billed. Yet, the office's books were in such a sorry condition that their only office assistant quit rather than attempt to bring order to the chaos.

Enter our heroine, Miss Annie Filings, legal office assistant extraordinaire. Miss Filings had been trained in the principles of legal office accounting, and was in the position to make the necessary changes in office bookkeeping procedure to present an accurate financial picture to the partners. Upon arrival, she found that the firm's "books" consisted of a checkbook for the general account with Cash First State Bank and journal sheets, upon which not a single entry had been made. The only "balance sheet" available from the previous year showed a partnership equity in the amount of $25,000, cash in the bank in the amount of $7,500, furniture and equipment in the amount of $12,000, and no liabilities.

Since this is January 31, it is timely for the creation of a journal and income statement. The checkbook shows the following entries:

1/2 Mr. Land Lord, rent—$500.00

1/4 Bill Barge, draw—$4,000.00

1/4 Marge Charge, draw—$4,000.00

1/10 Midwestern Bell Tel. Co.—$170.00

1/17 Manila Office Supply—$86.23

1/20 Flying Fingers Court Reporters, File #1025, deposition—$250.00

1/26 Dick Sleuth, P.I., File #1275, invest.—$750.00

1/30 Fremont County Court, File #1222, filing fee—$50.00

Deposits:

1/3 File #1145, fee—$2,976.00

1/9 File #1782, fee—$4,500.00

In addition, February 1 saw opportunities for entries to be made on the office's time records. On that date the following billable events occurred:

1. Telephone call from Judge Rashidmore on the motion for dismissal on the Cline case, #1068

2. Telephone call from Attorney Smallwood, re deposition on Wilson v. Child, #1087

3. Scheduling deposition of our expert witness on the Wilson case, #1087

4. Call to our expert witness regarding his report before deposition on Wilson, #1087

5. Research motion for dismissal on the Cline case, #1068, 2 hours

6. Preparation of a motion for rehearing on Davidson, #1183

7. Telephone call to opposing attorney to schedule hearing on Davidson, #1183

8. Office conference with client, Davidson, #1183, 1 hour

   A. From the student template retrieve act4.doc. This document contains forms for a journal and a timesheet. Key in the required information from the scenario to make the journal entries and the entries on the timesheet. Refer to the chapter for examples.

   B. Save this information on the template as account.doc.

   C. Print one copy for your instructor. Make sure your name appears for identification purposes.

Part 2
Court System

Chapter 5
Federal Court System

Chapter 6
State Court System

Chapter 7
Discovery

Chapter 8
Appellate Procedures

Chapter 9
Legal Research

Chapter 5

Federal Court System

And perhaps of even greater importance, it is essential that we recognize that the Rules were intended to embody a unitary concept of efficient and meaningful judicial procedure, and that no single Rule can consequently be considered in a vacuum.

Nasser v. Isthmian Lines, 331 F.2d 124, 127 (1964)

Objectives

After completing this chapter, you will be able to:

1. Discuss the levels of the federal court system.

2. Explain the nature of jurisdiction in the federal courts.

3. Outline the types and purpose of pleadings.

4. Identify the elements of a complaint for a federal court case.

5. Discuss service of process in the federal court system.

6. Explain the purpose of the answer in a federal court case.

7. Discuss counterclaims and cross-claims.

8. Summarize the nature of motions in the federal court system.

9. Outline the basic types of motions.

COURT SYSTEM

The federal court system is separate and distinct from that of the state courts. Of primary importance is that the lawsuit be presented to the proper court. Lawsuits are filed in federal court or state court, depending on various factors that provide proper jurisdiction. A case filed in the wrong court will be dismissed for a lack of proper jurisdiction, and any judgment entered by a court without jurisdiction is unenforceable. Therefore, it is essential for legal office assistants to understand that cases must be filed in the court with proper jurisdiction. This chapter will address requirements for a case with federal jurisdiction. Chapter 6 will address requirements for determining state jurisdiction.

❋ FEDERAL COURT SYSTEM

The federal court system is structured in three levels:

- United States district courts

- United States courts of appeal

- United States Supreme Court

U.S. district courts are the trial courts where lawsuits are commenced. The courts of appeal and the U.S. Supreme Court are the appellate courts, providing review on questions of law that arise in the lower courts. See Illustration 5-1.

❋ United States District Courts.
The court in which a lawsuit is commenced is called the **trial court.** In the federal court system, the district courts are the trial courts. They are occasionally referred to as the courts of **original jurisdiction,** which is another way of saying that the lawsuit was started and the trial took place at this level.

There are federal district courts located in each state, with more than one district court in the larger states. The courts are designated by the state and region within each state. For example, the district court that resides in the city of Detroit, Michigan, is designated as the "United States District Court for the Eastern District of Michigan."

❋ United States Courts of Appeal.
The U.S. courts of appeal review the decisions of the district courts that are located within their respective geographic territory. An **appeal** is the right of a superior court to review the correctness of the decision of a lower court on questions of law.

The U.S. courts of appeal are divided into thirteen **circuits,** or territories. Twelve of the circuits are geographical territories, some covering several states. The thirteenth circuit is the U.S. court of appeals for the federal circuit. It is not a geographical territory as are the others, but is a specialized circuit covering only appeals from certain types of federal courts. See Illustration 5-2.

❋ United States Supreme Court.
The U.S. Supreme Court is the highest court in the land. It has appellate jurisdiction from the federal courts of appeal and from state courts involving a constitutional question. Appeals to the Supreme Court are granted with what is termed a **writ of *certiorari,*** which is an order of the court agreeing to hear a case. The court agrees to hear fewer than two hundred appeals a year, only accepting those cases it deems to have sufficient importance from a legal precedent standpoint.

trial court
original jurisdiction

appeal

circuits

writ of *certiorari*

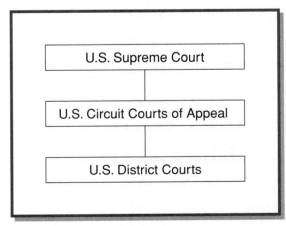

Illustration 5-1
The Federal Court Structure

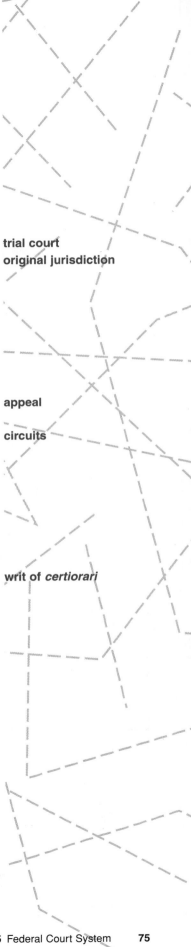

FIRST CIRCUIT
Maine, New Hampshire, Massachusetts, Rhode Island, Puerto Rico

SECOND CIRCUIT
New York, Connecticut, Vermont

THIRD CIRCUIT
New Jersey, Pennsylvania, Delaware, Virgin Islands

FOURTH CIRCUIT
Maryland, Virginia, West Virginia, North Carolina, South Carolina

FIFTH CIRCUIT
Texas, Louisiana, Mississippi, Canal Zone

SIXTH CIRCUIT
Michigan, Ohio, Kentucky, Tennessee

SEVENTH CIRCUIT
Illinois, Indiana, Wisconsin

EIGHTH CIRCUIT
Minnesota, North Dakota, South Dakota, Iowa, Nebraska, Missouri, Arkansas

NINTH CIRCUIT
Washington, Oregon, California, Idaho, Nevada, Montana, Arizona, Hawaii, Alaska, Guam

TENTH CIRCUIT
Colorado, New Mexico, Utah, Wyoming, Kansas, Oklahoma

ELEVENTH CIRCUIT
Alabama, Georgia, Florida

DISTRICT OF COLUMBIA
District of Columbia

FEDERAL CIRCUIT
Appeals from specialized federal courts

Illustration 5-2
Circuit Courts of Appeal

The U.S. Supreme Court is the court of original jurisdiction in limited situations involving (1) suits between two states, (2) suits between the United States and a state, and (3) suits by a state against citizens of another state for aliens. It also has original jurisdiction in matters involving ambassadors or other ministers of foreign states.

JURISDICTION

jurisdiction

Most courts have the power to hear only certain types of cases. **Jurisdiction** is the term applied to the power of a court to hear a case. A court must have jurisdiction over the parties before its orders and judgments have any legal effect. Those cases filed in a court without proper jurisdiction are subject to dismissal.

There are three fundamental types of jurisdiction:

- subject matter jurisdiction

- personal jurisdiction

- *in rem* jurisdiction

A court must have at least one of these types of jurisdiction for an action to be maintained.

Subject Matter Jurisdiction. **Subject matter jurisdiction** refers to the power of a court over a particular type of lawsuit and the relief sought. It also may refer to a dollar amount limitation for which the court is authorized to render judgment.

In the federal courts, subject matter jurisdiction refers to those cases that involve a federal question, a question that arises pursuant to a federal law. Title 28 of the United States Code grants the district courts "original jurisdiction of all civil actions arising under the Constitution, laws, or treaties of the United States" (28 U.S.C.A. § 1331). Persons filing a lawsuit in federal court must state the particular federal law under which the matter is brought.

Subject matter jurisdiction in federal courts has a second requirement. That requirement is the existence of **diversity of citizenship.** Diversity of citizenship exists where the case involves citizens of different states or is between citizens of a state and those of a foreign country (28 U.S.C.A. § 1332).

Diversity of citizenship alone is not sufficient to create subject matter jurisdiction. There is an additional requirement that the matter involve an amount of recovery in excess of $50,000. This jurisdictional amount is called the **amount in controversy,** and must exist before any federal district court will have civil jurisdiction.

Subject matter jurisdiction in the federal courts also exists where a federal law is at issue in the case. For instance, if a claim is made for a federal civil rights violation under Title VII of the Civil Rights Act of 1964, then the federal district court would have subject matter jurisdiction. Also, the same can be said of matters involving bankruptcy, admiralty, or any other purely federal domain.

Where there is no statute that specifically requires that a federal court have jurisdiction, then there may exist **concurrent jurisdiction.** Concurrent jurisdiction exists where *either* a federal or a state court may hear the matter. For instance, if a particular case involved a claim under a federal statute involving more than $50,000 and arose between citizens of two states, the plaintiff may still choose to file in either federal district court or in a state court. The only limitation would be the existence of a statute requiring that the particular type of case be heard in a designated court.

Personal Jurisdiction. In addition to subject matter jurisdiction, in order for a court to enter an enforceable judgment against a person, it must also have jurisdiction over the defendant's person. **Personal jurisdiction** refers to the authority of a court over a person and is sometimes called *jurisdiction in personam.*

Ordinarily, personal jurisdiction exists if the defendant to the action is a resident of the state in which the federal district court is located. Physical presence alone, without actual residence, can satisfy personal jurisdiction. Also, it may exist if the defendant agrees in writing to be subject to the jurisdiction of the court. Furthermore, personal jurisdiction may be present as a result of some statutory authority giving the court jurisdiction because of some minimal contact with the state. A statutory provision for acquiring jurisdiction over nonresident defendants is called a **long arm statute.**

***In Rem* Jurisdiction.** Courts that have power over a particular thing within its geographic borders are said to have *in rem* **jurisdiction.** It refers to the court's power to

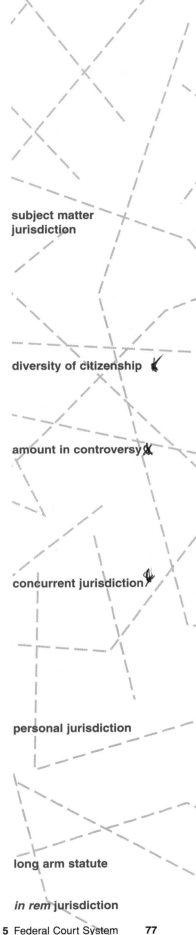

subject matter
jurisdiction

diversity of citizenship

amount in controversy

concurrent jurisdiction

personal jurisdiction

long arm statute

in rem jurisdiction

render a judgment against a particular thing, such as land, located within the state. If the relief sought is related to the particular *thing,* as opposed to the *person,* then the court has *in rem* jurisdiction.

VENUE

venue

🌿 **Venue** is a requirement similar to jurisdiction. Venue is a reference to the particular county, or geographical area, in which a court may hear a case. The purpose of the venue requirement is to have the parties try a lawsuit in a location that is fair to the defendant. This would avoid a situation where the defendant might have to incur the expense of litigation in a court located some distance away.

Venue is determined by statute in most jurisdictions. In the federal courts, 28 U.S.C.A. § 1391 addresses proper venue in diversity of citizenship cases as either:

- the location where all plaintiffs reside
- the location where all defendants reside
- the location where the cause of action arose

In a situation where proper venue exists in more than one court, it will be incumbent on the court to decide which district is most convenient.

NATURE OF FEDERAL PLEADING AND PRACTICE

Federal Rules of Civil Procedure

All procedure necessary for preparing a lawsuit before the United States District Courts is governed by the ***Federal Rules of Civil Procedure.*** The rules consist of a group of procedural rules governing all civil actions in the federal courts. Most states have modeled their rules of procedure after the Federal Rules. The United States Supreme Court established the *Federal Rules of Civil Procedure* in 1938. The rules can now be found in Title 28 of the United States Code. Each local district court has its own set of procedural rules that compliment the *Federal Rules* for local issues surrounding procedure. The legal office assistant must consult these rules when preparing any federal pleading.

PURPOSE OF PLEADINGS

🌿 **pleading**

The *Federal Rules of Civil Procedure,* state procedural rules, and any statutory law governing jurisprudence, have one common goal: the efficient administration of justice on matters deserving merit. The rules for the administration of justice are based on fairness and equity. It is through the proper use of pleadings that justice is administered fairly and equitably without arbitrary discrimination. A **pleading** consists of any document filed with the court containing the claims of a party, with the purpose of giving notice of the issues to be presented at trial.

The rules governing the construction of pleadings serve the following purposes:

- to introduce the allegations of a claim
- to narrow the issues in dispute
- to place the defendant on notice of the claim
- to invoke the jurisdiction of the court

Pleadings must not be a lengthy recitation of detail, but must serve to place the other party on notice of the claim in a concise manner. Rule 8 requires a "short plain statement of the claim showing the pleader is entitled to relief." The details surrounding the claim are a matter for later concern through the discovery process.

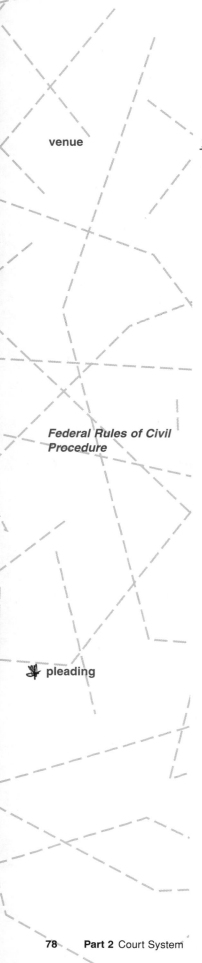

ALLEGATIONS AND ISSUES

A pleading must contain clear statements of the facts upon which a party's claim is based. The facts should reveal the proof that will be offered at the time of trial in the form of an **allegation.** An allegation is an assertion made by a party in a pleading setting out what is to be proven at trial.

It is through the allegations contained in a pleading that each issue in a case may be determined and narrowed. An **issue** is a disputed question to which parties to a lawsuit are requesting a decision of the court.

An **issue of fact** occurs where there exists a dispute over the existence of a particular fact alleged in a pleading. An **issue of law** is when the facts are not in controversy, and the matter may be decided by the court through the application of legal principles.

The court will base its decision on the facts and law resulting in a decision on the **ultimate issue,** which is the question that must be finally answered to support a claim.

✂ COMPLAINT

The initial pleading filed in a lawsuit by the plaintiff to commence an action is called the **complaint.** It is sometimes known as the *statement,* or the *declaration.* Its purpose is to formulate the plaintiff's claim and place the defendant on notice of that claim.

✑ CHECKLIST

An essential element in the preparation of any pleading is the gathering of information necessary to formulate the claim. Information must be gathered from the client and any external sources. It is the duty of the preparer to verify the information in the pleading. A checklist is an essential tool in the information-gathering process. Illustration 5-3 provides the basic elements of a good personal interview checklist to prepare the complaint.

REQUIREMENTS FOR A FEDERAL COMPLAINT

A well-drafted complaint requires the following four elements:

- a proper identification of all parties with names and addresses
- a statement of jurisdiction
- a statement of the claim giving rise to a cause of action
- a prayer for relief

There will be some variation between local federal district courts as to the specific requirements for any complaint. Those local rules *must* be consulted by the legal office assistant before any pleading is prepared.

Identification of the Parties. In the opening numbered paragraphs of the complaint, each of the parties should be identified with name and address. For an individual party, it is sufficient to state only the name and address. In the case of a corporate party, its principal place of business, along with the address of its corporate headquarters, is required. If the party is a public official, then the complaint must state the individual's official capacity, as seen in Illustration 5-4.

The proper identification of the parties, along with their representative capacity, and address, is necessary for purposes of establishing jurisdiction.

Statement of Jurisdiction. Since jurisdiction exists in federal courts under very specific guidelines, it is necessary to set forth the jurisdiction of the particular court. The

allegation

issue

issue of fact
issue of law

ultimate issue

complaint

CLIENT INFORMATION CHECKLIST

PERSONAL
1. Name
2. Address
3. Date of birth
4. Social Security number
5. Occupation
6. Employment history
7. Education
8. Income
9. Marital Status
10. Spousal information
11. Children
12. Assets
13. Liabilities
14. Medical history

FACTS OF THE CASE
1. Date
2. Place
3. Witnesses
4. Addresses/phone numbers
5. Reports/statements
6. Corporate officers
7. Insurance coverage
8. Narrative of incident(s)

DAMAGES
1. Personal
2. Property
3. Mitigation
4. Preexisting conditions
5. Experts
6. Valuation

RECORDS
1. Tax
2. Banks, brokerages
3. Insurance
4. Police
5. Medical
6. Corporate
7. Contracts
8. Statements

Illustration 5-3
Client Information Checklist

IN THE UNITED STATES DISTRICT COURT
FOR THE EASTERN DISTRICT OF MICHIGAN

CONRAD P. CROWN and
OYSTERDENT, INC.,
a Michigan corporation,

    Plaintiffs,

v.   C.A. No. 99-23456

CYBERNET, INC.,
an Ohio corporation,

    Defendant.
_____/

COMPLAINT

(For an individual)

    1. CONRAD P. CROWN resides at 13 Bridge Lane, Detroit Michigan.

(For a corporation)

    1. OYSTERDENT, INC., is a Michigan Corporation, with its principal place of business located at One Incisor Lane, Detroit, Michigan.

(For a public official)

    1. ALFRED M. CABLE is the Secretary of State of the state of Ohio, residing at 486 Ether Court, Columbus, Ohio.

Illustration 5-4
Manner of Identifying a Party

JURISDICTION

3. Plaintiff is a corporation incorporated under the laws of the state of Michigan having its principal place of business in the state of Michigan, and defendant is a corporation incorporated under the laws of the state of Ohio having its principal place of business in a state other than the state of Michigan. The matter in controversy exceeds, exclusive of interest and costs, the sum of Fifty Thousand Dollars and No Cents ($50,000).

Illustration 5-5
Statement of Jurisdiction

caption of the pleading establishes the court for which jurisdiction is deemed proper. The complaint itself must set forth the reason(s) for qualification for federal jurisdiction. If the question arises under a provision of the U.S. Constitution, then the constitutional section must be cited. Where the federal question arises pursuant to a law of the United States, the appropriate statutory citation must be cited. If jurisdiction arises from diversity of citizenship, an appropriate allegation must be made. See Illustration 5-5.

Statement of the Claim. The statement of the claim is a recitation of the facts that entitle the plaintiff to judicial relief. Facts entitling a party to judicial remedy constitute a **cause of action.** A cause of action is frequently based on negligence, fraud, or breach of contract. All of the facts necessary to constitute a cause of action must be alleged in the complaint. If a material element of the cause of action is omitted, the complaint may be subject to dismissal. For instance, the material elements of a claim for a breach of contract would be:

- the existence of the contract
- a failure without legal excuse to perform the contractual obligation by defendant
- damage as a result of the breach

A complaint must reflect an allegation of fact as part of its statement of claim that supports each material element of the cause of action. If an additional cause of action arises out of the same set of facts, then an additional theory of recovery would be added in the complaint.

Prayer for Relief. The complaint concludes with a request of the court for judicial relief or damages. Such a request is called a **prayer for relief** or *demand for judgment.* Rule 8(a) of the *Federal Rules of Civil Procedure* refers to the prayer for relief as a demand for judgment that is used by the court as a guide in deciding the nature and extent of the recovery sought.

Signature. Rule 11 of the *Federal Rules of Civil Procedure* requires that the complaint be signed by an attorney, or by the plaintiff if unrepresented. The purpose behind this requirement is to hold the attorney, as an officer of the court, to a professional standard that would prevent filing of a frivolous or fraudulent lawsuit. The requirement constitutes a certification by the attorney that the facts are true.

cause of action

prayer for relief

SERVICE OF PROCESS

After the completion of the complaint, and its filing with the court, the court must acquire jurisdiction over the defendant. Reasonable notice to the defendant of the pending proceedings is accomplished by means of delivery of the summons and complaint in accordance with Rule 4 of the *Federal Rules of Civil Procedure.* Delivery of the summons and complaint to the defendant is termed **service of process.**

service of process

Service of process must be accomplished within 120 days of the filing of the complaint, and can be accomplished by:

- mail

- personal service by a process server

- service by a U.S. marshal

Service of process by mail is performed by mailing the summons and complaint to the defendant, along with two copies of the notice and acknowledgment form provided in the rules. First-class postage is allowed, although most legal offices prefer certified mail. If the defendant does not accept service or does not acknowledge receipt within twenty days, then an alternative means of service must be employed.

Where it is necessary to effect service of process, an individual process server may be retained. The person must be eighteen years of age and not have any stake in the outcome of the litigation. Following completion of the service, the process server must complete the return of service form that is on the reverse side of the preprinted summons form.

The rules also provide for service of process by a U.S. marshal in limited circumstances. Those occasions exist when the United States is the serving party, or under special circumstances.

Rule 4 provides an explanation of whom the proper person to be served may be, and should be consulted to avoid dismissal of the action for improper service. Generally, the rule provides for service upon:

- an individual other than an infant or incompetent person by personal delivery or leaving a copy with a person of suitable age and discretion at the individual's dwelling place or usual abode

- a guardian of an infant or incompetent person

- a corporation or partnership by delivery to an officer or managing partner

- the United States by delivery to the district attorney or to the agency that is the party

- a municipal governmental body in the manner provided by state law

If the service of process is defective in some manner, the defect may form the basis for a dismissal of the action, resulting in a costly delay or the total loss of the action.

For the court to acquire jurisdiction over an individual or corporation that does not reside within its geographical jurisdiction, the court must obtain personal service through the use of a long arm statute. The long arm statute is used to obtain service on nonresident defendants in situations where there have been certain minimum contacts with that state. In general, those contacts must have been:

- the transaction of business within the jurisdiction

- an act of negligence within the jurisdiction

- ownership of real property within the jurisdiction
- limited contact of a specially defined nature

Service of process through the use of a long arm statute is performed through substituted service, such as the U. S. mail. In the federal courts, the long arm statute of the state in which the court sits is the statute used to obtain jurisdiction.

RESPONSIVE PLEADINGS

Once the plaintiff has filed the claim in the appropriate federal district court, it is then necessary for the defendant to respond to the claim. The response may be in one of the following forms:

- a motion to dismiss the action
- the assertion of certain defenses
- an admission of the claim

The defendant must assert a response within twenty days of the service of the complaint.

ANSWER

Rule 8 of the *Federal Rules of Civil Procedure* governs the defendant's response to a complaint. An **answer** is the defendant's responsive pleading stating the grounds for defense. In federal courts, allegations that are not denied in response to the complaint are deemed admitted. The answers of the defendant should be set forth in a clear and plain statement. The defendant may respond with:

- an admission or denial of the allegation
- a combination of an admission in part and a denial in part
- a claim that the defendant is without sufficient knowledge or information to form a belief as to the truth of an allegation, having the effect of a denial

The defendant's responses must be drafted without any ambiguity as to the matter being admitted or denied. The answer should contain a caption to the matter, a title designating the nature of the pleading, and numbered paragraphs corresponding to the numbered paragraphs of the complaint. Illustration 5-6 provides an example of the defendant's responses in an answer.

In the formulation of the answer, the defendant analyzes the complaint for the following:

- technical defects (i.e., jurisdiction, service)
- factual errors
- possible defenses
- addition of parties
- substantive law

An analysis of the complaint in light of the foregoing will assist the legal office assistant in the preparation of the answer along with potential defenses, dismissal, or the addition of parties.

AFFIRMATIVE DEFENSES

Where the defendant has a defense to the complaint based on a matter not mentioned in the complaint, then the defendant may assert that new matter as an **affirmative defense.**

answer

affirmative defense

IN THE UNITED STATES DISTRICT COURT
FOR THE EASTERN DISTRICT OF MICHIGAN

CONRAD P. CROWN and
OYSTERDENT, INC.,
a Michigan corporation,

    Plaintiffs,

v.   C.A. No. 99-23456

CYBERNET, INC.,
an Ohio corporation,

    Defendant.
_____/

DEFENDANT'S ANSWER

The Defendant, for answer to Plaintiff's Complaint, states as follows:

1. Paragraph 1 is admitted.

2. Paragraph 2 is admitted.

3. Paragraph 3 is admitted.

4. The Defendant denies the allegations contained in paragraph 4 for lack of sufficient information of knowledge to form a belief as to the truth thereof.

5. Paragraph 5 is denied.

Illustration 5-6
A Sample Answer

The basis for an affirmative defense may be found in the fact that the plaintiff failed to file the action within a specified length of time. The defendant would have an affirmative defense of the statute of limitations. Rule 8 provides additional affirmative defenses based on questions of fraud, res judicata (already decided), contributory negligence (the plaintiff was also at fault), release and waiver (the claim has been paid), and discharge in bankruptcy. Each affirmative defense should be set forth in the answer as a separate matter and should plead separate from the numbering of the paragraphs to conform to the complaint.

MOTION TO DISMISS

Rule 12(b) of the *Federal Rules of Civil Procedure* provides the defendant with alternatives to the filing of an answer in response to the plaintiff's complaint. Rule 12(b) gives the defendant an opportunity to have the court dismiss the complaint for one of seven different defenses through the filing of a motion pursuant to the rule. Those seven defenses are:

- lack of jurisdiction over the subject matter
- lack of jurisdiction over the person
- lack of proper venue
- lack of sufficiency of the process (defective summons)
- insufficiency of service of process
- failure to state a claim upon which relief can be granted
- failure to join an essential party to the action

The motion to dismiss can be made a part of the answer or it can be filed as a separate responsive pleading. If filed as a separate pleading in lieu of filing an answer, then it must be filed within the twenty days allowed for the filing of the answer to avoid a judgment on the plaintiff's complaint.

COUNTERCLAIM

The federal district courts are consistent in seeking to make a decision on *all* claims between the parties to an action, thus preventing multiple lawsuits over the same transaction. If the defendant to an action has a claim against the plaintiff in opposition or reduction of the plaintiff's claim, that claim may be asserted in the form of a **counterclaim.**

In the counterclaim, the original defendant essentially becomes the plaintiff for purposes of the counterclaim, while remaining the defendant on the original action. The counterclaim must be filed within the time prescribed for filing an answer and may be made part of the answer. The plaintiff must then respond with a reply within twenty days. The drafting of the counterclaim, whether as a part of the answer, or a separate pleading, is accomplished in the same form as the complaint. The necessary elements to state a cause of action must be pleaded in a paragraph allegation form.

CROSS-CLAIM

Rule 13 of the *Federal Rules of Civil Procedure* covers the situation where a party to a lawsuit initiates an action against a coparty. Such an action is called a **cross-claim.**

counterclaim

cross-claim

A cross-claim can exist between two or more defendants or between two or more plaintiffs. The claim exists where a party to one side of the case files a claim against another party on the same side of the lawsuit. The opportunity for a cross-claim exists only in the situation where there are coparties, and where the claim against a coparty arises out of the same transaction or event. The validity of the cross-claim may be contingent on the validity of the initial claim against the party filing the cross-claim. That is, if the defendant is found to have liability, then liability may exist for the cross-defendant. But, if the defendant is found to have no liability on the initial claim, then there can be no liability for the cross-defendant.

Cross-claims must be filed within the twenty-day time limit prescribed for filing the answer. It is usually filed as part of the answer, and should be pleaded in the same manner as if it were a complaint. The pleading requirements of Rule 8 apply in mandating a clear and concise statement of the claim.

THIRD-PARTY PRACTICE

In addition to the original parties to an action, the *Federal Rules of Civil Procedure* also provide a procedure for the addition of third parties to the action. The procedure set forth in Rule 14 is called **impleader,** and involves the assertion by the defendant that a person not already a party to the action is in fact liable to the defendant. The distinction between a situation involving the original parties (counterclaim and cross-claim) and an impleader is the involvement of a third party, a person not a party to the original lawsuit.

MOTIONS

The *Federal Rules of Civil Procedure* provide for certain forms of relief by the order of the court through a process of petition. The petition to the court for an order directing some act is called a **motion.** Rule 7 (b) (1) of the *Federal Rules of Civil Procedure,* provides:

> An application to the court for an order shall be by motion that, unless made during a hearing or trial, shall be made in writing, shall state with particularity the grounds therefor, and shall set forth the relief or order sought. The requirement of writing is fulfilled if the motion is stated in a written notice of the hearing of the motion.

A motion is frequently accompanied by further documentation to support the allegations or claims upon which the motion is based. The document may be an **affidavit,** which is a sworn statement of facts by the signer acknowledged by a notary. The motion may also be accompanied by a memorandum of law called a **brief**, providing the court with relevant statutory and case law support for the moving party's position.

Motions must be served upon all parties at least five days before the scheduled hearing, along with all supporting affidavits and briefs. Some motions require a longer notice period, and local district court rules should be consulted. The rules provide for many motions that control the flow of the litigation on a lawsuit.

DEFAULT JUDGMENT

If the defendant fails to file an answer within the twenty days prescribed by the *Rules,* then the plaintiff is entitled to a judgment on the complaint. The defendant's

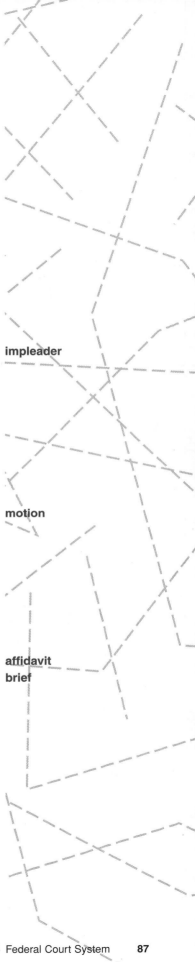

impleader

motion

affidavit

brief

default judgment

failure to defend the matter has left the defendant in a state of default. This allows the plaintiff to take a **default judgment** against him.

Rule 55 provides that the plaintiff must first file a Request to Enter Default, supported by an affidavit from the plaintiff's attorney to the effect that service was perfected and that the twenty-day period for response has elapsed. If the documentation is complete, then the clerk of the court will enter an Entry of Default.

MOTION FOR SUMMARY JUDGMENT

motion for summary judgment

Rule 56 of the *Federal Rules of Civil Procedure* provides for an end to the case upon motion by either party where there is no genuine issue as to any material fact. The moving party can be either the plaintiff or defendant, and can be entitled to judgment as a matter of law where such a situation exists. That dispositive motion is called a **motion for summary judgment.** The moving party's entitlement to a grant of the motion is based on a question of law, as opposed to any question of fact. Once the motion has been granted by the court, the matter is terminated. The burden is on the moving party to show that there is no genuine issue of any material fact. If any doubt exists, resulting in a disputed fact, the matter is resolved against the moving party.

The motion for summary judgment may not be filed by the plaintiff until twenty days has elapsed from the service of the summons and complaint. The defendant may file the motion for summary judgment at any time. The motion itself is usually accompanied by one or more affidavits establishing the lack of any factual issue and also by a brief or memorandum of law in support of the motion, as shown in Illustration 5-7.

MOTION FOR JUDGMENT ON THE PLEADINGS

Closely related to a motion for summary judgment is the procedure governed by Rule 12(c) of the *Federal Rules of Civil Procedure* allowing for the entry of judgment by the court solely on the pleadings. Such a judgment is granted only in limited circumstances where the court considers the pleadings in a light most favorable to the nonmoving party and bases its decision on the lack of any disputed fact. If any question of fact exists, the motion will not be granted.

COURT ORDERS

court order

interlocutory

final order

It is a fundamental rule of pleading that a court speaks only through its orders. A **court order** is a written direction of the court determining a step in the proceedings. An order is considered **interlocutory** if it only decides some intervening matter, but not the ultimate outcome in the case. If the court's order is a ruling that terminates the action, the order is considered a **final order.**

Proposed orders are usually submitted to the court along with the filing of motion and its supporting documents. Local district court rules should be consulted for both procedure and form for proposed orders given the wide divergence between court rules.

judgment

It is important to recognize the distinction between an *order* and a **judgment.**

An order resolves specific issues that are the subject of a motion or request of a party. A judgment provides for a termination of the lawsuit and the granting of the ultimate relief sought.

IN THE UNITED STATES DISTRICT COURT
FOR THE EASTERN DISTRICT OF MICHIGAN

OYSTERDENT, INC.,
a Michigan corporation,

    Plaintiff,

v.   C.A. No. 99-23456

CYBERNET, INC.,
an Ohio corporation,

    Defendant.
_____/

MOTION FOR SUMMARY JUDGMENT

      Defendant, CYBERNET, INC., moves for an order pursuant to *Federal Rules of Civil Procedure* 56 for summary judgment to be granted against Plaintiff in the above-captioned action on the grounds that there is no genuine issue to any material fact and that defendant, CYBERNET, INC., is entitled to judgment as a matter of law. Defendant attaches its Brief In Support of Motion.

                              _____

                              I. M. SHARPE, 12345
                              Attorney for Defendant
                              10 Tennace Court Street
                              Detroit, Michigan 48226-1254
                              (301) 555-5678

Illustration 5-7
A Motion for Summary Judgment

SUMMARY

The federal court system is a three-level structure, with the federal district court constituting the court of original jurisdiction in most situations. The U.S. courts of appeal and the U.S. Supreme Court exist for purposes of review on questions of law. The initial pleadings in a lawsuit are filed in the district court in preparation for litigation of the issues.

The proper federal district court in which to start a lawsuit is determined on the basis of jurisdiction. Jurisdiction is determined by either subject matter, personal, or *in rem* jurisdiction. For federal jurisdiction, there must be a diversity of citizenship and an amount in controversy in excess of $50,000.

Pleadings in federal court are designed to introduce the plaintiff's allegations, narrow the issues, place the defendant on notice, and invoke the court's jurisdiction. Regardless of the nature of the document, pleadings should be drafted in language that contains a short, plain statement of the matter.

A well-drafted complaint contains a proper identification of the parties, a statement of the court's jurisdiction, a statement of the claim, and a prayer for relief. The complaint must state a cause of action upon which relief may be granted and must, therefore, contain all of the necessary elements of the cause.

The preparation of answers, motions, and other responsive pleadings follow the same construction rules in requiring a short, plain statement. The legal office assistant must be sure to follow the proper format required by local federal court rule and prepared in a timely fashion.

Chapter Activities

Review Questions

1. What are the three levels in the federal court system?
2. What are the courts of original jurisdiction?
3. What are the basic types of jurisdiction?
4. Describe the difference between jurisdiction and venue.
5. List the four purposes of a pleading.
6. List the elements that make up a complaint.
7. Define a long arm statute.
8. List the five purposes of the filing of an answer by the defendant.
9. Describe the difference between a counterclaim and a cross-claim.
10. What is the fundamental ground behind a Motion for Summary Judgment?

Computer Activity

In May 1997, Margaret "Large Marge" Mack began her employment with Pitt Bull Freight Lines as an over-the-road driver. In November of that same year, upon review of Large Marge's personnel file, Pitt Bull's chief dispatcher, Owen "Stretch" Jingo, discovered that he had mistakenly hired a female. From that point on, she was allowed to haul only hogs or their byproducts. She was denied any decent jobs and was even told that no more members of her club, The Gear-Jammin Mommas, would be hired by Pitt Bull. Finally, after succumbing to "hog-aroma" in December, Large Marge was forced to quit her employment.

Your legal office has filed a lawsuit against Pitt Bull Freight Lines, Inc., in the local federal district court in your jurisdiction on behalf of Marge Mack. You have been asked by Mr. Cole Hahn, of the law firm of Cole Hahn, P.C., and your supervising attorney, to prepare a Motion for Summary Judgment in the matter. Mr. Hahn has already prepared the Brief in Support of Motion.

A. From the student template retrieve act5.wpd. This document contains a sample of a Motion for Summary Judgment form, accompanied by a time sheet for the firm. Key in the required information from the scenario to prepare the motion and the entries on the timesheet. Refer to the chapter for examples.

B. Save this information on the template as depo.doc.

C. Print one copy for your instructor. Make sure your name appears for identification purposes.

Chapter 6

State Court System

Objectives

After completing this chapter, you will be able to:

1. Compare civil practice and procedure between federal and state courts.

2. Describe jurisdiction in state courts.

3. Explain the significance of a statute of limitation.

4. Summarize the general rules of pleading in state courts.

5. Outline the defenses available in state courts.

6. Discuss pleading special matters in state courts.

7. Summarize the filing of amended pleadings.

8. Describe class actions.

9. Explain survivorship and substitution of parties.

10. Discuss the role of mediation and arbitration in state court.

The state court systems are separate and distinct from the federal court system. Although the federal courts operate within the borders of the state, they are an independent system with separate jurisdiction. Each state court system contains many different courts, but all systems have some basic characteristics in common. For the legal office assistant to provide the professional support required by the legal office, an understanding of the court system is essential.

THE STRUCTURE OF STATE COURT SYSTEMS

Every state has its own court system with general jurisdiction over matters concerning the state, its residents, and their property. The state court system is established by the state constitution. The court of last resort is most frequently referred to as the *Supreme Court*. The Supreme Court hears cases on review from the *courts of appeal,* the review courts that examine the proceedings in the trial court. The *trial courts* are the courts of original jurisdiction. See Illustration 6-1.

The duties and power of each court are set forth in the rules of civil procedure called the **rules of court.**

Most state rules of court are patterned after the *Federal Rules of Civil Procedure,* having been enacted by either the state legislature or issued by the state's highest court. These rules govern procedure in all courts of the state. There is a difference in procedure between the states. The rules of court of each individual state must be consulted before proceeding.

rules of court

JURISDICTION

Jurisdiction in state courts, as with the federal courts, can be based on the subject matter of the action, personal jurisdiction, or it may be *in rem,* as seen in chapter 5 in the federal court system. Any judgment rendered by a state court without proper jurisdiction is unenforceable. In the state court system, the court of original jurisdiction, or the trial court, is most frequently called the **circuit court.**

circuit court

Depending on the state, the court may be called the district court, superior court, county court, or common pleas court. Generally, each county of the state has its own circuit court. The circuit courts are considered to be the state **courts of general jurisdiction**, which are empowered to hear cases concerning personal injury, property damage, contracts, domestic relations, and any other general cause of action.

courts of general jurisdiction

Courts of limited jurisdiction are those state courts that are permitted to hear only cases of a specific type. These courts are limited to a designated subject matter jurisdiction, such as probate matters, misdemeanor criminal cases, lesser civil matters with a dollar amount limitation, municipal courts, and workers' compensation. A special court of limited jurisdiction found in most states is the **small claims court.**

courts of limited jurisdiction

small claims court

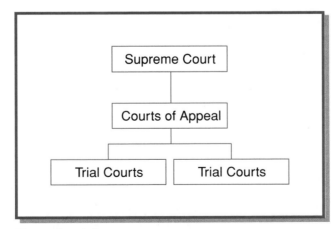

Illustration 6-1
A State Court System

The small claims court is a court of limited jurisdiction where the value of the matter at issue cannot exceed a maximum dollar amount, for example, $1,500. These courts generally litigate matters without attorneys and offer reduced filing fees and simplified procedures.

STATUTES OF LIMITATION

statute of limitation

Federal and state laws have established various maximum time limits during which an action may be maintained. Once that maximum time has expired, no lawsuit may be filed, regardless of its merit. A law establishing the time limitation to the right of filing an action is called a **statute of limitation** or *limitation of action.* It prohibits the commencement of a lawsuit and provides the defendant with an affirmative defense that must be pleaded.

The statute of limitations begins to run at the time the cause of action arises. For example, with a personal injury claim, the cause of action would arise on the day of the accident, and the statute of limitations would begin to run the following day. For a contract, the cause of action would arise at the time of the breach, or when the first payment is overdue, and the statute would begin to run the next day. If the cause of action arises over a period of time or through a series of events, the statute begins to run the day of the last event. The number of days constituting the statutory period begins the day after the accrual of the cause of action. For instance, if a failed payment on a note were due on November 15, then the statute of limitations would commence running on the following day, November 16.

toll

If the statutory period for limitation expires on a weekend or holiday, then the statute does not expire until the next business day. In that case, the statute is said to **toll**, which means that it is prevented from expiring until the next business day. Typical of statutes of limitation for civil actions in many states, the Florida statutes shown in Illustration 6-2 provide the limitations of action on various causes of action.

All states have deadlines for filing certain pleadings set forth in the rules of court that function in a manner similar to a statute of limitation. The filing deadlines in the rules of court are of a procedural nature, as opposed to a matter of substantive law. The filing of a particular pleading may be prevented by the court rule, eliminating a valuable right by a party. Professional responsibility requires that actions are commenced within the statutory period for filing and that pleadings are filed within the limitations established by the rules of court. It is the responsibility of the legal office assistant to be aware of these limitations and monitor their compliance. The docket control systems discussed in chapter 3 provide the vehicle to monitor a statute of limitations.

PLEADING IN STATE COURTS

The *Federal Rules of Civil Procedure* provide the model from which most states have patterned their respective procedural rules. Most state rules of civil procedure set forth the requirements for such matters as the caption, complaint, counterclaims and cross-claims, service of process, answer, and motions. Typical of many state rules, Illustration 6-3 states the intended scope of the *Florida Rules of Civil Procedure.*

The fundamental rule of pleading in any state court is the same as in the federal system. Pleadings require a short, plain statement as to the nature of the relief sought and its grounds. That requirement extends not only to the complaint, but also includes any other pleadings filed pursuant to the rules.

Limitation	Action
20 years	Action on a judgment
7 years	Action to quiet title on real property
5 years	Action on a written contract
	Foreclosure on a mortgage
4 years	Negligence actions
	Title to personal property
	Paternity
	Oral contract
	Products liability
2 years	Professional malpractice
	Defamation action
	Wrongful death
1 year	Specific performance on a contract
	Violation of a provision of the UCC

Illustration 6-2
Florida Statutes of Limitation

These rules apply to all actions of a civil nature and all special statutory proceedings in the circuit courts and county courts except those to which the probate and guardianship rules or the summary claims procedure rules apply. The form, content, procedure and time for pleading in all special statutory proceedings shall be as prescribed by the statutes governing the proceeding unless these rules specifically provide to the contrary. These rules shall be construed to secure the just, speedy and inexpensive determination of every action. These rules shall be known as the *Florida Rules of Civil Procedure*.

Illustration 6-3
Florida Rules of Civil Procedure, 1.010

THE CAPTION

In state courts, the caption requires basically the same information as required by the federal rules:

- name of the court

- the file number

- the name of the parties on each side of the case with their proper designation

All pleadings must contain some indication as to the nature of the pleading, clearly stating the subject matter of the document. For instance, if the pleading is a complaint, then *complaint* must clearly be in its title (see Illustration 6-4).

COMPLAINT

State court rules provide that a complaint must state a claim upon which relief may be granted. It is the responsibility of the legal office assistant in preparing a complaint to ensure that it contains the following:

- an identification of the parties

- a statement of jurisdiction

- a statement of the claim giving rise to a cause of action

- a demand for relief

The actual format of a complaint is a matter of local court rule and custom. Every legal office assistant should have samples available to be tailored to the particular facts of a given case.

SERVICE OF PROCESS

Proper service of process gives the defendant notice of the proceedings and provides an opportunity to appear and defend. The form of process may vary, depending on the state and the nature of the case. Process can be serviced in any of the following ways:

- by personal delivery to the defendant by an authorized individual

- by mail

- by publication under specific statutory guidelines

- pursuant to the state's long-arm statute

proof of service

Regardless of the form of the service, the court will require a **proof of service**, which is merely a written indication by the process server that service has been made upon the defendant as prescribed.

ANSWER

In the answer, the defendant must state in short, plain terms a response to the allegations in the complaint. The defendant may:

- admit the allegation

- deny the allegation

- state that he/she is without sufficient knowledge to form a belief

A response to an allegation may be an admission in part and a denial in part, as long as the defendant clearly states the portion admitted and denied. Some states allow a

```
                          STATE OF GEORGIA
               IN THE CIRCUIT COURT FOR ORANGE COUNTY


DAVID B. ROUNDSTONE,

      Plaintiff,

v.                                        File No:

GOLIATH, INC.,
a Georgia corporation,

      Defendant.

_____/

                            COMPLAINT

      NOW COMES DAVID B. ROUNDSTONE, Plaintiff herein, and says the

following:

      1.   He is a resident of the county of Orange, state of Georgia.

      2.   The Defendant, GOLIATH, INC., is a corporation incorporated under

the laws of the state of Georgia and has its principal place of business in

the county of Orange, state of Georgia.

      3.   On or about November 8, 1999, the Defendant did slander, defame,

and otherwise bring to disparagement the good name and reputation of the

Plaintiff, to wit:
```

Illustration 6-4
A Sample Caption

general denial to all matters asserted, including jurisdiction. If so, then the procedure is a simple statement to the effect that the defendant denies all the allegations in the plaintiff's complaint.

DEFENSES

It is the responsibility of the legal office and the legal office assistant to ensure that every defense be asserted by the defendant, whether it is of a factual nature or a matter of law. The timing and the form of the assertion are matters that vary from state to state and at the option of the pleader.

When Presented. The time for filing an answer is always a specified time from the service of the original process. An extension of time in which to file an answer is frequently granted by the court on motion by the defendant.

In the case of a cross-claim, most court rules provide the cross-defendant with the same time to answer the cross-complaint as with the original pleading. If a defendant files a counterclaim against the plaintiff, the plaintiff shall have the same period in which to file an answer to the counterclaim. If a reply is required, the same time constraints apply.

Presenting Defenses. Both legal and factual defenses must be asserted in the responsive pleading. The answer will contain the defendant's response to each specific allegation in the complaint. The defendant may have other defenses available, as opposed to a specific response to an allegation. In that case, most states allow the certain defensive issues to be pleaded by motion. Illustration 6-5 presents a list of defensive issues that can be pleaded by motion rather than answer.

A motion that pleads any of these defenses must set forth specifically the grounds upon which the motion is based. The motion must also be supported with an affidavit and legal brief setting forth the law.

Failure to Deny. Any allegation in a pleading that requires a response from the other party is deemed to be admitted unless specifically denied in a responsive pleading. If the plaintiff alleges a certain fact in the complaint, and the defendant fails to admit or deny the allegation, then for purposes of the current case the allegation is admitted. Therefore, the legal office assistant must be aware that *all* matters requiring a response are addressed in one of the responsive pleadings. If the matter does not require a response, then the matter is considered denied.

---

1. Lack of jurisdiction over the subject matter
2. Lack of jurisdiction over the person
3. Improper venue
4. Service of process
5. Failure to state a cause of action
6. Failure to join indispensable parties

Illustration 6-5
Defensive Issues

Affirmative Defenses. A defense to the complaint based on a matter not mentioned in the complaint is an **affirmative defense**. The underlying basis for an affirmative defense is that it attacks the legal right of the plaintiff to present a claim. Under most state court rules, the affirmative defenses are set out as a separate section to the answer. Illustration 6-6 provides a list of affirmative defenses allowed by most state courts.

affirmative defense

Waiver of Defenses. The court rules of most states provide for a waiver of defenses for those matters not submitted in a responsive pleading. If a party does not present a defense by way of pleadings, then the court will consider that defense waived and will not allow its later consideration. This does not include those matters that are brought before the court after pleadings are closed, such as a motion for judgment on the pleadings. Also, in most states this provision would not cover motions at trial. The legal office assistant should keep in mind the legal principle that a defense of lack of jurisdiction may be raised at any time.

MOTIONS

The procedure for bringing a motion before the state courts varies greatly. A hearing is not required for every type of motion. There are some forms of motion that are considered to be *ex parte*, which is a hearing by the court attended only by the moving party.

ex parte

Those motions requiring a hearing for both sides of a dispute are scheduled by the judicial assistant on the court's motion calendar. Certain days or specific times of the week may be set aside for the hearing of motions. The notice of the motion is usually furnished to the opposing party through the use of a pleading, called a **notice of hearing**.

notice of hearing

The notice must provide "reasonable" notice of the time and place of the hearing and identify the nature and grounds for the motion. Some states require the use of a writ called a *praecipe*, which is an order in the form of a writ from the clerk of the

praecipe

accord and satisfaction	laches
arbitration and award	license
assumption of the risk	master-servant
contributory negligence	payment
discharge in bankruptcy	release
duress	*res judicata*
estoppel	statute of frauds
failure of consideration	statute of limitations
fraud	waiver
illegality	

Illustration 6-6
Affirmative Defenses

court to a party to show why something should or should not occur. It serves as the court's official notice of the pending hearing and must be served upon the opposing party.

Motion for Judgment on the Pleadings. The motion for judgment on the pleadings in most state courts is patterned after Rule 12(c) of the *Federal Rules of Civil Procedure.* The proper time to file the motion is after the period for filing pleadings has expired. At that time, the court may determine the sufficiency of the pleadings. The court is required to view the pleadings in a light most favorable to the party against whom the motion is brought.

Motion for a More Definite Statement. A situation may arise where a party to an action is unable to frame a response to an allegation or defense due to some ambiguity or vagueness in the form of the pleading. It is reasonable that a party be able to understand the nature of an allegation before being required to admit or deny its correctness. The party may request sufficient information upon which to form a response. To facilitate that end, many state court rules provide a procedure through **motion for more definite statement**.

Once the court has granted the motion, then the responding party is given a set period of time in which to comply with the court's order for a clarification. In some states, this motion may be referred to as a *bill of particulars.*

Motion to Strike. Available to all parties at the state level as well as the federal level is an opportunity to have the court order the opposing party to strike any material from a pleading that is considered "redundant, immaterial, impertinent, or scandalous." The purpose behind the provision is to keep such material from potentially influencing the opinions of a jury at the time of trial. The opportunity is presented through the use of a motion to strike the offending material from the pleading.

JOINDER OF PARTIES

Consistent with the goal of litigation to resolve all claims between parties to a lawsuit, it is necessary that *all* parties to that action be added. The **joinder of parties** is the addition as parties to an action of all those persons or entities that have the same rights or interests as coplaintiffs or codefendants.

The court rules generally require that those parties who are united in interest *must* be added. Parties that were not included in the original pleadings may be added by amended pleadings within the time allowed by the rules of court for such amendments. If a person not named as a party wishes to join in the action, it is possible to move to be added as a party through a procedure termed **intervention**.

The rules also provide a solution for the situation where a party was added by mistake. A motion may be dismissed from the action by a party wrongfully added, termed **misjoinder**.

If possible, it is important that all parties with any potential exposure be added in the original pleadings to avoid the delay and expense that accompany the procedure of joinder and intervention. In all cases, judgment will be rendered according to the party's respective rights and liabilities.

PLEADING SPECIAL MATTERS IN STATE COURTS

Pleadings must properly reflect the basic laws of the state. To do otherwise is to violate the professional responsibility to which a client is entitled. The law of a particular state may require that certain legal principles, if relevant to the action, must

motion for more definite statement

joinder of parties

intervention

misjoinder

be pleaded separately. For example, many states require that the following substantive issues be alleged separately within a pleading:

- capacity
- fraud, mistake of fact, state of mind
- conditions precedent
- official document
- prior judgment or decree
- special damages

CAPACITY

In those states with special pleading practices for these issues, the court rules will define the issue and require its assertion.

If **capacity** must be pleaded separately, the court rules will specifically require it. Capacity refers to the level of mental competence required by law to understand the nature of one's acts. If the state's rules do not refer to a requirement of pleading capacity specifically, the opposing party may still raise the issue as an affirmative defense.

capacity

FRAUD OR MISTAKE

Causes of action involving an intentional misrepresentation of a material fact, either by words or conduct that lead to a detrimental reliance thereon, must be pleaded separately in many states. Actions involving the state of mind of a party, whether intentional or negligent, may be pleaded generally. Illustration 6-7 provides an example of a typical court rule relating to state of mind.

CONDITION PRECEDENT

A **condition precedent** is an event that must occur before some right that depends on the event may arise. Such conditions are frequently seen in the law of real property or are associated with contractual obligations. Most state court rules allow the existence of a condition precedent to be pleaded in a general manner, merely stating that all conditions precedent to filing the action have been performed. If done so, then the denial of the condition by the defendant in his or her responsive pleading must be made specifically.

condition precedent

Fraud, Mistake, Condition of Mind. In all averments of fraud or mistake, the circumstances constituting fraud or mistake shall be stated with such particularity as the circumstances may permit. Malice, intent, knowledge, mental attitude, and other conditions of mind of a person may be averred generally.

Illustration 6-7
Florida Court Rules

OFFICIAL DOCUMENTS

official documents

Official documents and official acts are those that are performed or kept in the performance of an official's authorized duties.

Such acts or documents, if material to the cause of action, are sufficiently pleaded by alleging that the document was issued or the act done in compliance with its authorizing statute.

PRIOR JUDGMENT

The judicial pronouncements of other courts, foreign or domestic, may form a relevant element of a particular cause of action. Such judgments or decrees need only be pleaded through a general allegation without establishing the court's jurisdiction to render such a judgment. If there is to be an attack on that judgment for any reason, it must take place in the court issuing the decree, not in the new forum. Such an attack is called a **collateral attack**, and it is prohibited in all states.

collateral attack

SPECIAL DAMAGES

special damages

Special damages are those actual damages flowing from an act or breach due to special circumstances. For instance, in the breach of a contract, there may be damages resulting that were not contemplated by the parties to the contract at the time of its formation. To be recoverable, they must flow directly from the breach. Special damages must be pleaded separately in federal and most state courts.

AMENDED AND SUPPLEMENTAL PLEADINGS

The need may arise during the course of a lawsuit to change pleadings because some material fact has been discovered or has been omitted. The *Federal Rules of Civil Procedure* and the court rules of most states allow a procedure for the filing of amended pleadings, as found in Rule 15 of the *Federal Rules of Civil Procedure.*

PROCEDURE

A party may amend a pleading as a matter of course when there has been no filing of a responsive pleading. If no responsive pleading is required, and the matter has not been placed on the trial calendar, then the plaintiff may amend the complaint within a specified number of days from service of process.

In all other circumstances, in most state courts and in federal court, leave of the court must be obtained before an amended pleading may be filed without the written consent of the opposing party. Most rules state that leave of the court shall be freely given when the ends of justice require, and the other party is not materially prejudiced.

SURVIVORSHIP

Amendment of the pleadings becomes necessary where the original plaintiff is no longer available to carry on the action, yet the cause of action remains alive. State laws provide for the circumstances where the cause of action survives beyond the death or incompetency of the plaintiff. Such statutes are called **survival statutes**, and provide that the cause of action is not extinguished due to death of a party.

survival statutes

Either by statute or court rule, the states generally provide a procedure for the filing of a motion for **substitution of parties** for the maintenance of an action after the original plaintiff is no longer available.

substitution of parties

Most court rules allow substitution under the following circumstances:

- death in cases where the survival statute prevents the extinguishing of the claim

- incompetency of a party

- transfer of interest in property or of a right allowable as a matter of law

- in the case of a public official who is a party to the action, upon death or removal from office

The procedure for the substitution of parties is the same for filing any amended pleading, namely, through the motion procedure. The amendment will be allowed as long as there is no material prejudice to the opposing party.

CLASS ACTION LAWSUITS

A **class action** is a lawsuit maintained by a large group of individuals with the same characteristic legal rights against a particular defendant.

The class action is a difficult and complex action to be maintained because of the volume of documented proof required. The purpose of a class action is to allow a large group to bring a lawsuit on behalf of themselves and other members of the group through a representative plaintiff.

In order for a class action to be maintained, the following conditions must be met:

- The number of members of the class is so large that joinder of the members is impracticable.

- There must be questions of law or fact common to the class.

- The claims or defenses of the representative party are common to the class.

- The representative party can fairly protect and represent the interests of each member of the class.

The court rules of most states will address the specific requirements for pleading a class action, as in Rule 23 of the *Federal Rules of Civil Procedure.* You should consult these rules before preparation of any class action pleading.

MEDIATION AND ARBITRATION

As an alternative means for the resolution of a lawsuit, many states have provisions in their court rules to submit the matter to a neutral third party or panel for decision. This process is called **mediation.** The procedure is usually not binding on the parties, but serves to bring the parties to a resolution posture without the expense, delay, and formalities of a trial.

Another alternative to a full trial of the lawsuit is a procedure known as **arbitration,** which involves the submission of the issues to a neutral third person for decision.

Arbitration provisions are found in many contracts to provide a less costly means of resolving a conflict. The decision of the arbitrator will be binding on the parties if the procedure is voluntary and will be nonbinding if the procedure is mandatory.

There is a wide degree of variance between states and court rules on the mediation and arbitration procedures. The local court rules must be consulted to avoid the loss of certain valuable rights.

SUMMARY

Civil procedure in most state courts is modeled after the *Federal Rules of Civil Procedure.* It is important for the legal office assistant to understand state procedure. The

class action

mediation

arbitration

basic procedures from the filing of the complaint through the pretrial pleading stages involve close adherence to the specific court rules of the individual state.

The preparation of pleadings by the legal office assistant serves the underlying purpose of adequately framing and narrowing the issues for decision by the court. Its goal is the efficient administration of justice. With close adherence to the general rules of pleading and through a careful use of the defenses available to a party, the issues can be significantly narrowed and defined before trial.

Chapter Activities

Review Questions

1. Define the model for the court rules of most states.

2. In the state court system, what are the courts of original jurisdiction?

3. List the courts of limited jurisdiction.

4. What is the significance of a statute of limitation in the preparation of a responsive pleading?

5. What is the fundamental rule of pleading in state courts?

6. List the four basic elements that must be contained in a complaint.

7. In the preparation of an answer, what are the alternate pleas that a defendant may use?

8. What is the effect of a failure to deny an allegation in a complaint?

9. List some affirmative defenses that a defendant may use.

10. What is the purpose behind a joinder of parties?

11. List the special matters to be pleaded in most state courts.

12. Define a class action.

Computer Activity

In November 1997, Ray Moon contracted a fatal illness. To provide for the disposal of his remains, he and his wife, Honey, entered into a contract with Eternal Wave Cremation Society for the disposal of his remains by cremation. It was set forth in the agreement dated November 13, 1997, that under no circumstances were his ashes to be disposed of at sea due to his unremitting fear of the water and of becoming an unwilling participant in a seafood buffet.

Ray succumbed to his disease on February 14, 1998. Pursuant to the agreement, his remains were transferred to Eternal Wave. The cremation was delayed for a week, causing Honey to experience Freudian nightmares. When seeking to obtain her husband's ashes, she was told that they could not be found. After some delay, an unlabeled urn was produced by Eternal Wave purportedly containing Ray's ashes. With ashes "in hand," Honey began a sentimental journey, returning to all of their romantic venues to distribute a small portion of his ashes at each site. As she was to place the remaining ash at a family burial plot, she discovered some dental bridgework in the urn. Immediately realizing that her husband had never had any dental bridge, she contacted Eternal Wave and was finally told that her husband's ashes had been mistakenly scattered over the Gulf of Mexico. Since that time, she has required around-the-clock medical attention for multiple neuroses.

The prestigious law firm of Bargin & Sale, P.C., has just hired you as its legal office assistant. The firm has been retained by Honey Moon to file a lawsuit against Eternal Wave for breach of contract. You have been informed that the contract was valid and that there was a breach of that contract by the defendant, resulting in damages to Mrs. Moon.

Preliminary contact with the defendant, Eternal Wave, resulted in correspondence received from their attorneys. That letter sets forth the affirmative defenses that will be asserted by Eternal Wave if this matter proceeds to litigation.

A. From the student template retrieve act6.wpd. This document contains a sample of a memorandum form accompanied by a letter from defendant's attorney. From the information in the scenario, prepare a memorandum to your supervising attorney, A. Bargin, outlining the matters that must be considered to prepare the complaint. Review the correspondence and underscore the defenses of merit. Refer to the chapter for examples.

B. Save this information as memo.doc.

C. Print one copy for your instructor. Make sure your name appears for identification purposes.

Chapter 7

Discovery

The purpose of our modern discovery procedure is to narrow the issues, to eliminate surprises, and to achieve substantial justice.

Greyhound Lines, Inc. v. Miller, 402 F.2d 134 (1968)

Objectives

After completing this chapter, you will be able to:

1. Discuss the general nature of discovery.
2. Explain the purpose of discovery.
3. Describe the scope of discovery.
4. Identify the various discovery tools.
5. Discuss the use of the various discovery tools.
6. Explain the purpose of a protective order.
7. Summarize the necessary authorizations for information gathering.

The litigation process depends on formal information gathering pretrial devices that can be used by the legal office to obtain facts and information about a case from another party to assist in the preparation for trial. It is necessary for the legal office assistant to understand the discovery and its purpose in the litigation process in order to assist the attorney.

DISCOVERY PROCESS

Preparation for the trial of a lawsuit mandates that each party obtain as much information as possible concerning the opposition's case. The process used to secure the information necessary to prepare for trial is termed **discovery.**

The discovery procedure for each state is provided by its rules of court that are patterned after the *Federal Rules of Civil Procedure.* The rules set forth the procedure for the discovery process and govern its limitations and timing.

discovery

107

Since there may be a wide divergence regarding individual state rules, these local rules must be consulted before attempting the use of any of the discovery tools.

PURPOSE OF DISCOVERY

As a legal office professional, it is your responsibility to learn everything allowed under the court rules about an opponent's case. To this end, discovery serves the following purposes:

- narrow the issues
- obtain facts for trial
- learn an opponent's contentions
- reveal the identity of witnesses
- locate and preserve evidence
- learn the extent of damages
- impeach witnesses

Depending on the nature of the cause of action, the emphasis will be on one or more of the purposes of discovery. For instance, the identity of witnesses and the preservation of evidence may not be as critical in a breach of contract action as in a personal injury lawsuit.

SCOPE OF DISCOVERY

scope of discovery

material

The **scope of discovery** refers to the depth and breadth of the inquiry, permitting any matter relevant to the case and not subject to privilege.

The scope of discovery must always answer the test of *materiality.* If an inquiry is **material,** it relates to an issue of fact necessary to decide the question.

If a fact, once established, can decide the outcome of a case, then the question is considered material. The scope of discovery is very broad, allowing inquiry into any matter relevant to the subject, and is not privileged. This general rule is usually set forth in state rules of court, most of which are modeled after Rule 26 of the *Federal Rules of Civil Procedure.*

ADMISSIBILITY

In order for information to be obtained through the discovery process, it does not necessarily need to be admissible in court at a trial. The requirement is that the information sought need only be "reasonably calculated" to lead to admissible evidence, as provided by Rule 26 of the *Federal Rules of Civil Procedure* (see Illustration 7-1).

It is not grounds for objection that the information sought will be inadmissible at the trial if the information sought appears reasonably calculated to lead to the discovery of admissible evidence . . .

Illustration 7-1
Rule 26, *Federal Rules of Civil Procedure*

In effect, this means that the information sought must meet the mutual tests of (1) relevancy to the subject matter, and (2) not be privileged. For instance, the content of a conversation between two individuals who are not parties to the action may be considered hearsay evidence at the time of trial, yet would be a proper matter of inquiry in discovery.

EXPERT WITNESSES

Complicated technical subjects require the testimony of individuals who have education and experience in a field beyond the scope of knowledge of the lay person. Such an individual is referred to as an **expert witness.**

If a party to a lawsuit uses an expert, the discovery of the existence and identity of such an expert may be obtained through the use of one of the discovery tools. The inquiry may be made at the time of a deposition of the party, or it may be asked as part of a written interrogatory. Most federal and state rules of court allow the discovery of expert witnesses only if they are to testify at trial. If an expert has been employed only for investigatory purposes and is not to be called as a witness, then this expert is not a proper subject for discovery.

PRIVILEGED INFORMATION

Chapter 1 discussed the law of privilege as it relates to communication between an attorney and client. Essentially, privilege is an exemption held by a particular person or class of persons. Privileged information is that information held by a person with the privilege and is not subject to discovery. Depending on the state, a privileged communication may exist within any one of several relationships, as shown in Illustration 7-2.

The information received by written or spoken communication *between* persons with the privilege is also not subject to disclosure. The purpose is to allow the physician to practice without fear of judicial intervention, to allow the priest to absolve without secular interference, to preserve the sanctity and privacy of the marital relationship, and to allow the attorney and client to prepare for a trial without revelation of strategy.

As discussed in chapter 1, a form of privilege seen frequently is that of work product, which consists of the papers, memoranda, and any other materials existing to assist an attorney in preparation for trial. These materials are not subject to discovery. Work product includes the attorney's own legal research, witness statements, correspondence, and personal recollections of his client. The law of a particular state must be reviewed to find out the scope and extent of the privilege.

expert witness

- physician–patient
- husband–wife
- attorney–client
- clergyman–parishioner
- executive privilege
- journalist privilege
- state secrets privilege

Illustration 7-2
Privileged Communication Relationships

PROTECTIVE ORDER

protective order

The court may issue its order upon motion by a party to protect information that is not privileged, but that would cause annoyance, embarrassment, oppression, or undue burden or expense. Such an order is termed a **protective order.**

Depending on the jurisdiction, the order may prevent any discovery, limit the disclosure terms, limit the persons to whom the information may be disclosed, or seal the information so that only the court may open it.

An example of the type of information subject to a protective order would be a trade secret. Suppose the lawsuit involved the potential for the revelation of a trade secret held by one of the parties. To reveal the trade secret in open court documents would compromise its value to the party holding it and cause additional burden. On motion, the court could enter an order limiting the disclosure of the secret to no one beyond counsel for the respective parties.

DISCOVERY TOOLS

Six discovery tools are available to the parties to a lawsuit. The method employed is determined by the need for disclosure of certain information, the time available, and the cost. These discovery tools are:

- deposition
- interrogatory
- request for production
- request for admission
- physical and mental examination
- request to enter land

The nature of the information being sought and the source of that information are also factors that control the particular discovery tools to be employed.

DEPOSITION

deposition

The testimony of a witness taken upon oral examination through the use of question and answer before an officer of the court is called a **deposition.**

A deposition is the only discovery tool that may be used to take the testimony of an individual who is not a party to the action. Although it may be either written or oral, the most common form is oral examination, closely paralleling courtroom testimony. During the deposition, a party's demeanor and veracity may be evaluated for courtroom presentation.

Depositions may be taken before any judicial officer, such as a notary public authorized to make an acknowledgment. The officer may not be an employee or relative of any of the parties or attorneys.

In federal court, and in most states, permission of the court to take a deposition must be obtained within the first thirty days of service of process. After permission is granted, and during the time allowed by the court rules for discovery, a deposition may be taken upon reasonable notice of the time, place, and the person or persons to be deposed. Illustration 7-3 provides an example of a notice of taking deposition of a party to a lawsuit.

If the individual being deposed is to make certain documents or records available for examination at the time of the deposition, then those documents must be requested in

```
                         IN THE CIRCUIT COURT
                      FOR THE COUNTY OF MOSQUITO


BELLE BLISS,

        Plaintiff,

v.                                                    Case No. 34567

THE THIRSTY TURTLE,

        Defendant.

_____/



                    NOTICE OF TAKING DEPOSITION



TO:     Barnwell Boozer
        Attorney for Defendant
        1234 South Drainage Street
        Orange, Georgia 45091-9876


     PLEASE TAKE NOTICE that the undersigned will take the deposition upon

oral examination of BUD WISER, at 2:00 p.m. at his office, located at One

Harmony Drive, Orange, Georgia, on November 30, 1999, before a notary public

or other authorized person by law to take depositions. This deposition is

being taken for purposes of discovery, for use at trial, or for any other

purpose allowed by law.

     YOU ARE INVITED TO ATTEND.


                                   _____
                                   WILL PURVALE 65432
                                   Attorney for Plaintiff
                                   One Harmony Drive
                                   Orange, Georgia 45090-6540
```

Illustration 7-3
Notice of Taking Deposition

subpoena
subpoena duces tecum

writing. A **subpoena** is a command to appear at a certain time and place. If the order is for documents or records, then a subpoena is termed a **subpoena duces tecum.**

The subpoena for records or documents to be examined at the time of the deposition is usually contained within the body of the notice of taking deposition.

Persons not a party to an action must be served with a subpoena before they can be required to appear for a deposition. Any of the witness's documents sought for review should also be listed in the subpoena.

Depositions are generally held in an office with all parties to the lawsuit represented by counsel. A transcript of the testimony is made by a court reporter. Objections to questions are reflected in the transcript of the hearing and exhibits are introduced as they are in the trial.

INTERROGATORIES

interrogatories

A pretrial discovery tool consisting of a set of written questions propounded to a party is called **interrogatories.**

The interrogatories may be issued to parties only, and are a common initial discovery tool to be used to obtain information from an opponent. The interrogatories may be used for any purpose allowed for discovery in general by the court rules of most states and the *Federal Rules of Civil Procedure.*

Many states have rules that limit the length of interrogatories or have prescribed sets of interrogatories for various causes of action. If there is to be a deviation from the standardized forms, permission of the court must be obtained.

The original of the interrogatories must be served upon the party to whom the questions are propounded, with copies of both interrogatories and answers to be delivered to all other parties. The answers must be returned to the party propounding the questions.

Preparation of interrogatories involves drafting a set of questions that is clear, concise, and without ambiguity. Questions should be framed to avoid yes or no answers. The document should contain a caption, as with any other pleading, signed by the attorney for the party, and furnished with a certificate of service.

Under oath, the recipient of the interrogatories must answer each question in writing. The answers should be placed in the space provided on the original of the interrogatory form. Attachment of records or lengthy documents is permissible. See Appendix A for an example of a set of interrogatories.

REQUEST FOR PRODUCTION

request for production

The rules of court of all states allow for a party to request documents and other things that are relevant to the subject matter and not privileged. This procedure, a **request for production,** is available only against a party.

The request may not be directed toward an individual who is not a party to the action. Rule 34 of the *Federal Rules of Civil Procedure* forms the model for most state rules for production. It is the intent of the rules that the request encompass more than mere documents. The request may include such things as drawings, graphs, charts, photographs, and data compilations.

The rules permit the production of documents and tangible things to allow their inspection and testing. The material may be examined, copied, sampled, tested, photographed, measured, or preserved. The original of any document or object must be preserved for trial.

In order for a party to request the production of a document or any other tangible thing, the document or object must be in the possession, custody, and control of the party from whom it is requested. The production requested must be reasonable in allowing copies or making something that is not easily transferrable available for inspection. In some lawsuits, the physical transfer of voluminous records can be a substantial task requiring cataloging and organization. If such a situation exists, some rules also provide for the reimbursement of the costs involved in production of documents.

The procedure in most states is to allow the issuance of a subpoena after proper notice has been given to the opposite party. The party to whom the request is made has a set time limit within which to respond with delivery or with objections, typically thirty days. The request should list the documents sought with reasonable particularity and without vagueness or ambiguity (see Illustration 7-4).

Requests for production are usually the next step in the discovery process following the submission of interrogatories. A review of the opposing party's responses to the interrogatories may reveal the existence of documents or other tangible objects that are material and require inspection.

REQUEST FOR ADMISSION

Each state provides the procedure for a party to request of another party the admission of the truth of any matter within the scope of allowable discovery. The matter sought to be admitted may fall within any of three categories:

- truth of statements or opinions of fact

- application of law to facts

- genuineness of documents

A request for admission serves to narrow the issues to be litigated at the time of trial, eliminating those matters that are not in dispute. The effect of an admission by a party is to conclusively establish that fact for purposes of the current action only, not for any other matter. An admission cannot be used against a party in another lawsuit.

The responding party may admit a fact completely, or the fact may be admitted in part and denied in part. It is important that the matters sought to be admitted be drafted with as much clarity as possible to avoid ambiguity of an answer. Vague requests are of no value to the party seeking the admission, and are likely to be denied by the responding party.

The request for admission is a tool employed in the discovery process after interrogatories, production, and deposition. Once the information from the other tools has been revealed, then strategic admissions can be of real value to a party from a tactical standpoint.

PHYSICAL AND MENTAL EXAMINATION

In cases where the physical or mental condition of a party is in controversy, the court rules of every state, as well as the *Federal Rules of Civil Procedure,* allow for an examination of that condition. Some jurisdictions allow for the examination without leave of the court, while others require an order of the presiding judge. The results of the examination must be forwarded to the opposing party in a report setting forth the physician's findings, diagnosis, and conclusions.

```
                    IN THE CIRCUIT COURT
                 FOR THE COUNTY OF MOSQUITO


BELLE BLISS,

       Plaintiff,

v.                                              Case No. 34567

THE THIRSTY TURTLE,

       Defendant.

_____/
```

PLAINTIFF'S REQUEST FOR PRODUCTION OF DOCUMENTS

PURSUANT TO Rule 409 of the Georgia Rules of Civil Procedure, BELLE BLISS, Plaintiff, requests that Defendant, THE THIRSTY TURTLE, produce for inspection and copying at the office of BUD WISER, at his office, located at One Harmony Drive, Orange, Georgia, or at a time and location to be mutually agreed upon by the parties, the documents requested herein:

1. All records of account of the business of Defendant for the years 1998 and 1999, related to premises maintenance and repair.

2. All photographs of the front entrance to Defendant's place of business taken at any time during the years 1998 and 1999.

```
                              _____
                              WILL PURVALE 65432
                              Attorney for Plaintiff
                              One Harmony Drive
                              Orange, Georgia 45090-6540
```

Illustration 7-4
Request for Production of Documents

The notice of the examination or the time and place set by the court must specify a reasonable time, place, and manner of examination. If costs for travel are involved, many jurisdictions provide for reimbursement of expenses.

In those cases where the physical or mental condition of a party is not in issue but evidence from a party is desired, as in a domestic relation case, then the examination must be requested by motion to the court. Good cause must be shown as to the reasons for requiring the examination.

REQUEST TO ENTER LAND

In many states, it is necessary to file a motion specifically to obtain court permission to enter the land of a party to a lawsuit. If good cause can be shown to the court for the need to examine land, the court will issue an order allowing the entry. The legal office assistant must prepare a motion disclosing the reasons constituting good cause to enter the land of the opposing party. This motion is closely related to the motion for production, and in many states it is covered within the same rule of court.

AUTHORIZATION

In the preparation of most lawsuits, documentary evidence is needed to support the claims of a party. Documentary evidence may be secured through the use of any one of the discovery tools above, but is also obtainable through the use of an authorization provided by either party. An **authorization** is merely the granting of authority to another to do or obtain something.

authorization

In the case of a lawsuit, an authorization may be used to obtain such information as:

- physician's records

- hospital records

- federal and state income tax records

- employment records

The authorization to obtain these records is usually sent by mail to the custodian of the records, along with a letter of explanation. The letter should also specify that any costs in the preparation of the records will be reimbursed. Illustration 7-5 provides an example of a letter of explanation.

The legal office assistant will find that the medical authorization form is one that most offices will have already prepared for the client's or party's signature. The authorization will be drafted in such general terms as to be flexible enough to cover the particular needs of most situations, as shown in Illustration 7-6.

An authorization for the release of income tax records or employment records can be an invaluable tool for the verification of claims related to the action. These records, like medical records, are confidential, and an authorization is required. Employment record authorizations should request the individual's employment application, payroll records, termination status, and any relevant notes. Income tax records may be obtained from the nearest Internal Revenue Service office.

Authorizations are generally used in the early stages of litigation. They may serve to streamline the discovery process and reduce the expense of litigation. The forms may require certain modification to meet the demands of a particular type of case. If there is going to be a substantial cost in the preparation of the records, it may be necessary to make arrangements for payment of those costs.

WILL PURVALE
Attorney at Law
One Harmony Drive
Orange, Georgia 45090-6540

February 29, 1999

Orange Memorial Hospital
Medical Records Department
P.O. Box 987
Orange, Georgia 45091-9871

Re: Belle Bliss v. The Thirsty Turtle   No. 34567

Dear Records Custodian:

I represent Ms. Belle Bliss in regard to injuries she sustained in a fall
which occurred on June 31, 1998. I am enclosing a medical authorization
form for your records that permits you to furnish all medical records you
possess concerning her treatment.

Please forward copies of the patient's medical chart, nurses' notes, x-ray
reports, consultation reports, physicians' notes, laboratory results, and any
charges for the treatment. Please bill me for any charges for this request.

Thank you very much for your cooperation.

Sincerely,

WILL PURVALE, Esquire

WP:xx

Enclosure

Illustration 7-5
Authorization Cover Letter

MEDICAL AUTHORIZATION

This is to authorize you to furnish to WILL PURVALE, Attorney at Law, any and all information and records that he may request regarding medical treatment. This authorization hereby cancels any prior authorizations.

DATED this _____ day of _____, 19__.

_____
WILL PURVALE

SUBSCRIBED AND SWORN to before me this

_____ day of _____, 19__.

_____
Notary Public

My commission expires:_____

Illustration 7-6
Medical Authorization

SUMMARY

Discovery is the process through which each party to a lawsuit is entitled to obtain certain facts, documents, physical evidence, and information to assist in the proof of allegations. Its purpose is to eliminate surprise, narrow the issues, reduce the expense of litigation, and assist the court in its docket. The legal office assistant must appreciate the fact that it is through the discovery process that a party is entitled to information to assist in the preparation for trial. Information of any nature may be sought as long as it is material to the action and not subject to a privilege.

It is only through the use of the subpoena and deposition that an individual not a party to the action is subject to the discovery process. Parties may find themselves subject to each of the tools of discovery at various stages of the litigation process. From interrogatories through requests for production, admission, and examination, each party is attempting to obtain as much information as possible about the opponent's case. Through the use of the deposition, that information is further defined and evaluated for purposes of trial. The ultimate goal is to place each party in a posture to try a lawsuit as expeditiously as possible.

Chapter Activities

Review Questions

1. Describe the discovery process.

2. What is the general purpose of the discovery process?

3. What is the scope of discovery?

4. What constitutes privileged information?

5. List the six primary discovery tools.

6. How is a deposition different from the other means of discovery?

7. Describe the difference between depositions and interrogatories.

8. What is the primary concern in the preparation of interrogatories?

9. What is the effect of a request for admission on that fact for purposes of trial?

10. What is the purpose of obtaining authorizations from a party?

Computer Activity

You are employed as a legal office assistant for the aggressive personal injury law firm of Landum & Fryim, P.C. The firm has been retained by Mr. Purvis Gomer to file an action against the Wet N' Wooly Water Park, Inc. Mr. Gomer sustained personal injuries resulting from his attempt to ride the "Cracker Barrel." The ride is the park's latest effort to separate the unsuspecting tourist not only from his last dollar, but also from his sanity.

It seems that on November 30 last year, Purvis was attempting to impress his best girl, Charlene McSly, with his manhood by riding the Cracker Barrel. The ride involved a trip in an enclosed barrel from a 160-foot waterfall into a small pool at speeds approaching terminal velocity. For Purvis, this folly left little intact but his stupidity.

The complaint filed by Mr. Gomer alleges that he sustained severe personal injuries from the fall and emotional distress from the loss of Charlene, who apparently was not too impressed. He claims that Wet N' Wooly's attempt to create a thrill ride in defiance of Newton's Law of Gravity and the Second Law of Thermodynamics amounted to a negligent act, for which losses he should be reimbursed.

A. From the student template retrieve act7.doc. This document is a sample Request for Production of documents. Prepare the request for the production of the defendant's safety inspection records for the Cracker Barrel. Key the changes to the template. Refer to the chapter for examples.

B. Save this information on the template as depo.doc.

C. Print one copy for your instructor. Make sure your name appears for identification purposes.

Chapter 8

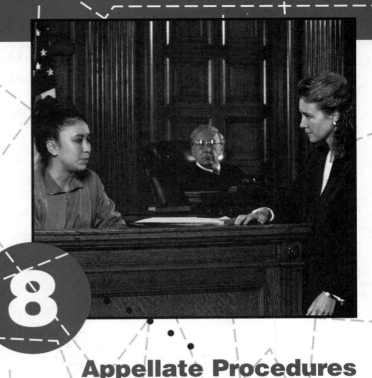

Appellate Procedures

Law never is, but is always about to be.

Justice Benjamin Cardozo (1921)

Objectives

After completing this chapter, you will be able to:

1. Define an appeal.

2. Describe the nature of the appellate process.

3. Classify the basic elements of an appellate brief.

4. Identify the content of each section of the appellate brief.

5. Summarize the motion process on appeal.

From the filing of the initial complaint to the final resolution of the matter by a higher court, the legal office assistant plays a key role in a lawsuit. Once the case has been to trial and a judgment has been rendered, the case may continue to progress to another court. The legal office assistant provides support to the legal office in the processing of that case. The interests of the client must be protected in the appeal with an emphasis on accuracy and thoroughness in the preparation of the necessary documents. It is the role of the legal office assistant to assist in the preparation of those documents and to ensure the accuracy and thoroughness of their contents.

NATURE OF THE APPELLATE PROCESS

The appellate process reviews the action of a lower court to decide whether or not there has been an error of law. Some types of appeal are discretionary with the appellate court—appeal is not automatic. Other types of appeal are a matter of right, where the case must be heard by the appellate court upon request by a party. Questions of fact that were decided by the trial court are not presented as issues on appeal. If the appellate court is convinced that there has been an error of law, then the court may reverse the decision of the trial court. If there has been no error of law, then the appellate court will merely affirm the decision of the trial court.

A challenge to the judgment of a trial court is called an **appeal.** The appeal takes place once there has been a final disposition of the case at the trial court level. The court to which an appeal is taken is called an **appellate court.** Appellate courts do not retry the case, but merely review the issues raised by the parties to determine the existence of any errors of law. The party filing the appeal is called the **appellant,** and the party against whom the appeal was filed (usually the prevailing party at the trial court level) is called the **appellee.**

An appeal is taken to the court of appeals in the district in which the case was tried. In federal courts, appeals from a U.S. district court are appealed to a U.S. circuit court of appeals. Appeals from that court are then taken to the U.S. Supreme Court if accepted. At the state level, appeals are taken from the trial court to a court of appeals and then to the state's supreme court. Court rules must be carefully reviewed in all questions of appellate procedure.

In all appeals, the appellate court is limited to the record of the case made at the time of trial, called the **record below.**

It is the responsibility of the legal office assistant to maintain a tickler file and copies of the materials that constitute the record. The record consists of:

- case docket

- transcripts of the proceedings

- exhibits

- pleadings

- motions and briefs

Almost without exception, the appellate court will refuse to hear any "new" evidence that was not submitted to the trial court for its decision.

In addition, the appellate court will limit its consideration of the case to only those issues that were presented at the trial court level. The theory is that the trial court must have had a specific issue presented for decision before it can be considered to have made an error. For instance, if a particular piece of damaging evidence against a party was introduced at the time of trial and that party failed to object to its introduction, then that party may not raise the objection on appeal for the first time. The scope of appellate review is limited to those questions that were before the trial court.

The appellate court will not disturb a ruling of a trial court unless there has been an error of law that has materially affected the outcome of the trial. The scope of appellate review is limited to **material error,** that is, error that may have influenced the decision of the court in a particular direction. If the error is harmless or supported by other competent evidence, then the decision will remain undisturbed.

Unless a decision of the trial court is final, and all matters before the trial court are completed, the appellate court will refuse to hear the appeal. This rule allows the appellate court to hear *all* of the issues at one time rather than piecemeal. There are certain limited exceptions where a party may appeal an interim decision of a court, but these are rare. The court rules will set out the grounds for such appeals.

The procedure for appeals in the federal courts has been simplified in recent years. The district court clerk provides the attorneys with the appropriate forms and copies of the local court rules. The court clerk also supervises the preparation of the record of proceedings in the trial court.

An appeal is started with the filing of a **notice of appeal** by the appellant and prepared by the legal office assistant. The notice of appeal is a formal request for a

appeal

appellate court

appellant
appellee

record below

material error

notice of appeal

hearing before the appellate court. Rule 4(a) of the *Federal Rules of Appellate Procedure* mandates that the notice of appeal be filed with the district court clerk within thirty days of the entry of judgment. It is the responsibility of the legal office assistant to calendar the dates. Local court rules determine the form, although most notices contain the following information:

- the identity of the appealing party
- the identity of the appellee
- the judgment or order appealed from
- the court to which the appeal is taken

In some courts, the appealing party must also file a bond to provide security to ensure payment of costs on appeal. Illustration 8-1 presents a sample Notice of Appeal for a matter appealed in federal court. State court rules closely follow the rules in federal court as to form and content.

After filing the notice of appeal, the legal office assistant must request the **transcript** from the court reporter within ten days.

The transcript is the official daily record of the proceedings before the lower court. The legal office assistant must also notify the court clerk that the transcript has been ordered for the appeal, with a copy for the opposing party.

ELEMENTS OF AN APPELLATE BRIEF

An **appellate brief** is a lengthy, written legal document submitted to an appellate court to persuade the court that an error has occurred in a lower court.

The preparation of the appellate brief represents both an art and a science. The artistic aspect of the appellate brief is beyond the scope of this text, but the scientific side of the brief is one that lends itself to analysis. The appellate brief is structured in a similar manner in both federal courts and state courts, although court rules must be consulted before preparation. The legal office assistant will make sure that the brief consists of the following components:

- cover page
- table of contents
- index of authorities
- statement of jurisdiction
- statement of issues
- statement of facts
- argument
- conclusion
- relief
- appendix

It is the responsibility of the legal office assistant to make sure all the components are in the brief and properly kept. The court rules of both the state courts and the federal courts are very specific as to the form and contents of the brief. Illustration 8-2 provides the requirement set forth in Rule 28 of the *Federal Rules of Appellate Procedure.*

transcript

appellate brief

UNITED STATES DISTRICT COURT
FOR THE EASTERN DISTRICT OF CALIFORNIA

I. M. HURT,

    Plaintiff,

v.   CIVIL NO. 23654

H. E. DIDDITT,

    Defendant.

_____/

NOTICE OF APPEAL

    Notice is hereby given that H. E. Didditt, Defendant above named, hereby appeals to the United States Court of Appeals for the First Circuit from the final judgment entered in this action on June 31, 19__.

Dated:

                                        _____
                                        M. N. SHURRED #81234
                                        Attorney for Defendant
                                        12 Fortune Place
                                        Orange, CA 22330-9876
                                        (901) 453-9999

Illustration 8-1
Notice of Appeal

(a) BRIEF OF THE APPELLANT. The brief of the appellant shall contain under appropriate headings and in the order here indicated:

(1) A table of contents, with page references, and a table of cases (alphabetically arranged), statutes and other authorities cited, with references to the pages of the brief where they are cited.

(2) A statement of the issues presented for review.

(3) A statement of the case. The statement shall first indicate briefly the nature of the case, the course of the proceedings, and its disposition in the court below. There shall follow a statement of the facts relevant to the issue presented for review, with appropriate references to the record. . . .

(4) An argument. The argument may be preceded by a summary. The argument shall contain the contentions of the appellant with respect to the issues presented and the reasons therefor, with citations to the authorities, statutes and parts of the record relied on.

(5) A short conclusion stating the precise relief sought.

(b) BRIEF OF THE APPELLEE. The brief of the appellee shall conform to the requirements of subdivision (a)(1)–(4), except that a statement of the issues of the case need not be made unless the appellee is dissatisfied with the statement of the appellant.

(c) REPLY BRIEF. The appellant may file a brief in reply to the brief of the appellee, and if the appellee has cross-appealed, the appellee may file a brief in reply to the response of the appellant to the issues presented by the cross appeal. No further briefs may be filed except with leave of the court.

Illustration 8-2
Rule 28, *Federal Rules of Appellate Procedure*

COVER PAGE

The cover page of the brief is similar to the headings and captions on pleadings identifying the court and the matter before it. It should contain the following information:

- the identity of the court
- the identity of the parties
- the case number assigned
- the name of the lower court
- the name of the brief
- the name of the attorney

Illustration 8-3 presents a sample of a cover page in state court.

TABLE OF CONTENTS

The table of contents of the appellate brief sets out the sections of the brief and their respective locations providing the court with convenient access to any component.

IN THE
SUPREME COURT OF THE STATE OF CALIFORNIA

No. 95-6749

MAJOR GASTROCNEMIUS,

Petitioner,

v.

PUMP-U-UP HEALTH SPAS, INC.,
Respondent.

ON APPEAL TO THE SUPREME COURT
OF THE STATE OF FREMONT FROM
THE COURT OF APPEALS

BRIEF OF PETITIONER

MARLIN MILQUETOAST, #234980
Attorney for Petitioner
Suite 40
1122 Garden Lane
Walden, CA 22334-9887

Illustration 8-3
Cover Page for State Court

Table of Contents

Index of Authorities 1

Statement of Jurisdiction 2

Statement of Issues 3

Statement of Facts 4

Argument 5

Conclusion 16

Relief 17

Illustration 8-4
A Sample Table of Contents

The legal office assistant should make this element one of the final steps in the preparation of the brief due to the fact that the contents and their locations are not known until completion. A table of contents may appear as presented in Illustration 8-4.

INDEX OF AUTHORITIES

Most jurisdictions require that the appellate brief contain a list of the citations of the legal authorities relied upon to support arguments made on behalf of a party. The index of authorities, sometimes called a table of authorities, provides the appellate court with a list of authorities arranged by category. Proper legal citation form discussed in chapter 9 should be adhered to throughout the brief. The index should include the following types of authorities if used in the brief:

- case law

- constitutional provisions

- statutes

- regulations

- secondary authority

Cases are listed in alphabetical order, and statutes are listed in their order of appearance in the brief. Chapter 9 will discuss each of these types of legal authority and the nature of legal research involving their use. Illustration 8-5 presents a sample index of authorities.

STATEMENT OF JURISDICTION

The statement of jurisdiction section of the brief is a short statement of the court's jurisdiction to the appeal. The purpose is to advise the court that all of the preliminary

Index of Authorities

Cases

Carson v. Johnson, 660 F.d 1042 (3rd Cir. 1980) 9

Hardy v. Smith, 490 F. Supp 10 (D.Fl, 1984) 13

Statutes

15 U.S.C.A. § 1368 15

15 U.S.C.A. § 1370 17

Illustration 8-5
A Sample Index of Authorities

appellate steps have been satisfied for jurisdiction, and that the court has jurisdiction to render an opinion. The statement may be as short and clear as:

This Honorable Court has jurisdiction pursuant to 12 U.S.C.A. § 1290.

The procedural steps involved in the appeal will be recited in the statement of facts portion of the brief.

STATEMENT OF ISSUES

This section of the brief, also referred to as the *statement of issues* or *statement of questions involved,* provides the statement of the issues of law involved in the appeal. The manner of the phrasing of the question(s) involves some degree of advocacy and will significantly impact how the court views the arguments. The **legal issue** is a question of law phrased in the best light for the party submitting the brief and constitutes a valuable tool of persuasion.

legal issue

STATEMENT OF FACTS

The statement of facts, also called the statement of the case, presents the factual picture of the case to the appellate court. The facts should include:

- a narrative of the essential facts as disclosed at trial

- a statement of the prior proceedings

- a short summary of the lower court's decision

The facts and summary of proceedings must be based on the record below. They must be set forth in a clear, concise, and unbiased manner. The legal office assistant must be concerned with the accuracy and comprehensiveness of the facts. In this section of the brief, the court is interested in the facts alone, not argument or advocacy.

argument

conclusion

relief

ARGUMENT

The **argument** is the advocacy portion of the brief devoted to a discussion of the issues and their legal support. It is in this section of the brief that the interests of the client are presented by the legal office. The party offering the argument is seeking to have the court adopt its reasoning in holding for that position offering case law and statutory authority in support. Counsel for a party present an argument in a well-reasoned and logical manner. The attorney will offer the authorities used in support of the position, citing legislative history, custom and usage, and a direct attack on an opponent's authorities. The legal office assistant should be aware that the argument is the bulk of the brief and it should be of sufficient length as to thoroughly present the authorities without being laborious.

CONCLUSION

The **conclusion** is the section of the brief constituting a summary of the party's position and arguments.

It should be a short, concise, and direct statement of the party's position without rearguing the case, and may consist of nothing more than a single sentence on each issue. The arguments on behalf of the client will have already been presented in the argument section of the brief. The conclusion is intended to be a summary only.

RELIEF

The **relief** section of the brief is the request by the proponent of an argument that the court hold in a certain manner on behalf of that party. The relief is a statement of the remedy sought from the appellate court. It should not include any argument or advocacy and should not address any of the specific issues. See Illustration 8-6.

APPENDIX

The appellant must file an appendix with the brief to provide the court with the relevant procedural documents from the lower court. In the appendix portion of the brief, the legal office assistant will include:

- relevant docket entries from the lower court

- relevant pleadings

- orders, judgments, decisions or rulings

- relevant portions of the record

Relief

WHEREFORE, Defendant respectfully requests that this Honorable Court reverse the

decision of the Court of Appeals and remand this matter for further proceedings consistent

with its opinion.

Illustration 8-6
A Sample Relief

Pursuant to most court rules, the content of the appendix is a matter of agreement between the attorneys for all parties. If the parties cannot agree, then each may submit a proposed appendix for consideration and ruling. The attorneys must only agree on the appendix, not the content of any brief. If exhibits of evidence used in the trial are to be included in the appendix, they should be designated as such upon agreement of the attorneys.

MOTIONS ON APPEAL

Any application for relief or order from the appellate court must be made by motion with service upon all parties. The motion must contain the grounds for relief and be supported by briefs. You must be aware of local court rules for filing of a motion on such matters as:

- extension of time
- procedural orders
- costs
- emergency relief

The motion form and the grounds allowable are dictated by court rule. Illustration 8-7 provides a sample motion for extension of time to be filed in an appeal where more time is needed to file a brief. The legal office assistant should be familiar with local court rules prior to the preparation and filing of any motion.

ORAL ARGUMENT

Once the case has been submitted to the appellate court for consideration of the briefs, the court will schedule the case for **oral argument.** The court may decide to hear a case without oral argument, and in some states oral argument may occur only upon request of one of the parties.

oral argument

At the oral argument session, the court will allow each party a set time to state a position and argument. That time limit is usually thirty minutes. Each side to the appeal presents the legal arguments in support of the client's position to the panel of appellate judges. Once the arguments have been presented, the case is considered to have been submitted to the court for a decision.

SUMMARY

The legal office assistant may play a significant role in the preparation and filing of an appeal. The interests of the client must be protected in the appeal, with an emphasis on accuracy and thoroughness in the preparation of the necessary documents. After the filing of the notice of appeal, the preparation of the brief is the most significant effort for the appellant, and the responsive brief is the appellee's greatest task. The motion practice on appeal is quite limited in most states and in the federal courts. The substantive issues of law forming the grounds for appeal and providing the basis for reversible error in the eyes of the appellant are the focus of the appeal. The entire process is an emphasis on the substance and accuracy of the documents necessary to accomplish the appeal.

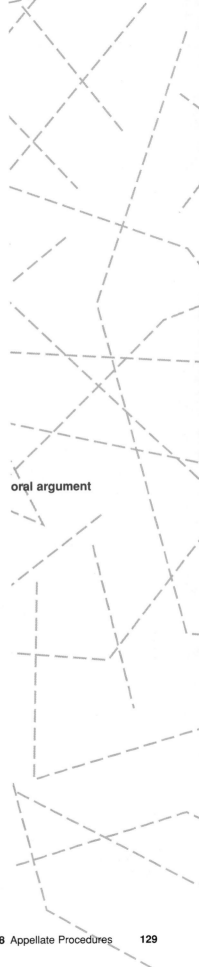

UNITED STATES COURT OF APPEALS
FOR THE FIRST CIRCUIT

I. M. HURT,

    Plaintiff,

v.   File No. 99-1234

H. E. DIDDITT,

    Defendant.

_____/

MOTION FOR EXTENSION OF TIME

    NOW COMES H. E. DIDDITT, Defendant herein, and moves this
Court for a 30-day extension for the filing of his Brief in the above-
captioned matter.

    This motion is made pursuant to Local Circuit Rule 11-2 (a), and an
Affidavit in support thereof is attached hereto.

Dated:

                                        _____
                                        M. N. SHURRED #81234
                                        Attorney for Defendant
                                        12 Fortune Place
                                        Orange, CA 22330-9876
                                        (901) 453-9999

Illustration 8-7
Motion for Extension of Time

Chapter Activities

Review Questions

1. Define an appeal.

2. Identify the parties on appeal.

3. What issues are generally considered by the appellate court?

4. List the documents that form the record below.

5. Identify the main sections of an appellate brief.

6. What material is presented in the statement of facts?

7. Describe the purpose of the argument.

8. List the motions typically filed during an appeal.

Computer Activity

When Ernest Winter, Sr., contracted for his subscription to *The Liver Spot,* he did so in response to representations in the advertising campaign of its publisher, Senectitude Press, that he would be provided with health tips designed to lengthen his "golden years." In his nineties at the time his first issue arrived, Ernest was ready to believe anything that this literary Ponce de Leon had to serve up. Therefore, when the article appeared in the travel section describing the "Liver Spot of the Month" travel designation, Ernest was ready. The "Spot" turned out to be a hot springs near Worthy, Arkansas. Rather than providing the proverbial pool of Bethesda-like healing waters, the only thing that Ernest got was second- and third-degree burns over 40 percent of his already decrepit body. The resulting medical treatment ran into the tens of thousands, leading him to the U.S. District Court for the District of Arkansas in an action against *The Liver Spot* and its publisher, Senectitude Press. Alas, the jury felt that our modern-day Don Quixote was merely jousting at windmills, and found his action to be without merit. His attorney, Malcom de Mise, has requested your assistance in the preparation of the appeal. Malcom's office is located in your city at 100 Capital Avenue. Ernest is now seeking an appeal of the lower court judgment to the U.S. court of appeals.

A. From the student template retrieve act8.doc. This document is a notice of appeal. Prepare the pleading for submission to the court with the following information:

   • proper local federal district court

   • names of parties

   • name and address of attorney for appellant

   Refer to the chapter for examples.

B. Save this information on the template as appeal.doc.

C. Print one copy for your instructor. Make sure your name appears for identification purposes.

Chapter 9

Legal Research

I read my eyes out and can't read enough. . . . The more one reads the more one sees we have to read.

Vice President John Adams (1794)

Objectives

After completing this chapter, you will be able to:

1. Discuss the sources of the law.

2. Understand the nature of case law.

3. Identify the types of court reports.

4. Describe how to find case law.

5. Summarize the researching of statutes.

6. Discuss shepardizing statutory and case law.

7. Identify the secondary sources of the law for legal research.

8. Compare the function of secondary sources.

9. Discuss computerized legal research.

10. Summarize legal research technique.

An understanding of the basic principles of legal research, along with an understanding of the tools used in that research, is an essential skill for the legal office assistant. Although it is rare for a legal office assistant to actually perform simple legal research, knowing the basic principles will allow you to give professional support to the attorney actually doing the research. This can involve checking simple procedures, reviewing citation format, and maintaining a small library in a law firm. This chapter will provide the legal office assistant with a basic understanding of the tools used to perform legal research, including the sources of the law, case law, statutory law, secondary sources, shepardizing, and research techniques.

LEGAL RESEARCH AND THE LEGAL OFFICE ASSISTANT

Considering the complexity of the law, and the volume of new law written daily, no one can possibly know all of the law. A knowledge of where to find the law is essential to any legal office.

Legal research is the procedure of locating and analyzing the answer to a legal question. It involves a systematic, step-by-step search for a specific answer to a particular legal question to support a client's case. The legal question usually involves a matter of **substantive law.**

Substantive law is that part of the law that establishes rights, duties, and obligations. It covers such areas as domestic relations, torts, criminal law, wills, trusts, contracts, business organizations, real estate, and bankruptcy.

The legal office assistant may reasonably ask, "Why do I need to know how to perform legal research when the attorney or the paralegal will be the one actually doing it?" It is a good question, and can be answered quite simply by stating that the role of the legal office assistant is to support the legal office and the attorney in every manner available. Although the attorney or paralegal will most likely be the individual in the office performing the research, the legal office assistant must understand what is involved for the following reasons:

- to be able to review the accuracy of citations

- to review simple procedural requirements

- to understand the nature of the authorities used in briefs and memorandum of law

- when called upon, to locate individual volumes to assist in the research process or for litigation

- to maintain a small firm's law library, including properly filing pocket parts

Whatever the demands of the legal office may be in terms of research support, it is the responsibility of the legal office assistant to be able to offer that support. Therefore, a knowledge of the process of legal research is essential for the expert legal office assistant.

SOURCES OF THE LAW

As discussed in chapter 3, the law library contains the written materials to research the law. The materials used to conduct legal research can be separated into three categories:

- primary sources of the law

- secondary sources of the law

- finding tools

These sources of the written law aid the legal researcher in answering the legal question at issue.

PRIMARY SOURCES

Sources of the law that are termed **primary sources** are those that are considered binding on the court. Courts are "bound" to apply a certain law, meaning that its application is mandatory, if the law stems from one of the primary sources. Primary sources are categorized as case law, statutory law, and administrative rules and regulations. Each of the primary sources has its origin from a particular branch of the government. Case law comes from the judicial branch, statutory law from the legislative branch, and administrative law from the executive branch.

legal research

substantive law

primary sources

SECONDARY SOURCES

secondary sources

Secondary sources of the law are those sources that, for legal research purposes, discuss and analyze the law. It can be said that secondary sources are "about the law," and that primary sources "are the law." Examples of secondary sources of the law are legal encyclopedias, law dictionaries, legal thesauruses, treatises, periodicals, and loose-leaf services. These sources will be discussed in detail later in this chapter.

Although secondary sources are not binding upon a court, they are extremely useful for the purpose of legal research. Courts consider secondary sources to be "persuasive" in making a decision on a legal question. Therefore, in the development of a legal argument, the legal researcher must present primary sources that will require the court to make a particular decision if possible. If there is no binding legal authority, then the legal researcher must present secondary sources to persuade the court to rule a certain way.

FINDING TOOLS

finding tools

Finding tools are legal research aids used to locate primary and secondary sources of the law. With the large volume of new law produced daily in the United States, both primary and secondary, the legal researcher is presented with a tremendous task of sifting through material to locate the authority necessary to support an argument. It is through the use of finding tools that access to primary and secondary sources is gained. Finding tools consist of digests, indexes, and computerized research tools for case law, and citators and indexes for statutory law. These will be discussed in greater detail later in this chapter.

CASE LAW

case law

stare decisis

As seen in chapter 3, **case law** consists of the written opinions of appellate courts contained in large, multivolume sets of books. The importance of case law stems from the legal doctrine of *stare decisis,* which states that a court will stand by the precedent set down by another court on a similar legal question. It is a matter of tradition that one court will follow the leading principles of another when not in conflict with its own laws.

Two principles determine the extent to which a court must follow the decisions of another court. The first principle is that the decision of a higher court is considered **binding authority** on the lower courts within the same court system, meaning that the lower courts within the same system "must" abide by the legal principles established by the higher courts.

binding authority

For instance, if the North Carolina Supreme Court rendered a decision on a certain legal issue, then all of the lower courts in the state are bound to follow that authority. Every appellate court and every trial court must abide by the U.S. Supreme Court's opinion.

persuasive authority

The second principle is that if there is no binding authority, then the court may rely upon **persuasive authority** in making its decision. Persuasive authority is the reliance by a court on the decisions of another court on the same legal issue, but not one that it is bound to follow. All secondary authority is persuasive only and can never be considered binding. In the previous example, if the North Carolina Supreme Court were to issue the same decision, while it would not be binding upon the courts of another state, the other state courts may elect to follow it, having been "persuaded" by the soundness of its legal reasoning.

COURT REPORTS

court reports

Case law is published in **court reports,** which are the multivolume sets of books containing the written opinions of the appellate courts of a particular jurisdiction.

Court reports are organized by arranging the opinions reported in three different ways:

- Jurisdiction—the opinions of a particular court are arranged by jurisdiction chronologically in a multivolume numbered series such as the *Michigan Reports* that covers the decisions of the Michigan Supreme Court.

- Geography—the opinions of a group of geographically adjacent states are published in a set of reports. For example, the *Northwestern Reporter* includes the opinions of the states of Iowa, Michigan, Minnesota, Nebraska, North Dakota, South Dakota, and Wisconsin.

- Subject Matter—the opinions of courts on certain subjects that may range from abandonment to zoning. An example would be the *CCH Labor Law Reporter,* which reports decisions from many jurisdictions on the issues involved in labor law.

Case law is usually published in official, unofficial, and annotated versions for legal research purposes.

Official Court Reports. The published reports of the written opinions of cases that are authorized by the state or federal government are considered the **official court reports.**

The authorization for the reporting of cases on an official basis must come from the legislature or the state's supreme court under its rule-making authority. As an example, the *United States Supreme Court Reports* is the name of the official court reporter for the decisions of the U.S. Supreme Court. The authorization comes from a law passed by Congress and found in § 411 of the *U.S. Code.*

Unofficial Court Reports. In most jurisdictions, a private publisher will offer a version of the actual written opinions of the court called **unofficial court reports.**

West Publishing Company publishes the most widely used unofficial court reports, presenting the cases in chronological order and arranged by jurisdiction in sets that make up the **National Reporter System.**

This system of unofficial reports has three main divisions:

- opinions of state courts

- opinions of federal courts

- opinions of special courts

The state reporting system consists of seven unofficial regional reporters containing the opinions of adjacent states. Illustration 9-1 shows how the National Reporter System is arranged by state court decision.

The National Reporter System for the opinions of the federal courts includes the *Supreme Court Reporter, Federal Reporter, Federal Supplement,* and *Federal Rules Decisions.* The system for the opinions of special courts includes West's *Bankruptcy Reporter, Military Justice Reporter,* and others.

Annotated Law Reports. To compliment the official and unofficial versions of court reports, there is also an annotated version published by Lawyer's Cooperative Publishing Co. The *American Law Reports,* or *A.L.R.* as it is known, is an **annotated law report** containing the text of selected cases, along with an in-depth discussion on the law of the particular case. The discussion on the law is called an **annotation.**

The *A.L.R.* reports come in sets of volumes, arranged in a series, which at this time consists of *A.L.R.1st, A.L.R.2d, A.L.R.3d, A.L.R.4th, A.L.R.5th,* and *A.L.R.Fed.* Each series is supplemented to update the decisions and the discussion.

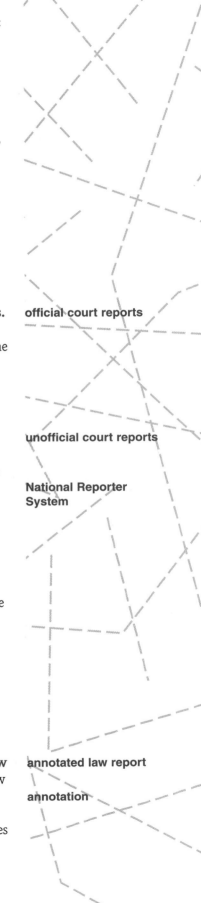

official court reports

unofficial court reports

National Reporter System

annotated law report

annotation

REPORTER

Atlantic A., A2d	North Eastern N.E., N.E.2d	North Western N.W., N.W.2d	Pacific P., P.2d	South Eastern S.E., S.E.2d	South Western S.W., S.W.2d	Southern So., So.2d
Connecticut	Illinois	Iowa	Alaska	Georgia	Arkansas	Alabama
Delaware	Indiana	Michigan	Arizona	North Carolina	Kentucky	Florida
Maine	New York	Minnesota	California	South Carolina	Missouri	Louisiana
Maryland	Ohio	Nebraska	Colorado	Virginia	Tennessee	Mississippi
New Hampshire	Massachusetts	North Dakota	Hawaii	West Virginia	Texas	
New Jersey		South Dakota	Idaho			
Pennsylvania		Wisconsin	Kansas			
Rhode Island			Montana			
Vermont			Nevada			
			New Mexico			
			Oklahoma			
			Oregon			
			Utah			
			Washington			
			Wyoming			

Illustration 9-1
The National Reporter System

OPINION FORMAT

The particular format of a judicial opinion printed in a court report will vary, depending on the court. Most opinions will contain the citation, caption, court, docket number, date, syllabus, headnotes, name of attorneys, names of judges, and the opinion.

Citation. The citation is an abbreviation of the name of the case, including the volume number and reporter series in which it appears, followed by the page number and date of issue.

Caption. The caption is the name of the case (1). (Numbers in parentheses refer to corresponding numbers in the illustration.) It consists of the names of the parties to the case and a designation as plaintiff and defendant. Usually, the appealing party is named first in the caption.

Court. The opinion contains the name of the court that heard the case and rendered the decision (2). Frequently the name of the court appealed from will also be named.

Docket Number. The docket number is the number assigned to the case by the court clerk when the appeal is filed (3). It appears on most opinions and is used for internal court docket control.

Date. This is the date that the opinion of the court was issued. Cases are reported chronologically through the use of this date (4).

Syllabus. The case syllabus is a synopsis of the case prepared by the publisher of the opinion (5). It consists of a brief summary of the case, including its facts, its history through the court system, and the decision of the court.

Headnotes. A headnote is a summary paragraph on a point of law discussed in the written court opinion (6). It is a convenient means of determining if a case has a discussion on a point of law that is relevant to the issue at hand. The headnotes of the West National Reporter System cases include a symbol of a key followed by a numerical reference to and index of cases on the identical legal issue.

Names of Attorneys. The names of the attorney or attorneys representing each party to the appeal appear in the written opinion following the headnotes (7).

Names of Judges. The opinion also includes the names of the appellate judges involved in the decision of the case (8). The name of the judge writing the opinion will appear at the beginning of the opinion, and the names of the judges concurring with the opinion are listed at the end.

Opinion. The opinion of the court is the written statement on the case, along with a discussion of the law and reasoning upon which the decision is based (9).

The opinion may consist of only a few lines, or it may be many pages in length with a detailed analysis of the court's reasoning and the law relied upon. The actual decision of the court is the majority opinion, which is the opinion that decides the case and is agreed upon by a majority of the judges of that particular appellate court.

Another judge may agree in the result reached by the majority, but not agree with the reasoning, and issue a concurring opinion, which consists of a statement of reasoning different than the majority.

The dissenting opinion is the written opinion of a judge disagreeing with the result reached by the majority of the judges in the decision.

The concurring and dissenting opinions are also printed in full, along with the majority opinion, but it is only the law as stated in the majority opinion that is binding upon the lower courts.

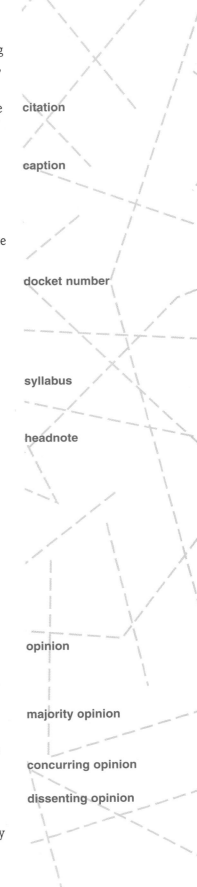

citation

caption

docket number

syllabus

headnote

opinion

majority opinion

concurring opinion

dissenting opinion

CASE FINDING

With the large volume of appellate decisions issued annually and reported in chronological order in their respective court reports, the task of locating an opinion with a discussion of a particular legal issue becomes significant. It is through the use of the finding tools of digests, indexes, and computerized research tools that the case law is accessed.

Digests. As seen in chapter 3, a digest is a multivolume set of books that provides a reference to case law by topic. The set of volumes of the digest is arranged alphabetically by subject matter. Each subject is broken into subtopics that provide a brief summary of the opinions on cases related to that topic. The summaries are a duplication of the headnotes of the cases.

key number system

West Publishing Company digests offer a **key number system** for locating the topics. The key number system assigns a number to each topic and its subtopics, corresponding to the key numbers used in the West legal encyclopedia, *Corpus Juris Secundum,* and other West publications, as shown. When a headnote is written by the reporter, it is assigned a key number from the system. With that key number, the legal researcher can then access any other cases with headnotes similarly designated through the use of the digest.

Indexes. Each of the major legal publishing companies offer indexes to their respective digests and publications. If the legal researcher has a very specific topic in mind, it can be accessed through the use of one of these indexes. These are particularly useful when researching case law that has appeared in periodicals which would not have been subject to digest treatment.

Computerized Research. On-line databases of the law are available through the use of the WESTLAW and LEXIS/NEXIS systems. Each service is capable of accessing federal and state case law as well as statutory law, offering access as soon as the opinions and law have been issued. Access is gained by a specific word search through the use of words or phrases that lead the legal researcher to an appropriate legal opinion.

CASE CITATION

As previously seen, a case citation is a method of identifying the location of a case through the use of a legal shorthand. The legal researcher has the ability to locate a particular case by looking at the information contained in the citation and then retrieving the case from its particular court report. A case citation contains the following information:

- name of the case

- volume, name, and page number of the court report

- year of the decision

For example, consider the case of *Barliant v. Follett Corp.,* 483 N.E.2d 1312 (1985). The name of the case is *Barliant v. Follett Corp.;* the volume of the court report is number 483; the name of the court report is *North Eastern Reporter, 2d Series;* the page number at which the case begins is 1312; and the year of the decision is 1985. This citation offers the location of the case in the unofficial court report from the National Reporter System. The case is also located in the official reporter for its state, Illinois, in the *Illinois Appellate Reports.*

A *Uniform System of Citation* is the standard reference book on the proper form for all legal citation including case law. Look once again and note that abbreviations, spacing, and punctuation are very specific. There are no spaces in N.E.2d and no period after the "d" in the citation. The *Bluebook* spells out how all cites should be keyed. This citation book should be on the desks of all legal office assistants. It is published by The Harvard Law

Review Association and is now in its sixteenth edition. The *Bluebook,* as it is known, should be consulted by the legal office assistant for the correct format for all cites.

STATUTORY LAW

Thorough legal research involves a consideration of statutory law as well as case law. A **statute** is the formal written law enacted by Congress or a state's legislature. The legal researcher must consider applicable statutory law in performing legal research for the following reasons:

1. The most current legislative enactments may impact a client's rights.

2. The statutory law of the appropriate jurisdiction may differ from another.

3. Statutes are frequently interpreted by appellate judges in written legal opinions.

FORMAT OF A STATUTE

The actual format of a statute will depend on the publisher of the volumes of statutory law. Some offer annotations to the text of the statute, while others provide only the statutory text. In either case, the text will be the same. The format will include (numbers in parentheses refer to corresponding numbers in the illustration):

- Title or section number—statutes are arranged in numerical order by title or section number and can be located by looking in the appropriate volume if the number is known (1).

- Statutory text—following the number will be the actual language enacted by the legislative body (2).

- Statutory history—the history of the statute follows the text, offering information as to the dates of enactment and amendment that can materially affect a client's rights (3).

- Reporter's notes—used in the annotated versions of statutes, the reporter's notes offer comments on the sources of the law, former provisions, and revisions (4).

- Cross-references—a reference to other pertinent statutes or treatises provides the legal researcher with convenient references for expansion of the search (5).

The legal researcher is well advised to consider all of the information offered rather than just the statutory text in performing a thorough search.

FEDERAL STATUTES

Federal statutes are the legislative enactments of the U.S. Congress. Each law as it is enacted is first published in a version known as a **slip law.**

A slip law is the first printed form of the new congressional enactments published in loose-leaf or pamphlet form. They are available through the U. S. Government Printing Office, through numerous loose-leaf services offered by private organizations, and through WESTLAW and LEXIS/NEXIS.

Once the congressional session has ended, the slip laws containing the session's enactments are compiled and published in the official bound statutory law of the United States, the *Statutes at Large.*

statute

slip law

Statutes at Large

codified

U.S. Code

titles

The *Statutes at Large* are a compilation of the session's laws arranged chronologically, which makes them difficult to use for legal research. To remedy this problem, the U.S. Government Printing Office offers a **codified** version of the laws of Congress called the ***U.S. Code.***

A codified version of a set of laws refers to the process of rearranging the previous chronological order into a subject matter format. The *U.S. Code (U.S.C.)* is arranged by subject into fifty **titles,** or subjects, which are accessed by a general index. Since 1926 it has been the official version of federal statutes, originally arranged into forty-eight titles. Illustration 9-2 provides a list of the titles of the code.

The unofficial versions of the federal statutes are contained in the *U.S. Code Annotated (U.S.C.A.)* published by West Publishing Co., and the *U.S. Code Service (U.S.C.S.)* published by Lawyers Cooperative Publishing Co. Each of these versions are arranged into the same fifty titles as the *U.S.C.,* followed by annotations and cross-references. The annotations contain the case law interpreting that particular statutory provision. Both of the annotated versions provide an excellent index for accessing the statutes.

TITLES

1. General Provisions	26. Internal Revenue Code
2. The Congress	27. Intoxicating Liquors
3. The President	28. Judiciary and Judicial Procedure
4. Flag and Seal, Seat of Government, States	29. Labor
5. Government Organization and Employees	30. Mineral Lands and Mining
	31. Money and Finance
6. Surety Bonds	32. National Guard
7. Agriculture	33. Navigation and Navigable Waters
8. Aliens and Nationality	34. Navy
9. Arbitration	35. Patents
10. Armed Forces	36. Patriotic Societies and Observances
11. Bankruptcy	37. Pay and Allowances of the Uniformed Services
12. Banks and Banking	38. Veteran's Benefits
13. Census	39. Postal Service
14. Coast Guard	40. Public Buildings, Property, and Works
15. Commerce and Trade	41. Public Contracts
16. Conservation	42. Public Health and Welfare
17. Copyrights	43. Public Lands
18. Crimes and Criminal Procedure	44. Public Printing and Documents
19. Customs Duties	45. Railroads
20. Education	46. Shipping
21. Food and Drugs	47. Telegraphs, Telephones, and Radiotelegraphs
22. Foreign Relations and Intercourse	48. Territories and Insular Possessions
23. Highways	49. Transportation
24. Hospitals and Asylums	50. War and National Defense
25. Indians	

Illustration 9-2
U.S. Code Titles

Federal statutes are cited to the *U.S.C., U.S.C.A.,* or *U.S.C.S.* The citation should include the title, the code version, and the section number. For example, 28 *U.S.C.A.* § 1102, would be the correct citation to access § 1102 of title 28 of the annotated version of the federal statute.

STATE STATUTES

The process for the enactment and publishing of state statutes is similar to that of the federal system. The legislative enactments first appear as slip opinions, then session laws, and finally as bound volumes of statutes. They appear in both official and unofficial versions, the latter usually being annotated with case law. Appendix B provides a convenient list of each of the state statutory official and unofficial sources.

The citation of state statutes generally adheres to the format of providing the official source with the statutory section following. For instance, *Mich. Stat. Ann.* § 201, refers to section 201 of the unofficial version of the compiled laws of the state of Michigan published by Callaghan Publishing Co.

UPDATING LEGAL RESEARCH

The final step in the completion of any legal research project is to determine whether or not the legal authority that has been located is still good law. To do this, each statute and case to be relied upon must be updated. This is a seemingly impossible task, given the volume of new law decided and enacted each year. Updating the legal authorities that have been located is accomplished primarily through the use of two legal research tools: shepardizing and pocket supplements.

SHEPARDIZING IN GENERAL

Shepard's Citations, shown here, offers the best solution to the problem with its system for updating the law. The term for the updating of research through the use of *Shepard's Citations* is called **shepardizing.**

Shepardizing refers to the use of *Shepard's Citations* to find out the subsequent treatment of cases, statutes, court rules, and other sources of the law. Sets of books used to provide the subsequent historical treatment of a case or statute are called **citators.**

Shepard's publishes many different citators depending upon jurisdiction. For instance, *Shepard's United States Citations* covers the decisions of the U.S. Supreme Court, while *Shepard's Federal Citations* covers decisions of the court of appeals. There are also citators for each state as well as for specialty courts.

SHEPARDIZING CASE LAW

To shepardize the previously referred to case of *Barliant v. Follett Corp.,* 483 N.E.2d 1312 (1985), follow these steps:

1. Locate the proper jurisdictional *Shepard's* citator for the *North Eastern Reporter, Second Series.*

2. Within the citator, locate the proper volume where the case is located by following the volume numbers appearing at the top corner of each page of the citator in bold print.

Vol. 483

3. On the pages of the citator headed with the volume number, locate the page number of the case appearing in bold print between two dashes:

-1312-

4. Review the cases cited under the page number.

shepardizing

citators

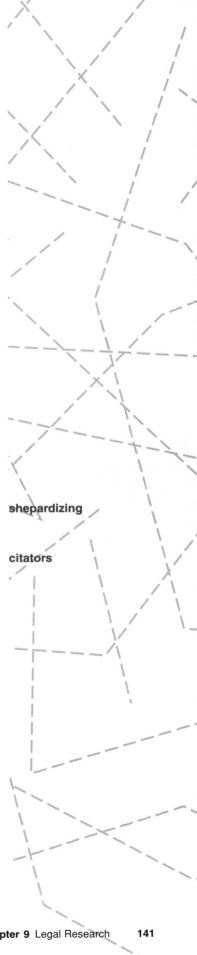

The legal researcher's reviewing task is facilitated further by abbreviations offered by the citator that help to determine which, if any, of the cases are necessary to review. Some of the cases may merely agree with the result, some may disagree, and others may overrule the point of law. For instance, if one of the cases subsequently addressing the legal issues of the *Barliant* case were to criticize the soundness of the decision, then the citation would be preceded by a "c" followed by the citation of the criticizing case:

-1312-
c453FS904

The example shown indicates that a case located in the *Federal Supplement Reporter,* volume 453 at page 904, criticizes the reasoning of the *Barliant* case.

The citator further assists the research by providing a reference to the particular headnotes of the principle case that receive treatment in the subsequent case by placing a small number within the citation. The small number refers to the corresponding headnote in the principle case. For instance, a citator may show the following for the *Barliant* case:

-1312-
c453FS3904

The small number indicates that the reasoning of the *Barliant* case was criticized on the point of law contained in the third headnote of the case and not on the other points of law addressed in the other headnotes.

The other abbreviations offered by the *Shepard's* citators assist the legal researcher in knowing just which of the cases provided in the history of subsequent treatment need to be reviewed to fully update the research. Illustration 9-3 provides a list of the abbreviations that can be found in each volume of the citator.

SHEPARDIZING STATUTORY LAW

Shepardizing statutory law is similar to that of case law. The process involves the following steps:

1. Locate the proper volumes referring to the appropriate statutes.

2. Locate the statute by section or title number printed in bold type at the top of the page:

T. 28 § 2204

3. Review the case citations under the appropriate statutory section:

§ 2204
849F2d297
912F2d560

The statutory listing may be further divided by statute subsection number. The history of the statute section provides information regarding repeal or amendment.

POCKET SUPPLEMENTS

pocket supplements

The second major tool available to the legal researcher for updating legal authority is through the use of **pocket supplements.**

Once legal authority is printed in a hardbound volume, it is updated by placing a small pamphlet inside the back cover of the volume inside a pocket especially for this purpose. Another term for pocket supplements is *pocket parts.* The supplements contain updated information on specific new law addressing subjects covered in the hardbound volume, allowing the legal researcher access to the latest law. In many legal offices it is the responsibility of the legal office assistant to update the volumes with pocket supplements.

ABBREVIATIONS—ANALYSIS

History of Case

a	(affirmed)	Same case affirmed on appeal.
cc	(connected case)	Different case from case cited but arising out of same subject matter or intimately connected therewith.
D	(dismissed)	Appeal from same case dismissed.
m	(modified)	Same case modified on appeal.
r	(reversed)	Same case reversed on appeal.
s	(same case)	Same case as case cited.
S	(superseded)	Substitution for former opinion.
v	(vacated)	Same case vacated.
US	cert den	Certiorari denied by the U.S. Supreme Court.
US	cert dis	Certiorari dismissed by U.S. Supreme Court.
US	reh den	Rehearing denied by U.S. Supreme Court.
US	reh dis	Rehearing dismissed by U.S. Supreme Court.

Treatment of Case

c	(criticized)	Soundness of decision or reasoning in cited case criticized for reasons given.
d	(distinguished)	Case at bar different either in law or fact from case cited for reasons given.
e	(explained)	Statement of import of decision in cited case. Not merely a restatement of the facts.
f	(followed)	Cited as controlling.
h	(harmonized)	Apparent inconsistency explained and shown not to exist.
j	(dissenting opinion)	Citation in dissenting opinion.
L	(limited)	Refusal to extend decision of cited case beyond precise issues involved.
o	(overruled)	Ruling in cited case expressly overruled.
p	(parallel)	Citing case substantially alike or on all fours with cited case in its laws or facts.
q	(questioned)	Soundness of decision or reasoning in cited case questioned.

Illustration 9-3
Shepard's Abbreviations

In addition to pocket parts, some publishers offer pamphlets to replace pocket supplements that have become too large. Also, pamphlets can be used in advance of the publication of a hardbound volume. The legal office assistant will update all legal authority to be relied upon through the use of pocket supplements, advance pamphlets, and shepardizing for the attorney.

SECONDARY SOURCES

Secondary sources consist of legal reference material "about" the law. They are not binding upon any court, but are of a persuasive nature because of their scholarly

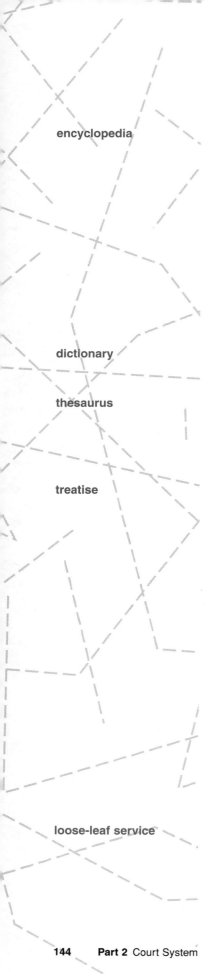

encyclopedia

dictionary

thesaurus

treatise

loose-leaf service

reputation. Secondary sources of the law include the legal encyclopedia, dictionary, thesaurus, treatise, periodical, loose-leaf service, and restatement of the law.

ENCYCLOPEDIA

A legal **encyclopedia** is a multivolume work that describes systematically the entire body of legal doctrine. There are two widely used legal encyclopedias: *Corpus Juris Secundum (C.J.S.)* and *American Jurisprudence 3d (Am. Jur. 3d)*. Both encyclopedias present comprehensive coverage of all legal subjects with annotations referring to cases, statutes, and other legal authority. Each is updated with pocket supplements to maintain their value as a current resource. The encyclopedia is considered to be a good tool with which to commence a research project in an area of the law about which the researcher knows little.

DICTIONARY AND THESAURUS

Legal dictionaries and legal thesauruses provide the legal researcher with resources for the terminology of the law. The law has many terms and phrases that are not common to the lay person, requiring the legal office assistant to seek the technical definition of legal terminology to support legal argument and understand its principles. The legal **dictionary** offers the definition of terms for use in legal argument and reasoning. The two primary legal dictionaries are: *Black's Law Dictionary* and *Ballentine's Law Dictionary.*

The legal **thesaurus** offers the legal office assistant alternative terminology for legal research in the form of synonyms and antonyms. One good legal thesaurus available for the legal researcher is *Ballentine's Thesaurus for Legal Research and Writing.*

TREATISES

A **treatise** is a single or multivolume work on one specific area of the law providing a discussion of all aspects of the particular topic. Treatises are provided by an authority in a given area of the law, such as a legal scholar, attorney, or judge. Treatises can be useful for the legal researcher because of the comprehensive and in-depth coverage of a subject with case analysis. Treatises can be found for all areas of the law, including contracts, evidence, real property, and taxation. Widely used types of treatises are books containing legal forms offering the legal office assistant access to many different types of legal forms for general practice.

PERIODICALS

An essential legal research tool for the law library is the legal periodical. Periodicals come in the form of the local legal news, the journal of the state bar association, and the law reviews of various schools of law. The periodicals provide news about the profession, information about new legislation, analysis of recent case law, and a survey of recent changes in the law. Most major law libraries contain *The Index to Legal Periodicals (IPP)* and the *Index to Periodical Articles Related to Law (IPL)*. Both indexes provide the legal researcher with convenient access to articles appearing in legal periodicals by topic and title. Additional access can be obtained through WESTLAW and LEXIS/NEXUS.

LOOSE-LEAF SERVICES

A **loose-leaf service** consists of a set of binders containing case law, statutes, administrative rules, discussion of the law, and cross-references on a particular area of the law. The popularity of loose-leaf services arises from the ease of updating accomplished by the replacement of an old page with the updated page. Frequent updating serves to make the loose-leaf service one of the best sources for current law. Loose-leaf services cover virtually every major area of the law including taxes, labor relations, environment, family law, criminal law, bankruptcy, and securities regulation. Major publishers include the Bureau of National Affairs (BNA), Commerce Clearing House (CCH), Mathew-Bender, and Prentice-Hall.

LEGAL RESEARCH TECHNIQUE

Legal research involves primarily the same technique regardless of the legal issue to be researched. The experienced legal researcher will have a method of research that will ensure that the question is fully explored and the most recent law is accessed. A sound legal research technique should include four basic steps:

- identify and analyze the significant facts

- frame the legal issues to be researched

- research the issues presented

- update

If these four basic steps are followed for each research project, the legal researcher will be more likely to have accessed all of the necessary information.

SUMMARY

The legal office assistant offers primary support to the attorney in the process of legal research. Although not usually performing the research, the legal office assistant must review citations, access procedural rules, understand the nature of the topic, furnish specific research tools upon request, and maintain small law libraries.

The process of legal research involves a thorough review of primary sources of the law in the form of case law and statutory law. It also involves extensive use of secondary sources to analyze and explain the primary sources upon which legal argument can be based.

Chapter Activities

Review Questions

1. Describe the reasons why a legal office assistant should understand the principles of legal research.

2. List the three categories of materials to be used for legal research.

3. Identify and define the three types of court reports.

4. What is a citation?

5. List the elements of a court opinion.

6. Describe the reasons for considering statutory law in performing legal research.

7. List the elements contained in the format of a statute.

8. What are the two tools that the legal researcher uses in updating legal research?

9. Identify the major secondary sources of legal research.

10. List the four basic steps for sound legal research.

Computer Activity

Your legal office manager has provided you with a list of citations from *Shepards.* Each of the citations for the case in question contains several abbreviations that require interpretation. Your manager has expressed a lack of understanding of these abbreviations and requires your assistance.

A. From the student template retrieve act9.doc. This document is a list of abbreviations. Key in the interpretation of the abbreviations for your instructor. Refer to the chapter for examples.

B. Save this information on the template as shepard.doc.

C. Print one copy for your instructor. Make sure your name appears for identification purposes.

Part 3
Substantive Law

Chapter 10

Domestic Relations

Happy and thrice happy are they who enjoy an uninterrupted union, and whose love, unbroken by any complaints, shall not dissolve until the last day.

Horace (65–8 B.C.)

Objectives

After completing this chapter, you will be able to:

1. Describe the nature of a marriage.

2. Summarize the contractual nature of a marriage.

3. Prepare and draft a separation agreement.

4. Explain the nature of a dissolution of marriage.

5. Distinguish between the various types of divorce.

6. Discuss the grounds for divorce.

7. Describe the judicial standards for custody, alimony, and property division in a divorce.

8. Prepare and draft a complaint for dissolution of marriage.

9. Prepare and draft the responsive pleadings in a divorce action.

10. Prepare and draft the final judgment for divorce.

The legal office assistant can be exposed to the field of domestic relations in almost any legal office setting. If the legal office does not specialize in the field, it often will find itself handling domestic matters for its clients as a service complimenting its area of specialization. Thus, the legal office assistant must be familiar with the principles of the law of domestic relations and the documents that are an integral part of that practice.

MARRIAGE

The concept of a marriage between a man and wife stands at the foundation of social organization in the United States today. Marriages are no longer "arranged" on the basis of property interests or for political reasons. Since the nineteenth century, women have begun to be placed on an equal footing with men in the eyes of the law. The enactment of women's property acts, both allowing women to own property in their own name, gave women more freedom in the selection of a mate and after the consummation of the marriage.

Marriage is the legal status of a man and woman existing as husband and wife and united for life. Marriage is viewed as a matter of contract between a man and a woman to live as husband and wife. It carries with it the legally guaranteed freedom of choice regarding such issues as employment, property, and procreation.

marriage

DOMESTIC RELATIONS CONTRACTS

The marriage of a man and woman involves a contractual relationship with its attendant requirements of legal capacity, consideration, and offer and acceptance. The enforceability of the contractual relationship has been eroded by the laws of most states abolishing an action for a breach of a covenant to marry, called an **anti-heart balm statute,** the term used for such statutory provisions.

anti-heart balm statute

Yet, the law of contracts is very much in evidence within the marital framework, involving such matters as an agreement before marriage addressing certain rights and obligations during marriage and upon death or divorce. Contracts may also address the rights and obligations of persons cohabiting, an agreement to separate without a divorce, and an agreement for reconciliation.

ANTENUPTIAL AGREEMENT

A contract between prospective spouses in contemplation of marriage is called an **antenuptial agreement.** It is also called a *premarital agreement* or a *prenuptial agreement.* Its purpose is to define the rights, duties, and obligations of the spouses during the marriage and to outline any possible divorce and the disposition of property. An antenuptial agreement is one that is usually undertaken by individuals with substantial property before marriage.

antenuptial agreement

Antenuptial agreements must be in writing to satisfy the statute of frauds in most states because real property is often a subject of the contract. The agreement must meet the formal requirements for the execution of a contract in that particular state and must contain a full and frank disclosure of all assets. Many states have enacted the Uniform Premarital Agreement Act (UPAA), a uniform law drafted by the Committee on Uniform Laws of the American Bar Association. Section 3 of the UPAA specifies those matters that may be the subject of the agreement:

- the rights and obligations of each of the parties in any property whenever acquired

- the right to acquire or dispose of any property

- the disposition of property upon separation, divorce, or death

- spousal support

- child support

- the creation of a will or trust

- life insurance

- choice of law governing the agreement

- any matters not in violation of public policy

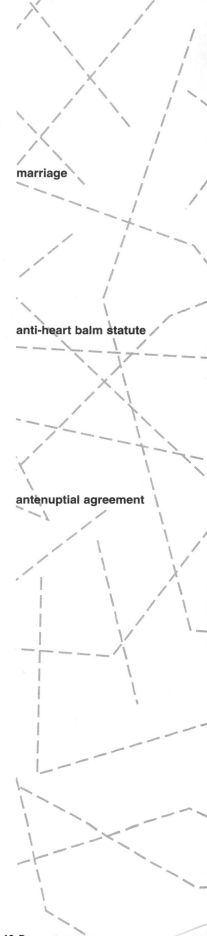

It must be kept in mind that not all states will permit an antenuptial agreement without limitations. Some states take the position that an antenuptial agreement violates the public policy of that state because it encourages or facilitates divorce. Such states are reluctant to uphold certain provisions of the agreement due to the possibility of a change in circumstances from the time of the execution of the agreement and the ultimate divorce.

Antenuptial agreements can be very lengthy. Refer to Appendix B for a sample antenuptial agreement between Winston P. Blansford, III, and his betrothed, Arcadia Hollowell.

SEPARATION AGREEMENT

separation agreement

A **separation agreement,** also referred to as a *postnuptial agreement,* is a contract between a husband and wife establishing their respective rights and obligations while they are separated. The agreement is prepared instead of going through the process of litigation, and in those situations where divorce is contemplated but not a certainty. Its purpose is to avoid the uncertainty of an oral understanding on such issues as child support, alimony, and property division.

The separation agreement can be a complex document, depending on the nature of the relationship, the extent of the property interests involved, and the care and support of children and spouse. The development of a thorough checklist can serve to ensure that the parties have considered each topic, and can provide the preparer with the necessary information to draft the agreement. A checklist should include the following items:

- personal data on the parties
- identification of children
- inventory of real property
- inventory of personal property
- antenuptial agreement
- financial statement
- provision for existing debts and contractual obligations
- alimony considerations
- child custody agreement
- disposition of property
- living arrangements during separation
- child support understanding
- health insurance and medical provision
- life insurance
- income tax
- attorney fees
- divorce
- reconciliation

The separation agreement is a contract and must comply with the requirements of its particular state regarding legality, capacity, consideration, offer, and acceptance. It will also be subject to individual state law on such questions as fraud, duress, or undue influence, which are particularly sensitive questions in a separation where emotions play a significant role.

The custom and rules regarding the form and content of the separation agreement may vary significantly from state to state due to the ongoing changes in the law of domestic relations. The specific matters to be addressed in a basic separation agreement should consist of:

- caption and identification of the parties

- purpose of the separation

- child support provisions

- child custody provisions

- provision for alimony

- property division

- responsibility for debts

- insurance

- wills

- modification

The format for the agreement should consist of numbered paragraphs similar to a formal contract. Subheadings are advisable for individual topics.

Caption and Identification of the Parties. The introductory provisions of the agreement should reflect those matters under state law that provide for the validity of the agreement. The agreement must conform with the public policy of the state, not be collusive in nature, and must not be in contemplation of a divorce. Since all contracts require a recitation of consideration, the separation agreement should reflect the mutual exchange of promises as fulfilling that requirement. Illustration 10-1 provides a sample caption and introduction for the marital separation agreement.

Separation Clause. In order to satisfy the public policy of most jurisdictions stating that it will tolerate nothing that fosters divorce, the separation agreement must reflect that the marriage is best served by a permanent separation. A timely effort on the part of the marriage partners avoids judicial interference. The parties must be in fact living separated, and must express an intent to remain so, electing to not act as husband and wife. Illustration 10-2 presents a sample clause expressing the intention of the parties.

Provision for Alimony Clause. In the English common law, a wife had a right to be supported by her husband. The modern state of the law views the obligation of support to be mutual, whereby each is responsible for the support of the other. This complies with the Fourteenth Amendment and avoids discrimination on the basis of sex. The duty of spousal support in the form of an allowance for maintenance is called **alimony.**

alimony

That allowance may take the form of a lump sum, or it may be in periodic payments. A lump sum alimony payment must be clearly designated as such to avoid any confusion with a property division, which may have certain tax consequences.

The amount of alimony provided, if any, will depend on the level of need and the ability to pay. The Uniform Marriage and Divorce Act, § 308, provides guidelines to be considered in determining alimony in both separation situations and divorce (see Illustration 10-3).

In preparation of the maintenance provisions of the agreement, it is necessary to consider the periodic nature of the payments, the dollar amount, termination upon death, and any limitations on the period or amount. Modification should also be considered. Illustration 10-4 provides language suggested for the provision for maintenance in the form of alimony.

MARITAL SEPARATION AGREEMENT

THIS AGREEMENT, entered into this 30th day of November 1999, between FOSTER SPLITT, hereinafter referred to as Husband, residing at 14 Freedom Circle, Johnstown, Florida, and WANDA SPLITT, hereinafter referred to as Wife, residing at One Limbo Lane, Johnstown, Florida.

WHEREAS, the parties were married on June 31, 1990, and a daughter, FAITH, was born on July 4, 1991;

WHEREAS, as a result of irreconcilable differences, the parties have been living apart since February 29, 1999; and

WHEREAS, the parties wish to enter into this Agreement to settle all custody, support, and property rights between them. Both parties have had independent advice of legal counsel, and have not been coerced into entering into this Agreement.

NOW THEREFORE, in consideration of the promises and the mutual obligations contained in this Agreement, the parties agree as follows:

Illustration 10-1
Caption and Introduction

Husband and Wife shall continue to live separate and apart, each free from interference, authority and control, either direct or indirect, of the other, except as may expressly be in this Agreement, and intend to do so permanently.

Illustration 10-2
Parties' Intention

(a) In a proceeding for dissolution of marriage, legal separation, or maintenance following a decree of dissolution of the marriage by a court which lacked personal jurisdiction over the absent spouse, the court may grant a maintenance order for either spouse only if it finds that the spouse seeking maintenance:

(1) lacks sufficient property to provide for his reasonable needs; and

(2) is unable to support himself through appropriate employment or is the custodian of a child whose condition or circumstances make it appropriate that the custodian not be required to seek employment outside the home.

(b) The maintenance order shall be in amounts and for periods of time the court deems just, without regard to marital misconduct, and after considering all relevant factors including:

(1) the financial resources of the party seeking maintenance, including marital property apportioned to him, his ability to meet his needs independently, and the extent to which a provision for support of a child living with the party includes a sum for that party as custodian;

(2) the time necessary to acquire education or training to enable the party seeking maintenance to find appropriate employment;

(3) the standard of living established during the marriage;

Illustration 10-3
Uniform Marriage and Divorce Act, § 308

(4) the duration of the marriage;

(5) the age and the physical and emotional condition of the spouse seeking maintenance; and

(6) the ability of the spouse from whom maintenance is sought to meet his needs while meeting those of the spouse seeking maintenance.

Illustration 10-3
Uniform Marriage and Divorce Act, § 308 (continued)

ALIMONY

Husband shall pay to Wife as alimony or separate maintenance payments the sum of One Thousand Five Hundred Dollars ($1500) per month on the first day of each month, commencing on the first month following the date of the execution of this Agreement. Payments shall terminate upon death of Husband or upon the remarriage of Wife. All payments shall be made in cash. Husband shall have the obligation to make alimony or separate maintenance payments for a period of thirty-six months following the execution of this Agreement.

Husband and Wife intend that all payments made pursuant to this paragraph shall be included as income on Wife's income tax returns, and shall be a deduction on Husband's income tax return pursuant to the Internal Revenue Code beginning in the year of the execution of this

Illustration 10-4
Alimony Provision

Property Division Clause. Any property division must be fair and equitable, but not necessarily equal. The division of the property must concern itself with the nature of the property, its source, and how it is currently held.

The property that may be subject to division can be either real or personal property. The source of the property, whether real or personal, may vary as in a gift, bequest, or purchase by one spouse or by both spouses jointly. The property may be held in the name of one of the spouses, or it may be held jointly with rights of survivorship, as in the marital home.

The general rule for property division in most states that base their law on English common law is that property acquired by a spouse before the marriage is deemed separate property and is not subject to division. Property acquired solely by one spouse as through a gift or bequest is similarly treated as not divisible. Property acquired in this manner is considered **nonmarital property.**

If such property gains in value during the period of the marriage, that **appreciation** may be subject to division. Any other property, whether real or personal, acquired during the marriage, will be subject to division upon separation or divorce, and is considered **marital property.**

The general rule is that the division must be equitable even if not equal. The separation agreement should reflect a fair distribution of marital property mutually agreed upon by the parties. Illustration 10-5 provides suggested language for an equitable split of the property.

Custody Clause. In a separation agreement, the issue of custody is a matter of agreement between the parties as to what form is in the best interest of the child. The agreement cannot contravene the public policy of each state, which is to assure that each minor child has frequent contact with both parents and that those parents share the

nonmarital property
appreciation

marital property

PROPERTY

Husband and Wife hereby agree to divide equitably between them their marital property vested during their marriage, as follows:

(a) *Residence.* Husband and Wife are co-owners of real property located at 1 Limbo Lane, Johnstown, Florida, and agree to sell the property as soon as practicable and to divide the net proceeds therefrom equally.

(b) *Personal Property.* Husband and Wife have amicably divided their personal property and each shall be the owner of any such property in their custody and control.

Illustration 10-5
Property Division Clause

```
CHILD CUSTODY AND VISITATION

    (a) Wife shall have the permanent custody and control of the minor

children subject only to the rights of visitation hereunder vested in

husband.
```

Illustration 10-6
Child Custody Clause

shared parental responsibility

responsibilities of child-raising, called **shared parental responsibility.** The issues that form the focus of the court in awarding child custody in a contested matter do not appear in this clause of the separation agreement (see Illustration 10-6).

Child Support Clause. Children are entitled to be maintained by law until they reach the age of majority, usually eighteen. In a separation agreement, the maintenance of a child is the responsibility of the noncustodial parent. Most state legislatures have adopted child support guidelines, which form the basis for an equitable means of determining the amount of support. They should be considered by the parties in formulating the separation agreement. The clause will vary significantly, depending on the understanding of the parties on such matters as the amount of support, visitation, and holidays. The agreement should also maintain a provision for health insurance for the child where it is reasonably available through a group insurance plan (see Illustration 10-7).

The support options available to the parties are solely a matter of agreement, and may depend on:

- the amount of support
- the method of payment
- the time of payment
- the termination of payment

A well-prepared agreement will anticipate the changing needs of the child, including the payment for a college education if that is contemplated by the parties.

Responsibility for Debts Clause. In any separation, there will be joint financial obligations that must be met by one party or the other. The responsibility for the debts should be addressed in the agreement in a separate paragraph that addresses the issues of:

- identity of the creditor
- account or loan number
- balance owed
- payment
- party responsible

```
                        CHILD SUPPORT

    Husband shall pay wife for the support and maintenance of the child

the sum of One Hundred Fifty Dollars ($150) per week on the first day

of each week, commencing upon the first day of August 1999, and

continuing until said child marries, dies, attains the age of majority,

or until custody of said child is awarded.
```

Illustration 10-7
Child Support Clause

The debts should each be listed in the agreement or made the subject of an exhibit to be attached to the agreement. Each creditor should then be notified by the parties as to the party responsible for the payments.

Insurance Clause. The preparer of the agreement may want to consider the necessity of maintaining the existence of life, health, and disability policies in effect at the time of separation. A separate clause should provide for the continuation of premium payment and an obligation to keep the policy in effect. The beneficiary designation may change, depending on the agreement of the parties, specifically designating a child as the beneficiary with the proceeds of the insurance held in trust for the child until the age of majority (see Illustration 10-8).

Wills Clause. The separation agreement should concern itself with the matter of the Last Will and Testament of each of the parties. Because of the unlikelihood of either party wishing to benefit the other, and with the intention to provide for the children, the wills clause is necessary to provide for the distribution of property, should either party die. It will be incumbent upon the husband and wife to decide how the property is to be held until the children reach the age of majority, and then to implement that decision with the necessary instruments. It will be necessary to incorporate those concerns in the agreement. A sample wills clause may begin as follows:

> Husband and wife agree that each will maintain a Last Will and Testament which provides that his or her estate be divided and distributed, at the time of death, in such manner that the full value of the estate be placed in trust for the use and benefit of the minor child until such time as the minor child shall attain the age of majority (18). The parties' heirs, administrators, executors, trustees, and assigns shall be bound by this Agreement, whether or not such Last Will and Testament is, in fact, executed.

Modification Clause. Provisions of a separation agreement providing for periodic changes in the amount of alimony or child support may be incorporated in this clause. The parties may wish to provide for an increase in the amount of support based on changes in the consumer price index or for a reduction if the noncustodial parent should become unable to earn a living because of a disability. The variations in the way a modification is handled will depend on the desires of the parties and the creativity of the preparer.

```
                        LIFE INSURANCE

    Husband  agrees  to  maintain  the  life  insurance  policies  listed  in

 Exhibit A attached hereto and made a part of this Agreement and to pay

 all premiums thereon due until the child support obligations under this

 Agreement are fully performed. The insurers will be instructed to change

 the beneficiaries of each policy to the minor child.
```

Illustration 10-8
Life Insurance Clause

DIVORCE/DISSOLUTION

divorce
dissolution

The termination of the legal status of marriage, whereby a man and woman no longer coexist as husband and wife, is known as **divorce.**

Dissolution is another term that means the same thing and is found in the statutes of many states in an attempt to soften the impact of disruption of the social institution. Regardless of the terminology used by the state, the effect is to terminate the bonds of matrimony within the limitations established by the public policy of the state.

NATURE AND TYPES

Most divorces in the United States are uncontested, which means that the parties are in agreement as to the necessity of the termination of the marital relationship. They are also in agreement on the issues of child custody, support, alimony, and property division. The form of the divorce will vary with the circumstances, giving rise to various types of divorce. Some of those types are:

default divorce

- **Default divorce**—a divorce where no appearance is made by the defendant, so that the plaintiff is granted the dissolution without contest.

ex parte divorce

- ***Ex parte* divorce**—a divorce where the court did not have jurisdiction over the defendant and only one party is present in court.

migratory divorce

- **Migratory divorce**—a divorce where the husband and wife travel to another state to obtain a divorce because of the laxity of the laws in that state.

foreign divorce

- **Foreign divorce**—a divorce obtained in a state other than the current state where enforcement is being sought.

It is in these types of divorce that the procedure is merely one of a formality involving none of the issues surrounding the grounds for divorce or the questions of property, custody, and support.

GROUNDS

grounds

fault

For a court to grant a divorce or dissolution of marriage, the party seeking the divorce must show **grounds,** or sufficient legal justification for the action. Historically, the courts would only terminate a marriage if the moving party could show grounds constituting **fault,** or responsibility for wrongful behavior.

The fault grounds for divorce were considered to be:

- **Adultery**—a sexual relationship by a married person with someone other than the spouse.

- **Cruelty**—the intentional infliction of mental and physical harm.

- **Abandonment** or **desertion**—the act of terminating marital cohabitation without consent or justification.

Frequently there would be insufficient facts to support any one of the fault grounds for divorce. As a result, the parties would be compelled to fabricate the grounds. Today, most state legislatures recognize the fact that there can be a breakdown of the marital relationship without any of the fault grounds existing. This recognition has given rise to **no-fault** grounds for divorce, which is an acknowledgment that the bonds and ends of matrimony no longer exist.

The no-fault grounds for divorce in most states are:

- irreconcilable breakdown

- incompatibility

- living apart

- mental incompetence

With no-fault grounds, the party filing the action for divorce has a significantly reduced burden of proving sufficient justification for the termination of the marriage. Neither party is forced to prove something that may not exist.

CHILD CUSTODY AND SUPPORT

The court determines all matters related to the questions of child custody and support. The general overriding concern of the court is the "best interest of the child." In determining what might be the best interest of the child, the court will consider such matters as:

- moral fitness of the custodial parent

- physical condition of the custodial parent

- age of the child

- emotional ties with one parent or the other

- capacity of the custodial parent to provide for the needs of the child

- home, school, and community environment of the custodial parent

In preparing any document relative to the question of child custody, sufficient facts must be alleged to support the claim of the parent seeking custody on the above factors.

Child support is based on the ability and resources and circumstances of the parents. Either party may be asked to pay support, depending on earnings. Most states have established certain written guidelines to determine the amount of support due on behalf of the child based upon an equitable determination of the means of both parties. The support guidelines may be varied by the court if the circumstances warrant special consideration.

PROPERTY

In determining an equitable distribution of property between the spouses, the court will first set aside all property that is considered to be nonmarital property that was not the product of the marriage. In distributing marital assets, the general rule is that the

adultery

cruelty

abandonment, desertion

no-fault

distribution will be equitable and fair, although it may not be equal. In deciding the disposition, the court will consider:

- duration of the marriage
- contribution of each spouse to the development of a marital asset
- economic circumstances of the parties
- interruption in the career of one for the educational career of the other
- need for the retention of a particular asset for a business
- need to retain the marital home for a child

There will be many other equitable issues that arise, depending on the nature of the asset itself requiring the decision of the court. Facts sufficient to present a question of fairness should be alleged in any pleadings addressing property distribution.

ALIMONY

The court has the option of awarding support for one spouse in a dissolution proceeding. As discussed earlier, spousal support is termed *alimony* and is a separate consideration from either child support or property division. Fault can be considered by the court in awarding alimony, along with the following factors:

- standard of living to which the parties have become accustomed
- duration of the marriage
- financial well-being of the parties
- physical condition of the parties
- time and resources needed to rehabilitate a spouse for the workplace
- relative contribution of the parties to the marriage

Alimony may be awarded on a periodic basis, or it may be granted as a lump sum within the discretion of the court. The duration of the periodic payments in a rehabilitative alimony situation will depend on the length of time required to render the spouse capable of finding suitable employment.

PROCEDURE

The preliminary step to the filing of any pleading in a dissolution of marriage is to obtain as much information as possible. The development of a good checklist will facilitate the process. Most law offices that specialize in domestic relations matters will have interview forms and checklists available for the information gathering process.

COMPLAINT

The complaint in a domestic relations matter, in some states referred to as a petition, is the initial pleading filed to commence the cause of action. As in any other civil matter, it must state a claim upon which relief may be granted. It must contain a statement of the jurisdiction of the court, the grounds for granting the divorce, and the relief being sought. Other matters for the court's consideration must be plead if at issue, such as: child custody, child support, alimony, and property division.

A complaint for dissolution of marriage should contain the following:

- caption
- identification of the nature of the cause of action

- jurisdiction and venue of the court

- details of the marriage

- identification of the children of the marriage, if any

- allegations regarding child custody

- allegations regarding child support

- allegations regarding alimony

- allegations regarding property division

- grounds for the divorce

Illustration 10-9 provides a sample of a petition for dissolution of marriage.

ANSWER

The answer is the responsive pleading filed by the defendant or respondent in a divorce action constituting the first appearance of record in the matter. In all cases, the defendant will have a specified period of time to file the answer outlined in state's statutes, typically twenty days after service of the complaint. The answer either admits, denies, or pleads insufficient knowledge regarding each element of the complaint, and may contain a counterclaim for any matter deemed necessary. For instance, if the plaintiff is seeking child custody, and the defendant is also seeking child custody, then an allegation sufficient to warrant the granting of custody to the defendant must be plead.

The answer contains the following:

- caption

- identification of the parties

- admission or denial of the allegations in the complaint

- any counterclaims to be asserted

- prayer for relief

If only a portion of any specific allegation is to be denied, the answer must state specifically the portion to be admitted.

SIMPLIFIED DIVORCE

In many states, the domestic relations procedural rules contain provisions for the submission of a "simple" divorce to the court for dissolution. Usually, these simple divorces are available in the situation where there are no minor children involved and the property of the parties, if any, is not at issue. In such cases, the complaint is a simplified version of the full complaint, and the proceedings are shortened to the scheduling of a quick hearing to enter the decree. The complaint should contain the following:

- caption

- identification of the nature of the cause of action

- jurisdiction of the court

- date of the marriage

- allegations regarding property division

- grounds for the divorce

IN THE CIRCUIT COURT
FOR BOONE COUNTY, FLORIDA

IN RE: The Marriage of

FLORENCE LAURENCE,

     Petitioner,

and   CASE NO.

LAWRENCE LAURENCE,

     Respondent.

_____/

PETITION FOR DISSOLUTION OF MARRIAGE

Petitioner, FLORENCE LAURENCE, petitions for the dissolution of the marriage between herself and LAWRENCE LAURENCE, hereinafter referred to as Respondent, and in support thereof, states:

1.   This is an action for dissolution of marriage between Petitioner, FLORENCE LAURENCE, and Respondent.

2.   Petitioner has been a resident of the state of Florida for more than six (6) months.

3.   Petitioner and Respondent were married to each other on November 12, 1989, at Boone Valley, Florida, and lived together as husband and wife until June 30, 1999.

4.   There was one child born of this marriage: PATIENCE LAURENCE, born April 25, 1991.

5.   Petitioner has not participated as a party, witness, or in any other litigation or custody proceeding, in this or any other state, concerning custody of the child subject to this proceeding.

Page 1 of 3--Petition for Dissolution of Marriage

Illustration 10-9
Petition for Dissolution of Marriage

6. Petitioner has no information of any custody proceeding pending in a court of this or any other state concerning the child subject to this proceeding.

7. Petitioner does not know of any person not a party to this proceeding who has physical custody or claims to have visitation rights with respect to the child subject to this proceeding.

8. Petitioner states that she is a fit and proper person to have permanent care, custody, and control of the minor child, PATIENCE LAURENCE.

9. Respondent is well and able to provide for, and Petitioner requires financial support of the minor child of the parties.

10. There is personal property to be divided equitably between the parties.

11. There are debts and obligations owing by the parties that should be equitably divided by the Court.

12. The marriage between the parties is irretrievably broken.

WHEREFORE, Petitioner, FLORENCE LAURENCE, requests that this Court enter a Final Judgment dissolving the marriage between the parties and granting unto Petitioner:

1. Take jurisdiction of this cause and enter an order dissolving her marriage to Respondent.

2. Temporary and permanent care, custody, and control of PATIENCE LAURENCE.

3. Temporary and permanent support money for PATIENCE LAURENCE.

Page 2 of 3--Petition for Dissolution of Marriage

Illustration 10-9
Petition for Dissolution of Marriage (continued)

4. An equitable division of the personal property owned by the parties.

5. Enter any order that the Court deems proper and just in this matter.

_____
FLORENCE LAURENCE, Petitioner

_____
MAVIS MAVEN #238765
Attorney at Law
1234 Marvin Place
Boone, Florida 54890-8123
(309) 555-1212

Page 3 of 3--Petition for Dissolution of Marriage

Illustration 10-9
Petition for Dissolution of Marriage (continued)

FINAL JUDGMENT

The final judgment, also known as a divorce decree or decree of dissolution in some states, is the order of the court granting the divorce along with any other relief sought by the parties and deemed appropriate by the court after hearing the facts. The final decision of the court addresses the matter of jurisdiction over the parties and the subject matter of the litigation. The court orders the dissolution of the marital relationship, child custody, support, alimony, and property division (see Illustration 10-10).

The final decision of the court may be rendered after a hearing, trial on the merits, or agreement by the parties.

SUMMARY

The marital union is considered a matter of contract between the spouses, yet is treated in manner unlike the typical contractual agreement in the eyes of the court. Each state has a public policy interest in preserving the marital union. If a breakdown of that marital union occurs, the state has a vested interest in securing the procedural safeguards for each spouse. The primary concern of the laws surrounding domestic relations is to equitably divide the property, provide for the welfare of minor children, and present an opportunity for the spouses to proceed on an even footing. The legal documents necessary to ensure these values from a procedural standpoint are governed by the rules of procedure for domestic relations of each state. The form and content of the documents is governed by court rule or statute. The preparer of the document must consult local and state rules where available.

IN THE CIRCUIT COURT
FOR BOONE COUNTY, FLORIDA

IN RE: The Marriage of

FLORENCE LAURENCE,

      Petitioner,

and   CASE NO. 12345

LAWRENCE LAURENCE,

      Respondent.

_____/

FINAL JUDGMENT OF DISSOLUTION OF MARRIAGE

From the evidence, the Court finds:

The Court has jurisdiction of the parties and the subject matter of this action, and,

The marriage of the parties, FLORENCE LAURENCE and LAWRENCE LAURENCE, is irretrievably broken.

IT IS ORDERED AND ADJUDGED:

1. The marriage of FLORENCE LAURENCE and LAWRENCE LAURENCE is dissolved; and each spouse is restored to the status of being single and unmarried.

2. The property of the parties is hereby divided pursuant to the agreement of the parties attached to the petition herein.

DONE AND ORDERED at Boone, Florida, this _____ day of _____, 1999.

_____
Circuit Judge

Illustration 10-10
Judgment of Dissolution of Marriage

Chapter Activities

Review Questions

1. Define the concept of a marriage.
2. Describe the difference between a marriage and a contract.
3. Discuss the matters that form the subject of the antenuptial agreement.
4. What is a separation agreement?
5. List the elements of a good checklist to be used before drafting a separation agreement.
6. List the various types of divorce.
7. List the fault grounds for divorce.
8. Identify the no-fault grounds for divorce.
9. What is the general rule used by the court to distribute property in a divorce?
10. What factors are considered by the court to determine whether alimony is proper?

Computer Activity

The law firm of Elliott & Ness, by Elvin Elliott, has requested your services in the handling of a recently acquired domestic relations matter. The heavenly bonds of marriage between Bonnie and Clyde Barker have broken down irretrievably, due to the excessive stress placed upon their relationship as a result of years of pursuit by law enforcement authorities throughout the southern Midwest. The Barkers have been "on the lamb" for the better part of six years, having dragged their son Junior on their odyssey since his birth on April 1, 1990. They had recently settled in your community, only to be ratted out by Bonnie's hairdresser, Bruce Phlough, a material witness at their trial. The Barkers are now serving twenty years to life in the state penitentiary, and Junior has been temporarily living with Clyde's mother, Ma.

The Barkers want to end their years of marriage on as peaceful a note as possible, and want Junior to be raised by Ma, since she seems to have done so well with Clyde. Their property consists of one 1984 Ford Bronco II 4x4 with air conditioning, and an unspecified amount of cash and securities hidden in an unknown location to be divided equally.

A. From the student template retrieve act10.doc. This document is a Petition for Dissolution of Marriage. Prepare a Complaint for Divorce reflecting the grounds for dissolution, the custody of Junior, and the property settlement. Refer to the chapter for examples.

B. Save this information on the template as petition.doc.

C. Print one copy for your instructor. Make sure your name appears for identification purposes.

Chapter 11

Law of Torts

Objectives

After completing this chapter, you will be able to:

1. Discuss the nature of torts.

2. Identify the categories of torts.

3. Understand the concept of negligence.

4. Discuss the elements of negligence.

5. Summarize the defenses to an action for negligence.

6. Identify intentional torts resulting in injury to a person.

7. Identify intentional torts resulting in injury to property.

8. Summarize the defenses to intentional torts.

9. Understand the concept of strict liability.

NATURE OF TORTS

In many legal office settings, the legal office assistant must be familiar with the concept of torts. The duties of the legal office assistant will be essentially the same, whether employed in a plaintiff's firm (representing the injured individual) or a defense firm (representing the wrongdoer or the insurance company). Those duties will be basically that of litigation support, as discussed in the chapters of Part 2.

TORTS DEFINED

To understand the nature of the field of torts, it is necessary to begin with a definition of the term. A **tort** is a wrongful act resulting in

tort

injury to a person or property. The individual that performs the wrongful act resulting in injury is known as the **tortfeasor.**

The field of law of torts is concerned with the individual rights of the injured person or property owner and the remedies available. There are many different types of torts for which the law provides a remedy, and each tort has its own distinctive elements rooted in history.

Tort law originated in the English common law, whereby the king's justices attempted to remedy any breach of the peace. Today, tort law allows the individual injured as a result of a breach of the peace to seek his redress in a court of law against the wrongdoer.

CATEGORIES OF TORTS

Tort law consists of the separation of torts into three broad categories. The separation is based on the degree of blame to be placed on the tortfeasor. The level of blame to be placed ranges from responsibility for mere carelessness to liability, regardless of fault. The three categories of torts are:

- **Negligence**—the failure to use reasonable care to avoid injury to another.

- **Intentional torts**—actions in which the tortfeasor has the intent or purpose to injure another.

- **Strict liability**—responsibility for actions regardless of intention or fault, also called *absolute liability.*

This chapter will provide the legal office assistant with an understanding of the basic elements of the torts for each category. The defenses available for each category will also be discussed.

NEGLIGENCE

The concept of negligence involves the failure to use reasonable care to avoid injury to another. The essence of the tort of negligence involves the following elements:

- duty of reasonable care

- breach of duty of reasonable care

- proximate cause

- damages

The tortfeasor may be liable for negligence either as a result of doing some act or as a result of failing to do some act. The failure to act is called an **omission** and can form the basis for liability for negligence.

DUTY OF REASONABLE CARE

The first step in determining the existence of the tort of negligence is a determination of whether or not the tortfeasor owed a duty of reasonable care to the injured person or property. A **duty** is an obligation to do or not do something.

A duty of **reasonable care** is the responsibility to act or not act reasonably under the circumstances to avoid injury. The measure of whether an act or omission is reasonable is based on the behavior of an imaginary reasonable person and has come to be known in tort law as the **reasonable person standard.**

The act or omission of the tortfeasor is to be measured against the prudent acts or omissions of a reasonable person under the same or similar circumstances. The jury has the responsibility to determine the reasonableness of an act or omission.

tortfeasor

negligence

intentional torts

strict liability

omission

duty
reasonable care

reasonable person
standard

foreseeability

A limitation on the liability of the tortfeasor for negligence is provided by the principle of **foreseeability.** Foreseeability refers to the concept that a specific act or omission would have an anticipated result. If the result could not reasonably have been anticipated, then the tortfeasor does not face liability for the act or omission.

BREACH OF DUTY OF REASONABLE CARE

breach of duty

Once it is established that one individual owes a duty of reasonable care to act or omit an act toward another so as not to cause harm, the next question to be resolved is whether or not there has been a **breach of duty** of reasonable care.

A breach of duty occurs with any violation of an obligation. Where a tortfeasor owes a duty of reasonable care, and violates that duty through an act or omission, then there may be liability for negligence. The breach occurs with the failure to act or not act as a reasonable person would under the same or similar circumstances.

PROXIMATE CAUSE

causation

A critical element to the tort of negligence is that of **causation,** which refers to an act or omission that produces a result. A tortfeasor cannot be held accountable for an act or omission if he or she did not "cause" the injury to person or property. In order to be held liable for acts or omissions, a tortfeasor must have been the **proximate cause** of the injury.

proximate cause

Proximate cause, or *legal cause,* as it is sometimes referred, is present when the tortfeasor's act or omission is the foreseeable cause of the injury. It is that causative event without which the injury would not have occurred. In a chain of events leading to injury, the proximate cause is the nearest in effect but not necessarily in time. It is sometimes said to be the last negligent act leading to injury or harm.

DAMAGES

damages

In order to maintain a lawsuit for negligence, the law requires that the plaintiff sustain some harm as a result of the breach of a duty of reasonable care as a result of the act or omission of the defendant. **Damages** is the term used in the law to refer to the harm or injury to person or property. A court of law is unable to compensate a victim of negligence if no damage has occurred as a proximate cause of the tortfeasor's actions. Usually, this means that there must have been some monetary loss as a result of the harm to a person or property.

There are two basic categories of damages allowed by law: *compensatory* and *punitive.* To maintain an action for negligence, the plaintiff must prove the existence of one or both form(s) of damages.

compensatory damages

Compensatory damages refers to the monetary loss to compensate the plaintiff for the harm to person or property. For personal injury, the monetary loss can be measured in actual out-of-pocket expenses, plus economic impairment in the future as a result of the injury. They may consist of lost income, pain and suffering, or loss of bodily function. For property, the monetary loss can be measured in a loss of value or out-of-pocket repair costs. The legal office assistant may be called upon to track the actual out-of-pocket losses of the injured person as the expenses are incurred.

punitive damages

Punitive damages, or *exemplary damages,* refers to money awarded in cases involving an intentional tort (discussed later) or in cases of extremely gross negligence. Punitive damages are not usually awarded to a plaintiff in cases involving ordinary negligence. Local state law should be reviewed carefully to determine the types of cases for which punitive damages are awarded to punish or make an example of the tortfeasor.

DISTINCTIVE NEGLIGENCE ACTIONS

Tort law has developed distinct rules for certain types of negligence actions. The basic theory of negligence involving a duty, a breach of that duty, proximate cause, and damage all apply. But each of the following areas of liability have their own distinct rules:

- premises liability
- bailment liability
- vicarious liability
- negligent infliction of emotional distress

PREMISES LIABILITY

Tort law is in a state of change regarding the liability for negligence for owners of property. The courts have traditionally held that there is a different standard of liability for owners of property, depending on the status of the injured person. Illustration 11-1 provides the traditional view of the courts still held by many states. As shown, there is a different standard traditionally imposed, depending upon whether the injured person is a:

- **trespasser**—an individual who enters another's property without consent.

- ***child***—for an **attractive nuisance,** a condition on the premises that is considered a source of danger to a trespassing child and that may be expected to attract them to play, resulting in injury.

- **licensee**—an individual who has permission to be on the premises.

- **invitee**—an individual who has been invited on the premises, sometimes called a *business invitee.*

The difference between a licensee and an invitee is that the owner does not necessarily have to invite the licensee on the premises but the invitee has been specifically invited. The difference is in the active role of the owner to get them on the premises. For instance, the owner of a business encourages individuals to come on the premises, and is thus held to a different and higher standard than a homeowner.

trespasser

attractive nuisance

licensee

invitee

Trespasser	No duty of reasonable care required to avoid intentional injury
Children	Duty of reasonable care to protect trespassing children from attractive nuisance
Licensee	Duty of reasonable care to correct known dangers on the property
Invitee	Duty of reasonable care to discover and correct unknown dangers on premises
Negligence Theory	Duty of reasonable care to act as a reasonable person would under the circumstances

Illustration 11-1
Traditional Premises Liability

Following recent decisions in the state of California, courts in many states have eliminated the trespasser/licensee/invitee approach and have adopted a pure traditional negligence theory to cover all three. The individual state laws must be consulted to determine the status of the law on this issue.

BAILMENT LIABILITY

bailment

bailor
bailee

A **bailment** occurs when an owner of personal property delivers possession of that property to another to keep until the item is returned or delivered to someone else. The owner of the property that is the subject of the bailment is called a **bailor,** and the recipient of the bailment is called the **bailee.** An example of a bailment situation would be the delivery of an automobile to a parking garage for pay.

As with premises liability, the liability for a bailment differs, dependent on who benefits from the bailment relationship. Illustration 11-2 presents the distinction between bailments and the respective liability of the bailee.

The recent trend has been to abandon the multilevel approach to liability and impose traditional negligence theory as a standard for the bailee. This approach involves the sole question as to whether or not the bailee used reasonable care in safeguarding the property, rather than analyzing who may have benefited.

VICARIOUS LIABILITY

vicarious liability

Vicarious liability is the liability of one person, called the *principal,* for the wrongful conduct (torts) of another subordinate individual, called the *agent.* The most common example of a situation where this form of liability exists is between an employer and an employee acting within the scope of employment. In addition to *employer–employee* liability, it is also known as the law of *principal–agent, agency,* or *master–servant.* Regardless of the terminology, the principle remains the same; that is, one individual is responsible for the acts or omissions of another. Of course, the principal is not liable for the acts of the agent if the agent is outside the scope of his employment or before and after the normal work hours while the employee travels to and from work. Also, the principal is not liable if the "agent" is an **independent contractor.**

independent contractor

An independent contractor is one who has been contracted for a specific purpose and differs from an employee because the employer does not control the independent contractor.

Bailment for Sole Benefit of Bailor	Bailee owes a duty of slight care to safeguard property from harm
Bailment for Mutual Benefit	Bailee owes a duty of ordinary, reasonable care to protect property from harm
Bailment for Bailee's Sole Benefit	Bailee owes a duty of great care to protect property from harm
Negligence Theory	Bailee owes a duty of caring for the property as a reasonable person would under the circumstances

Illustration 11-2
Traditional Bailment Liability

NEGLIGENT INFLICTION OF EMOTIONAL DISTRESS

Emotional distress is mental anguish caused by a tortfeasor. Examples of emotional distress are fear, anxiety, grief, shock, shame, embarrassment, and mental suffering. The tort of negligent infliction of emotional distress involves the following elements:

- outrageous conduct by the tortfeasor
- reasonable anticipation of emotional distress
- emotional distress in the victim

Most courts currently hold that the victim must undergo some physical manifestation of the mental suffering. This rule prevents fraudulent practices involved in this type of claim. There is a wide diversity of formulas and criteria to be used in emotional distress cases between state jurisdictions requiring a consultation of local law.

DEFENSES TO NEGLIGENCE

Negligent conduct as seen above imposes liability upon the defendant/tortfeasor for damages. But the law provides the defendant with certain defenses that are aimed at an analysis of the conduct of the injured plaintiff and that offer an excuse for the defendant's behavior. Even though the tortfeasor may have been negligent toward the plaintiff, the tortfeasor's acts or omissions are forgiven because of certain behavior by the plaintiff. The defenses available to a claim for negligence are:

- statutes of limitations
- contributory negligence
- comparative negligence
- assumption of risk
- governmental immunity

STATUTES OF LIMITATIONS

As previously seen, **statutes of limitations** are laws that establish a time limitation to the right of filing a lawsuit for a particular type of case. Each state has a statute or statutes that regulate the time limit for the filing of certain types of negligence actions. For instance, one state may have a statute of limitations for filing an action for medical malpractice claims of two years, while another state may have a limitation of three years. The legal office assistant should become familiar with the various statutory periods for filing negligence claims in an individual state.

CONTRIBUTORY NEGLIGENCE

English common law stated that if the plaintiff's action contributed to the injury even slightly, then there was no recovery. This has come to be known as the doctrine of **contributory negligence.**

The elements of contributory negligence are:

- duty of reasonable care for oneself
- breach of that duty
- plaintiff's act or omission that proximately contributed to the injury
- harm to plaintiff

emotional distress

statutes of limitations

contributory negligence

The basic principle behind the doctrine of contributory negligence is that every individual has a duty to not injure oneself. If there is a breach of that duty, then there has been negligence toward oneself. Regardless of the tortfeasor's negligence, if the plaintiff contributed to the injury with a negligent act of omission, then there is a bar to recovery.

Although this doctrine provides the defendant with a defense in a claim for negligence, the plaintiff also has a counterargument against a claim for contributory negligence. That argument is the principle of **last clear chance.**

The theory is that although the plaintiff was contributorily negligent in causing the injury, if the defendant had the "last clear chance" to avert the harm, and through negligence failed to do so, then the plaintiff may still recover. The last clear chance doctrine nullifies the contributory negligence defense.

COMPARATIVE NEGLIGENCE

The common law doctrine of contributory negligence has been criticized as unduly harsh to a plaintiff that may have only been marginally involved in the injury. In response, the courts and legislatures of many states have adopted a modification of the common law rule with the theory of **comparative negligence.**

The theory of comparative negligence is a measure of comparison of the negligence of the plaintiff against that of the defendant in causing the injury. It allows an adjustment of the liability of the defendant by the plaintiff's contribution to the injury. The theory mandates a calculation of the percentage of contribution of the negligence of each party and apportioning liability accordingly. For example, if the defendant were found to be 60 percent responsible for the injury to the plaintiff, and the plaintiff found to be 40 percent responsible, then the defendant would be liable for 60 percent of the damages.

Although this defense has been criticized as unduly arbitrary in assigning percentages, the net effect is a result that approaches fairness more than the theory of contributory negligence. Again, the laws of each individual state must be consulted to determine which defenses are allowed.

ASSUMPTION OF RISK

Another defense to a claim of negligence is the defense of **assumption of risk.** Clearly stated, this theory is that the plaintiff assumed the risk of an act or omission that resulted in injury. The defense involves two principles:

- plaintiff voluntarily assumed a known risk

- plaintiff fully appreciated the danger in facing that risk

This defense is an absolute bar to a plaintiff's claim for negligence. For instance, if an individual were to attempt a "bungee jump" from a bridge over a river, that individual can be said to have voluntarily assumed the risks inherent in bungee jumping and could fully appreciate the dangers. In the event of an injury, a recovery against defendant would be barred by the plaintiff's assumption of risk.

GOVERNMENTAL IMMUNITY

A defense to a claim for negligence that is not aimed at the plaintiff's own culpability, yet serves as a complete bar to any action, is the doctrine of **governmental immunity.** Also called *sovereign immunity,* the doctrine arises from the English common law theory that the king could not be sued for negligence. In twentieth-century practice, the doctrine holds that a governmental unit is immune from liability for the torts of its employees.

The courts have drawn distinctions between which actions of the employees are covered by the doctrine. If the employee were engaged in a purely governmental function,

last clear chance

comparative negligence

assumption of risk

governmental immunity

then the government could not be sued. Such purely governmental functions would include police and fire protection. If the employee were engaged in a proprietary governmental function such as providing sewer or electric service, a function more resembling a business function, then there is no immunity from a claim for negligence.

State legislatures are now moving away from the governmental/proprietary function distinction, holding governmental units liable for the torts of their employees. It is an area of the law that is in a state of change, mandating a review of the most recent changes in the individual states.

INTENTIONAL TORTS: INJURY TO PERSON

The law of *intentional torts* involves those acts or omissions that are considered intentional and injurious. Two elements are necessary in determining the existence of an action for intentional torts:

- the tortfeasor intended the act or omission

- the act or omission was injurious behavior

The essence of all intentional torts is that the tortfeasor intended to accomplish the harmful results of the behavior. **Intent** refers to the desire to bring about a harmful result.

Intentional torts can be directed at either the individual or property. Those directed at the person or individual include:

- defamation

- infliction of emotional distress

- invasion of privacy

- assault and battery

- false imprisonment

- fraud and misrepresentation

- malicious prosecution

- abuse of process

While the essence of these torts is the element of intent, the intent can often be inferred from the behavior. If the tortfeasor's behavior is reckless, then the tortfeasor should have known that such behavior would produce injurious results.

DEFAMATION

The intentional tort of **defamation** consists of the communication of an intentionally false statement about another to a third person. Defamation can be subdivided into two separate types: **slander,** which is an oral false statement, and **libel,** which is a written false statement.

The essence of the tort is the communication to a third person that results in an injury to the person's reputation in the community. The elements of the tort are:

- intentionally false written or oral statement

- communication to a third person

- harm to the victim's reputation

Truth is an absolute defense to the tort of defamation. Since a principle element of the tort is a "false" statement, if the statement is true, then there is no cause of action.

intent

defamation

slander
libel

INFLICTION OF EMOTIONAL DISTRESS

As discussed earlier, the negligent infliction of emotional distress is certainly grounds for a cause of action against the tortfeasor. This tort involves the same elements, yet adds an additional element of intent. The essence of this tort is that the victim suffers some emotional trauma proximately caused by the intentional act of the tortfeasor. The conduct must be so outrageous that a reasonable person would suffer the same or similar harm if so confronted.

INVASION OF PRIVACY

invasion of privacy

The intentional tort of **invasion of privacy** consists of the public exploitation of another person's private affairs in an unreasonably intrusive manner.

This tort has four separate types:

- appropriation—use of a person's name or likeness without permission

- unreasonable intrusion—an excessive and highly offensive invasion of another person's solitude

- public disclosure of private facts—communication of private information without permission

- false light in the public eye—publicly attributing spurious statements or opinions to another in an embarrassing manner

With modern technology it is increasingly difficult to maintain any level of privacy. To be actionable, the invasion must have been intended to harm the individual.

ASSAULT AND BATTERY

assault
battery

An **assault** is an attempt by one person to make harmful contact with another without consent. It differs from a **battery** in that it does not involve physical contact.

It is physical contact that converts an assault to a battery. A battery is an intentional touching of another without consent and in a harmful manner. Both of these torts have certain elements in common:

- intent

- lack of consent

- harmful or offensive contact

Assault and battery are fairly straightforward for an intentional tort. The existence of the tort is to be measured by the reasonable person standard to determine if the resulting harm is actionable.

FALSE IMPRISONMENT

false imprisonment

The tort of **false imprisonment** occurs where an individual is intentionally confined without consent.

This tort seeks to guarantee an individual's freedom of movement and when that has been intentionally impaired, then an actionable tort arises. The tort has the following elements:

- confinement without consent

- intent to confine

- confinement for an appreciable period of time

- no reasonable means of escape

The essence of the tort is the intention to restrict the individual's movement, resulting in injury—usually of an emotional nature.

FRAUD AND MISREPRESENTATION

Fraud occurs when false statements are intentionally used to entice the victim to give up something of value. **Misrepresentation** occurs when the tortfeasor intentionally makes false statements or behaves in a manner intended to deceive the victim.

The two torts are very similar in nature and involve these elements:

- false statements intended to deceive

- knowingly false

- victim is harmed by the deception

The critical elements of both torts involve intent and knowledge on the part of the tortfeasor.

MALICIOUS PROSECUTION

The intentional tort of **malicious prosecution** is directed at the groundless filing of a criminal complaint against another person.

The tort must contain a groundless complaint, malice in filing the charges, the accused's acquittal or dismissal, and injury to the accused. The essence of this tort is the concept of malice directed at the victim manifested through the use of a criminal complaint.

ABUSE OF PROCESS

Similar to malicious prosecution, the tort of **abuse of process** involves the use of civil legal proceedings to achieve an unlawful objective, resulting in harm to the victim.

This tort is based on the intentional misuse or the threat of civil legal proceedings to obtain an objective to which the tortfeasor would not have been entitled. For instance, the tortfeasor may threaten civil litigation to extract money for a disputed claim that would not have been successful if properly pursued. The essence is the misuse of a legal proceeding to gain a benefit to which the tortfeasor would not have been entitled.

INTENTIONAL TORTS: INJURY TO PROPERTY

Property and property rights can also be the object of an intentional tort. When a tortfeasor intentionally interferes with the enjoyment and rights associated with property ownership, then the owner of that property has a cause of action against the tortfeasor for the damage sustained. The common intentional torts resulting in injury to property and property rights are:

- trespass to land

- toxic torts

- trespass to chattel

- conversion

- slander of title

- commercial disparagement

- defamation by computer

Each of these torts involves the intention of the tortfeasor and resulting interference with the property interests of the victim.

fraud
misrepresentation

malicious prosecution

abuse of process

trespass to land

toxic tort

chattel
trespass to chattel

conversion

slander of title

TRESPASS TO LAND

Trespass to land occurs when the tortfeasor enters the land of another without the owner's consent. The trespass occurs with the entry on to the land. Entry can occur either through personal presence on the land of another or by physically depositing an unwanted substance on the land of another. Either form interferes with the owner's right to peaceful enjoyment of the property. The entry must be without the consent of the owner and need not result in any physical harm or damage to the property. Also, the trespass may occur in the sky above the land and beneath the surface of the property.

TOXIC TORTS

Closely related to trespass to land is the relatively modern **toxic tort** involving an action for pollution and hazardous waste disposal involving toxic chemicals.

Environmentally sensitive issues are raised when the trespass to land is in the form of the introduction of toxic substances to the land of another. The entry can occur in the form of dumping, seepage, or accumulation. Intent can be inferred from the disposal method. For instance, if a tortfeasor buried toxic chemicals in containers that deteriorate quickly, intent is inferred because the tortfeasor should have taken sufficient precautions. The ultimate interference with the owner's enjoyment and use of the property is seriously impaired as a result.

TRESPASS TO CHATTEL

A **chattel** is another name for personal property. The tort of **trespass to chattel** occurs when the tortfeasor possesses the property of another without consent.

The tort involves an intent on the part of the tortfeasor to deprive the owner of possession or exclusive use of the property without consent. For instance, if a tortfeasor took his neighbor's wheelbarrow without consent, then a trespass to the chattel would have occurred. The property would have been possessed by the tortfeasor without consent and with intent to deprive the owner of the use and enjoyment of the property.

CONVERSION

Closely related to trespass to chattel is the intentional tort of **conversion.** Conversion occurs where a tortfeasor deprives a personal property owner of possession of property without consent, and converts the property to the tortfeasor's own use. The elements of the tort of conversion are:

- depriving the owner of possession of a chattel

- intent to convert the property to the tortfeasor's own use

- without the owner's consent

The essence of the tort of conversion is the concept of converting the property to the tortfeasor's own use, thus differentiating this tort from the tort of trespass to chattel. If a tortfeasor takes the other's property to possess but not use, then the tortfeasor has committed the tort of trespass to chattel. But, when the tortfeasor intends then to use the chattel, then the tort of conversion arises. The concept of conversion also carries with it a criminal offense within the meaning of the statutes of many states under the term *theft*. More will be discussed on that subject in the next chapter.

SLANDER OF TITLE

The intentional tort of **slander of title** is concerned with the defamation of title to property by the tortfeasor making false statements about the ownership of property.

The tort is aimed at the interference with the owner's ability to use the property as a result of aspersions cast by the conduct of the tortfeasor. The most common occurrence of this type of intentional tort is through the abuse of liens by the tortfeasor. For instance, suppose the tortfeasor files a lien against the property of an individual that does not owe the tortfeasor any money. The owner's right to enjoyment and use of the property has been impaired through the filing of a false lien.

COMMERCIAL DISPARAGEMENT

Closely related to slander of title is the tort of **commercial disparagement** that is concerned with false statements communicated to third persons regarding the victim's goods, services, or commercial enterprise.

As with slander of title, this tort interferes with the victim's ability to perform the commercial enterprise. The essence is the intentional interference through the publication of knowingly false statements.

DEFAMATION BY COMPUTER

With the increase in the use of computer databases to store information about an individual, there is an increasing chance for erroneous information to be stored. The tort of **defamation by computer** is the inclusion of false information about an individual's credit rating in a computer recordkeeping system.

This tort is concerned with the knowingly false nature of the information and the resulting harm to an individual's ability to obtain credit.

DEFENSES TO INTENTIONAL TORTS

A defense to an intentional tort occurs when the tort is legally justified in some manner. That legal justification gives the potential tortfeasor a defense to any claim for the intentional tort. The defense occurs in response to a legal action filed by the plaintiff for damages for the tort. Illustration 11-3 provides a summary of the intentional torts and their applicable defenses.

The most common defenses to intentional torts are:

- **statutes of limitations**—as a defense to all intentional torts, statutory time limits within which a plaintiff may file an action.

- **self-defense**—use reasonable force to repel an attack upon oneself or to avoid confinement.

- **defense of persons or property**—the use of reasonable force to defend a third person or property.

- **rightful repossession**—the right of an owner to retake possession of property through the use of reasonable force if necessary where the property has been wrongfully taken or withheld.

- **consent**—the voluntary acceptance of the tortfeasor's actions by the victim.

- **mistake**—a good-faith belief on the part of the tortfeasor based on false information of justification in committing the tort.

- **privilege**—a legal justification to engage in a tort to accomplish a socially justified goal.

- **necessity**—the justification of the tortfeasor to engage in intentionally tortious conduct to prevent serious injury from an external source.

commercial disparagement

defamation by computer

self-defense

defense of persons or property

rightful repossession

consent

mistake

privilege

necessity

INJURY TO PERSON		INJURY TO PROPERTY	
TORT	DEFENSE	TORT	DEFENSE
Defamation	Statute of Limitations, Truth, Consent, Privilege	Trespass to Land	Statute of Limitations, Rightful Repossession, Consent, Mistake, Privilege, Necessity
Emotional Distress	Statute of Limitations, Consent	Toxic Torts	Statute of Limitations, Consent, Mistake, Privilege, Necessity
Invasion of Privacy	Statute of Limitations, Consent, Mistake, Privilege, Necessity	Trespass to Chattel	Statute of Limitations, Rightful Repossession, Consent, Mistake, Privilege, Necessity
Assault and Battery	Statute of Limitations, Self-defense, Defense of Persons, Public Officer, Discipline, Rightful Repossession	Conversion	Statute of Limitations, Rightful Repossession, Consent, Mistake, Privilege, Necessity
False Imprisonment	Statute of Limitations, Consent, Mistake, Necessity, Public Officer, Warrantless Arrest, Discipline	Slander of Title	Statute of Limitations, Consent, Mistake, Privilege, Necessity
Fraud and Misrepresention	Statute of Limitations, Rightful Possession, Consent, Mistake, Privilege, Necessity	Commercial Disparagement	Statute of Limitations, Consent, Mistake, Privilege, Necessity
Malicious Prosecution	Statute of Limitations, Consent, Mistake, Public Officer	Defamation by Computer	Statute of Limitations, Consent, Mistake, Privilege, Necessity
Abuse of Process	Statute of Limitations, Rightful Possession, Consent, Mistake, Necessity		

Illustration 11-3
Defenses to Intentional Torts

- **public officer's immunity**—the justification of tortious activity by public officials due to authorization by law.

- **warrantless arrest**—the commission of an intentional tort while in the performance of proper enforcement of legal process.

- **reasonable discipline**—the use of reasonable force by a parent, guardian, or authorized individual, against a child, to maintain order or punish unacceptable misconduct.

STRICT LIABILITY

public officer's immunity

warrantless arrest

reasonable discipline

strict liability

With the torts that fall under the categories of negligence and intentional torts, the concept of fault underlies the determination of liability for tortious conduct. In the case of **strict liability,** the question of fault is unnecessary to establish liability. Strict liability refers to the responsibility of the tortfeasor for conduct regardless of fault. Another term often used for strict liability is *absolute liability.* The concept of strict liability is restricted to a few activities that are considered dangerous or those that involve defectively manufactured products.

ABNORMALLY DANGEROUS ACTIVITIES

Strict liability attaches to those activities that the law considers to be abnormally dangerous or inherently perilous because of the actions or devices involved. Activities included in many jurisdictions are:

- explosives

- flammable substances

- noxious gas

- poison

- hazardous wastes (toxic torts)

- electricity

- water in unprotected utility lines

Such activities are referred to in some jurisdictions as *ultrahazardous activities,* but the term is synonymous.

The *Restatement (Second) of Torts* § 520 states that persons engaged in abnormally dangerous activities shall be strictly liable for injuries caused by their actions. The criteria are:

- The abnormally dangerous activity created a high risk of substantial injury to an individual or property.

- The risk could not be removed through proper care.

- The activity is not commonly undertaken.

- The activity was inappropriately undertaken in the place in which the victim was harmed.

- The hazards of the activity outweigh the benefits that the activity brings to the community.

The legislatures of many states have enacted statutes that limit the liability for certain dangerous activities. Such legislation is justified on the basis of serving the public interest in the construction of public works and related benefits.

ANIMAL OWNERS' LIABILITY

Owners of domestic animals may be held strictly liable for injuries caused if the animal has exhibited vicious tendencies. This is called the **vicious propensity rule** and refers to the animal's reputation for viciousness.

The ownership of wildlife, as opposed to domesticated animals, carries with it the burden of strict liability. English common law presumed that wild animals were dangerous by nature and attached strict liability for ownership. There is a presumption of a vicious propensity in such cases.

Most states have enacted specific legislation that addresses an owner's liability for dog bites. A state's statute can materially affect the liability of the owner of a dog relative to injuries sustained by a victim of an attack. Some statutes do not require that the dog need to have shown a dangerous propensity, attaching liability for any injury regardless of propensity. Local statutes must be reviewed to determine the extent of liability.

PRODUCTS LIABILITY

Another form of strict liability is **products liability.** The theory of products liability is that the manufacturer or seller of a product is absolutely liable for injuries caused by a defect in the product. The concepts of negligence and fault play no part in a determination of the liability for manufacture or distribution of defective products. There are basically five elements to the tort of products liability:

1. A defect renders the product unreasonably dangerous to use.

2. A seller or manufacturer is engaged in the business of the sale or distribution of products such as the defective one.

3. No substantial change is made to the product from the time that it left the manufacturer's hands.

4. The defect must be the proximate cause of the injuries.

5. The product must have been used in the manner for which it was designed.

Some state jurisdictions require additional elements to maintain an action. State law should be carefully consulted to maintain an action.

DEFENSES AVAILABLE

Although the negligence and intentional tort defenses are not available for strict liability cases, some defenses are still provided in some states. The defenses that are available for strict liability cases may be:

- assumption of risk

- contributory or comparative negligence

- consent

These defenses, along with some that are particularly related to the specific tort, are used to defend an action for strict liability. Once again, state law must be consulted, because the states vary substantially on the defenses permitted.

SUMMARY

Tort law is concerned with civil remedies for wrongful conduct, acts, or omissions. Where there has been harm suffered as a result of negligence, intentional conduct, or with certain inherently dangerous situations, the law provides a remedy for the wrong. The

vicious propensity rule

products liability

remedies available are monetarily offering the victim compensation for any loss sustained to property or person. The roots of tort law are buried in the English common law and survive in every state today with modern trends ever evolving to meet changing lifestyles. The entire field of tort law is in a constant state of change to meet technological and environmental changes in a fast-growing world. This constant evolution will make this area of the law exciting and challenging for a legal office assistant.

Chapter Activities

Review Questions

1. What are the three basic categories of torts?

2. List the elements of the tort of negligence.

3. Describe the standard of care in negligence cases.

4. List the defenses to an action for negligence.

5. What is the difference between contributory negligence and comparative negligence?

6. What are the categories of intentional torts?

7. List the intentional torts involving injury to person.

8. List the intentional torts involving injury to property.

9. What defenses are available to intentional torts?

10. List the torts of strict liability.

Computer Activity

Big Wayne Tamper saw the state of Florida as one giant sandbar suitable for paving. He had taken Florida Landscape and Paving, Inc. (FLAP) from little more than a "truck and trailer" operation to the state's largest environmental reengineering company. Tamper knew that the way to capitalize on the state's massive influx of the cold and weather-beaten Yankee was to take the home of the heron and backfill it. A coat of asphalt over sand over wetland made the ideal platform for another development, be it single family, condo, or governmental complex. To obtain the land to reengineer, FLAP contributed heavily to every little politico running for every conceivable office, creating a large following of the finest politicians that money could buy. When FLAP was ready to expand into another area, the political infrastructure was already in place. Nothing stood between FLAP and a new parking lot, other than a few recalcitrant landowners that could be summarily dealt with through the heavy hand of the local law, the palm of which was greased by Tamper. FLAP's political agenda was simple enough: change the state tree to the "greased palm," the state bird to the "building crane," and the state flower to the "yellow traffic cone."

Luvenia Culpepper's family farm stood in the way of the new Bile River Retirement Home under development by FLAP, and supported by its usual coterie of political lackeys. FLAP had acquired all of the acreage surrounding the Culpepper farm but was unable to bring sufficient "pressure" upon Luvenia and her two children, Brandy and Randy, also part owners of the property, to part with the plat. In typical Tamper style, FLAP backfilled the neighboring wetlands, displacing thousands of resident waterfowl and flooding the Culpepper acreage, hoping to force a sale of the soggy homestead. The actual result was the visit by the Culpepper clan to the law offices of one Virgil Verdant, Attorney at Law, and specialist in environmental torts. Mr. Verdant has furnished you with a rough draft of a complaint against FLAP. He has requested that you prepare a draft of a complaint for the Culpeppers, citing damages in excess of $150,000 for decrease in value to the land.

A. From the student template retrieve act11.doc. This document is a rough draft of a complaint. Key the changes necessary to file the action. Refer to the chapter for examples.

B. Save this information on the template as complaint.doc.

C. Print one copy for your instructor. Make sure your name appears for identification purposes.

Chapter 12

Criminal Law

There are few better measures of the concern a society has for its individual members and its own well being than the way it handles criminals.

Attorney General
Ramsey Clark (1967)

Objectives

After completing this chapter, you will be able to:

1. Discuss the role of the legal office assistant in a criminal law office.

2. Summarize the criminal justice system.

3. Classify the elements of a crime.

4. Distinguish the crimes against persons.

5. Distinguish the crimes against property.

6. Discuss the defenses available to a criminal defendant.

7. Discuss the issues surrounding the Fourth Amendment guarantee of freedom from illegal search and seizure.

8. Describe the procedure in a criminal case.

9. Understand the rights of the criminal defendant in a trial.

10. Understand the issues involved in sentencing a criminal defendant.

Although the goal of civil law is the compensation of the individual injured by the behavior of another, it is the goal of criminal law to prevent undesirable behavior and punish those whose acts are prohibited. The criminal law is found in the statutory law of the United States government, the statutory law of each state, and the ordinances and regulations of the many municipalities. The U.S. Constitution provides the fundamental authority for the establishment of laws to establish justice and protect individual freedoms. The Preamble of the U.S. Constitution recognizes the principle of justice to secure freedom (see Illustration 12-1).

> We, the People of the United States, in Order to form a more perfect Union, establish justice, insure domestic Tranquility, provide for the common defense, promote the general Welfare, and secure the Blessings of Liberty to ourselves and our Posterity, do ordain and establish this Constitution of the United States of America.

Illustration 12-1
Preamble to the U.S. Constitution

THE ROLE OF THE LEGAL OFFICE ASSISTANT

The legal office assistant may be employed in a legal office that represents the criminal defendant or in an office of the prosecuting attorney. The tasks required will vary, depending on the type of office, although some basic functions will be consistent with either legal office. Those tasks are:

- collect facts, statements, records, and reports

- prepare pretrial motions

- organize evidence

- assist with legal research

- prepare post-trial motions

- maintain calendar and/or tickler file to remind attorney of important dates

The role of the legal office assistant is one of support for the attorney, whether defense or prosecution, and to provide the clerical assistance necessary. The variety of motions and pleadings is not as great as in a civil case, but they are just as important in terms of their effect on a client's case.

CRIMINAL JUSTICE SYSTEM

The responsibility for the administration of the criminal justice system rests with the executive branch of the government at both the federal and state level. Crime is investigated by a law enforcement agency such as the Federal Bureau of Investigation or the state police. When the investigation is completed, the results are turned over to a **prosecutor** for proceeding with the criminal case against the accused.

prosecutor

The prosecutor is an attorney representing the interests of the public in the criminal case. In the federal system, the prosecutor is referred to as the *United States attorney.* In state cases, the prosecutor is known as the *district attorney, county attorney, prosecuting attorney,* or the *city attorney.*

JURISDICTION

The vast majority of criminal cases fall under the jurisdiction of the state laws pursuant to the delegation of authority to protect the general welfare by the U.S. Constitution. A large body of federal statutory criminal law that overlaps with the state laws, creating a

concurrent jurisdiction

situation involving **concurrent jurisdiction.** Concurrent jurisdiction is where both the federal government and the state government have jurisdiction over a criminal defendant for the same act.

Most criminal cases are heard in the courts of general jurisdiction at either the federal level or the state level. U.S. district courts are the courts of general jurisdiction for federal crimes, and the local circuit courts are the courts of general jurisdiction for state cases. Many municipalities have a separate level of specialty court to hear criminal cases involving matters that are not serious crimes, such as traffic offenses and minor criminal offenses.

CLASSIFICATION OF CRIMES

crime

A **crime** is the term used to refer to an act that is in violation of a law. Crimes are classified into two broad categories:

felony

- **felony**—a serious crime usually punishable by imprisonment for more than one year or death.

misdemeanor

- **misdemeanor**—offenses of a less serious nature usually punishable by a fine and/or imprisonment for a period less than one year.

State laws vary greatly as to the classification of crimes within these two broad categories. Some states classify the seriousness of the felonies in determining the punishment to be administered.

ELEMENTS OF A CRIME

Regardless of the classification of a crime as a felony or a misdemeanor, crimes defined by most statutes involve the same two elements. A crime consists of both the mental aspect—*mens rea*—and the physical aspect—an act.

MENS REA

mens rea

Mens rea refers to the mental aspect of the commission of a crime. The state of mind of the criminal required for there to be criminal liability for certain behavior is the essence of *mens rea*. Another way to view the concept is to look to the criminal intent of the accused; if the individual intended the act, although not necessarily the result, then there is criminal liability. For instance, suppose an individual fired a pistol into the air with no intent to kill anyone, merely to fire the weapon. The bullet, however, struck an unsuspecting bystander, causing that person to die. The individual did not intend to kill anyone, but did intend to fire the pistol, resulting in criminal liability.

AN ACT

act

The second aspect of criminal liability is the requirement of an **act,** that is, the physical movement engaged in by the accused. Generally, individuals are not considered to be criminally liable unless there is voluntary conduct in the form of a criminal act. A mere thought alone is not considered a criminal act, nor is a bodily reflex or convulsion. Also, criminal liability does not apply to an individual's status, gender, race, or religion.

CRIMES AGAINST PERSON

Criminal activity is generally classified as crimes against the person and crime against property, depending on the focus of the intent of the accused. If the focus of the accused's conduct is toward a person, then it is considered a crime against the person. If the focus of the accused's behavior is against property, then it is considered a crime against property.

HOMICIDE

Homicide is the act of one human being killing another. Most states classify homicide into degrees. First-degree murder is the highest form of homicide, generally requiring an act that was willful, deliberate, and premeditated. For second-degree murder, the accused lacks the specific intent of first degree. The laws of the individual states will vary significantly on the distinctions between the degrees of murder.

ASSAULT AND BATTERY

As discussed in chapter 11, an assault is an attempt by one person to make harmful contact with another without consent. It differs from a battery in that it does not involve physical contact. It is physical contact that converts an assault to a battery. A battery is an intentional touching of another without consent and in a harmful manner. All states have made each of these acts criminal by statute where the necessary *mens rea* exists. A negligent act cannot form the basis for a conviction. Many states have also classified assault into degrees of severity, depending upon the seriousness of the act.

SEX-RELATED CRIMES

There is a wide variety of sex crimes that are considered to be crimes against the person, based on the motivation of the accused. Some examples of sex-related crimes against a person are:

- **rape**—sexual intercourse by force or by putting the victim in fear or in circumstances under which there can be no resistance.

- **statutory rape**—sexual intercourse with a female under the age of consent, usually sixteen years of age.

- **sodomy**—statutorily defined unnatural sexual conduct.

Other forms of criminal activity of a sex-related nature include prostitution, pornography, and public nudity. The requirements for such conduct to be considered criminal vary greatly from state to state.

KIDNAPPING AND FALSE IMPRISONMENT

Kidnapping is the act of taking and detaining a person against the individual's will by force or intimidation. The crime requires an unlawful confinement following a "taking" of the individual by force or threat. If the individual is taken across a state line, the crime becomes a federal offense in violation of the Federal Kidnapping Act.

Closely related to kidnapping is the crime of false imprisonment. As seen in chapter 11, false imprisonment is where an individual is intentionally confined without consent.

The crime has the same elements as the tort:

- confinement without consent

- intent to confine

- confinement for an appreciable period of time

- no reasonable means of escape

The distinction between false imprisonment and kidnapping is the "taking" of the individual from one place to another.

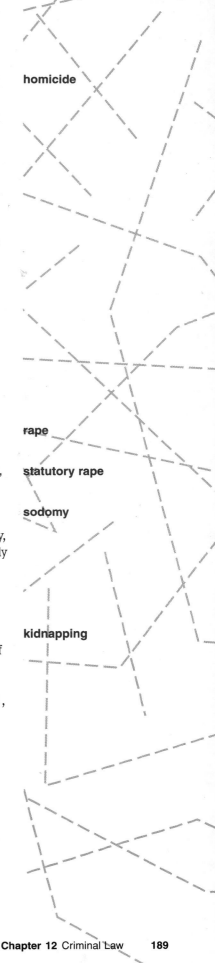

homicide

rape

statutory rape

sodomy

kidnapping

CRIMES AGAINST PROPERTY

Crimes against property are those crimes where the focus of the accused is toward the property of an individual as opposed to bodily harm to the individual. Although the owner of the property may be hurt financially, if there is no physical harm, the crime is considered a crime against property.

ARSON

arson

Arson is the willful burning of a building of another. Originally, the crime of arson required that the act be directed at a dwelling of another, but most states now apply the criminal behavior to any building. The severity of the crime is based on whether the building was occupied, and also whether the accused owned the structure.

BURGLARY

burglary

Burglary is the unlawful entry of a building for the purpose of stealing from the premises. The crime of burglary originally required that the building was a dwelling and that the entry occurred at night. Now, states have eliminated the requirement of a dwelling, and consider burglary at night to be an aggravation of the crime resulting in more severe treatment. In many states, the intention of the accused can be assumed merely from the entry of a building.

THEFT

theft

Under the English common law, **theft** consisted of the unlawful taking of the property of another and included the following crimes:

larceny

- **larceny**—the unlawful taking and carrying away of the property of another with the intent to permanently deprive the owner of possession.

embezzlement

- **embezzlement**—the conversion of the property of another by one who has acquired lawful possession with an intent to trick the owner.

receiving stolen property

- **receiving stolen property**—knowingly receiving property that has been stolen with the intent to deprive the owner of possession.

robbery

- **robbery**—the unlawful taking and carrying away of property from the person of another by threat or force with intent to steal.

false pretense

- **false pretense**—a false representation made to trick the victim into conveying title to property.

extortion

- **extortion**—the threat of future harm to acquire the property of another.

Illustration 12-2 provides a breakdown of the theft crimes and a summary of their elements.

Many states have now done away with the common law distinctions between the theft crimes, replacing them with a single category of theft. Local state law must be consulted.

CRIMINAL DEFENSES

defense

A **defense** in a criminal case is a term for an assertion of innocence. The defense is used by the accused to avoid criminal liability. The criminal defense is more than a mere assertion of innocence and involves a legal excuse for the act. These are common criminal defenses:

insanity

- **insanity**—a defense related to the requirement of *mens rea* whereby, depending on the jurisdiction, because of the disease the defendant did not

	Taking	Carrying Away	Property of Another	Intent to Steal/ Possess	Convert	Intent to Defraud	Knowing	Threat/ Force
Larceny	X	X	X	X				
Embezzlement			X	X	X	X		
Stolen Property			X	X			X	
Robbery	X	X	X	X				X
False Pretenses			X	X		X	X	
Extortion	X		X	X				X

Illustration 12-2
Theft Crimes

know that the act was wrong, could not control actions because of an irresistible impulse, or lacked the capacity to understand the nature of the act.

- **duress and necessity**—the defendant was threatened and had to commit the crime to avoid serious personal injury.

- **self-defense**—the defendant was forced to resort to force to avoid harm.

- **intoxication**—the defendant's mental or physical abilities were impaired because of drugs or alcohol.

- **entrapment**—law enforcement officers encourage the defendant to commit a crime with the intent to make an arrest.

- **alibi**—the defendant claims that he or she was not at the scene at the time the crime was committed.

duress and necessity

self-defense

intoxication

entrapment

alibi

The defenses available to the criminal defendant may vary from state to state, requiring consideration of local state law.

SEARCH AND SEIZURE

The U.S. Constitution guarantees certain rights that are available to the criminal defendant. The Constitution prohibits unreasonable searches and seizures in the Fourth Amendment, which reads:

> The right of the people to be secure in their persons, papers and effects, against unreasonable searches and seizures, shall not be violated, and no warrants shall issue but upon probable cause, supported by oath or affirmation, and particularly describing the place to be searched and the persons or things to be seized.

In order to comply with the Fourth Amendment, law enforcement officers must exercise extreme care for the rights of the defendant. If evidence is obtained through an illegal search, it cannot be used against the defendant at the time of trial.

SEARCH WARRANTS

search warrant

A **search warrant** is a court order allowing a law enforcement officer to search for evidence. The law enforcement officer requesting the warrant must establish the following elements necessary to the satisfaction of the judge:

- The evidence must establish probable cause to believe that the items will be found within the area to be searched.

- There must be probable cause to believe that the evidence is linked to criminal activity.

- The area to be searched must be described in detail.

- The facts must be established by oath.

- The warrant must be issued by a neutral judge.

The specific language of the warrant will contain any restrictions or limitations on the search. The following circumstances do not require a search warrant for a legal search if:

- There is a voluntary consent to the search.

- The officer is in a position to see the evidence in plain view.

- An inventory may be conducted of an impounded vehicle.

- Searches at a U.S. border do not require a warrant.

- The defendant's person may be searched at the time of a lawful arrest.

- Evidence might be destroyed if a search is delayed while a warrant is obtained.

- The police officer is in hot pursuit.

- An emergency exists.

Warrants are traditionally used to obtain any item that constitutes evidence that a crime has been committed or is the fruit of the crime.

ARREST

arrest

An **arrest** is any deprivation of freedom by a legal authority. An arrest occurs when an individual has reason to believe that freedom to leave does not exist. For an arrest to be upheld, the law enforcement officer must show probable cause that: a crime was committed, and that the person arrested committed the crime.

Once the arrest has been properly executed, a lawful search may be performed. The search may include the defendant and the area within immediate control of the defendant. The scope of the search is limited to areas where a weapon may be reached.

ADMISSIONS AND CONFESSIONS

The Fifth Amendment to the Constitution guarantees the right of an individual against self-incrimination by stating in part:

> No person shall be held to . . . nor shall be compelled in any criminal case to be a witness against himself, nor be deprived of life, liberty, or property, without due process of law . . . .

The interrogation of an accused individual is an important law enforcement tool aimed at securing a **confession** of a crime.

confession

A confession is a statement confirming the commission of a crime by an accused individual. If the individual under interrogation does not admit the crime but makes a

The following rights and facts must be conveyed to the defendant:

1. You have the right to remain silent.

2. Any statements may be used against you to gain a conviction.

3. You have the right to consult with a lawyer and to have a lawyer present during questioning.

4. You have the right to a lawyer. If you are unable to afford a lawyer, one will be provided without cost.

Illustration 12-3
Miranda Warnings

statement that would tend to show involvement in the crime short of a confession, such a statement is considered to be an **admission**.

In the landmark case of *Miranda v. Arizona,* 384 U.S. 436 (1966), the U.S. Supreme Court stated that before a person in custody may be interrogated, warnings are required. Illustration 12-3 presents the *Miranda* warnings.

There is no presumption in the law that any defendant knows these rights; therefore, the warnings must be read to all persons who are to be interrogated. Any statement obtained in violation of the *Miranda* warnings will be inadmissable in a trial against that defendant.

admission

CRIMINAL PROCEDURE

A legal office assistant working with a prosecutorial or defense legal office must be knowledgeable about the pretrial procedure in criminal cases. That procedure will vary greatly between the federal system and that of the various states, among which there will also be a great divergence of procedure. Local criminal procedural rules must be carefully consulted regarding the steps taken following the arrest of the defendant.

PRELIMINARY PROCEEDINGS

Once a law enforcement agency has completed its investigation to the point that an arrest can be made, the first step is the issuance of a **complaint**. The complaint is the initial instrument filed with the court charging an individual with a crime. The *Federal Rules of Criminal Procedure* provide:

complaint

> The complaint is a written statement of the essential facts constituting an offense charged. It shall be made upon oath before a magistrate.

Illustration 12-4 provides an example of a federal criminal complaint.

After arrest, the defendant is taken before the nearest available federal magistrate. Rule 5 of the *Federal Rules of Criminal Procedure* provides that the initial appearance before a magistrate must be accomplished "without unnecessary delay." This has been interpreted to mean within twenty-four hours. At the initial hearing, the court must assure itself that the defendant is the individual named in the complaint. The defendant is informed of the right to remain silent and the right to the assistance of counsel. A date for a preliminary hearing is then scheduled.

UNITED STATES DISTRICT COURT
SOUTHERN DISTRICT OF ALABAMA

UNITED STATES OF AMERICA

v.

ERNEST BLEDSOE   CASE NO.: 98-87655
_____/

CRIMINAL COMPLAINT

I, the undersigned Complainant, being duly sworn, state the following is true and correct to the best of my knowledge and belief. On or about February 12, 1998, in the county of Hawkins, Defendant did manufacture, sell, and distribute alcoholic beverages without license or consent in violation of 27 U.S.C.A. § 203, to wit:

I shall be unlawful, except pursuant to a basic permit issued under this chapter by the Secretary of the Treasury, to engage in the business of the manufacture or sale of distilled spirits, wine, or malt beverages . . .

I further state that I am an agent of the Federal Bureau of Alcohol, Tobacco and Firearms, and that this Complaint is based upon the facts contained in the attached sheet.

Contained on the attached sheet and made a part hereof: ❑ Yes ❑ No

_____
Complainant

Sworn to before me and subscribed in my presence.

                                          at
Date   City and State

_____
Name and Title of Judicial Officer   Signature of Judicial Officer

Illustration 12-4
Criminal Complaint

The **preliminary hearing** is the defendant's second appearance before the court. The preliminary hearing is generally used to determine if there is probable cause to formally accuse the defendant of the crime. The court must make a preliminary decision that a crime has been committed and that there is a reasonable basis for believing that the defendant committed it. This stage of the proceedings varies between states. Generally, the case is either referred to a grand jury to review the evidence and to issue its own charge or it is referred for trial.

FORMAL CHARGE

There are two formal charges commonly seen in criminal cases. The first formal charge is an **information,** which is a formal charge prepared by the prosecutor. It consists of a formal accusation of the commission of a crime sworn to by a prosecutor to bring a defendant to trial. Once it is filed, then the information replaces the complaint as the formal charging instrument.

The other formal charge is the **indictment,** which is a formal accusation of the commission of a crime made in writing by a grand jury based on evidence presented to it. Like the information, the indictment replaces the complaint as the formal charging instrument. A grand jury indictment is not required of the states by the U.S. Constitution, and is not necessary to formally charge a defendant.

Both the information and the indictment must state in plain and concise terms the essential facts constituting the offense charged. It must contain all of the essential elements of the crime, as well as the applicable statutory authority for the crime.

ARRAIGNMENT

After the formal charge has been filed with the court, the defendant is then brought before the judge for an **arraignment**. The arraignment is a formal hearing at which the charge is read and the defendant is asked to enter a **plea,** which is the formal response of the defendant to the accusation. The defendant may either plead guilty, not guilty, or *nolo contendere,* meaning that the defendant will not contest the charges and will not defend against them.

DISCOVERY

Pretrial discovery in criminal cases is not as broad in scope as in civil cases, and the discovery tools are different. The pretrial criminal discovery tools are:

- bill of particulars
- statements of the defendant
- criminal record of the defendant
- documents and tangible objects
- scientific reports and tests
- statements of witnesses
- depositions

Although the law in each particular state may vary on the criminal discovery tools, there is some general area of agreement with respect to these. Local statutes and case law must be consulted.

Bill of Particulars. A **bill of particulars** is a discovery tool for the criminal defendant to use to obtain information about the prosecution's case by requesting that the

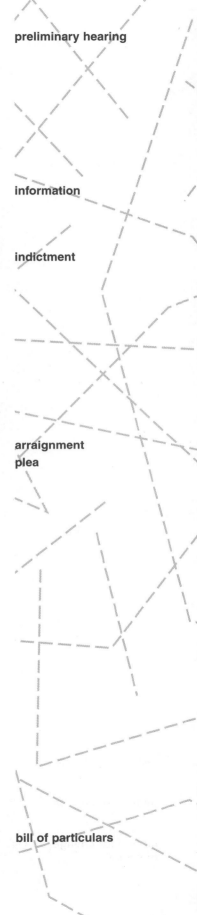

preliminary hearing

information

indictment

arraignment
plea

bill of particulars

information or indictment be made more specific. As with all discovery tools, the purpose of the bill of particulars is to avoid prejudicial surprise at the time of trial.

Statements of the Defendant. The *Federal Rules of Criminal Procedure* and all state rules of criminal procedure allow for the defense to inspect, copy, or photograph all prior relevant written and recorded statements of the defendant. Summaries of statements made by law enforcement officers are also discoverable.

Criminal Record of the Defendant. The defendant's criminal record must also be furnished to the defendant. This includes those records that are not only available to the prosecutor, but are easily obtainable through reasonable efforts.

Documents and Tangible Objects. The *Federal Rules of Criminal Procedure* also allow the defendant to inspect, copy, photograph, and examine tangible objects, papers, buildings, and places that are under the control of the prosecution. These may be examined if the item:

- is material to preparation of a defense
- will be used by the prosecution at trial
- was obtained from or belongs to the defendant

This rule also permits the prosecution the same privilege.

Scientific Reports and Tests. All scientific reports and tests in possession of the prosecution must be turned over to the defense. These include:

- medical and psychological evaluations of the defendant
- autopsy reports
- drug tests
- fingerprint analysis

Statements of Witnesses. In the federal system, the defendant is *not* entitled to statements of witnesses before they testify, but the defendant may review any prior written or recorded statement after the witness has testified. The result is to cause a considerable delay in the trial process. State law must be consulted as to treatment of the statements of witnesses.

Depositions. The *Federal Rules of Criminal Procedure,* Rule 15, allows for a deposition to be taken under "exceptional circumstances." The anticipated absence of an intended witness would be one such circumstance, allowing the deposition to be used at the time of trial.

MOTIONS

As in civil cases, the motion practice in criminal cases is a request made to the court to enter an order for a particular purpose. The motions frequently filed in criminal cases include:

- **motion to dismiss**—used when the defendant believes that the indictment or information is inherently flawed, such as a lack of jurisdiction.
- **motion to suppress**—used to suppress evidence obtained in an unconstitutional manner.
- **motion for change of venue**—used if the defendant cannot obtain a fair and impartial trial at the location where the case is pending (e.g., prejudicial pretrial publicity) in order to persuade the court to change the trial location.

motion to dismiss

motion to suppress

motion for change of venue

- **motion for severance**—used to request a separate trial where one or more defendants are charged in the same indictment or information.

The motions filed in criminal cases are to ensure the constitutionally guaranteed rights of the defendant. Local rules and statutes must be consulted to determine the permissibility of a particular motion.

TRIAL

In the criminal trial process, the defendant is guaranteed a certain body of rights before a conviction can be obtained. The U.S. Constitution guarantees the right to a jury trial, the right to a public trial, the right to confrontation and cross-examination of witnesses, the presumption of innocence, the right to a speedy trial, and the right to be represented by counsel.

SIXTH AMENDMENT

The Sixth Amendment to the U.S. Constitution provides:

> [i]n all criminal prosecutions, the accused shall enjoy the right to a speedy and public trial, by an impartial jury of the State and district wherein the crime shall have been committed . . .

In that clause, the Sixth Amendment guarantees a right to a trial by jury, a speedy trial, and a public trial. The trial by jury guarantee means that the defendant may have a jury determine guilt or innocence, and may even determine sentencing.

The right to a speedy trial has not been interpreted into a specific number of days, but means that four factors must be considered in determining if the defendant has been denied a speedy trial:

- the length of the delay

- the reason for the delay

- whether the defendant has requested a speedy trial

- the seriousness of the prejudice

The time for a speedy trial commences with the formal charge and generally prohibits a trial within thirty days to allow the defendant time to prepare a defense.

The guarantee of a public forum for both the trial and any preliminary hearings serves to keep the prosecution honest. By placing the actions of the prosecutor under theoretical public scrutiny, the defendant's chances of a fair trial are improved.

Another section of the Sixth Amendment also guarantees the defendant the right to confront and cross-examine any witness. This means that the defendant has a right to have the witnesses personally appear in court and guarantees the right of the defendant to be personally present at the time of trial. The right to cross-examine any witnesses by the defendant's counsel affords the defendant a valuable protection.

Another of the guarantees of the Sixth Amendment is the right to counsel. It states:

> . . . in all criminal prosecutions, the accused shall enjoy the right . . . to have the Assistance of Counsel for his defense.

If the defendant lacks the financial ability to pay an attorney for the defense, then the court will appoint counsel. The defendant does not have to be destitute, only unable to afford representation by counsel. Of course, the defendant always has the option to self-representation, as long as courtroom behavior and demeanor is acceptable to the court.

PRESUMPTION OF INNOCENCE

A fundamental right underlying all criminal cases is the concept that the defendant is presumed innocent until proven guilty. For this reason, the criminal defendant has no duty to say anything and need not even testify at the time of trial. The prosecutor cannot call the defendant to testify, nor mention the failure of the defendant to testify to the jury.

Closely related to the principle of the presumption of innocence is the **burden of proof** that must be met by the prosecutor to obtain a conviction. The burden of proof is the requirement of offering the necessary evidence to prove a fact or guilt. In the case of a criminal defendant, the prosecution must prove the defendant's guilt beyond a reasonable doubt. This means that if a reasonably prudent person would question the guilt of the accused, then the prosecution has failed to meet its burden. The burden extends to every element of a charge in order to obtain a conviction.

burden of proof

SENTENCING

After a conviction has been obtained in a criminal case, a sentence must be imposed. The legislature of each state determines the ranges within which the court may act in imposing an appropriate sentence. The Eighth Amendment to the U.S. Constitution prohibits cruel and unusual punishment; however, the state legislatures have great latitude in establishing sentencing guidelines to be followed by the court in imposing sentence.

The federal and state sentencing guidelines should be reviewed for any conviction, as there will be a wide divergence between jurisdictions.

SUMMARY

In the specialized area of criminal law, the legal office assistant will be presented with the task of assisting the attorney in the preservation of constitutional rights. The collection of information, preparation of motions, and legal research are essential contributions to the criminal case. The legal office assistant may be employed in the office of the prosecutor or a legal office representing the defendant. The tasks required are similarly important and involve an understanding of the nature of the crime and its related constitutional guarantees.

Chapter Activities

Review Questions

1. What are the responsibilities of the legal office assistant in a criminal law office?

2. Define the two major elements of every crime.

3. List the categories of the crimes against persons.

4. Summarize the elements of theft crimes.

5. List the major criminal defenses.

6. What is the guaranteed individual right of the Fourth Amendment?

7. Describe the difference between an information and an indictment.

8. List the individual freedoms guaranteed by the Sixth Amendment.

9. What is the presumption of innocence?

10. Who determines the sentences to be imposed after conviction?

Computer Activity

You are employed in the office of the prosecuting attorney. As the facts will disclose, the assistant prosecutor has been creative in finding a "crime" with which to charge the defendant, Mr. Rufous S. Towhee. He has elected to charge this defendant under a state statute that classifies an individual guilty of a felony if he projects a missile, designed to cause bodily harm, at a building or occupied dwelling. The statute reads as follows:

> § 806.1 A person commits the offense of criminal mischief if he willfully and maliciously injures or damages by any means any real or personal property belonging to another.

The relevant facts are that Rufous S. Towhee was proceeding north on S.R. 434 when a squadron of four sandhill cranes swooped down in front of his automobile as if preparing to land. Believing that the sandhill crane is possessed with the spirit of the deceased, Rufous became fearful of possibly striking one of his ancestors and swerved to avoid hitting the birds. In so doing, his car left the highway and stopped on the lawn of St. Audubon's Church. Thinking that he could safely exit the property before angering the parishioners who were enjoying a Mother's Day service, Rufous attempted to slam the gear shift into reverse. He failed to find that gear and hit forward instead, causing his automobile to enter the church through a large stained glass window in front. Dazed and confused, Rufous climbed from his car, only to be beaten almost senseless by a very angry mob of "mothers" dressed in their finery. He managed an inglorious retreat but was later arrested on the strength of the vigilance of one of the matriarchs who had copied his license tag number. The investigating and arresting officer was Sergeant Bob White.

A. From the student template retrieve act12.doc. The document is a form for a criminal complaint to be prepared by the arresting officer. Prepare the criminal complaint against Mr. Rufous S. Towhee from the facts given. Refer to the chapter for examples.

B. Save this information on the template as criminal.doc.

C. Print one copy for your instructor. Make sure your name appears for identification purposes.

Chapter 13

Law of Wills and Trusts

This time, like all times, is a very good one, if we but know what to do with it.

Ralph Waldo Emerson (1864)

Objectives

After completing this chapter, you will be able to:

1. Identify the characteristics of a will, along with its advantages and disadvantages.

2. Apply the basic guidelines for the preparation and execution of a will.

3. Outline the basic format for drafting a will.

4. Discuss the nature of will contests.

5. Summarize the nature of a trust.

6. Outline the elements of a trust.

7. Distinguish between the various trust instruments.

8. Discuss the provisions of the various trust instruments.

estate planning

Estate planning is the creation of a method for the orderly handling, disposition, and administration of an estate when the owner dies. To develop an estate plan that satisfies the intent of the owner of an estate requires the use of a will and, in many cases, a trust. This chapter will focus on the basic requirements of the law of wills and trusts for estate planning purposes and will provide for the creation of the necessary documents.

WILLS

will

A **will** is an instrument that declares the intended distribution of one's property at death. It is intended to accurately reflect the intent of the maker

testator

testate
intestate
Laws of Intestate
Succession

heirs at law

of the will, called the **testator,** in a written document and to provide for the orderly distribution of the property of the testator that makes up the estate.

An owner of property who has created a valid will providing for the distribution of an estate is said to have died **testate**. An owner of property who does not provide for its orderly distribution on death or fails to create a valid will is said to have died **intestate**. If an individual dies intestate, that person's property is distributed through the **Laws of Intestate Succession**.

Every state has a body of statutes that determine the manner of the distribution of a decedent's property when there is no valid will concerning that particular property. The terms used to describe that body of law may be the *laws of intestate succession* or may be called the *law of descent and distribution*. Whichever term is used, the intention of the legislature is the same; namely, to provide for the orderly distribution of property upon death without a will.

Difficulty may arise with a distribution of property by intestate succession, in that the decedent may not have intended for the property to be distributed in the manner provided by such statutes. Individuals entitled to receive a portion of the estate as provided by state laws of intestacy are known as **heirs at law**. These individuals are considered heirs solely because of legislative designation. Heirs at law may experience considerable delay because of the failure of the owner of property to provide for its orderly distribution.

TYPES OF WILLS

The orderly distribution of an estate may take varying forms, depending on state law. While all states provide statutory requirements for the creation of a written will, some states also allow other forms of wills to be valid and enforceable expressions of the testator's intent. These other types of wills allow for distribution of a decedent's estate in an alternative form.

holographic

Holographic Will. Many states recognize the validity of a **holographic** will. Traditionally, a will drawn in the testator's own handwriting is said to be holographic. Those states recognizing a holographic will, demand that it meet other statutory requirements for execution. Most states mandate that all wills must be executed by a competent testator and witnessed.

nuncupative

Nuncupative Will. A **nuncupative** will, or one that is entirely oral, is recognized in some states. It is a will spoken in the presence of witnesses, and generally only with an imminent expectation of death. Such wills are occasionally called *speaking wills* or *deathbed wills*. This type of will is not valid in many jurisdictions because of the opportunity for inaccuracy. Those states that allow nuncupative wills consider them valid only for the conveyance of personal property, rather than real property.

joint will

Joint Will. A **joint will** arises where the same instrument comprises the will of two or more persons. In states permitting joint wills, they are most frequently used where the bulk of the estate of each of the joint testators consists of property held as a joint tenancy or tenancy in common. The purpose of a joint will is to provide for the testamentary disposition of joint property upon the death of both parties.

mutual will

Mutual Will. A **mutual will** occurs where two persons create their respective wills with provisions that favor each other. These wills are also known as *reciprocal wills*, and are frequently seen within a marital relationship where each party wishes the other to have all, or a significant portion, of the estate.

ADVANTAGES AND DISADVANTAGES OF WILLS

The primary advantage in the preparation and execution of a valid will is the fulfillment of the testator's intent for the disposition of the property. Most individuals desire some control over the ultimate distribution of their property and do not want the state Laws of Intestate Succession to dictate its disposal. They wish to avoid the situation where some heirs at law receive no portion of the estate, while others may receive an inequitable portion. The will gives the testator the opportunity to select the recipients of the estate and to determine the extent of the portion of the estate for each.

A will also provides the testator with an opportunity to reward the long-term loyalty of an individual who may not be considered an heir at law by state statutes. Someone such as a trusted housekeeper, ward, or even an educational institution may be a recipient of a gift to which it may not be entitled under the laws of intestate succession.

In addition, a will affords the testator an opportunity to select the **personal representative** of the estate. The personal representative is the individual named in the will to carry out the testator's wishes and enforce the provisions of the will.

Beyond appointing the personal representative, the testator may provide for the protection and care of any minor children through the appointment of a **guardian**. A guardian is an individual designated by will who has the legal responsibility for the care and management of a person, such as a minor child, while that person remains a minor, or an incompetent person, as long as the incapacity lasts.

Federal and state tax laws will apply to most distributions of property, testate or intestate. The provision for the payment of those taxes from certain assets may protect some property from liquidation and allow its transfer within the intentions of the testator. Careful planning through a trust, gifts, or a will can also serve to lessen the effect of taxes on the entire estate.

To safeguard the provisions of a will, all states require that there be court supervision of the distribution through the **probate** process. Probate is a court procedure involving the collection of the decedent's assets, payment of debts, and the distribution to heirs. It is a legal process required by the probate code of all states. Probate can be costly and time-consuming, delaying the achievement of the testator's intent. Elimination of this expense and delay is a valid goal of a well-constructed estate plan.

An ill-fitting, poorly drafted, or inadequate will can cause a testator and the heirs more difficulty than an intestate death, which sometimes gives rise to the principal disadvantage of a will. If a will is not properly drafted with careful consideration to the testator's intent within the framework of the various applicable laws, considerable time and assets may be wasted.

A further disadvantage of a will occurs because of the manner in which estates are taxed by the state and federal governments. Taxes in the form of estate taxes and inheritance taxes are imposed upon the value of the property of a decedent at the time of death. The greater the value of the decedent's property, the greater the tax consequence. If property is to pass to one's heirs through a will, for tax purposes that property is considered to be part of the decedent's estate and subject to taxation. But, if the decedent had restructured the estate through the use of trusts and gifts during the decedent's lifetime, then there may not be the same need for a will and any exposure to taxes will be reduced. This is where effective estate planning can assist an individual in lessening the estate's tax burden. Therefore, many testators find that certain forms of nontestamentary disposition of assets are more efficient. A gift of property during an individual's lifetime can avoid the delay and expense of probate, as can the use of a trust as a dispositive vehicle.

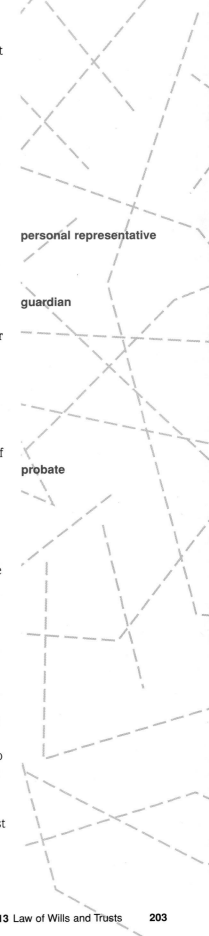

personal representative

guardian

probate

EXECUTION OF A WILL

The statutory requirements for the preparation and execution of a will may vary from state to state. However, all states share certain elements needed for the creation of a valid will. Those requirements are established by state statute in each state's probate code or its equivalent. Since a will is a legally enforceable declaration of property distribution, the procedure to create a legally enforceable document must be followed. The probate code for the state of Texas provides:

> Every person who has attained the age of eighteen years, or who is or has been lawfully married, or who is a member of the armed forces of the United States or of the auxiliaries thereof or of the maritime service at the time the will is made, being of sound mind, shall have the right and power to make a last will and testament, under the rules and limitations prescribed by law. Texas Statutes Annotated § 57.

Each state's probate code should be consulted for specific compliance.

Writing. Most states require that wills be in writing as evidence of an expression of the testator's intent. The written document may be typed or in the testator's own handwriting. Either form will be allowed if the writing is legible and otherwise meets the statutory guidelines for the creation of a will.

Legal Capacity. The validity of a written will is dependent upon the **capacity** of a testator to create the document. Capacity in the law refers to that level of mental competence necessary to understand the nature of one's acts. A lack of competence can be based on either age or sanity. Nearly all states require that the testator reach the age of majority, which is eighteen in most states. A testator with sufficient soundness of mind to understand the nature and extent of the property owned is considered competent. The testator can then formulate an intention as to its distribution. It is important to note that the capacity need exist only at the time of the creation of the will, and need not exist at the time of death.

Signatures. The testator's signature must appear at the end of the will. If the testator is unable to execute a signature, then another individual may sign his, along with an indication as to the procedure. This must be done in the presence of the witnesses and reflected in the acknowledgment of the procedure. The signing of the will by the testator must occur in the presence of the witnesses, a fact to be attested to by those witnesses. **Attestation** is merely the act of witnessing the signing of a written instrument. Witnesses attesting to the signature of the testator must sign the will in the presence of each other.

Most states require that at least two witnesses attest to the testator's signature. Although the original of the will must be executed by the testator and the witnesses, it is not a formal requirement that each copy be executed.

The proper execution of the copies of a will acts to protect against the loss of the original and reduce the possibility of a fraudulent claim. Every page of the will should be signed or initialized by the testator and dated, but in some states it is not necessary that the witnesses attest to each page. This is done to avoid a later claim that some material portion of the will content may have been altered.

Witnesses. Generally, the formal statutory requirements for witnesses only include provisions that they are of sufficient age and of sound mind. The probate codes of most states merely require that a witness have the same qualifications of that required of a testator. A witness should be informed that he or she may be required to testify as to the validity of the will to decide its authenticity at probate. It is not required that a witness be made aware of the contents of the will, nor that the witness has had an opportunity to read the document.

Language. No particular language or phrasing is required by statute to achieve the testator's intent. If the intention of the testator is conveyed in a clear manner, the will

capacity

attestation

may be enforced. Every effort, then, should be made to ensure that the language used be simple and unambiguous.

Will Storage. A question arises frequently as to the best location for the storage of the original and copies of the will. Although state statutes are silent on this issue, there are certain practices adopted by most practitioners that well serve the testator's interests. Most testators insist on maintaining a copy of their own will for reference. They often choose to store the copy in a safety deposit vault. However, this form of storage may delay the probate of the will, should access to the vault be delayed due to banking procedures and local state laws.

If a banking institution is named in a will to act in a **fiduciary capacity,** then most banks will require that a copy of the will be deposited with them. A bank's fiduciary capacity, like any fiduciary capacity, is the duty to act in good faith with respect to the property of another. Most states make provision for the filing of a copy of a will with the appropriate probate court for safekeeping until probate is required. It is a common practice for most law firms to maintain a copy of any client's will in their vault for safekeeping. In that way, the presentation of the will may be facilitated when the need for probate arises.

fiduciary capacity

Living Wills. Some state laws allow a competent individual to provide for a contingency wherein he or she may become incompetent either physically or mentally in the future and to express a desire not to be kept alive by artificial means at such time. State statutes creating such health directives for a natural death attempt to spare family members the making of that decision under trying circumstances. It also serves to protect any treating physician or health care facility from potential liability. Each state has a public interest to protect with such legislation. It is necessary to consult each state's statutes for statutory restrictions. Some states even provide for the specific language to be used.

FORMAT FOR DRAFTING A WILL

Although there is no specific requirement that any standardized form or language be used in the drafting of a will, the primary focus is to draft a document that will best carry out the intent of the testator. Certain guidelines will help provide a clear expression of the testator's intentions. The preparer of the will can insure that the document conforms to the intent of the testator with careful attention to:

- clause revoking prior wills
- provision for debts and expenses
- provision for taxes
- clauses containing specific gifts of property
- residuary clause
- appointment of personal representative
- testimonium clause
- testator's signature
- witnesses' signatures
- self-proving language

Introductory Clause. The opening paragraph of a will should state the name of the testator along with a domicile. It should also indicate the nature of the document, and affirm that it is the testator's last will and testament. In addition, the introduction should declare that the testator is of a sound and disposing mind and thus competent to execute such a document. The execution of a will generally revokes any prior wills

general revocatory clause

or codicils, yet it is customary to state that it is the testator's intent to do so in what is termed the **general revocatory clause**:

> I, Alvin B. Alert, a resident of the County of Osceola, State of Florida, being of sound and disposing mind, memory and understanding, do hereby make, publish, and declare this to be my Last Will and Testament, hereby revoking all wills and codicils at any time heretofore made by me.

A clause such as this will serve to identify the testator, establish his competence, and validate the instrument as the last will and testament.

Article I. The testator will have certain debts that have accrued as of the time of death. It is customary to instruct the personal representative of the estate to pay those debts out of the funds of the estate. Included in those debts may be some expenses related to the last illness and associated with the funeral arrangements. Instructions for the payment of those expenses and any others that may reasonably be anticipated should be addressed in this initial article.

In conjunction with the question of funeral expenses, many testators chose to include directions for the funeral and burial arrangements. It is not uncommon to have a dispute arise between surviving relatives as to the testator's preferences. There may also arise the question of anatomical gifts to be made by the testator at the time of death. These considerations should be formally addressed in the will, along with instructions to the personal representative regarding these issues should disclosure of the will's contents be delayed:

> I direct that all my legally enforceable debts, funeral expenses, expenses of my last illness, and administrative expenses be paid by my personal representative from the assets of my estate as soon as practicable after my death.

A matter closely related to the estate's debts at the time of death is the question of the costs of the administration of the estate and their payments. The personal representative should receive specific instructions from the testator as to the payment of these expenses from the funds of the estate.

Article II. With an estate of substantial value, consideration must be given to the question of the payment of federal estate taxes and state inheritance taxes. If the size of the decedent's gross estate for federal tax purposes will create exposure to tax liability, it is advisable to include directions to the personal representative as to the payment of taxes from estate funds and assets. If there is any question that such liability may exist, such provisions should be made. The clause may read as follows:

> I direct that all my inheritance, transfer, succession and other death taxes, which may be payable with respect to any property includable as a part of my gross estate, shall be paid from my residuary estate, without any apportionment thereof.

The personal representative must have specific direction from the document if it is the intention of the testator that payment be made from a particular asset.

Article III—et. seq. It is at this point in the preparation of a will that an expression of the testator's intent should be made regarding each specific testamentary gift, called a **devise**. The term *devise* refers to any gift of property by will without any distinction as to whether the property is real or personal. The major concern of most testators is directed to the question of the ultimate distribution of the assets. Every individual testator will have their own reasons for their bequests, and the will should clearly set forth any intentions without ambiguity (see Illustration 13-1). Although it is not necessary that the testator's reasons behind his devises be set forth, it may be valuable should litigation develop in a will contest.

devise

Residuary Clause. It can be anticipated that property will be acquired by the testator after the drafting of a will through acquisition or appreciation in value of existing

```
I give, devise, and bequeath all of my property of whatever

kind, whether real or personal, and wherever located as follows:

(1) to my wife, ALICE B. ALERT;

(2) if my wife ALICE B. ALERT predeceases me, to such of my

children as survive me, in equal shares, provided however,

should a child of mine predecease me, survived by a child or

children who survive me, such grandchild or grandchildren of

mine shall take the share his or their parent would have taken

had such parent survived me;

(3) if my wife ALICE B. ALERT and all of my children predecease

me, to such grandchildren as survive me, in equal shares.
```

Illustration 13-1
Bequest Language

assets. It is the duty of the testator to anticipate such an eventuality and provide for the specific distribution of such property. The remainder of the testator's estate that is not subject to a specific devise must also be made the subject of direction. These **residuary** assets generally form the bulk of the decedent's estate and provide the source for the funds to pay debts, expenses, costs, and taxes.

residuary

Instructions for the distribution of the remainder of the testator's estate should be directed to the personal representative at this juncture. The residuary clause may read as shown:

> All the rest, residue, and remainder of my estate, of every nature and kind, which I may own at the time of my death, real, personal, and mixed, tangible and intangible, of whatsoever nature and wheresoever situated, I give, devise, and bequeath to my alma mater, MERIT U.

If there are insufficient assets in the estate to cover those payments requiring cash, then provision must be made for the sale of the fixed assets of the estate and the order of such liquidation or **abatement.** Abatement is the process by which the order of liquidation is decided and typically follows this order: (a) residual assets; (b) general devises of cash left to named individuals; (c) specific devises. The actual drafting of this clause requires care to protect the creditors of the estate and the specific devisees as well.

abatement

Personal Representative. The personal representative of the estate is responsible for collecting and preserving the assets of the estate at the testator's death, paying the debts, and distributing the property pursuant to the testator's wishes. The actual powers and responsibilities of the personal representative, also called an **executor** (male) or **executrix** (female), are enumerated by statute. For example, see § 234 of the Texas Probate Code (see Illustration 13-2).

executor/executrix

Powers To Be Exercised Under Order of the Court.

The personal representative of the estate of any person may, upon application and order authorizing same, renew or extend any obligation owing by or to such estate. When a personal representative deems it for the interest of the estate, he may, upon written application to the court, and by order granting authority:

(1) Purchase or exchange property;

(2) Take claims or property for the use and benefit of the estate, in payment of any debt due or owing to the estate;

(3) Compound bad or doubtful debts due or owing to the estate;

(4) Make compromises or settlements in relation to property or claims in dispute or litigation;

(5) Compromise or pay in full any secured claim which has been allowed and approved as required by law against the estate by conveying to the holder of such claim the real estate or personalty securing the same, in full payment, liquidation, and satisfaction thereof, and in consideration or cancellation of notes, deeds of trusts, mortgages, chattel mortgages, or other evidences of liens securing the payment of such claim.

Powers To Be Exercised Without Court Order.

The personal representative of the estate of any person may, without application to or order of the court, exercise the powers listed below, provided, however, that a personal representative under

Illustration 13-2
Texas Probate Code, § 234

```
court control may apply and obtain an order if doubtful of the

propriety of the exercise of any such powers:

    (1) Release liens upon payment at maturity of the debt secured

thereby;

    (2) Vote stocks by limited or general proxy;

    (3) Pay calls and assessments;

    (4) Insure the estate against liability in appropriate cases;

    (5) Insure property of the estate against fire, theft, and other

hazards;

    (6) Pay taxes, court costs, bond premiums.
```

Illustration 13-2
Texas Probate Code, § 234 (continued)

It is this clause that mentions the identity of that individual chosen to act as personal representative. To avoid the contingency whereby the chosen personal representative may be unable to act in such a capacity, a successor representative should also be named to avoid any delay or confusion. A clause appointing the personal representative may read as shown in Illustration 13-3. As a matter of law in most states, the powers conferred by statute also protect the personal representative from any personal liability while acting in an authorized capacity.

Testimonium Clause. It is customary to conclude the body of the will with a declaration that the testator is freely signing the will as the last will and testament and is requesting that the witnesses do similarly. The **testimonium clause,** as it is known, may also include a reference to the total number of pages of the will and refer to the date and place of the signing. This reflects the voluntariness of the will, avoiding any subsequent claim of fraud or duress.

testimonium clause

Testator's Signature. The signature of the testator must appear on the will to make it valid. The signing of the will by the testator must be done in the presence of the witnesses. Any signature will be invalid if the testator is not of the age of majority, not of sound mind, or is not performed before the witnesses. The presentation of the testator's signature should appear as shown in Illustration 13-4.

Witnesses' Signatures. The witnesses to the testator's signature indicate that they have so witnessed the signing in an **attestation clause.** The actual number of witnesses is controlled by statute, but usually consists of two or three. The witnesses must place their signatures, along with their addresses, on the will in the presence of

attestation clause

I appoint FAITH SCRUPLES as Personal Representative of my Will, with full power and authority to sell, transfer, and convey any and all property, real or personal, which I may own at the time of my death, at such time and place and upon such terms and conditions as my Personal Representative may determine, without necessity of obtaining a court order. If FAITH SCRUPLES does not survive me or if she fails to qualify for or, if having qualified should die, resign or become incapacitated, then in that event I nominate and appoint FIRST FIDELITY AND TRUST COMPANY as successor Personal Representative of my Will, with all the powers and duties afforded my Personal Representative herein.

Illustration 13-3
Appointment of Personal Representative

IN WITNESS WHEREOF, I have hereunto subscribed my name and affixed my seal at the city of _____, state of_____, this _____ day of _____, 19__, in the presence of the subscribing witnesses who I have requested to attesting witnessed hereto.

_____
Testator/Testatrix

Illustration 13-4
Testator's Signature

each other. Language to be employed may read as shown in Illustration 13-5. Additional language may also include an attestation to the effect that there was no undue influence or duress.

MODIFICATION OF A WILL

codicil

Modification of an existing, valid last will and testament is through a **codicil.** A codicil is a separate instrument that serves to alter or modify an original will without appearing to

```
    This instrument was, on the date hereof, signed, published, and

declared by ALVIN B. ALERT, to be his Last Will and Testament and we,

at the same time, at his request, in his presence and in the presence

of each other, have hereunto signed our names and addresses as

attesting witnesses.


_____          of  _____
Witness                                     (address)


_____          of  _____
Witness                                     (address)
```

Illustration 13-5
Witnesses' Signatures

be the entire will of the testator. It serves to "republish" the original will through reference to it, and also provides for any alterations or additions to that original.

Most states require that a codicil be executed in the same manner as a will in that it needs to be in writing and signed by the testator and witnessed. Any individual state requirements for the execution of the original must also be followed.

WILL CONTESTS

An action in court to challenge the validity of a will is called a **will contest.** While most wills are uncontested, most will contests are unsuccessful if the drafting and the execution of the will has been properly performed. A person with an "interest" in the estate may bring such an action. In most states, creditors are not considered to have an interest sufficient to effectively challenge the will. Most frequently, the challenge is initiated by a spouse, heir, or devisee of a prior will excluded from the current will.

will contest

Challenges generally are based on one or more of the following grounds:

- a lack of proper formal execution
- a lack of testamentary capacity
- claim that the will has previously been revoked
- claims of forgery
- fraud or undue influence in the creation of the will
- material ambiguities or errors

Challenges are costly to the estate, both from the standpoint of time and expenditure of the estate's assets for defense. The drafter's goal is to eliminate the possibility of an effective challenge through careful attention to the guidelines for the execution of the will.

TRUSTS

The orderly disposition and administration of property on death is the goal of an estate plan. As previously noted, a will is the basic estate planning tool to accomplish the orderly distribution of property at death. The other basic estate planning tool is the trust, which can be used to distribute property during the owner's lifetime or at his or her death.

NATURE OF A TRUST

trust

The fundamental nature of a trust consists of the creation of a separate legal entity to hold property for the benefit of another, resulting in a legal entity called a **trust.** The arrangement places legal title to property in the hands of one person who owes a fiduciary duty to administer that property for the benefit of another. A **fiduciary duty,** like fiduciary capacity, is the duty to act on another's behalf in good faith and trust. It is a legal obligation that one person owes, requiring prudence, care, and diligence. A trust represents the combination of a legal entity, in the form of a contractual property relationship, and an estate planning tool in one legal instrument.

fiduciary duty

An example of a trust can be illustrated by the following. Artemus Longreach decided that he wanted his daughter, Alene, to have the benefit and use of the family estate, Cypress Farms, until she turned twenty-five, at which time she was to receive title to the property. It was also his decision to have his long-time and trusted friend, Oswold Cosmold, administer the property on his daughter's behalf until she became old enough to handle the duties herself. The creation of a trust of the property, Cypress Farms, for the use and benefit of his daughter, Alene, until she reaches age twenty-five, would fully satisfy his intentions. Oswold Cosmold would be appointed as trustee with the attendant fiduciary responsibilities. The trust would terminate upon Alene Longreach attaining age twenty-five, at which time title to the property would pass to her. During the period of the trust, title to Cypress Farms would be held in the name of the trust; that is, The Alene Longreach Trust.

private express trust

In the law, a trust may take many forms, including trusts that are created solely by operation of law to correct some inequity. A trust of this type is called a **private express trust,** and requires a written instrument expressing an individual's intentions for the distribution of property.

ELEMENTS OF A TRUST

To create a private express trust, four basic elements are required. Those elements are:

- a settlor
- a trustee
- a beneficiary
- property

A valid private express trust will fail in its creation if any of the four elements are missing. There must be property to be transferred to a trustee for administration for the benefit of one who can enforce the relationship, created intentionally by the owner of the property.

settlor

Settlor. The **settlor** is that individual who is the owner of property that is to be placed in a trust. Additional terms that are used in various jurisdictions to describe the settlor may be: *creator, grantor,* or *trustor.* The individual creating the trust must meet certain requirements:

- competency
- owner of the property
- power to dispose of the property
- intention to create a trust

If the settlor satisfies these requirements, then he or she may proceed to create a trust, as long as it meets the statutory requirements of the state of domicile of the trust.

Each state has its own body of law with respect to trusts, and those laws must be consulted before the creation of the trust.

Trustee. In the trust relationship, the settlor is usually the one who appoints the trustee through the trust instrument. The **trustee** is the person that holds legal title to property for the benefit of another person, the beneficiary.

The trustee is considered to be the fiduciary of the trust and its administrator. The trustee might be a natural person, or it might be a legal "person" in the form of a corporate entity, so long as it has the power to hold title to property.

The trustee owes a fiduciary duty to the beneficiary of the trust, consisting generally of the duty to act in the beneficiary's best interest. The trustee must use ordinary care, skill, diligence, and prudence in the fulfillment of its duties. Among other things, those duties consist of:

- maintaining accurate records
- preserving trust property
- collecting receivables
- acting solely in the best interests of the beneficiary

In addition to an active fiduciary duty, it is also incumbent upon the trustee to avoid any conflict of interest between the trustee and the beneficiary. He or she may not profit from the trust to the detriment of the beneficiary. The trustee may be liable for any breach of fiduciary duty.

Beneficiary. The **beneficiary** of a trust is the individual recipient of the trust benefits or property. The trust must have a beneficiary to be valid. The beneficiary has the power to enforce the terms of the trust. While the trustee holds the legal title to the trust property, the beneficiary holds **equitable title,** or the beneficial title, which is the right to profit or benefit from the property.

The equitable title of the beneficiary entitles him or her to the rights and benefits of the trust property during the period of the trust. In some jurisdictions, the beneficiary is referred to as the *cestui que trust* or the *cestui que use,* meaning that he or she is the one for whom property is held.

The beneficiary need not be a particular person named at the time of the creation of the trust, as long as he or she is capable of being identified, as in the case of an unborn child. If the beneficiary is not capable of holding title to the property, as in the case of a minor or incompetent, then a guardian must be appointed for the beneficiary. In most states, the beneficiary may be a co-trustee, but may not be the sole trustee because there would no longer be anyone to enforce the terms of the trust against the trustee.

Property. The trust property is known as the **corpus** and consists of the property interest owned by the settlor and transferred to the trustee for the benefit of the beneficiary. Any transferable interest may be the subject of a trust. Depending on the jurisdiction, the trust property may be referred to as the *body, principal, res,* or *subject matter.* The property may be a transferable interest in real property, or it may be personal property, or a combination of the two. It may not consist of an interest that is not transferable. Since the validity of the trust depends on its enforceability, there must be an interest to be enforced.

TRUST INSTRUMENTS

Trust instruments take the form of a contract between the settlor and the trustee describing the principal and providing for the disposition of that principal to the beneficiary. The instrument must clearly express the intentions of the settlor that the trust property is held by the trustee over time and the income is applied to a designated beneficiary.

trustee

beneficiary

equitable title

corpus

A private express trust instrument may take one of three basic forms:

- an irrevocable living trust
- a revocable living trust
- a testamentary trust

It is the intent of the settlor that decides the type of trust. If the property is to be placed in trust during the settlor's lifetime, then a *living trust* is to be created. If the settlor intends to make that living trust subject to the right to revoke it, then the trust will be either an *irrevocable living trust* or a *revocable living trust*. If the settlor intends to place the property in trust only upon death, then the form of the trust to be used will be a *testamentary trust*.

IRREVOCABLE LIVING TRUSTS

living trust

irrevocable living trust

A **living trust** is a trust created during the settlor's lifetime and that becomes operative before his death. A living trust is sometimes referred to as an *inter vivos trust*. For estate-planning purposes, it may be advisable for the settlor to create a living trust that cannot be revoked once it has been established. An **irrevocable living trust** is a trust created and executed during the settlor's lifetime and that cannot be revoked by him or her at any time.

The trust document can be a complex instrument, depending on the nature of the property, the duties of the trustee, and the character of the beneficiary. A well-drafted irrevocable living trust should contain sections that provide for the following:

- an identification of the parties
- an identification of the trust property
- the distribution of income and principal
- the rights, powers, and duties of the trustee
- an irrevocability clause
- provision for a successor trustee
- the applicable state law
- the execution

As with any legal instrument, there must be compliance with the applicable state law, while the individual needs of the settlor will dictate the complexity of the agreement.

Parties. The trust instrument begins with an identification of the parties to the agreement in a form similar to that of a standard contract. The title of the trust should be followed by language establishing the date of the agreement and the identity of the settlor and trustee as shown in Illustration 13-6.

Trust Property. The property clause transfers title of the trust property to the trustee and authorizes collection of the trust assets and perfection of title to the trust property. The trust property, or *corpus,* must be identified with as much detail as possible. If the property is extensive, an attached "exhibit" may be used to list the items that constitute the principal. Real property should be identified by its legal description. The settlor should contemplate the addition of property to the principal during the life of the trust and so declare that contingency in the agreement as shown in Illustration 13-7.

Distribution of Income and Principal. An important function of the trust instrument is to describe in detail the manner in which income and principal are to be distributed. The directions must be clear and unambiguous to avoid confusion and ensure compliance with the intentions of the settlor (see Illustration 13-8).

<u>**THE ALENE LONGREACH TRUST**</u>

THIS AGREEMENT is made this 30th day of June 1998, by and between ARTEMUS LONGREACH, 111 Foxhunt Lane, city of Orange, state of California, hereinafter referred to as Settlor, and OSWOLD COSMOLD, 222 Scribe Court, city of Orange, state of California, hereinafter referred to as Trustee.

Illustration 13-6
Title and Opening Paragraph of a Trust

<u>**ARTICLE I**</u>

Settlor hereby transfers, and trustee hereby agrees to receive, certain assets described in Exhibit "A" attached hereto and incorporated by reference, constituting the initial principal of this Trust, thereby establishing this trust. Settlor declares that it is his purpose in establishing this Trust to provide a means for the conservation and management of income-producing assets and other properties and to provide for the comfort, maintenance, and support of the Beneficiary. Trustee is authorized to receive additional property added to the trust principal from any person acceptable to the trustee.

Illustration 13-7
Trust Property

Rights, Powers, and Duties of the Trustee. An essential section of the trust instrument is the section setting forth the rights, powers, and duties of the trustee (those powers are based in general upon the fiduciary duty of the trustee), along with those specific powers and rights authorized by the trust agreement. Individual state statutes will provide certain guidelines governing the authority of the trustee as well and should be consulted before the preparation of the instrument. The section detailing the trustee's authority should also contain any limitations that the settlor may wish to impose on the trustee. Illustration 13-9 provides an example of the provision for the powers of the trustee.

ARTICLE II

Settlor hereby authorizes Trustee to manage the trust principal and collect income therefrom. Trustee shall pay all taxes and assessments incident to the management thereof, and apply and dispose of the net income from the trust principal as follows:

During the life of beneficiary, ALENE LONGREACH, Trustee shall pay to or for the benefit of, any amounts of the net income she deems advisable for the care, maintenance, and general welfare of beneficiary after consideration of the standard of living to which she is accustomed at the time of the creation of this Trust;

When beneficiary, ALENE LONGREACH, reaches her twenty-fifth (25) birthday, she shall be empowered to appoint or withdraw up to one-half of the then-remaining trust property of her trust as of said date; when she reaches her thirtieth (30) birthday, she shall be empowered to withdraw the remaining trust property of her trust; if she predeceases the date of distribution of her trust, Trustee shall, as soon as practicable following her death, pay all debts, funeral expenses, expenses of last illness, administration expenses, and estate taxes, and shall distribute the remaining trust property to her surviving heirs, whereupon this Trust shall terminate.

Illustration 13-8
Distribution of Income and Principal

ARTICLE III

Trustee and his successor shall be governed by the provisions of the laws of the state of California not in conflict with this instrument, and shall have additional responsibilities granted and imposed by statute. In addition, without limiting any common law or statutory authority, and without the need to apply to any court, Trustee shall have the following powers and responsibilities:

To acquire, retain, improve, manage, protect, invest, reinvest, exchange, lease, sell or option to sell, borrow, mortgage, pledge, transfer, and convey trust property, real property, tangible personal property, and intangible personal property, without regard to any law, court ruling, or rule or regulation governing fiduciaries in that manner Trustee shall deem advisable.

To pay all expenses of management and administration of the trust estate, all or any part of which may, in Trustee's discretion, be charged either to income or principal.

To perform any and all acts, institute proceedings, and to exercise all other rights and powers that an absolute owner of the property would otherwise have the right to do, subject to the Trustee's fiduciary responsibility.

Any enumeration of rights, powers, and duties of Trustee in this Agreement shall not limit the general or implied powers of Trustee.

Illustration 13-9
Powers of the Trustee

```
                        ARTICLE V

    Settlor hereby appoints the SABAL BANK AND TRUST COMPANY as

successor Trustee in the event that Trustee shall die, resign, become

incapacitated, or for any reason fail to act as Trustee. The

successor Trustee shall have all the powers, rights, and duties of

the Trustee named herein.
```

Illustration 13-10
Successor Trustee

Irrevocability Clause. The trust instrument creating an irrevocable living trust must contain clear and unambiguous language expressing the intent of the settlor that the trust is to be irrevocable. The purpose of this section is to state clearly that the property is to be held for the benefit of another, without any reservation of authority by the settlor, as expressed here:

> Settlor hereby declares that the trust created by this Agreement shall be irrevocable and not subject to alteration, amendment, revocation, or termination by Settlor.

Provision for a Successor Trustee. The trust agreement must include a provision establishing the procedure for the appointment of a successor trustee, should the named trustee fail for any reason. The instrument must recognize the fact that the trustee might die, become incompetent, refuse the position, or otherwise become ineligible to act on behalf of the trust, thus creating the necessity for a successor (see Illustration 13-10).

Applicable State Law. In most jurisdictions, the law of the state of the domicile of the trust property will govern the provisions of the trust agreement. If there is property in multiple states, the state of domicile of the settlor will be the law of choice, as long as the laws of the states involved have received compliance (see Illustration 13-11).

Execution. The laws of the state of domicile of the settlor will control the formalities of the execution of the trust instrument. As a general procedure, it is advisable to provide for the signatures of the settlor, trustee, and witnesses, and for an acknowledgment of a notary public (see Illustration 13-12).

Miscellaneous Provisions. In addition to the various requirements of individual state statutes governing trust agreements, the specific intentions of each settlor will vary, depending on the nature of the property and the beneficiary. Some optional provisions to provide for a complete agreement may include such areas as:

- definition of terms
- spendthrift provisions
- Rule Against Perpetuities provision
- accounting procedures
- compensation of trustee

ARTICLE VI

This Agreement has been established pursuant to the laws of the state of California, and Settlor is a resident of the state of California at the time of its execution. Any interpretation of this Agreement, and any question concerning its validity, and all questions relating to its performance, shall be adjudged pursuant to the laws of the state of California.

Illustration 13-11
Applicable State Law

IN WITNESS WHEREOF, Settlor and Trustee have executed this Agreement at the city of Orange, state of California, on this 31st day of June, 1999.

_____   _____

Witness   ARTEMUS LONGREACH

_____   _____

Witness   OSWOLD COSMOLD

(acknowledgment of notary public)

Illustration 13-12
Execution

- bond of trustee
- transactions with third parties

The length and complexity of the agreement will be determined by the individual requirements of the creator of the trust. As always, care should be taken to avoid any ambiguity in providing for the settlor's wishes.

REVOCABLE LIVING TRUSTS

revocable living trust

A trust created by a settlor during his or her lifetime that reserves the right of revocation of the trust is called a **revocable living trust,** or a *revocable inter vivos trust.*

The right of revocation retained by the settlor can take the form of any power to change, alter, or amend the terms of the trust agreement during the settlor's lifetime. Upon the death of the settlor, the right of revocation is terminated, and the terms of the trust become irrevocable.

Estate planners find the revocable living trust to be a useful planning tool due to its flexibility, and for that reason, it has been termed a *will substitute.* It has certain advantages over a will in that it avoids the expense and delay of probate administration and still allows the settlor the power to manage the property during the settlor's lifetime.

The trust instrument used to create a revocable living trust is similar in most respects to the document used to create the irrevocable living trust. The exception comes with the clause referring to the revocable nature of the trust. In such trusts, the settlor usually serves as a co-trustee with another individual. The settlor not only exercises the powers of a trustee, but retains the sole right to revoke the trust at any time. The language used to establish the revocable nature of the trust should be clear and unambiguous (see Illustration 13-13). The revocable living trust does not result in a tax saving, but does allow the settlor to maintain control over the property until death.

TESTAMENTARY TRUSTS

testamentary trust

A trust created by a will and executed with the statutory formalities required by state law is called a **testamentary trust.** Since a will does not become effective until the testator's death, such a conveyance in trust does not become effective until the death of the testator.

Upon the testator's death, the trust becomes effective and operates as a typical trust situation with the property held by the designated trustee for the benefit of a named beneficiary. As with any will, there must be probate administration that includes the proving of the will prior to its contents taking effect. The validity of the trust arrangement will depend on the validity of the will itself.

```
                         ARTICLE IV

     Settlor reserves the power and right by written direction signed

by him, and effective on delivery to Trustees, to revoke this

instrument and the trust created by it and to receive back from

Trustees all the trust property. Upon receipt of such written notice,

Trustees shall surrender all trust properties belonging to the Trust

estate as described in such notice.
```

Illustration 13-13
Revocability Clause

SUMMARY

The last will and testament is one of the most important documents that will be prepared for an individual. It can best be described as the final written expression of the intended distribution of one's assets at death. The validity of the will lies in its execution; the integrity of the will lies in its expression of intention. The preparation of the will is extremely important, as is its execution. It is the task of the preparer of the document to ensure that the will not only reflects the desires of its maker, but also is executed in a form to withstand challenge. A failure in its execution will cost the estate unnecessary court costs and attorney fees.

The probate code of each state provides the formal requirements for the creation of a document that will be considered by a court. The content of the will is not covered by statute, and must remain the province of the testator and his counsel. No single format will serve to meet the needs of each testator. The content of each estate will differ, as well as the desires of the owner of that estate. Keep in mind the need to provide for the certain burden that debts, administration expenses, and taxes will impose. The effect on the size and direction of any devise must be measured in light of the possible depletion of the estate.

A trust is a basic estate-planning tool allowing the creator to distribute property for the benefit of heirs, or any other person or organization, without the delay and expense of probate administration (while the trust property is held by the beneficiary, which property will be managed for the benefit of the beneficiary due to the trustee's fiduciary duty). Once the terms of the trust have been satisfied, the beneficiary will receive legal title. The instrument is an expression in written form of the settlor's intentions, setting forth the specific powers of the trustee and the nature of the beneficiary's equitable interest. The document must declare the primary elements of a trust and set forth its revocability without ambiguity.

Chapter Activities

Review Questions

1. Describe the purpose and nature of a will.

2. Summarize the advantages and disadvantages of a will.

3. What formal language is necessary for the execution of a will?

4. Describe the requirements for a witness to a will.

5. What document is used to modify a will?

6. What is a trust used for?

7. List the four elements required to form a valid trust.

8. Summarize the primary duty of a trustee.

9. Distinguish between a revocable living trust and an irrevocable living trust.

10. What is the advantage of a revocable living trust?

Computer Activity

The Industrial Revolution of the nineteenth century brought with it not only the giants of American industry, but also the unsung heroes of primitive technology. One such notable was Ebenezer Coates, a full-time tinkerer. Prior to his demise, Ebenezer Coates perfected a device for hanging women's outer garments so that their shape was retained. The device was a thin wire formed into a loop in the shape of an isosceles triangle with a hook at the top. With the law about to terminate his gainful employment, Ebenezer had the foresight to patent his device with the U.S. Patent Office, calling it Coates Hanger. While old Ebenezer was never able to enjoy the economic prosperity resulting from his device, his family was able to take Coates Hanger to the American people, where it found immediate acceptance with that buttress of the U.S. economy, the housewife. It was not long before Coates Hanger became not only a household word, as has occurred with "Kleenex" and "Xerox," but also the source of a considerable fortune for Ebenezer's heirs.

Today, the Coates family has built upon the entrepreneurial tradition of their infamous heir. Having withstood the obvious threats presented by both plastic and polyester, the family is now on the verge of introducing the world's first digital coat hanger, with resident RAM to store personal information relative to the owner's dress size and hygiene. The Coates family fortune is now controlled by Ebenezer Coates IV, affectionately known to the family as "Top."

It is Top's intention to create a testamentary trust to be administered by his loyal attorney, Larsen S. Hart. Top does not think that his twin children, Rupert and Gretchen, will be competent to handle their own affairs until they have attained the age of thirty-five. Top's estate consists of: (1) the family home, Upside Downs; (2) 100 percent of the stock in Coates Hangers, Incorporated; (3) and a substantial stock portfolio with the brokerage firm of Catch & Lynch.

A. From the student template retrieve act13.doc. This document is a testamentary trust. Prepare a testamentary trust placing Mr. Top Coates's entire estate in trust for his children at his death, with Larsen S. Hart as trustee and the firm of Catch & Lynch as successor trustees. Use the scenario to help complete the document. Refer to the chapter for examples.

B. Save this information on the template as testrust.doc.

C. Print one copy for your instructor. Make sure your name appears for identification purposes.

Chapter 14

Law of Contracts

Objectives

After completing this chapter, you will be able to:

1. Describe the nature of a contract.

2. Define a contract.

3. Outline the five primary elements of a contract.

4. Identify the preliminary considerations in the preparation of a contract.

5. Detail the basic content of the provisions of a contract.

6. Identify the need for any of the optional provisions that a contract may contain.

7. Summarize the formalities required for the execution of the contractual agreement.

Contracts play a vital role in our personal lives, as well as occupying an integral role in the typical business relationship. Any agreement between two or more people involves some form of a contract. It is important for the legal office assistant to understand the fundamental principles of contract law, as well as the content of the basic provisions of a contract, if any work is to be done in a commercial setting. In drafting a contract that adequately represents the intentions of the parties and fully sets forth the agreement reached, it is essential that the objectives are clearly expressed in language that is easily understood. The focus of this chapter will be to present this expression of intention in its simplest form.

NATURE OF A CONTRACT

A **contract** is an agreement that creates legally enforceable obligations binding each party. Every contract has a common element of agreement in some form between the parties, resulting in a "meeting of the minds."

A **party** to a contract is that person or legal entity having an interest in the subject matter of the agreement and is legally bound by his or her promise. The party making a promise, which is the subject matter of the contract, is known as the **promisor,** or *obligor.* The party to whom the promise is made is known as the **promisee** or *obligee.*

The promisor and promisee stand in a relationship to each other called **privity of contract.** It was privity that allowed one party to maintain an action at law to enforce the terms of their agreement under the English common law. Privity refers to the relationship of the parties that constitutes the basis for a lawsuit.

The extent of the subject matter forming the basis of a contract is virtually unlimited. Just as any person or legal entity may be a party to a contract, so may any legally enforceable matter be the subject of the parties' agreement. For example, an agreement may call for the sale or manufacture of goods, for personal service such as an employment contract, or for the sale or lease of property. Although a contract may call for one party to actively perform an act or obligation, the subject matter of a contract may also require that a party refrain from performing some act. The term for the promise not to do an act is called **forbearance.**

The law recognizes the existence of a contract that is created by the action of the parties but not reflected in a writing. Such an agreement inferred by law is called an **implied contract.** The focus of this chapter is on its counterpart in the law, the **express contract.** An express contract is an actual (rather than implied) agreement between the parties stated in definite terms. It may be either written or oral.

Traditionally, an agreement that creates a legally enforceable obligation between the parties must satisfy certain basic requirements before it will be considered enforceable. For a contract to be legally enforceable, the following five elements must exist:

- The parties must have the *capacity* to enter into a contract.

- There must be an *offer* and an *acceptance* of that offer.

- *Consideration* must support the contract.

- The subject matter of the contract must be *legal* and not against public policy.

- Under certain circumstances, the contract must satisfy the *Statute of Frauds* with a written instrument.

A contract will not be enforceable unless each element is present.

CAPACITY

Before the formation of an agreement, each party to a potential contract must have established the legal age and mental ability to enter into a contract. The term referring to the competency of age and ability is **contractual capacity.**

If contractual capacity does not exist, then the contract is voidable in most cases at the discretion of the party lacking such capacity. A **voidable** contract is a contract that is valid, yet may be declared invalid at the option of a party to the agreement.

Historically, a minor has always been considered to lack sufficient wisdom and maturity to understand the nature of his or her acts and to display the ability to carry out his or her promises. A minor is any individual who has not attained the age of legal competence. Due to the lack of contractual capacity, a minor cannot enter into a legally enforceable agreement. If an agreement is executed before a party reaches the **age of majority** (usually 18 years of age), that agreement is voidable at the discretion of the minor.

contract

party

promisor
promisee
privity of contract

forbearance

implied contract
express contract

contractual capacity

voidable

age of majority

incompetent

guardian

authority

**principal
agent**

offer

offeror

offeree

consideration

Individuals who lack the mental ability to understand the nature and consequences of their acts are said to lack contractual capacity. Contracts executed by such individuals are considered voidable. An individual is said to be **incompetent** if he or she lacks the mental capacity to appreciate the nature and consequences of acts due to such things as insanity, imbecility, or the excessive use of drugs or alcohol. If such a person has periods of mental clarity and enters a contract at such a time, then the contract is valid and binding.

An individual who otherwise lacks contractual capacity because of age or incompetence may enter into a legally binding agreement through the use of a **guardian.** A guardian is a person invested by law with the power to manage the rights and property of another person who cannot manage on his or her own due to a lack of mental capacity or insufficient age.

Contractual capacity also refers to the authority to enter into an agreement that will legally bind the parties. **Authority** is the power delegated to one person by another, or by a legal entity such as a corporation, to act on their behalf. It is that power given by a **principal** (the one granting the authority) to an **agent** (the one receiving the authority) to act for his or her benefit and to be subject to his or her direction and control.

Within the structure of a corporation, authority is the power to act on behalf of the corporation within the limits prescribed by the corporate bylaws. In most situations, an individual may not legally obligate a corporation without the express authorization of the corporate bylaws.

OFFER AND ACCEPTANCE

The second major element of a contract goes to the very heart of an agreement and reflects mutuality of interest and intention where the parties have voluntarily bound themselves to act, as set out in the contract. The requisite "meeting of the minds" refers to the mutual agreement of the parties. That agreement exists in the requirement that there be first an *offer*, followed by an *acceptance* of that offer.

An **offer** is a proposal demonstrating a willingness to enter into an agreement and creating a power of acceptance in the person to whom the offer is conveyed. No offer exists if the **offeror** (the person making the offer) did not have an intent to enter into an agreement. The offer must be definite in nature and leave no uncertainty regarding any relevant element of the agreement. An offer must be such that its acceptance will create a contract. In addition, the offer must be communicated to the **offeree** (the person to whom the power of acceptance is given) in order for the contract to exist.

An offer creates in the offeree the power to bind the offeror to a contract through his or her acceptance. Acceptance is the agreement to the terms of the offer that results in an agreement to all material terms. As with the offer, in order for there to be an enforceable acceptance, an intent to accept the offer must be present. Ordinarily, if the offeree is silent or fails to act, no inference of acceptance is present.

CONSIDERATION

The third essential element that must exist for the formulation of a legally enforceable contract is the requirement of consideration. **Consideration** is the element of a contract that forms the inducement to a party to enter into the agreement.

Consideration is the motivating influence consisting of some right, interest, profit, or benefit accruing to one party, and some forbearance, detriment, loss, or responsibility sustained by the other party. In its essential nature, consideration is something of value that is considered the price paid for the promise that is the subject matter of the contract.

Consideration may consist of anything of value, including a promise, a payment, an act, or forbearance. If there is an absence or failure of consideration, then no contractual obligation exists. Certain exceptions are found in the law, however, such as a charitable contribution or a contract for the sale of goods under the Uniform Commercial Code, as well as many other situations governed by state statute.

LEGALITY

The fourth element necessary to the formation of an enforceable contract is a requirement that the subject matter of the agreement be legal and not in violation of any public policy. No contract will be enforceable if the agreement specifies conduct that would create civil or criminal liability. Such an agreement is considered void from the beginning and is unenforceable, as though it never existed at all. A violation of a statute or regulation creates a situation of illegality *per se*. Any agreement to conduct that would result in unlawful activity may not properly be contemplated by the contract.

Public policy is more difficult to define because of the lack of any statutory guidelines. The essence of public policy is that it is concerned with the public welfare or general goodwill of the people. The enforceability of a contract is measured by its effect on the public welfare. If that effect is detrimental, such as in a gambling contract, then the contract is void.

STATUTE OF FRAUDS

The final element of a contract involves the requirement that the contract be in writing. By statute in most states, certain contracts must be written to be enforceable. The English common law provided a historical precedent in the *Statute of Frauds and Perjuries,* adopted in 1677, which established the requirement of a written contract under certain circumstances. The *Statute of Frauds* required a written contract if the agreement involved a contract:

- for the sale of goods
- for the sale of land
- that cannot be performed within one year
- to guarantee the debts of another

Although the *Statute of Frauds* was repealed in England in 1954 except for the provisions relating to the conveyance of real property, its remnants exist in many states today. The Uniform Commercial Code, which has been adopted in some part by virtually every state, provides in § 2-201 that a contract for the sale of goods in excess of $500 is not enforceable by way of action or defense unless there is some writing sufficient to suggesting that a contract exists between the parties and is signed by the party against whom enforcement is sought.

The essence of the written agreement is the meeting of the minds of the parties that creates a mutuality of understanding in the formation of the agreement. If the essential elements are not met in the formation of the agreement, the parties will find themselves with an unenforceable document. As the preparer of the agreement, the legal office assistant must avoid the creation of an invalid agreement. Careful attention to the preliminary considerations will eliminate that occurrence.

FORMATION OF A CONTRACT

Certain preliminary concerns must be addressed before the actual agreement is written, or the agreement might not fully represent the intentions of the parties. Those considerations involve:

- parties to the contract
- property interests
- federal and state laws
- mutuality of the agreement
- conditions precedent

PARTIES TO THE CONTRACT

Initially, identification and participation of all parties to the contract is essential. To ensure its enforceability, the contract must reflect the identity by name of each party to be bound by the agreement. Fundamental contract law requires that no contract be enforced against an individual who has not agreed to be bound by the terms and conditions of the agreement.

Representation by legal counsel is not a prerequisite to the formation of an enforceable contract; but if the agreement involves substantial rights and duties, it is advisable that the parties obtain advice and counsel of one skilled in such matters. The complexities of a contract, along with the adverse interests of the parties, dictate a need for professional representation.

PROPERTY INTERESTS

A second preliminary concern in the formulation of a contract is to find the existence of any special property interests that may be the subject of the agreement. If the focus of the agreement pertains to any property, whether real or personal, a determination must be made initially as to the interest of each party in that property at the time of execution of the agreement.

FEDERAL AND STATE LAWS

The third preliminary concern requires a review of applicable federal and state statutes pertaining to the subject matter of the contract. These must be checked to ensure that the agreement will be valid through statutory compliance. If the agreement is going to affect the tax liability of one or more of the parties, that result should be taken into account as a preliminary step in identifying the intentions of the parties. Other statutory concerns that may arise would involve such concerns as the Federal Truth in Lending Act or the Consumer Protection Acts of most states. In addition, certain state statutes governing the form and content of certain types of contracts, such as a contract for the sale and purchase of real estate, must be considered.

MUTUALITY OF THE AGREEMENT

A fourth preliminary consideration concerns those matters that affect the validity or legality of the transaction because of the failure of a meeting of the minds. The validity of the agreement can be materially affected by such matters as:

- conflicts of interest of either party

- mistake of fact, either mutual or unilateral

- ignorance of any material fact by one or both parties

- fraud in any material element of the agreement

- duress in the formulation of the contract

- undue influence of one party to the agreement over any other party

Such matters go to the heart of the question of the existence of any "meeting of the minds" of the parties. Questions concerning the existence of any of the above conditions should first be resolved. Otherwise, the agreement may fail for a lack of mutuality.

CONDITIONS PRECEDENT

condition precedent

Finally, many contracts involve the performance of a certain **condition precedent** preliminary to the execution of an agreement. A condition precedent requires that a specified event occur before some right that is dependent upon the event may arise, (such as an obligation under the contract). If a party to a potential agreement is required to deliver certain property in escrow, provide an abstract or title, secure title insurance, obtain a license or permit, or provide a release of a special property interest, then such events must occur before the contract can take place.

For example, assume hypothetically that Leonard Loveless found himself in the throes of an unfortunate divorce. The terms of the divorce judgment provided that he was to pay his soon-to-be ex-wife a certain sum of cash, and to do so, he had to sell his most prized possession, the Bass Slayer 5000. Elrod Bream had offered to pay $8,500 for the boat, but title to the boat had been in the name of both Leonard and his wife, Luanne. Before Leonard could enter into the agreement to sell the boat to Elrod, he had to obtain title to the boat in his name from the court. Such a condition precedent exists if there is an event that makes the effect of an agreement conditional upon its occurrence.

It is important to remember that each state has its own set of statutes governing the form and content of certain types of contracts. Those statutes must be consulted before the drafting of any instrument to ensure its effectiveness.

STANDARD PROVISIONS

The preparation of any contract centers around the dual purposes of (1) communication of the intention of the parties and (2) clear and concise language. The order of presentation of the suggested areas of concern is a matter of style and in no way reflects upon the degree of importance of any paragraph. The following provisions should be considered when drafting a contract, although they may not apply to all documents. Each provision must be tailored to the specific needs of the parties to the agreement. See Illustration 14-1 for examples of the language to be used in the various contractual provisions.

TITLE

Each contract should have a title that in some concise manner reflects the nature of the subject matter of the agreement. If the contract is for the sale of goods, it may very well be titled "CONTRACT FOR SALE OF MACHINERY," or for a consultation agreement, "CONSULTATION AGREEMENT."

PARTIES

The initial paragraph of any contract should reflect the date of the agreement and fully identify the parties to the agreement. The parenthetical references suggest the terms to be used throughout the agreement to identify the parties. If the status of the parties is relevant, such as marital status or corporate office, that status may also be reflected in the first paragraph.

CONSIDERATION

A statement of the consideration that forms the basis of the contract should be included, following the identification of the parties. The nature of the consideration will vary, depending on the subject matter of the agreement. The statement must be specific in its identification of the terms of the consideration. The agreement may then go to a full description of the terms of the employment, including salary, benefits, and responsibilities, as agreed upon by the parties.

DESCRIPTION OF PROPERTY

A detailed description of any property that is the subject matter of the agreement is another requisite paragraph necessary to accurately reflect the parties' intentions. If the subject matter of the contract is a particular piece of property, either real or personal,

Identification of Parties:

THIS AGREEMENT ("Agreement") is made this __ day of _____, 19__, by and between _____, a Delaware corporation, having its principal office at _____ (the "Company") and _____, (the "Employee"), as follows:

Statement of Consideration:

CONSIDERATION. The Company hereby agrees to employ the Employee, and the Employee, in consideration of such employment, hereby accepts employment upon the terms and conditions set forth herein.

Property Description:

PROPERTY. The lathe to be conveyed pursuant to the terms and conditions herein set forth is a Smith & Williams, Type D, 1982 upright center bore, serial number KC6378239, located at the Seller's place of business.

Duration of Agreement:

TERMINATION OF AGREEMENT. This Agreement will terminate two (2) years from the date hereof, unless terminated sooner as provided herein. Either party may terminate this Agreement upon thirty (30) days written notice of termination to the other party, at which time this Agreement shall terminate immediately.

Definitions:

DEFINITIONS. It is the intention of the parties that for purposes of this Agreement, the meaning accorded terminology used herein shall be as follows:

Bond — an interest-bearing security

Broker — person who acts as intermediary

Conversion — exchange of bond into stock

Compensation:

COMPENSATION. In consideration for services, the Company agrees to pay an amount equal to two percent (2%) of the purchase price of said property, said amount to be paid at the time of the closing of the sale of said property.

Entirety of Agreement:

ENTIRE AGREEMENT. This Agreement constitutes the entire Agreement of the parties and supersedes all prior agreements, understandings and negotiations, whether written or oral, between the parties. This Agreement may not be changed orally but only by an agreement in writing signed by both parties and stated to be an amendment hereto.

Nonperformance:

NONPERFORMANCE. Should the Employee, for any reason, become physically or mentally incapacitated from the performance of his/her duties as set forth herein, this Agreement shall be considered null and void and shall terminate immediately.

Illustration 14-1
Contractual Provisions

that property should be identified in as much detail as possible regarding its location and description. If the property involved is real property, in addition to the postal address, a full, legal description of the property should be included. The legal description of a parcel of land is the official description by governmental survey, metes and bounds, or a plat map.

DURATION OF AGREEMENT

Since most contractual agreements are for a specified period, the agreement should reflect that fact under a paragraph labeled "Term" or "Termination of Agreement." If the term of the contract is to be for an indefinite period that ends upon the occurrence of some event, then the exact nature of the event should be clearly identified.

DEFINITIONS AND TERMINOLOGY

The subject matter of a contract may involve technical terms that are familiar to the parties but not to the general public. In order for the intention of the parties to be interpreted by anyone, the agreement should define any technical words, terms of art, or custom and usage, so that any reader may understand the parties' intentions. The purpose behind the inclusion of a detailed list of terminology is to eliminate the chance for either party to misconstrue any technical terms that are the subject matter of the agreement. It is also of benefit to both parties, should litigation occur over some breach of the terms of the agreement.

PAYMENT

Many contracts call for some form of payment of money, either in one lump sum at an agreed upon date, or the periodic payment of a set amount over time. Any paragraph referring to such payments must accurately and fully set forth the understanding of the parties concerning such items as time and place of payment, amount, terms, method, interest, and security if contemplated. The reference to the terms and conditions for payment of any monies is a particularly sensitive area of any contractual agreement where the accurate presentation of the parties' intentions is most critical.

ENTIRETY OF AGREEMENT

In most contractual settings, it is the intention of the parties that the written agreement should fully represent the complete understanding between them. It is preferable to state in the agreement itself that it is the entire understanding. This avoids any later claim that there exists certain material terms that are the subject of another agreement, either oral or written. The idea of having the written agreement encompass the entirety of the understanding between the parties means that the parties may only refer to that agreement should any question arise as to their respective rights, duties, and obligations. No unresolved matters outside the written agreement should remain to be negotiated.

EXCUSES FOR NONPERFORMANCE

The parties to a contract may reasonably contemplate circumstances beyond either's control that would make performance of a particular condition or term impossible. Excuses for nonperformance may be such things as an act of God, a labor dispute, an illness, or death. If such an occurrence is a part of the negotiated understanding between the parties, the agreement should so state. The situation to be avoided would be an impossibility of compliance by one party without fault, and an expectation of satisfaction by the other party. If the situation is addressed in the agreement, then future misunderstanding can be avoided.

OPTIONAL PROVISIONS

Each written contract is intended to contain the complete understanding between the parties as to the exact nature of their agreement. To adequately reflect that total agreement, a well-drafted document could contain any of several purely optional provisions to eliminate any uncertainty regarding the parties' intentions.

PASSAGE OF TITLE

If the subject matter of the contract involves property, either real or personal, then title to that property will be conveyed at some point during the term of the contractual relationship. The written agreement should specify when that passage may occur and under what conditions.

RISK OF LOSS

Any contract with property as its subject matter should address the question of which party must bear the burden of risk of some form of loss to that property. As a rule, that risk is born by the party controlling the use of the property in the form of insurance. If the risk has been the subject of negotiation, then the agreement should state which party pays for that insurance.

WARRANTIES

warranty

express warranty

implied warranty

In a contract for the sale of personal property or of goods, the transaction involves a warranty in most situations. A **warranty** is a representation made by the seller as to the quality, fitness, or title to goods, assuring the purchaser that certain facts are as represented.

An **express warranty** arises if there is any statement of fact in writing by the seller. The Uniform Commercial Code expressly governs transactions involving express warranties. If the agreement is silent concerning any express warranties made by the seller, then there may be an **implied warranty** created by the operation of law with respect to fitness for a particular purpose.

The Uniform Commercial Code and other applicable state and federal laws must be consulted for the applicable law concerning express and implied warranties.

INSURANCE AND BONDS

Commercially available insurance covering the risk of any loss, as well as bonds governing the performance of a party, may be contemplated in the negotiation between the parties. The document should reflect the provisions concerning the levels of coverage, risks contemplated, and the party to whom the burden of the cost will be born as shown in Illustration 14-2. Therefore, it is the responsibility of one or both parties to secure the necessary surety before any enforceable obligation arises.

SECURITY. It is understood and agreed that this contract is not to be binding upon either party until it is endorsed by some person, or firm, or corporation as security for the execution of the promises and conditions thereof, or until a satisfactory surety bond is furnished that the parties will carry out all of the promises and conditions of the contract.

Illustration 14-2
Security

TRANSFER AND ASSIGNABILITY OF RIGHTS

If there is to be some limitation on the transferability of the rights of a party, then the contract should reflect the terms and conditions for assignability as shown in Illustration 14-3. Frequently, it is the intention of the parties to a contract that rights are not assignable to any third party. These rights might include selling the right to receive payments to another entity or conditions that the interests of one of the parties not pass through his estate. If the contract does not address such contingencies, then an interest may be transferred or assigned as permitted by law.

SUBROGATION

The parties to certain agreements may wish to reserve the right of **subrogation.** This occurs where one person (who has paid an obligation that should have been paid by another person) retains the right to be indemnified by the other. Subrogation is the substitution of one person in the place of another concerning a certain right. **Indemnification** is the right of a person to be reimbursed for some loss.

Not all agreements lend themselves to either a reservation or release of any right of subrogation or indemnification, but if the question has been the subject of the negotiation between the parties, the document should reflect the parties' intentions.

subrogation

indemnification

ACCOUNTING

Many types of contracts require an accounting of a party's compliance with the terms of a contract. The recording of information and the retention of such records, if completed on a formalized basis, should be addressed in the written instrument as shown in Illustration 14-4.

The information may be as simple as recording a few periodic payments, or as complex as a full set of accounts for an elaborate commercial enterprise. The needs will vary, depending on the nature of the contractual relationship. A well-drafted agreement will provide for the maintenance of records, and will address the question of the retention of an independent accounting service if necessary.

ASSIGNMENT. This Agreement shall not inure to the benefit of the heirs, successors, and assigns of the respective parties hereto.

Illustration 14-3
Assignment

ACCOUNTING. The Company agrees to keep complete and accurate books or accounts, and to furnish monthly statements of receipts and disbursements, and such additional information as may be requested.

Illustration 14-4
Accounting

REMEDIES. The parties recognize that a breach of any of the restrictive covenants herein set forth may cause irreparable harm and that actual damages may be difficult to ascertain and in any event may be inadequate. Accordingly, the parties agree that in the event of such breach, the parties may seek to enforce their remedies through binding arbitration or any court of competent jurisdiction.

Illustration 14-5
Remedies

ATTORNEY FEES AND LITIGATION COSTS. If any legal action or other proceeding is brought for the enforcement of this Agreement, the successful or prevailing party shall be entitled to recover reasonable attorney fees and other costs incurred in that action or proceeding, in addition to any other relief to which that party would be entitled.

Illustration 14-6
Cost and Attorney Fees

ARBITRATION

An alternative process of dispute resolution by a neutral third party, known as an **arbitrator,** can be used to avoid the expense and delay ordinarily associated with litigation. As long as the arbitration process is agreed upon by the parties, arbitration provides a convenient means of resolving any conflict within the confines of the agreement. The language of the contract expressing the arbitration agreement should state that the agreement is mutual and based on a recognition of the possibility of a failure of a party to perform (see Illustration 14-5). The purpose of such a clause is not to prevent parties to a contract from having their day in court. It is merely to avoid the expense and delay of ordinary litigation.

arbitrator

COSTS AND ATTORNEY FEES

Should a dispute arise surrounding the contract or any of its provisions, legal expenses and related costs may be incurred. The agreement may anticipate such an occurrence with the inclusion of a paragraph that provides for the payment of such expenses by stipulation of the parties as shown in Illustration 14-6. Most agreements provide that such costs are born by the party who defaults.

LIQUIDATED DAMAGES

The sum that a party to a contract agrees to pay if he or she fails to perform as promised is called **liquidated damages** and is frequently the subject of consideration by the parties to an agreement. The contractual agreement should contain a clause that states the circumstances that constitute a breach and the cost of that breach in a specified dollar amount (see Illustration 14-7). The purpose is to ensure performance by fixing the amount to be paid in lieu of such performance.

liquidated damages

NOTICE

The method and necessity of the conveyance of any information called for by the terms of the contract is called **notice.** Such notice required by the contract may be oral or

notice

LIQUIDATED DAMAGES. In the event that either party to this Agreement should breach this contract, the parties hereby agree that the breaching party shall pay to the other party the sum of _____ Dollars ($_____) as liquidated damages.

Illustration 14-7
Liquidated Damages

NOTICES. All notices herein shall be in writing and may be delivered personally, or by mail, postage prepaid. Any notice sent by mail, postage prepaid, will be deemed received three days after it is mailed.

Illustration 14-8
Notice

APPLICABLE LAW. This Agreement shall be governed in all respects, including its construction and interpretation, by the law of the state of Delaware.

Illustration 14-9
Applicable Law

written and is generally required within a specified period to be effective. The notice clause should state the circumstances under which it applies, and it should provide for the specific notice period (see Illustration 14-8).

The time and circumstances under which notice must be given are a matter of agreement between the parties in most situations. Local state statutes should be consulted to determine the effect such statutory regulation may have on certain types of agreements.

CHOICE OF LAW

In contemplation of the potential for litigation over some term of the contract, it is advisable for the parties to identify the state laws that are to be applied to interpret the terms of the contract. The contract may establish the body of state law to be applied in the event of a dispute, as long as there is some rational basis for the selection of a particular state. The selection of a particular state, while a matter of negotiation, must have some basis in fact. The choice is generally determined by the residence of one or both parties to secure the jurisdiction of a particular court (see Illustration 14-9).

SEVERABILITY

The separate clauses of an agreement should be independent of each other. This is called **severability,** meaning that the terms of a contract are divisible. The clause should be drafted to reflect that the breach of one clause does not affect the validity of another; that the entire agreement is not breached. When an agreement contains a severability

severability

SEVERABILITY OF CLAUSES. Each section of this Agreement shall stand independently and severably, and the invalidity of any one section or portion thereof shall not affect the validity of any other provision. In the event any provision shall be construed to be invalid, no other provision of this Agreement shall be affected thereby.

Illustration 14-10
Severability

MODIFICATION. There may be no modification of any of the provisions of this Agreement, except in writing, executed with the same formalities as this instrument.

Illustration 14-11
Modification

clause, a breach of one portion of the agreement does not destroy the validity of the remainder of the agreement (see Illustration 14-10).

MODIFICATION

In the performance of a contract, circumstances beyond the contemplation of the parties at the time of the execution of the agreement may arise. A material change or **modification** in the terms of the agreement may be necessary.

If the introduction of a new element or the elimination of some existing element will not clearly change the basic purpose of the agreement, then the procedure for modification of the agreement may be set forth. It is typical of most contracts that the parties agree that no modification may take place without the written consent of the other party (see Illustration 14-11).

BREACH OF CONTRACT

Any failure to act or perform in a manner called for by the contract without legal excuse constitutes a **breach of contract.** There is a significant body of law surrounding the question of the nature of a breach of contract. Applicable federal and state laws should always be consulted to determine the consequences of any breach.

FORMAL REQUIREMENTS

The specific formalities of certain types of contractual agreements may be governed by either federal or state law. To formally execute the document regardless of any individual state regulation, you should consider the following:

- Number of copies—the original document should be maintained by one party, with photocopies distributed to all remaining signatories along with a file copy for the office.

- Incorporation of documents—any documents incorporated by reference or attached to the agreement as exhibits should be attached to the original document and each photocopy.

modification

breach of contract

- Date of execution—the date of signing the document should be reflected in the opening paragraph as well as on the signature page; the date of execution may differ from the date the agreement is to take effect or be performed.

- Signatures—all parties to the contract must sign the document either personally or through a legal representative.

- Attestation—the witnessing of the signing of a written instrument is frequently preferred by the signatories to an agreement.

- Acknowledgment—the authentication by a notary public should be attached to the document where required as a formality in the execution of such agreements.

- Seal—a **seal** is an impression made upon the original of an agreement to authenticate an act, such as that performed by a corporation; documents required to be sealed are prescribed by law in many states.

- Filing or recordation—federal and state laws require that certain documents, such as a financing statement, be filed with a particular governmental agency.

- Designation of custodian of records—if the agreement requires the maintenance of any form of records, the procedure for such maintenance should be agreed upon prior to the document's signing.

The formal execution of the contract demonstrates its legal existence and the applicability and enforceability of its terms. As previously explained, five basic elements are necessary for the existence of a legal and enforceable contract. It is the function of the preparer to further develop the actual understanding of the parties and reduce that understanding to writing.

SUMMARY

A contract is the written expression of the agreement between the parties. Its preparation and drafting must focus on the intention of the parties in a clear, concise, and simple manner. The basic elements of capacity, offer and acceptance, consideration, legality, and the *Statute of Frauds* must be met before an enforceable agreement exists.

Once the contract satisfies the basic five elements, then any other provisions are optional. It is the preparer's responsibility to include those optional provisions if they have been the subject of negotiation between the parties. Where those provisions have not been considered by the parties in their negotiations, it is advisable that the preparer recommend their inclusion. It is only through a full presentation of all of the options available that the party will be fully protected. Each provision of the contract must fully comply with federal and state laws where applicable. Therefore, it is the function of the preparer of the contract to not only provide for the basic elements of a contract, but also consider any of the optional provisions, as well as the applicable law.

seal

Chapter Activities

Review Questions

1. Define a contract.

2. List and discuss the two general types of contract.

3. List the five basic elements of a contract.

4. Describe the importance of the *Statute of Frauds* for modern contracts.

5. What information is necessary to identify the parties to a contract?

6. Summarize the mutual meeting of the minds that can affect the validity of an agreement.

7. List the standard provisions of a contract.

8. List and discuss five optional provisions considered the most important to any contract.

9. Define a breach of contract.

10. Summarize the formal requirements of a contract.

Computer Activity

Your employer, attorney Wayne Wannabey, has been contacted by Mr. Hugh Bilditt, president of Overnight Construction Company. Overnight wants to enter into an agreement with Mr. Les A. Thanaday, a local business consultant, to assist in the purchase, sale, construction, and completion of homes developed by the builder. Overnight plans to pay Thanaday 2 percent of the purchase price of any home for a period of two years. The parties are concerned about such provisions in the agreement as compensation, assignment, attorney fees and costs, termination of the agreement, entirety, severability, interpretation, notices, and any other provisions deemed advisable. Mr. Wannabey has asked you to prepare a draft of a contractual agreement between the parties from the form agreement.

A. From the student template retrieve act14.doc. This document is a contractual agreement form to be completed with the information provided in the scenario. Refer to the chapter for examples.

B. Save this information on the template as agrmnt.doc.

C. Print one copy for your instructor. Make sure your name appears for identification purposes.

Chapter 15

Law of Business Organizations

There is a tide in the affairs of men which, taken at the flood, leads on to Fortune; Omitted, all the voyage of their life is bound in shallows and in Miseries. On such a full sea we are now afloat, and we must take the current When it serves, or lose our ventures.

William Shakespeare, *Julius Caesar*

business enterprise

Objectives

After completing this chapter, you will be able to:

1. Describe a sole proprietorship.

2. Discuss the advantages and disadvantages of a sole proprietorship.

3. Understand partnerships.

4. Summarize the provisions of a general partnership agreement.

5. Discuss the characteristics of a corporation.

6. Understand the steps in the creation of a corporation.

The selection of a form of business ownership is determined by the nature of the business and concerns over control, taxes, and liability for claims against the business. The decision to start a commercial enterprise involves a choice as to the form of ownership. A **business enterprise** is the expenditure of time, labor, skill, technology, management, and capital in the commencement of an undertaking for profit.

The business enterprise may take one of three basic forms:

- sole proprietorship

- partnership

- corporation

The selection of the best form of ownership for an individual or group of persons will depend on a number of factors, including management preference, the number of owners, the method of financing, the cost of the undertaking, the continuity of existence of the venture, and the applicable federal and state tax laws.

239

SOLE PROPRIETORSHIPS

sole proprietorship

The **sole proprietorship** is the simplest form of business enterprise. A business enterprise in which one person owns all of the assets is a sole proprietorship. Along with being the sole owner of all the assets, the sole proprietor is also individually liable for the debts of the business and is entitled to all the profits.

The sole proprietorship provides the small business owner with a number of advantages over the other forms of business enterprise. The advantages of a sole proprietorship are:

- Full management authority—the sole owner has the authority to manage the business without needing to obtain permission from a partner or board of directors.

- Minimal formalities to operate the business—most states only ask that the name of the business be registered.

- Low cost of organization—the cost of organizing a sole proprietorship is minimal compared to other forms of business ownership.

- Income tax benefits—the sole owner is taxed at an individual tax rate, rather than a corporate rate, which may be higher.

The sole proprietorship has several disadvantages when compared to the other forms of business ownership. In addition to limited growth from restricted capital, the disadvantages of a sole proprietorship are:

- Unlimited liability—the owner is solely responsible for all debts and torts.

- Lack of business continuity—the business terminates upon the death or resignation of the sole proprietor.

- No diversity of management—there may be a lack of needed expertise to handle every aspect of the business.

- Difficulty of transferability—the business may not be marketable because it is so closely linked with the original owner's good will.

- Taxation—if the business is too successful, the sole proprietor may have to pay taxes at a high tax rate.

The sole proprietorship form of business ownership does not involve the creation of a separate legal entity, as with the partnership and the corporation. The business is an extension of the individual, who is responsible for all aspects of the enterprise.

PARTNERSHIPS

The foundation of the law of partnership arises from common law, the law of contracts, and from the Uniform Partnership Act. The National Conference of Commissioners on Uniform State Laws of the American Bar Association approved the act in 1914 and recommended its adoption by state legislatures. Most states have now ratified the Uniform Partnership Act in some form to apply to those situations where there is no written contractual agreement between the parties or where the written agreement fails to address some matter of concern.

GENERAL PARTNERSHIP

There are two basic partnership forms: the general partnership and the limited partnership. The essential nature of either type of partnership as a form of business ownership is the contract between the partners of the business that defines the relationship and determines its type. A **general partnership** is a contract between two or more individuals to commit their resources to a business enterprise and to share in the profits and losses.

A partnership may exist without the benefit of a written agreement, but the majority of formal partnership enterprises are based on a written contract. Thus, the nature of a general partnership can be described as consisting of:

- a mutual agreement in writing

- two or more competent persons

- a lawful business

- sharing of the profits and losses

A *mutual agreement* in a partnership refers to the contractual agreement between the partners. The principles of contract law apply to any partnership agreement requiring that the essential elements be present, including formal execution. To be valid, there must be a capacity to contract, an offer and acceptance, consideration, and legality. In other words, there must be a "meeting of the minds" essential to the formation of a contract.

A partnership exists between *two or more persons,* which distinguishes it from a sole proprietorship. Those "persons" are not limited to individuals, but may be other partnerships, corporations, or any other association. The concept is simply that of more than one entity acting together for a common goal.

Partnerships exist to carry on a *lawful business* for profit. That business may be a trade, occupation, manufacturing, profession, art, or other enterprise permitted by law and not in violation of public policy.

Finally, a partnership exists for the partners to *share in the profits and losses.* This is the essence of a partnership: an intention to earn a profit and share in the proceeds, along with a willingness to risk a loss and share in its burden. The benefit and the burden need not be equal between the partners. The agreement between the partners determines the proportionate distribution of the profits and the burden of any loss.

ADVANTAGES AND DISADVANTAGES

When compared with the sole proprietorship and the corporation, the partnership has certain advantages and distinct disadvantages. These matters should be evaluated by an attorney. The advantages of a partnership are:

- shared responsibility

- ease of formation

- greater talent and capital base

- income tax advantages

Each partner has equal authority with the other partners, unless otherwise stated in the agreement. Along with equal authority comes the ability to share in the management responsibilities associated with any business operation, allowing each partner the opportunity to better concentrate his or her efforts in the production aspects of the enterprise.

Many individuals are able to benefit from a partnership's multiple advantages. For others, it may present some disadvantages that make another form of ownership preferable. The potential disadvantages of a general partnership are:

- unlimited personal liability

- diffuse management

- dissolution through death or resignation

- income tax

The prospect of unlimited personal liability is the major disadvantage of the partnership form of business ownership. The primary concern with most individuals contemplating a partnership is that there is no protection of their personal assets from business debts. Each partner is personally liable for the debts of the partnership, including contractual obligations and acts of negligence committed by any partner on behalf of the business. Each partner is entirely liable for all of the debts, regardless of his or her proportionate share of the profits and losses. This operates to the disadvantage of a wealthy partner who may be called upon to carry a greater burden of debt.

Since each partner is on an equal level and is entitled to as much say in the management of the business as the other partners, confusion may arise unless a specific partner is designated to handle management. If there is no designation made for management, a majority of the partners try to agree on an issue to avoid difficulties.

The law in most states provides that a partnership dissolves upon the death or resignation of a partner. Unless contingencies are provided for such occurrences in the partnership agreement, the business can fall into a state of disarray and can require restructuring at the moment of dissolution. To avoid problems and maintain continuity of the business, provision should be made in the partnership agreement to cover such contingencies.

The income tax disadvantage can occur if the partners are earning a substantial income that places them in a tax bracket that exceeds the tax rate for corporations. The income from a partnership business that is passed through to the partners individually is taxed at a higher rate than if they had formed a corporation and were taxed at the corporate rate.

RIGHTS AND DUTIES OF GENERAL PARTNERS

The relationship of the partners is controlled by the terms of the partnership agreement. A well-drafted agreement will reflect the nature of that relationship concerning:

- fiduciary duty of a partner

- property interests of a partner

- management responsibilities of a partner

- right of indemnification of a partner

Each of the partners stands in a fiduciary relationship to the others—a duty to act on another's behalf in good faith and trust. The law imposes a duty on each partner to act in good faith, trust, and full disclosure to benefit the partnership and the other partners.

The property interests of the partnership specified in the agreement usually give each partner the status of co-owner. The interest in partnership property held by each owner is called a **tenancy in partnership.**

tenancy in partnership

Such a tenancy gives each partner an equal ownership interest in the property as a whole, but that interest may not be sold or assigned without the consent of the other partners.

A significant right of partners is the right of indemnification—the right that one partner has against the other to be made whole and to be reimbursed for some loss that has been incurred. In practice, this means that if one partner has had a judgment secured against him or her for a partnership obligation, he or she has a right to be reimbursed from the other partner(s) for the loss.

LIMITED PARTNERSHIP

A limited partnership is the other major type of partnership. The limited partnership offers certain advantages over a general partnership, yet also has certain disadvantages, and therefore is limited in its use. In most states, a limited partnership is governed by state statutes adopted from the Uniform Limited Partnership Act proposed by the American Bar Association.

A **limited partnership** is a form of partnership requiring at least one general partner and one limited partner. A limited partner is one who has contributed capital and shares in the profits but has no role in the management of the business. Limited partners face no liability beyond the original contribution. A limited partnership can be distinguished by the following characteristics:

- an agreement with one or more general partners and one or more limited partners

- a contribution of capital only

- a share in the profits

- no role in the day-to-day management of the business

- liability limited to the original contribution

Limited partners are not subject to the terms and conditions of the general partnership agreement. Their rights and obligations are determined by the limited partnership agreement and the laws of the state of the principal place of business of the enterprise.

The limited partner has certain advantages in his relationship with a general partner not found exclusively between general partners. Those advantages are:

- limited liability

- income tax

- transferability of interest

The primary advantage of entering into a limited partnership relationship is the *limited liability* faced by the limited partner. The role of a limited partner is more that of a passive investor than an active participant in the business enterprise. Should the general partnership incur substantial debts or liabilities, the personal assets of the limited partner cannot be used to satisfy those obligations, as can the assets of a general partner.

This type of partnership provides the limited partner with an advantage from the standpoint of *income tax* exposure. The limited partner is taxed on income from the partnership personally. Those in a relatively low income tax bracket will not be taxed on the partnership as much as on other forms of investment. Also, losses of the partnership may be used to offset any other income that may be received.

Unlike a general partner, a limited partner has an interest that is easily transferable in most cases. The interest may pass through an estate, be the subject of a gift, or be sold to another investor. Many limited partnerships are traded actively as a form of security and are subject to government regulation.

The distinct disadvantage in a limited partnership is based on the lack of any management role. The limited partner is said to be a "silent partner" when it comes to any active contribution to the running of the business. The direction of the partnership is controlled by the general partner or partners, and the limited partner must rely on the sound business management decisions of the general partner(s).

JOINT VENTURE

A **joint venture** is another form of business enterprise, similar to a partnership, that is engaged in the joint undertaking of a particular transaction for profit. A joint venture is a temporary contractual association of two or more individuals or businesses that agree to share in the responsibilities, profits, and losses of a common enterprise. The joint

limited partnership

joint venture

venture is different from a partnership because it does not involve a continuing relationship among the parties. It is characterized by the following:

- contractual relationship between two or more persons

- a one-time joint undertaking

- contribution of assets by all parties

- right to manage and direct policy by all parties

- sharing of the profits and losses

- personal liability of the parties

- limited duration

- taxed personally to the individual parties

A joint venture typically is a new business that exists only for the length of time required to complete the project. A joint venture is subject to the same principles and limitations of the general partnership in the preparation of the agreement. The elements of the agreement are the same, and consideration is given to each concern, but for a limited purpose and duration.

DISSOLUTION OF A PARTNERSHIP

dissolution

The **dissolution** of a partnership is distinguished from the termination or winding up of the partnership as contemplated by the partnership agreement. The term *dissolution* refers to a change in the relationship of the partners as a result of one or more partners leaving the partnership. The Uniform Partnership Act provides the rules for the orderly dissolution of a partnership. The partnership ceases to exist upon dissolution, but it is still necessary for the partners to proceed to terminate the business, satisfy obligations, and distribute the assets. Dissolution is the first step in an orderly process of the termination of a partnership relationship.

The orderly dissolution process is best accomplished through the execution of a dissolution agreement, which is a formal contractual agreement between the partners to wind up the partnership business and terminate its existence. A simple dissolution agreement will contain the following elements:

- an identification of the parties

- a statement of termination

- an agreement to liquidate

- an execution

Illustration 15-1 provides a simple dissolution agreement.

A partnership may face a termination other than the orderly voluntary dissolution by agreement, and, if so, then the provisions of the general partnership agreement regarding arbitration will apply. The dissolution agreement serves the purpose of providing an orderly termination of business without the expense and delay of litigation.

GENERAL PARTNERSHIP AGREEMENT

A partnership relationship is the product of a negotiated agreement among the principals. A written partnership agreement is advisable due to the complex nature of the agreement and the wide variety of its provisions. Although most states have enacted the Uniform Partnership Act establishing the rights and duties of the partners, that act serves only to enforce those rights where the agreement is silent or nonexistent. It is best to have the agreement specifically set forth the understanding between the partners.

DISSOLUTION AGREEMENT

THIS AGREEMENT made this 31st day of April, 1999, by and between REX KING, COURTNEY QUEEN, AND MARSHALL SQUIRE, of the city of Orange, state of Wyoming,

WHEREAS, the parties to this Agreement have conducted a Partnership under the firm name of KING, QUEEN & SQUIRE, and;

WHEREAS, the parties are desirous of withdrawing from the Partnership and all parties have agreed that the Partnership shall be dissolved and terminated, and;

WHEREAS, the parties have agreed that the assets of the Partnership shall be promptly liquidated and the Partnership terminated and closed;

NOW, THEREFORE, it is mutually agreed that the Partnership existing between the parties to this Agreement shall be liquidated and dissolved at as early a date as can be practically accomplished without loss to the parties in interest and the net assets realized, after paying all debts and expenses of liquidating the assets and caring for the property of the Partnership, shall be divided equally between the parties.

IN WITNESS WHEREOF, the parties have executed this Agreement.

_____
REX KING

_____
COURTNEY QUEEN

_____
MARSHALL SQUIRE

Illustration 15-1
Dissolution Agreement

A well-drafted general partnership agreement will specifically set forth the understanding of the partners on the following matters:

- Title—this will identify the nature of the agreement in establishing a partnership.

- Names and addresses of the partners—the first article of the agreement should contain the name and address of each of the general partners.

- Name and domicile of the partnership—the name of the partnership should be set forth fully, along with the principal place of business.

- Duration of the agreement—depending on the purpose of the business enterprise and the intention of the partners, the agreement should reflect the duration contemplated.

- Contribution of the partners—this reflects the amount of money and property, either real or personal, that each of the partners originally contributed to the business.

- Allocation of expenses—provide for the payment of the normal operating expenses of the business from the general account of the partnership, or from a separate account for wages if desired for accounting purposes.

- Ownership of partnership assets—the ownership of assets should be in the partnership name.

- Accounting procedures—this includes the understanding between the partners regarding the books and records of the business, the fiscal year, the accounting procedures, the right of inspection, and the location of the books of account.

- Distribution of profits and losses—this reflects the percentage share distributed to each partner.

- Liability of the partners to each other—make clear the conditions of liability among the partners and the liability of the partnership to others and any understanding as to the indemnification of one partner by the partnership for any obligation incurred in the ordinary course of business.

- Compensation of the partners—the partners' understanding of their salaries, draws, vacations, and other benefits should be spelled out.

- Effect of the death or resignation of a partner—detail the understanding of the partners as to the conditions of purchase and the reorganization of the partnership.

- An alternative form of dispute resolution—clarify the means of the resolution of disputes between the partners through arbitration.

- Termination of the partnership—any matter contemplated by the partners requiring termination, the procedures, and the distribution of assets may be established by the agreement.

- The execution of the agreement—all partners must sign and date the agreement for it to be valid.

A well-drafted general partnership agreement must reflect the nature of the partnership business. For instance, the provisions necessary for a real estate investment group will vary from those essential to commercial architects. The elements outlined are suggested for most situations and will meet most partnership needs. Some additional provisions to be considered are:

- notice provisions

- modification or amendment of the agreement

- construction of the agreement

- costs and attorneys fees

- voting

- limitations on partnership indebtedness

- life insurance on the partner's lives

No single agreement will suffice for all situations, and individual state laws must be consulted prior to the preparation of any general partnership agreement. Appendix D provides an example of a general partnership agreement.

CORPORATIONS

The transaction of business in the United States is unlimited in its scope and purpose. The enterprise established to accomplish that purpose may be for commerce and trade, manufacturing, banking or professional service. It may be a "for-profit" enterprise, as many are, or it may be a "not-for-profit" organization typically found with religious, educational, and charitable functions. The corporate form of business ownership may be for any purpose that is legal and permitted by state law.

CHARACTERISTICS OF A CORPORATION

The form of business ownership known as a **corporation** is a legal entity chartered by a state government having a legal existence separate and distinct from the person(s) who own it. It has the same rights and privileges guaranteed by law for citizens; it can sue and be sued, enter into contracts, and be punished for crimes.

A corporation has four distinguishing characteristics that separate it from the other forms of business ownership:

- limited liability

- centralized management

- continuity of existence

- ease of transferability of ownership

The concept of *limited liability* refers to the absence of personal liability of the owners of a corporation for corporate debts. The individual owners of the business risk losing only the amount of their initial investment. With sole proprietorships and partnerships, the owners face personal liability for all business debts.

The feature of *centralized management* also distinguishes the corporation from other forms of business ownership. The corporate governmental structure can best be compared to a pyramid, the base of which is formed by the owners of the business, the **shareholders.** The shareholder/owners elect the **board of directors**—the persons appointed to manage the affairs of the business.

The board of directors establishes corporate policy in accordance with the direction of the stockholders. The board of directors, in turn, appoints the **officers** of the corporation, who are those persons charged with carrying out the wishes of the board of directors for

corporation

shareholders
board of directors

officers

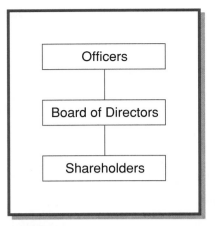

Illustration 15-2
Corporate Structure

the day-to-day management of the business. The pyramidal structure, where each level of the corporate governmental structure is directly responsible to the level below, would appear as presented in Illustration 15-2.

The third unique feature of a corporation is its *continuity of existence.* Most corporations are formed to exist perpetually until dissolved. Unlike a sole proprietorship or partnership, where the death or resignation of an owner terminates the business, a corporation continues to operate despite any turnover in its ownership through a transfer of its shares of stock.

The final distinguishing feature that separates a corporation from the other forms of business ownership is the *ease of transferability* of that ownership. An owner's interest in a corporation is represented by shares of stock. A **share** of stock is the unit into which the ownership of the business is divided.

Each individual owner of a corporation owns a specific number of units, represented by the number of shares of stock that have been purchased. Unless the owners have placed some restriction on the transfer of a share, stock may be freely bought and sold, devised by will, or given to another person as the subject of a gift or trust. Regardless of the type of transfer, the new owner of the stock takes the place of the previous owner, with all the rights and privileges of a shareholder.

These four unique features of a corporation distinguish it from the sole proprietorship and the partnership. It must be kept in mind that the corporation exists as a result of state statutory authorization. Most state corporate laws are patterned after the Model Business Corporation Act. The laws of an individual state must be consulted whenever any document related to the formation or government of a corporation is to be developed. In addition, there is a body of federal law arising from the Securities Act of 1933, along with the Securities Exchange Act of 1934, which governs the sale of shares of stock to the public. Also, corporations are subject to the tax laws of the United States and its individual states where applicable.

CORPORATE AUTHORITY

Consistent with the centralized management of a corporation and characteristic of its nature, a corporation has certain rights and powers separate from its owners, termed **corporate authority.** Illustration 15-3 presents § 3.02 of the Model Business Corporation Act, setting forth a model for the extent of corporate authority.

Corporate authority is statutory in origin and, therefore, does not find its origin in the common law, as do the rights of individuals. If there is no statutory authorization of authority to act in a certain manner, then the corporation does not have such authority.

share

corporate authority

General Powers

Unless its articles of incorporation provide otherwise, every corporation has perpetual duration and succession in its corporate name and has the same powers as an individual to do all things necessary or convenient to carry out its business and affairs, including without limitation power:

(1) to sue and be sued, complain and defend in its corporate name;

(2) to have a corporate seal, which may be altered at will, and to use it, or a facsimile of it, by impressing or affixing it or in any other manner reproducing it;

(3) to make and amend bylaws, not inconsistent with its articles of incorporation or with the laws of this date, for managing the business and regulating the affairs of the corporation;

(4) to purchase, receive, lease, or otherwise acquire, and own, hold, improve, use, and otherwise deal with, real or personal property, or any legal or equitable interest in property, wherever located;

(5) to sell, convey, mortgage, pledge, lease, exchange, and otherwise dispose of all or any part of its property;

(6) to purchase, receive, subscribe for, or otherwise acquire; own, hold, vote, use, sell, mortgage, lend, pledge, or otherwise dispose of; and deal in and with shares or other interests in, or obligation of, any other entity;

(7) to make contracts and guarantees, incur liabilities, borrow money, issue its notes, bonds, and other obligations (which may be convertible into or include the option to purchase other securities of the corporation), and secure any of its obligations by mortgage or pledge of any of its property, franchises, or income;

(8) to lend money, invest and reinvest its funds, and receive and hold real and personal property as security for repayment;

(9) to be a promoter, partner, member, associate, or manager of any partnership, joint venture, trust or other entity;

(10) to conduct its business, locate offices, and exercise the powers granted by this Act within or without this state;

(11) to elect directors and appoint officers, employees, and agents of the corporation, define their duties, fix their compensation, and lend them money and credit;

(12) to pay pensions and establish pension plans, pension trusts, profit sharing plans, share bonus plans, share option plans, and benefit or incentive plans for any or all of its current or former directors, officers, employees, and agents;

(13) to make donations for the public welfare or for charitable, scientific, or education purposes;

(14) to transact any lawful business that will aid governmental policy;

(15) to make payments or donations, or do any other act, not inconsistent with law, that furthers the business and affairs of the corporation.

Illustration 15-3
§ 3.02 of the Model Business Corporation Act

TYPES OF CORPORATIONS

The type of corporation may vary, depending on the nature of the business, the form of stock ownership, and its financing. There are five major types of corporate structure:

- Business corporation—the most common form found in the modern commercial setting, it extends from the smallest business for profit operating on a local level to the largest companies that are publicly owned and doing business on a global basis.

- Professional corporation—a corporation is formed for the purpose of rendering professional services within a recognized profession.

- Not-for-profit corporation—a corporation is created for some charitable, religious, educational, or benevolent purpose.

- "S" corporation—a small business corporation is formed under Subchapter S of § 1361 of the Internal Revenue Code, available in a situation where a limited number of shareholders elect to have the income and losses of the corporation taxed to each personally, thus avoiding the corporate income tax.

- Close corporation—in this corporation, shares of stock are owned by one person or a closely knit group of shareholders, such as a family.

The determination of the type of corporate structure is based on the form of stock ownership, the purpose of the corporation, and its financial basis. The documents used in the formation of the corporation are essentially the same for each type of corporate structure.

LIMITED LIABILITY COMPANY

limited liability company

A relatively recent development involves a hybrid unincorporated association known as a **limited liability company,** abbreviated LLC or LC. A limited liability company is an association combining the best of the Subchapter S corporation and the partnership into a new legal entity. In 1977 the state of Wyoming became the first state to offer the LLC, but it was not until 1988 that the Internal Revenue Service confirmed that the Wyoming legal entities would be treated as partnerships for taxation purposes.

States try to foster a favorable business climate by offering the LLC as a means to "pass through" the income of the business to the owners, as in a partnership. This can also be done in the form of an "S" corporation, but the Internal Revenue Service has placed a number of restrictions upon the makeup of that form of ownership.

Typically, the LLC has no limitation on the number of shareholders, does not ban nonresident ownership, and provides for multiple classes of shares of stock. As with the corporate form of ownership, the LLC has limited liability for its owners. The owner's personal assets are not at risk to business-related obligations, as they are with the partnership.

Another feature of the LLC that sets it apart from the partnership is the role of management for the "partners." In a true partnership, there are limitations in most states regarding the management role to be played by limited partners. In the LLC, there are no such restrictions. The LLC protects each of the partners personally, without imposing a limitation on their management role.

The statutes of the state of organization should be consulted before attempting to create this type of legal entity. The majority of the states providing for the LLC have a prescribed procedure for the establishment of the entity that includes the filing of its documentation. Although there may not be articles of incorporation, there will be requirements for the submission of the company's Articles of Organization before the issuance of its recognition. The statutes of the state of organization need to be consulted for the specific requirements.

FORMATION OF A CORPORATION

The formation of a separate legal entity created under the state laws governing corporations is a relatively simple process prescribed by state law. There are, however, certain preliminary concerns to be addressed between the attorney and the client seeking incorporation. Once those matters have been settled, then the preparation of the documents to form the corporation can be accomplished on a step-by-step basis.

A checklist should be developed as a preliminary step in the preparation of the documents needed to accomplish the formation of a corporation. Illustration 15-4 provides an example of a basic checklist to obtain the client information necessary to incorporate.

CHECKLIST FOR INCORPORATION

1. Name:
   - Call secretary of state for name availability
   - Reserve corporate name

2. Draft incorporation documents:
   - Articles
   - Designation of registered agent
   - Bylaws
   - Minutes and waiver or consent
   - Subscriptions
   - Stock certificates

3. Prepare necessary applications

4. Prepare miscellaneous letters:
   - Secretary of state/articles
   - City/Business licenses
   - IRS filing Subchapter S

5. Prepare minute books

6. Send articles to secretary of state

7. Send city/business licenses

8. Send application for IRS EIN

9. Send application for sales tax

10. Order corporate seal/corporate kit

11. Schedule organizational meeting of board of directors

12. Hold organization meeting of board

13. Prepare corporate bank account resolution

14. Prepare the waiver of notice of the annual shareholders' and directors' meeting

15. Prepare the annual shareholders' and directors' resolution

---

Illustration 15-4
Checklist for Incorporation

STEPS IN FORMATION OF A CORPORATION

After the type of corporation has been selected and the state of domicile has been chosen, there are procedural steps to be followed that are common to the laws of most states:

- preparation of a preincorporation agreement

- selection and reservation of the corporate name with the secretary of state

- preparation and filing of the articles of incorporation

- preparation of the stock subscription agreements and issuance of stock certificates

- preparation of the corporate bylaws

- first meeting of stockholders

- first meeting of board of directors

The laws of each state will vary slightly as to the formal requirements for each of these matters. The corporate laws of each state should be reviewed prior to formation.

ARTICLES OF INCORPORATION

articles of incorporation

Corporate existence begins with the filing of the articles of incorporation. The **articles of incorporation** is a legal instrument filed with the appropriate state agency, usually the secretary of state, which creates the corporate entity.

The document may also be referred to as the corporate charter, articles of association, certificate of incorporation, or articles of organization. The controlling state statutes dictate the contents of the instrument and usually include the following:

- Name and place of business of the corporation—the first article of the instrument should identify the new entity.

- Duration of the corporation—the corporation act of every state allows its corporations to have perpetual existence, meaning that if a death or disability should occur to an owner/shareholder of the corporation, the business will continue in existence.

- Purpose for which the corporation was formed—most states have very broad guidelines to encourage the expansion of commercial enterprise as long as the purpose is legal and does not violate public policy.

- Total number of shares of stock—most states require some information in the articles of incorporation regarding the shares of stock to be issued by the corporation.

- Board of directors—some states require an initial board of directors named in the formal articles of incorporation, which does not necessarily reflect the permanent board to be later elected by the shareholders pursuant to the corporate bylaws, and which may be for organizational purposes only.

- Identity of incorporators—the formal identification of the incorporators is accomplished with the incorporators clause in the body of the articles and the provision of their signatures for the execution of the instrument.

- Identity of registered agent—an individual is appointed by the corporation and is required by statute for the purpose of receiving service of process, giving the corporate entity a physical existence.

- Date of incorporation—this establishes the commencement of the existence of the enterprise.

Some states require only a minimum of information, while others demand more detailed information. The corporate statutes of each state must be reviewed before preparation of the articles of incorporation. Some states may provide form documents for the sole purpose of filing the articles.

STOCK

Ownership of a corporation and its assets is represented by **stock.** Stock is the capital or principal fund of a corporation formed by the contributions of subscribers or the sale of shares. For an individual to have an ownership interest in a corporate business enterprise, a portion of the corporate stock must have been acquired through purchase, gift, or devise.

stock

STOCK SUBSCRIPTION AGREEMENT

In the formation of a future corporation, the incorporators or promoters may agree to purchase shares of stock in the new venture once it has been formally established. The agreement to commit to the purchase of a set number of shares of stock of the new corporation at a stated price is called a **stock subscription agreement.**

The agreement is a contract to be performed once the corporation has come into existence. Once the corporation is established, the shares of stock will be issued to the parties to the agreement, and those shares will be paid for by those individuals creating the corporate capital structure.

The stock subscription agreement should contain the following basic information:

stock subscription agreement

- names and addresses of the parties to the agreement

- number and type of shares agreed to be purchased

- price to be paid for the shares of stock

- date for issuance of stock and payment of price

The corporate laws of many states contain a provision that the agreement to purchase stock pursuant to a stock subscription agreement is irrevocable for a set period of time, such as six months. Illustration 15-5 provides an example of a stock subscription agreement.

STOCK CERTIFICATE

The documentary evidence of an individual's ownership in a corporation is represented by the **certificate of stock.** This certificate represents ownership similar to a document of title, entitling the owner of the stock to all the rights and privileges guaranteed by law and set forth in the corporate bylaws. The certificate is generally a preprinted form, which may vary from state to state, and contains the following information:

certificate of stock

- name of the corporation

- name of the owner of the stock

- number of shares represented and their type

- certificate number

To be valid, the shares must be formally executed by a corporate officer designated as having such authority by the corporate bylaws, usually the secretary. The reverse side of most certificates of stock contains the language and space for the owner of the shares of stock to endorse a transfer of those shares by sale, gift, or devise.

The corporation must also maintain its own records as to the identity of the shareholders of record. This is done through the maintenance of the **stock transfer ledger.** This record contains the identity of each owner of the shares of the corporation, the date of his or her purchase, and the record of the transfer of any of those shares (see Illustration 15-6).

stock transfer ledger

SUBSCRIPTION AGREEMENT

The undersigned incorporators of the corporation, CYBERSPACE, INC., pursuant to the Preincorporation Agreement signed by them, do severally subscribe for the number of shares of said corporation set opposite our signatures, and agree to purchase same from the corporation at Ten Dollars ($10) per share. The obligation of each of the undersigned shall not be dependent upon performance by any of the other signatories.

All subscriptions shall be payable at such time or times as the board of directors may determine, and shall be paid in cash.

IN WITNESS WHEREOF the subscribers have executed this subscription at the city of Cascade, state of Wyoming, this 31st day of October, 19__.

_____   _____   _____
Name and Signature of Subscriber   Number of Shares   Amount

Illustration 15-5
Stock Subscription Agreement

Illustration 15-6
Stock Transfer Ledger

CORPORATE BYLAWS

The corporation law of most states requires that the corporation adopt a set of rules that govern the internal operation of the business. The **bylaws** of a corporation are the rules and regulations that define the corporate structure and provide the rights and obligations of the officers, directors, and shareholders. The bylaws may be adopted by either the incorporators, the board of directors, or the shareholders upon formation of the corporation.

A well-drafted set of corporate bylaws should be specific in defining the basic rules of the business, addressing such areas as:

- location of the corporate office
- shareholders' meetings
- rights of shareholders
- number, duties, and obligations of directors
- removal of directors
- meetings of directors
- number, duties, and obligations of officers
- capital stock and dividends
- fiscal year of the corporation
- corporate seal
- adoption and amendment of bylaws

The specific language of each provision of the bylaws will vary greatly, depending on the nature of the business and the individual needs of the corporate owners and directors.

Most law firms have preprinted sets of corporate bylaws that have proven themselves to be effective in the establishment of the corporate laws. The corporate law of some states may dictate the content of the bylaws on such matters as the shareholders' meetings and should be consulted before preparation. Also, there are a number of form books available with sample language appropriate for most corporate enterprises.

CORPORATE MINUTE BOOK

The corporate record of the actions of the shareholders and directors of a corporation is kept in the **corporate minute book.** The book is generally maintained by the corporate attorney and contains:

- articles of incorporation
- corporate bylaws
- minutes of the initial organizational meeting
- minutes of the annual shareholders' meetings
- minutes of the annual board of directors meetings
- stock transfer ledger

A corporate minute book can be purchased from any reputable office supply facility and will contain samples of the documents, along with individual state statutory guidelines and blank stock certificates. The corporate seal can also be ordered with the minute book and used to authenticate corporate acts and resolutions.

bylaws

corporate minute book

CORPORATE ANNUAL REPORT

Most states require each corporation doing business to file a report for stockholders every year to be furnished to the proper state agency. An **annual report** is a statutory report to be filed with the local secretary of state, providing the basic information regarding the corporation and an identification of its officers.

annual report

A typical report should include:

- name of the corporation and its state of incorporation

- date of incorporation

- address of the corporate office

- corporate federal identification number

- name and address of the corporate registered agent

- optional information relating to capital structure and corporate indebtedness

The annual report is a matter of public record for every corporation doing business within a state and is open for public inspection.

SUMMARY

A partnership is based on an agreement between two or more persons to engage in some lawful business enterprise. The partners must agree to share their talent and pool their resources in exchange for a proportional division of the profits and the losses. The essence of the partnership is the agreement. The partnership agreement is a complex document that begins with an understanding between the prospective partners on the fundamental nature of the partnership. The formation of the agreement begins with the resolution of each of the major areas of concern. The issues to be resolved extend from the simple matter of the partnership name to the detailing of the division of profits and losses. The Uniform Partnership Act has been passed in most states and is the law governing those partnerships that have no written agreement or where the written instrument is silent as to some material element of the business relationship. The laws of the state of domicile of the partnership must be consulted before preparation of any agreement.

The corporate form of business ownership is an association conforming with state statutory requirements establishing a distinct legal entity. That entity exists independent from its individual owners and survives their resignation or death. The corporation can sue and be sued, enter into contracts, and must pay taxes in its own right. The process of the formation of a corporation begins with a decision as to the type of corporation to be established, a decision dictated by the size of the enterprise and its purpose. The preincorporation agreement and the stock subscription agreement among the incorporators serves to bind them by contract to the completion of the formation process. The articles of incorporation filed with the state serve to charter the entity, providing it with a legal identity. The organizational meetings serve to organize the corporate government in order to commence operations following the adoption of the bylaws that provide the rules for conducting the business.

Chapter Activities

Review Questions

1. List the three forms that a business enterprise may take.

2. Discuss the advantages of a sole proprietorship.

3. What is a general partnership?

4. List the advantages of a partnership.

5. List the disadvantages of a partnership.

6. How does the partnership agreement reflect the nature of the relationship between the partners?

7. What is a corporation?

8. List and discuss the four distinguishing characteristics of a corporation.

9. Summarize the five major types of corporate structure.

10. List the procedural steps to be taken in the formation of a corporation.

Computer Activity

Your office has been contacted by three individuals to form a corporation in your state. The promoters are Lief Pyle, Arnold Prunes, and Stan Strait, Sr. They want to name their corporation Roaring Twenties, Ltd., and will be in the business of land development. In particular, they will be developing a senior citizen theme park called the Victorian Village to provide senior citizens with a unique return to a kinder, gentler time where the old values in entertainment can be appreciated without the commercialization of today. A shopping mall, condominiums, and single-family homes are also contemplated.

The three promoters will serve as the incorporators, directors, and stockholders. They plan to contribute $100,000 each for their stock and wish to authorize 100,000 shares with a value of $100. Pyle will be the designated registered agent.

A. From the student template retrieve act15.doc. This document is a sample articles of incorporation form. Key in the appropriate information to form Roaring Twenties, Ltd. with the information provided in the scenario. Refer to the chapter for examples.

B. Save this information on the template as articls.doc.

C. Print one copy for your instructor. Make sure your name appears for identification purposes.

Chapter 16

Law of Real Estate

As a man is said to have a right to his property, he may be equally said to have a property in his rights.

James Madison (1792)

Objectives

After completing this chapter, you will be able to:

1. Describe the classification of property and its form of ownership.

2. Identify the forms of conveyance of property.

3. Outline the requirements of a contract for the sale of real property and prepare the document.

4. Distinguish between the types of deeds and prepare the documents.

5. Identify the basic elements of a mortgage and a promissory note.

6. Prepare a mortgage and promissory note.

A legal office involved in property transactions requires a legal office assistant with an understanding of real property law. The legal office assistant must be aware of the types of property, estates, and forms of ownership before any preparation of deeds or mortgages can be commenced.

FUNDAMENTALS OF REAL PROPERTY LAW

Before considering the actual preparation of the necessary documents required to complete a real estate transaction, it is helpful to understand the basic concepts of real property law. The law of real property in the United States is an outgrowth of the **feudal system,** the social, political, and economic system that formed the basis of the English common law following the Norman Conquest in 1066.

The wealth of an individual in feudal England was measured by property ownership and its possession. The right of possession of real property is

feudal system

259

the basis for deciding the nature and extent of property ownership. To prevent the many fraudulent commercial practices of the day, the English Parliament enacted the *Statute of Frauds and Perjuries* in 1677, requiring that certain types of transactions involving property be formalized by a written instrument. Specifically, the *Statute of Frauds* requires that any **conveyance,** a transfer of an interest in real property, must be in writing. Nearly every jurisdiction in the United States has adopted the *Statute of Frauds* in some modified form.

The law of the particular state in which property is located governs the modern real estate transaction and its requirements. This chapter will address the various documents required to satisfy the statutory requirements of most states and accomplish the orderly transfer of an interest in real estate.

CLASSIFICATION OF PROPERTY

Basic to an understanding of the documents required in a real estate transaction is the manner in which the law classifies property itself. A knowledge of real property law involves an appreciation of the nature of an estate and its forms of ownership before there can be any transfer of an interest in that property.

There are two basic classifications of property: tangible and intangible. **Tangible property** is that which has some form or physical nature and that may be felt or touched. Tangible property may be either *real property* or *personal property* (i.e., the family farm or automobile).

Real property is land and whatever is built on or growing on or affixed to land. The owner of real property owns the land, anything growing on it, and any fixture permanently attached to the land. An **appurtenance** is the term applied to any structure permanently attached to the land, such as a shed or a fence surrounding an individual's backyard.

Personal property is all tangible property that is not considered real property. Property other than land and its appurtenances is considered personal property, a *chattel.* A chattel is an item of personal property that may be moved and that has no connection to real property, such as the very chair upon which an individual might sit. In this chapter we will concern ourselves with the law relating to real property and its documents.

Intangible property is that which has no physical existence of its own but stands as representative of something that is tangible and has intrinsic value. Promissory notes, certificates of stock, and copyrights are examples of intangible property, where the chief value exists in what the intangible property represents.

ESTATES IN REAL PROPERTY

An **estate in real property** refers to the type and extent of ownership that an individual has in the property. The owner of real property has three fundamental rights associated with ownership: (1) possession, (3) use and (3) disposition of the property. The person in whom these rights are vested is said to have **title,** consisting of the formal right of ownership of real property.

Evidence of a valid title to property is reflected in a document of transfer of title, known as a **deed.**

Estates in real property can be classified as **freehold** or **non-freehold estates.** A freehold estate is the right of title in land for an indeterminate period. A non-freehold estate exists where an individual is entitled to possession of real property, but does not have title to that property, nor is there an absolute right to dispose of the property.

FORMS OF OWNERSHIP

Real property may be owned either by an individual or by several individuals in one of a number of forms of joint or concurrent ownership. Ownership of real property by one

conveyance

tangible property

real property

appurtenance

personal property

intangible property

estate in real property

title

deed

freehold estate, non-freehold estate

person is called a **tenancy in severalty.** The owner of that property has all the rights of ownership, including possession, use, and disposition.

Concurrent ownership of real property occurs where two or more individuals own a single piece of property. The law treats the separate rights of ownership of the property—namely, possession, use, and disposition—differently, depending on the form of concurrent ownership and the relation of the owners to each other. There are four basic forms of concurrent ownership:

- tenancy in common

- joint tenancy

- tenancy by the entirety

- community property

A **tenancy in common** is the most basic form of concurrent ownership. It occurs where each owner of the property holds an undivided interest in all of the property. In this form of ownership, the parties are unified only by their right to possess the property. Each co-owner can obtain an interest by separate means, such as inheritance, gift, or purchase. If a co-owner dies, that owner's share passes to the owner's heirs and not to the co-owner, as occurs with other forms of concurrent ownership. By law in many states, if the necessary language and relationship are not specifically set forth to establish another form of concurrent ownership, then the law assumes that a tenancy in common exists as the presumed form of concurrent ownership.

A **joint tenancy** arises when two or more persons own property and are unified in their ownership based on these four unities:

- Unity of time—the interest originated at the same time.

- Unity of title—the interest was conveyed in a single title.

- Unity of interest—the interest of each owner is identical.

- Unity of possession—each owner has the right to occupy the property.

In addition, and most significantly, a joint tenancy carries with it a **right of survivorship,** meaning that at the moment of death of one joint owner, the property passes automatically to the remaining joint owner.

If any of the four unities fails, then the law presumes that a tenancy in common exists.

A **tenancy by the entirety** is a form of concurrent ownership that occurs between a husband and wife. It must have the four unities of a joint tenancy, along with a fifth unity, the unity of person. In most states, a dissolution of a marriage results in title to the property being held as a tenancy in common. The tenancy by the entirety carries with it a right of survivorship in which the death of one spouse results in the creation of a tenancy in severalty in the survivor.

Although the three forms of concurrent ownership already discussed come from the English common law, there is a fourth form of concurrent ownership that has its origins in the laws of Spain and France, namely, **community property.**

Community property creates a form of concurrent ownership for all property acquired by the husband and wife during marriage other than by gift or bequest.

CONTRACTS FOR SALE

The modern real estate transaction involves the transfer of title to real property through a sale of that property. The transaction commences with the decision of the owner to place the property for sale and proceeds through the negotiation of a contract for the transfer of

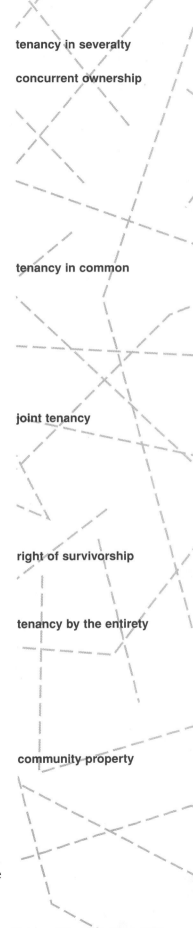

tenancy in severalty

concurrent ownership

tenancy in common

joint tenancy

right of survivorship

tenancy by the entirety

community property

title for a stated price to be paid by a willing buyer. A contract for sale and purchase of real property is a separate and distinct document from a deed. The function of the contract for sale and purchase of real property is to commence a process that results in the subsequent execution and delivery of the deed. This section will address the basic elements of a contract, as well as an analysis of the requirements for a contract for sale and purchase of real property. The form and nature of the deed will be considered separately.

ELEMENTS OF THE CONTRACT

Although chapter 14 examined the law of contracts in detail, for purposes of a discussion of the contract for sale and purchase of real property, some review is necessary. The contract becomes an agreement between the owner/seller and the purchaser/buyer to transfer title to a particular piece of land according to the terms of the contract. The *Statute of Frauds* in every state requires that the contract must be in writing where the subject of the contract is real property. The essence of a contract is to express that "meeting of the minds" necessary to establish an agreement.

PREPARATION OF THE CONTRACT

The contract for sale and purchase of real property must address multiple issues and, consequently, may be detailed and lengthy. Many states have simplified the procedure and now require that a standard form be used for all transactions. Whether a standard form is used or an original custom agreement is drafted, certain basic issues must be addressed. The following checklist is designed to assist in the preparation of the contract by illustrating the primary considerations:

- parties
- property description
- purchase price
- acceptance
- closing
- title
- warranties of the parties
- conditions of closing
- default
- mortgage
- miscellaneous provisions

Illustration 16-1 provides an example of a simple contract for the sale of real property. The contract for sale and purchase of real property represents the entire agreement between the parties and forms the basis for the transaction. The legal office assistant must exercise care and prudence in every detail of its preparation.

DEEDS

A deed is an important document in a modern real estate transaction because it is the formal, written instrument through which title to real property is conveyed. A deed is a conveyance of real property in writing when the title is transferred to another. Once that transfer has been completed, the deed becomes the evidence of ownership of real property. Each deed is subject to the law of the state in which the property is located.

CONTRACT FOR SALE OF RESIDENTIAL PROPERTY

This agreement is made in the county of Jay, state of Michigan, on July 30, 1999, by KIRTLAND WARBLE, of 14 Nest Egg Lane, Osceola, Michigan, hereinafter referred to as Seller, and FULVOUS GADWALL, of 919 Water Creek Road, Osceola, Michigan, hereinafter referred to as Purchaser.

In consideration of the covenants made each to the other, as herein set forth, the parties agree as follows:

SECTION ONE
PREMISES

Seller shall sell and convey and Purchaser shall purchase, on the terms and conditions hereinafter set forth, the real property, together with improvements thereon, consisting of a dwelling house, and all appurtenances thereto, situated in the city of Osceola, county of Jay, state of Michigan, at 919 Water Creek Road, more particularly described as Lot 22, Block Q, Audubon Preserve Estates, in the official records of the county of Jay, state of Michigan.

SECTION TWO
PURCHASE PRICE: TERMS OF PAYMENT

The full purchase price for the property is One Hundred and Twenty Thousand Dollars ($120,000), payable as follows: in cash or its equivalent at the time of closing.

SECTION THREE
DELIVERY OF DEED

DELIVERY OF DEED assurance of its payment satisfactory to Seller, Seller shall execute and deliver a deed describing the property and conveying the same to Purchaser or his nominee.

Illustration 16-1
Contract for Sale of Real Property

SECTION FOUR
TITLE

(a) Seller shall furnish for Purchaser's examination within thirty (30) days from this date a complete abstract of title or preliminary title report issued by Northern Gannet Title Company showing condition of the title of the property as of the date of issuance of the Abstract of Title. The Abstract of Title shall remain the property of Seller pending completion of this transaction.

(b) Title to the property shall be good and marketable, free and clear of all encumbrances, liens, restrictions, easements, defects and burdens, except unpaid taxes not delinquent and acceptable matters affecting title, if any.

(c) If any title restrictions, defects, or burdens appear on the Abstract of Title to which Purchaser objects, such objection shall be stated in writing to Seller, who shall be allowed a reasonable time, but not to exceed thirty (30) days, in which to correct the same. If Seller is unable or unwilling to do so, Purchaser at his or her option may either terminate this contract and recover his or her deposit and costs, or pursue any other remedy available to Purchaser in law or equity.

SECTION FIVE
CLOSING: TIME OF ESSENCE

Unless extended by written agreement of the parties, this contract shall be completed and the transaction closed on or before September 1, 19__. Time is of the essence in this contract.

Illustration 16-1
Contract for Sale of Real Property (continued)

SECTION SIX
TRANSFER OF PROPERTY

Possession of the property shall be delivered within ten (10) days after closing. Purchaser has inspected the property, including the improvements thereon, and accepts the same in their present condition. Seller shall maintain the improvements, including the plumbing, heating and electrical systems therein, in good working order to the time of transfer of possession, but all obligation of Seller with respect to maintenance shall terminate at the date of transfer. Risk of loss by fire or other casualty prior to closing shall be Seller's.

SECTION SEVEN
BINDING EFFECT

This contract shall insure to the benefit of and bind the heirs, personal representatives, and assigns of the respective parties.

Executed in duplicate on the day and year first above written.

_____
KIRTLAND WARBLE, Purchaser

_____
FULVOUS GADWALL, Seller

Illustration 16-1
Contract for Sale of Real Property (continued)

TYPES OF DEEDS

There are three types of deeds used to convey real property:

- general warranty deed

- special warranty deed

- quitclaim deed

The three are distinguished by the degree of promise by the seller to the buyer that the property may be used (enjoyed) free of the claims of others. A **general warranty deed** is one in which the seller guarantees the title against any defects.

The traditional covenants warranted by the seller to guarantee good, clear title are:

- right of possession

- quiet enjoyment—the right to use the land without fear of some adverse claim

- right to transfer ownership

- freedom from **encumbrances**—liens against the property

- defense of title—seller will indemnify the buyer for costs in defending title in a lawsuit

The legal office assistant should ensure that the language used is similar to the following covenant in a general warranty deed:

> AND grantor hereby covenants with said grantee that it is lawfully seised of said land in fee simple; that it has good right and lawful authority to sell and convey said land; that it hereby fully warrants the title to said land and will defend the dame against the lawful claims of all persons whomsoever, and that said land is free of all encumbrances.

The language necessary to achieve a valid warranty deed may be set by statute in many states. For instance, the state of Michigan provides the language of the warranty deed as shown in Illustration 16-2. With the provision of these warranties, the seller has guaranteed a clear title to the property to the buyer and will undertake to compensate the buyer for any loss. The general warranty deed is most commonly seen in the modern real estate transaction.

Similar to a general warranty deed is a **special warranty deed.** This type of deed is used where the seller only promises to defend the title against persons making a claim or demand through the seller.

That any conveyance of lands worded in substance as follows: "A.B. conveys and warrants to C.D. (here describe the premises) for the sum of (here insert the consideration)," the said conveyance being dated and duly signed, sealed, and acknowledged by the grantor, shall be deemed and held to be a conveyance in fee simple to the grantee, his heirs and assigns, with covenant from the grantor for himself and his heirs and personal representative, that he is lawfully seized of the premises, has good right to convey the same, and guarantees the quiet possession thereof that the same are free from all incumbrances, and that he will warrant and defend the title to the same against all lawful claims. M.S.A. § 565.151

Illustration 16-2
Michigan Warranty Deed Law

general warranty deed

encumbrances

special warranty deed

A **quitclaim deed** is merely a promise by the seller to release any claim that the seller may have had in the property. The seller makes no guarantees as to the title or any liens on the property. The effect of the quitclaim deed is to transfer only the title that the seller had in the property, however limited. Quitclaim deeds are commonly used to settle estate and divorce claims, as opposed to the sale and purchase of real property. Illustration 16-3 provides an example of a quitclaim deed.

PREPARATION OF THE DEED

Statutory forms for deeds exist in most states as the instrument to convey title to real property; while in other states, the bar association, title companies, real estate companies, or law firms will have prepared forms that comply with the state requirements for the preparation of a deed. Local statutes and forms should be consulted in the preparation of deeds. Most deed forms will include:

- caption
- preamble
- language of conveyance
- property description
- warranty clause
- proper execution

Caption. The caption to the deed form is the entitlement portion, indicating the type of deed that the document represents.

Preamble. The preamble of the deed sets forth the date of the execution of the document and the identity of the seller and buyer. The preamble should read:

> THIS WARRANTY DEED made and executed this 30th day of June 19__, by Martin Partwithitt of 123 North Main Street, city of Orange, county of Osceola, state of Michigan, hereinafter called the grantor, to Sandra Gottitall of 543 South Avenue, city of Orange, county of Osceola, state of Michigan, hereinafter called the grantee:

The preamble may then proceed to represent that not only are the parties to the instrument bound, but their successors, heirs, and assigns are also bound.

Language of Conveyance. The language of conveyance contained in the deed is the necessary portion stating that it is the intention of the seller to transfer an interest in the property. This clause of the deed may also be the appropriate place to recite the consideration. It should state:

> WITNESSETH: That the grantor, for and in consideration of the sum of One Hundred and Twelve Thousand Dollars ($112,000) and other valuable considerations, receipt whereof is hereby acknowledged, by these presents does grant, bargain, sell, alien, remise, release, convey, and confirm unto the grantee, all that certain land situated in . . .

The specific language may vary, depending on the extent of the interest conveyed by the grantor. If the deed is merely a quitclaim deed releasing only the grantor's interest, then the language will vary accordingly.

Property Description. The property description portion of the deed is part of the conveyance clause, providing an accurate and full legal description of the property. For instance:

> . . . all that certain land situated in the county of Osceola, state of Michigan, viz:
> Lot 11 in Block 79 of Harbor Sludge Estates, as per map or plat thereof, recorded in Plat Book 7, Page 382, of Public Records of Osceola County, Michigan.

QUITCLAIM DEED

THIS QUITCLAIM DEED, Executed this 30th day of June 1999, by KIRTLAND WARBLE, first part to FULVOUS GADWALL, whose post office address is 2254 Garden Path Lane, Storytown, Michigan, second party:

WITNESSETH, that the said first party, for and in consideration of the sum of Ten Thousand Dollars ($10,000) in hand paid by the said second party, the receipt whereof is hereby acknowledged, does hereby remise, release, and quitclaim unto the said second party forever, all the right, title, interest, claim, and demand that the said first party has in and to the following described lot, piece, or parcel of land, situate, lying and being in the county of Longago, state of Michigan, to-wit:

Lots 6 and 7, Block 105, Forest Estates, Fourth Addition, Longago County Public Records, Plat 435, Book U, Page 94.

TO HAVE AND TO HOLD the same together with all and singular the appurtenances whereunto belonging or in anywise appertaining, and all the estate, right, title, interest, lien, equity and claim, whatsoever of the said first party, either in law or equity, to the only proper use, benefit, and behalf of the said second party forever.

IN WITNESS WHEREOF, the said first party has signed and sealed these presents the day and year first above written.

Signed, sealed, and delivered

in the presence of:

Illustration 16-3
Quitclaim Deed

The abbreviation form "viz" is seen in formal documents and used in place of the word *namely.*

Warranty Clause. The warranty clause is that portion of the deed where the seller obligates himself or herself to defend the title conveyed against any lawful claims. It is in this clause that the grantor makes a specific representation as to the title:

> AND the grantor hereby covenants with said grantee that he or she is lawfully seized of said land in fee simple; that he or she has good right and lawful authority to sell and convey said land; that he or she hereby fully warrants the title to said land and will defend the same against the lawful claims of all persons whomsoever and that said land is free of all encumbrances.

The warranty language will vary slightly with the special warranty deed, and, of course, is not included in the quitclaim deed.

Proper Execution. The execution portion of the deed is the language that exists immediately above the signature lines at the end of the deed, depending on the number of sellers, and whether the seller is a corporation or not. With one seller, it should read:

> IN WITNESS WHEREOF the grantor has caused these presents to be executed in his or her name, and by his or her signature hereunto affixed, the day and year first above written.

Some states have mandatory statutory language that should be consulted before the preparation of any of the deed forms.

Every real estate transaction involves a contract for purchase and sale of real property and a deed. It is essential that the preparer of these documents consult the real estate law of the state in which the property is located or reference it on specific matters.

PROPERTY DESCRIPTION

All transactions involving real property necessitate an accurate identification of the exact parcel of property. Each document referring to a specific piece of property, whether it be a deed, mortgage, easement, or lease, requires a description of that parcel of property to identify it as the subject of the transaction. Therefore, the **legal description** of a piece of property becomes important in determining the enforceability of any document detailing the transaction.

legal description

The legal description of real property identifies a specific parcel of land with certain boundaries in a uniform and consistent manner, although that manner may vary from state to state.

An evaluation of real property to determine its boundaries and physical limits is called a **survey.** A surveyor gives an opinion about where a particular piece of property is located, following a review of written descriptions and field evaluation. The survey should contain:

survey

- an identification of the state and county where the surveyed property is located

- an indication of north

- a point of beginning

- courses and distances for each property line

- an identification of the surveyor

- the scale used

- a legend

The survey will supply a precise identification of the property involved in the transaction and will use a system of description uniform to that particular state.

Records required by law to be kept by a county clerk or other official are known as **public records.** These records are kept in an official capacity to give the general public notice of the information contained in those records. The effect of recording documents with the county clerk is to protect the parties to a transaction against the claims of a subsequent purchaser, creditor, or encumbrancer. The transaction between the parties need not be recorded to be valid. Most records of real property transactions are now kept on computers, facilitating their accessibility to the public.

PROMISSORY NOTES AND MORTGAGES

A real estate transaction may involve a large sum of money requiring that the purchaser obtain a loan to complete the sale. To obtain a loan for the purchase of real property, the purchaser must provide some guarantee to the lender that the money will be repaid as agreed in the contractual agreement between them. Therefore, the modern real estate transaction requires that the loan of money be evidenced by a written document in the form of a contract, known as a promissory note, and that security for the repayment of that money be provided for in a security document, called a mortgage. Mortgage transactions are subject to federal and state consumer credit protection laws which should be consulted before any transaction.

PROMISSORY NOTES

A **promissory note** is a promise in writing to pay a certain sum of money at a time stated, or on demand, to a person. In a real estate transaction, the note states the relationship of the parties to the loan. The lender is called the **mortgagor** and the borrower is called the **mortgagee.**

The note will also provide for a specified interest rate, along with a repayment schedule. A promissory note should include the following:

- identification of the parties

- the amount of the loan

- a repayment schedule

- default provisions

- security statement

- the signature of the borrower/mortgagor

Illustration 16-4 provides an example of a promissory note for a real estate transaction.

Parties. After the caption of the note, in some form identifying the nature of the document, comes the identification of the parties to the agreement. Not only should the contract represent the names of the lender/mortgagee and the borrower/mortgagor, it should also state their corporate and marital status.

> FOR VALUE RECEIVED, the undersigned Gideon P. Gordon and his wife, Gladys Q. Gordon, jointly and severally, promise to pay to the order of The Great Summit Savings and Loan Company, . . .

Further information may also be included in this clause to identify the parties, including their respective addresses and corporate status of the signer.

public records

promissory note

mortgagor
mortgagee

PROMISSORY NOTE

$80,000.00   Osceola, Michigan

Payable: November 30, 1999

FOR VALUE RECEIVED, I, ROSEY SPOONBILL, promise to pay to the order of ALVIN C. KESTREL, of 597 Wilderness Park Lane, Osceola, Michigan, the sum of Eighty Thousand Dollars ($80,000) with interest at the rate of seven (7) percent per annum on the unpaid balance, and said principal and interest shall be payable as follows:

Payable in equal monthly installments of Six Hundred Twelve Dollars ($612.00), principal and interest inclusive, for 130 months, commencing on the first day of December 1999, and continuing on the first day of each month thereafter, until fully paid; however, prepayment in full or a portion of the principal balance may be made at any time.

Additional payments may be made at any time and interest will be charged on the unpaid balance.

It is agreed that time is of the essence of this contract and that in the event of default in the making of any payment as herein provided for a period of thirty (30) days, the holder of this note may, at his option, declare all the remainder of said debt due and collectible, and any failure to exercise the said option shall not constitute a waiver of the right to exercise the same at any other time.

In the event of default in the making of any payments herein provided and in the event the whole of said debt is declared to be due, interest shall accrue on such past due interest at the rate of ten (10) percent per annum. I further waive demand, protest, and notice of demand, protest, and nonpayment.

GIVEN under the hand and seal of each party, the day and year first above written.

_____
ROSEY SPOONBILL

Illustration 16-4
Promissory Note

Amount of Loan. The promissory note must state the exact amount of the loan that constitutes the mortgage amount. In addition, this portion should also state the interest rate on the note, as well as whether it is an adjustable rate or fixed rate of interest.

> . . . promise to pay to the order of The Great Summit Savings and Loan Company the principal sum of Ninety-four Thousand Dollars ($94,000) with interest thereon from date at the fixed rate of 8.75 percent, per annum until maturity, payable as follows:

Repayment Schedule. Once the note has stated the principal and interest of the obligation, then the note should provide details regarding the agreed upon schedule for repaying the loan. The precise terms of the repayment schedule will vary greatly, depending on the size of the loan and the length of time over which payments are to be made.

> SAID principal and interest being payable in lawful money of the United States in equal monthly installments of Seven Hundred and Nine Dollars ($709) commencing on the 31st day of June 19__, and being payable monthly on the first day of each and every month, both principal and interest, until fully repaid, at lender's place of business, prepayment in full or a portion of the principal balance may be made at any time.

It is significant to note that any prepayment is to reduce the principal and not for the purpose of the prepayment of the interest.

Default Provisions. The promissory note must address the question of the remedies of the lender if there is a breach of the agreement by the borrower through nonpayment. If there is such a default, then the balance of the loan becomes due immediately through an *acceleration clause,* allowing the lender to proceed to judgment on the entire principal balance.

> IT IS AGREED that time is of the essence of this contract and that in the event of default in the making of any payment as herein provided for a period of thirty (30) days, the holder of this note may, at his/her option, declare all the remainder of said debt due and collectible, and any failure to exercise the said option shall not constitute a waiver of the right to exercise the same at any time.

This clause may also provide for any late charges, costs, or attorney's fees that may be incurred as a result of a default.

Statement of Security. The promissory note is secured by a mortgage on the property that is the subject of the transaction. That fact must be reflected in the note to provide for its enforceability. It may read as follow:

> This note is secured by a first mortgage of this date herewith, and is to be construed and enforced according to the laws of the state of Michigan, upon default in the payment of principal and/or interest when due.

The security is provided in the form of an assurance that the mortgagee will be furnished with a resource to be used in case of a failure of the mortgagor to pay the indebtedness on the note. The mortgage itself is enforceable only to the extent of the validity of the underlying obligation.

Signature of Borrower/Mortgagor. The note must bear the signature of the borrower/mortgagor to be binding on him or her. It is a form of a contractual agreement and must be executed with the same formalities as any other contract. It is not a requirement in most states that the note be acknowledged by a notary public, but the provision of the notary's signature aids in its enforcement.

MORTGAGES

A **mortgage** is a written instrument creating an interest in real property as security for the repayment of a debt. Under the English common law, mortgages were considered a type of conveyance of title. When the mortgage was paid in full, then the title was returned to the mortgagor.

The type of mortgage most commonly used in modern real estate transactions is known as a **conventional mortgage.** This is a security device used by the mortgagor to transfer a lien to the mortgagee or lending institution in return for part of the purchase price of the property. Such mortgages are referred to as **purchase money mortgages** when the parties to the transaction are private parties, as opposed to the involvement of a commercial lending institution. The conventional nature of the mortgage stems from the fact that the mortgagee looks only to the mortgagor and the property for security, and not to a third party such as the government for a guarantee of satisfaction.

Some creativity in mortgage loans has occurred with the recognition of the fact that a fluctuating economy causes significant changes in interest rates. Rather than offer a **fixed rate mortgage,** where the interest rate on the loan remains the same for the life of the mortgage, some lending institutions offer an **adjustable rate mortgage,** sometimes referred to as an ARM.

ARMs have a variable interest rate that is tied to an economic index, resulting in the rate moving up or down on a periodic basis. There is usually a limitation, such as 2 percent, on the extent to which the rate may vary. These mortgages also contain a provision that allows for conversion to a fixed rate mortgage.

Frequently observed in today's mortgage market is the form of loan that is insured or guaranteed by the government. An **FHA mortgage** involves a loan that is insured by the Federal Housing Administration. A **VA mortgage** is one in which the loan is insured by the Veterans' Administration.

These guaranteed loans consist of a conventional loan that involves a third party, the government, as the insurer of the obligation. This encourages lending institutions to consider the extension of a loan to individuals who might fail to qualify for a pure conventional loan based on a poor credit rating.

A mortgage loan requiring periodic payments for a specific length of time with the full principal balance due on maturity is termed a **balloon payment mortgage.** Such mortgages occur where the balance due is more than twice the amount of the regular installment payment. Most states have a balloon mortgage law that specifically states the requirements that the parties must follow. Failure of compliance usually results in an automatic extension of the maturity date until principal and interest are paid in full.

PREPARATION OF THE MORTGAGE

To create an interest in real property as security for a loan, certain requirements must be satisfied in order for the instrument to be valid. In general, the mortgage must meet the basic requirements of a deed, including the following:

- the names of the mortgagor and the mortgagee

- language sufficient to create a lien or constitute a conveyance

- a valid legal description of the property

- proper execution

- delivery to the mortgagee

mortgage

conventional mortgage

purchase money mortgages

fixed rate mortgage

adjustable rate mortgage

FHA mortgage
VA mortgage

balloon payment mortgage

Preprinted forms are available for most typical real estate transactions. Lending institutions and law firms have their own forms covering the basic provisions just outlined that have been proven to meet state law. Appendix E provides an example of a mortgage.

In the normal course of most real estate transactions, the formal mortgage document will be preprinted, with the basic requirements stated by section. The actual, specific terms will vary according to the individual transaction.

SATISFACTION AND DISCHARGE

Satisfaction of Mortgage

A mortgage is discharged or released once the debt has been paid. Although the interest in the property created by the mortgage has been discharged, the mortgage continues to appear as a matter of public record, preventing conveyance by the mortgagor. Therefore, it is necessary for the mortgagor to prepare and file a formal document called a **Satisfaction of Mortgage,** also known as a Release of Mortgage. The drafting of the Satisfaction of Mortgage document, as shown in Illustration 16-5, requires that the following concerns be addressed in a brief manner and simply stated:

- identification of the mortgagee
- reference to the underlying indebtedness
- mortgage
- legal description of the property
- language reflecting the satisfaction and discharge
- date of execution of the document
- signature and acknowledgment

Local statutes frequently regulate the form and content of the satisfaction and discharge. They should be consulted before preparation. In every state, it is necessary that the satisfaction be recorded to inform subsequent purchasers, creditors, and encumbrancers.

FORECLOSURE

foreclosure

When the debt underlying the mortgage is in default (the mortgagor has not paid), then the mortgagee has certain rights available to satisfy the debt. **Foreclosure** is the legal means available to the mortgagee to require that the property be sold and that the proceeds of the sale be applied to satisfy the debt.

equity of redemption

The mortgagor who is in default has a statutory right to redeem the mortgage and pay the indebtedness to date. This right is called the **equity of redemption.** The concept is basically the right of the mortgagor to make a late payment without having the property lost to a sale.

There are basically two types of foreclosure: (1) judicial foreclosure and (2) power of sale. The law of the state where the property is located will determine which remedy is available to the mortgagee. Most states allow a judicial foreclosure.

judicial foreclosure

Judicial foreclosure involves the filing of an action in court to obtain a court order approving the sale. This is a lengthy and costly procedure that allows the mortgagor an opportunity to obtain other financing or to repay the debt.

power of sale foreclosure

Under a **power of sale foreclosure,** there is an out-of-court sale based on a provision in the mortgage document allowing for the sale without court supervision. This procedure is regulated by state statute and is prohibited in some states.

By statute, approximately half the states allow the mortgagor to redeem the mortgaged property after the foreclosure sale. This procedure, known as the period of

SATISFACTION OF MORTGAGE

The undersigned, NORTHERN PARULA STATE BANK, of 5400 South Atlantic Drive, city of Osceola, county of Jay, state of Michigan, hereby certifies that the mortgage, dated June 30, 19__, executed by BELVA GREBE, as mortgagor, to mortgagee, and recorded in the office of the county of Jay, state of Michigan, in Book 54 of mortgage, page 112, together with the debt secured by such mortgage, has been fully paid, satisfied, released, and discharged, and that the property secured thereby has been released from the lien of such mortgage.

In witness whereof, the undersigned has executed this release at the city of Osceola, county of Jay, state of Michigan, on December 7, 19__.

NORTHERN PARULA STATE BANK

By:_____
HOWARD JUNCO, President

Illustration 16-5
Satisfaction of Mortgage

statutory redemption

statutory redemption, generally allows the mortgagor a period of one year, depending on the jurisdiction, to exercise the equity of redemption.

SUMMARY

The legal office assistant plays a significant role in the preparation of any documents affecting real property. The responsibility for the accuracy and content of the documents may fall to the legal office assistant in the preparation of those documents. With a thorough understanding of the nature of interests in real property, the legal office assistant can assist in the preparation of deeds, legal descriptions, notes, and mortgages.

Chapter Activities

Review Questions

1. Identify the name of the system that forms the basis for the law of real property in the United States.

2. Discuss the significance of the *Statute of Frauds* regarding real property transactions.

3. Why is the form of ownership of real property important?

4. List the basic considerations in the preparation of a contract for sale of real property.

5. List and discuss the three types of deeds.

6. Summarize the principal areas to be emphasized in the preparation of any deed.

7. Why is a legal description of property important?

8. Discuss the documents most commonly prepared to finance the purchase of real property.

9. What are the basic forms of a mortgage?

Computer Activity

You are employed by Mr. Norman Conquest, Attorney at Law, representing Mr. Bill B. Pade and his wife, Willa. The Pades have recently retired and are purchasing a house located in the Harmony Homes Retirement Village at 711 Bluehair Boulevard. The legal description locates the property as follows: Lot 50, Block N, Prune Lake Estates. The home is being purchased from Mr. Sherwood Forest for the asking price of $72,000, for which the Pades wish to tender a deposit of $2,000. The Pades have already sought a mortgage from The Liens and Loans Savings Bank in the amount of $60,000. They have arranged for the title examination and insurance with Marshland Title Company, who, in turn, arranged for the survey with Metes and Bounds, Inc. The Pades have requested that your office prepare a contract for sale and purchase. The mortgage, loan documents, and the title documents have already been arranged.

A. From the student template retrieve act16.doc. The document is a form for a contract for sale of real estate. Key the necessary information to prepare the contract from the facts in the scenario. Refer to the illustrations in the chapter for examples.

B. Save this information on the template as contsale.doc.

C. Print one copy for your instructor. Make sure your name appears for identification purposes.

Chapter 17

Law of Bankruptcy

But the restructuring of debtor-creditor relations, which is at the core of the federal bankruptcy power, must be distinguished from adjudication of state-created rights. . . .

Northern Pipeline Construction Co. v. Marathon, 458 U.S. 50 (1982)

Objectives

After completing this chapter, you will be able to:

1. Define the nature of bankruptcy.

2. Discuss the jurisdiction of the bankruptcy courts.

3. Identify the debtor and his estate.

4. Identify the creditor and his claim.

5. Distinguish between the types of bankruptcy.

6. Discuss bankruptcy procedure.

7. Prepare a checklist for an individual bankruptcy.

8. Prepare a bankruptcy petition and schedules.

The legal office assistant plays an integral role in the bankruptcy process. A legal practice that involves the handling of a bankruptcy matter requires a legal office assistant knowledgeable in the field to prepare the documents and ensure the accuracy of the information. Therefore, it is imperative for a legal office assistant that may handle a bankruptcy matter to have a basic understanding of the process.

DEBT

A well-ordered legal environment is based on the protection of the rights of creditors from the dishonest acts of debtors. The rights of creditors find their origin in the English common law and their guarantee in the U.S. Constitution with its prohibition against any impairment of the obligation of contracts. The law of creditors' rights is based on the concept of the permission of the creditor to claim property of the debtor in payment of the debt.

NATURE OF DEBT

A **debt** is a fixed obligation owed by one person to another. The obligation most frequently arises out of a matter of contract, but it also can originate as a result of some legal action that has been reduced to a judgment.

Three basic elements constitute a debt. The debt must be:

- Certain—the debt must not consist of a contingency, but be certain and currently definable.

- Liquidated—the debt must be for a certain amount of money, and not for a sum to be determined at a later date.

- Enforceable—the normal process of law must be available for enforcement of the debt.

When all three elements exist, then a debt in the legal sense exists, whether based on a court-ordered judgment or contractual agreement.

debt

DEBTOR–CREDITOR RELATIONSHIP

The relationship between a debtor and creditor arises as a result of the terms of a contract, or in some instances by operation of law. A **debtor** is one who owes money to another. The one to whom the money is owed is called the **creditor.** If the relationship has arisen as a result of a contractual relationship, then the debtor is the party to the contract who is obligated to pay money in exchange for receipt of something of value.

Also, the debtor–creditor relationship may occur as a result of the operation of law. The creditor may achieve the status of a **judgment creditor,** whereby the creditor has obtained a money judgment against the debtor upon which he can then force collection. A judgment creditor is also called an *execution creditor* in some jurisdictions.

debtor
creditor

judgment creditor

NATURE OF BANKRUPTCY

The reality of our modern commercial environment provides protection for an individual from creditors and for the orderly settlement of his or her obligations. The bankruptcy system has evolved to protect both debtor and creditor, equitably balancing their respective interests.

HISTORY

Article I, § 8 of the U.S. Constitution, the highest law of the land, gives Congress the power to enact "uniform laws on the subject of bankruptcies throughout the United States." This clause, known as the Supremacy Clause, preempts state laws on the subject of bankruptcy, making federal law superior.

In the United States during the early nineteenth century, imprisonment for debts was still a common remedy of the courts to protect creditors and demand payment of debts. Several unsuccessful attempts at reform were made throughout the century, until Congress enacted the Bankruptcy Act of 1898, establishing the system found today. The Bankruptcy Reform Act of 1978, found in Title 11 of the U.S. Code and known as the Bankruptcy Code, governs all bankruptcies in the United States today.

DEFINITION

The term **bankruptcy** refers to something more than a situation of one's liabilities exceeding one's assets. Bankruptcy is the condition of a person, either an individual, a partnership, or a corporation, being unable to pay its debts as they become due. It

bankruptcy

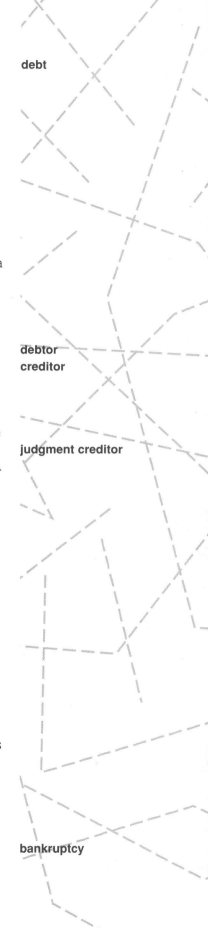

specifically refers to the legal process available to an individual who requires relief from burdensome debts and is seeking relief through court supervision guaranteed by the Bankruptcy Code.

PURPOSE

The purpose of the bankruptcy system is based on sound public policy. It has evolved from a creditor-favored system, designed to ensure payment and punish the debtor, to a system with two distinct purposes:

- to provide the debtor with relief from the unmanageable burden of his or her debt
- to provide the creditor with an equitable distribution of the debtor's assets that are not exempt

The dual purpose of the bankruptcy laws provides distinct benefits to both the creditor and the debtor. The debtor benefits from bankruptcy by:

- obtaining a discharge of his or her debt obligations
- preserving as many of his or her basic assets as possible

The creditor benefits from the bankruptcy law by:

- receiving maximum distribution of the debtor's property
- a guarantee that there will be no discharge of those debts that are not dischargeable under the bankruptcy law

The bankruptcy system presents a compromise position that favors neither the creditor nor the debtor, but gives each a guarantee in exchange.

JURISDICTION

The Bankruptcy Reform Act of 1978 gave exclusive jurisdiction to the Bankruptcy Court over any matter having any relationship to a bankruptcy estate. Jurisdiction, as has previously been discussed, is the term applied to the power of a court to explore facts, apply the law, and make judgments. Under some circumstances, a party may seek to have a case removed from the Bankruptcy Court to the federal district court.

core matters, noncore matters

The Bankruptcy Court hears two types of matters: **core matters** and **noncore matters.** Core matters are those issues that are governed by a specific provision of the Bankruptcy Code. Noncore matters are those questions that are not governed by a specific section of the Bankruptcy Code, but are related to the debtor and his estate. A party may request that the Bankruptcy Court abstain from hearing a noncore matter, which will then be heard by a court with the appropriate jurisdiction. For example, suppose Will Dodge decided that it was in his or her best interest to file a petition for protection from his creditors with the Bankruptcy Court. As the debtor, Dodge was entitled to have all matters concerning his debts and assets heard by the Bankruptcy Court. These would be the core matters. In addition, suppose Dodge had a personal injury action available to him as a result of a recent automobile accident. He would have the right to request the Bankruptcy Court to abstain from hearing the merits of the personal injury lawsuit, a noncore matter, allowing it to be resolved by another court.

DEBTORS

Under the Bankruptcy Code, the term *debtor* is used to designate the person who has filed a voluntary petition or had an involuntary petition filed against him or her.

The Bankruptcy Code also specifies the eligibility requirements to qualify as a debtor (11 U.S.C.A § 101):

1. The debtor must reside or have domicile, a place of business, or property in the United States.

2. The debtor must not have been a debtor in any case within the preceding 180 days if the case was dismissed at the debtor's request or by the court for a failure of the debtor to cooperate.

3. A person who has received a discharge within the last six years may not become a debtor.

Any individual, partnership, or corporation, that fails to qualify on the basis of all three requirements will not have the protection of the Bankruptcy Court.

DEBTORS' ESTATES

With the filing of a petition in bankruptcy, an **estate in bankruptcy** is established. The estate in bankruptcy is any legal and equitable interest owned by the debtor that is subject to administration. The property of the estate includes real and personal property, and also a legal or equitable interest in either. The Bankruptcy Court has jurisdiction over the property, regardless of the location of the property. In addition, any property acquired by the debtor within 180 days of the filing of the petition is also included in the estate.

EXEMPT PROPERTY

Individual debtors under the Bankruptcy Code may protect certain assets from seizure by a creditor or the trustee in bankruptcy. Such assets are known as **exemptions** under the Code. They serve to allow the debtor the opportunity to claim a "clean start" to be rehabilitated financially. Exempt property is not subject to administration by the court, and is, therefore, one of the most important considerations in filing a petition in bankruptcy.

An exemption operates in the following manner: Suppose that Will Dodge elected to file a petition in bankruptcy. At the time of the filing, he owned his home and automobile, both of which were financed. His equity in his modest home $7,500, and his equity in his car is $1,200. The Bankruptcy Code allows an exemption on one's equity in his home up to $7,500, and on one's automobile up to $1,200. Therefore, Dodge would have an exemption available in his home and automobile, excluding those items from his estate in bankruptcy. Property that is subject to a lien or security interest may be exempt. The value is determined by the fair market value at the time of filing. Illustration 17-1 suggests a summary of the federal exemptions under the Bankruptcy Code.

Exemptions must be claimed by the debtor to be valid and that claim must be filed at the time of the filing of the petition. A creditor may, in turn, file an objection to the exemption, requiring a decision by the court.

DISCHARGEABLE AND NONDISCHARGEABLE DEBTS

The Bankruptcy Code provides a release of a debtor from all his debts that have been proven in court. The release of the debtor from an obligation is called a **discharge,** after which the debtor is free from the burden of the charge allowing the debtor a "clean start."

Public policy dictates that release from certain types of debt not be permitted. Under the Bankruptcy Code, debts from which there is no discharge are termed **nondischargeable debts.**

Upon such debts, a creditor may proceed to collection without effect from any action in bankruptcy. Also, a debtor's exemptions under the Code will not serve to prevent a creditor from proceeding to collect for nondischargeable debts.

estate in bankruptcy

exemptions

discharge

nondischargeable debts

Residence of debtor	$7,500
Motor vehicle	$1,200
Household goods, furniture, wearing apparel	$200 per item, up to $4,000 in aggregate
Personal jewelry	$500
Other property	$4,150
Tools of trade	$750
Insurance	no set value
Cash value of insurance	$4,000
Prescribed health aids	no set value
Social Security, welfare, VA benefits, alimony, disability	will vary
Personal injury claim	will vary

Illustration 17-1
Exemptions

Under the Bankruptcy Code, the following debts are nondischargeable:

- some tax claims
- unlisted debts
- alimony, child support, property settlement
- guaranteed student loans
- fines, penalties, or forfeitures payable to a governmental unit
- damages from a conviction for driving under the influence
- debts not discharged in a prior bankruptcy
- fraud, larceny, embezzlement
- damages for willful or malicious injury

When a debt has been found by the court to be nondischargeable, the bankruptcy will not provide the debtor with any relief or protection from collection.

CREDITOR

claim

As already seen, a *creditor* is any person or legal entity to whom a debt is owed. Under the Bankruptcy Code, a creditor is a party in interest to the action as is the debtor. The creditor's interest is expressed in a **claim,** which is a right of payment, whether or not such right has been reduced to judgment. In any bankruptcy proceeding, the emphasis is on the nature of the claim, rather than the creditor.

TYPES OF CLAIMS

Under the Bankruptcy Code, creditors hold three types of claims:

- secured claims

- priority claims

- unsecured claims

Creditors with a **secured claim** are those that hold a security interest in property. That security interest may take the form of a mortgage securing real property, or it may take the form of a security interest in personal property. As with any security interest, the creditor has the right to have the property sold to satisfy the underlying obligation. Pursuant to the Bankruptcy Code, those creditors with a secured claim have a right to property that takes precedence over those of other creditors.

A creditor with a **priority claim** is one with a preference granted by some statutory authority. Under the Code, priority claims are considered superior to claims that are *unsecured,* and thus receive payment first. A priority claim includes claims by Internal Revenue Service, state tax authorities, or claims by employees for compensation.

A creditor with a claim that is unrepresented by a security interest in property, and without any statutory priority, is said to have an **unsecured claim.** Generally, unsecured creditors are individuals who have lent the debtor money without requiring collateral, or those who performed services for the debtor and have yet to receive payment.

PROOF OF CLAIM

The creditor's claim is submitted to the Bankruptcy Court in the form of a pleading called a **Proof of Claim.** It is a legal document submitted under oath, which sets forth the amount owed and the details forming the basis for the claim. As with any standardized form, the Proof of Claim must be tailored to meet the individual creditor's particular situation. The principal amount of the claim, interest, security, and expiration of the debt are factors that will vary with each claim.

TYPES OF BANKRUPTCY

The decision to file a proceeding in bankruptcy is one that must be made with the advice of counsel and should not be taken lightly by any individual. Often there are alternate solutions available to the debtor and the creditor short of bankruptcy. These must be carefully explored to decide which of the alternatives, if any, would be in the individual's best interest.

VOLUNTARY AND INVOLUNTARY PETITIONS

A proceeding in bankruptcy begins with the filing of a legal pleading in the form of a **petition,** similar to a complaint form in civil proceedings. If the filing of the petition is initiated by the debtor under one of the provisions of the Bankruptcy Code, then the petition is said to be a **voluntary petition.** If the petition is filed by a creditor that is forcing the debtor into the proceeding, then it is said to be an **involuntary petition.**

The filing of a petition in bankruptcy has a broad effect. It serves to place the creditors on notice that the debtor is seeking relief under the protection of the court and is attempting to obtain a discharge. The petition also serves as an automatic **stay of proceedings** that may be pending in another court.

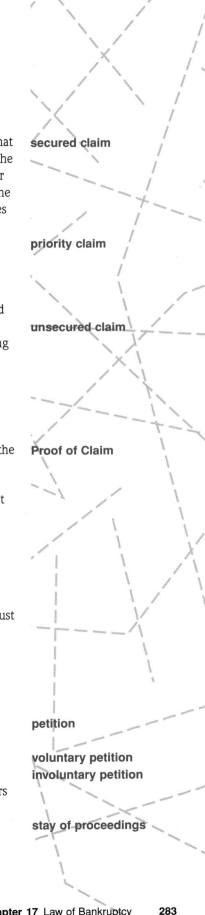

secured claim

priority claim

unsecured claim

Proof of Claim

petition

voluntary petition
involuntary petition

stay of proceedings

A stay of proceedings in this case means that no further action may be taken in any other court involving this particular bankrupt person. Upon the filing of a petition in bankruptcy, all actions in other courts are automatically stayed until the matter has been resolved in the bankruptcy court. Any collection efforts against the debtor are barred as of the moment of filing. An additional effect of the filing of a petition is the creation of the estate in bankruptcy at that time. Those assets that are not exempt become the property of the court.

The Bankruptcy Code provides for three basic types of petitions to initiate a proceeding:

- Chapter 7 liquidation
- Chapter 11 reorganization
- Chapter 13 plan

CHAPTER 7 PETITION

A petition filed for the liquidation and distribution of the debtor's estate is filed under Chapter 7 of the Bankruptcy Code. This procedure is available to any debtor, whether individual, partnership, or corporation. Under Chapter 7, the trustee collects all nonexempt assets of the debtor, sells or liquidates them, and makes a distribution of the proceeds to the creditors.

Once the liquidation has been accomplished, the debtor may receive a formal discharge, or release from debt. Following the issuance of the discharge, the debt is no longer a charge against the debtor or any remaining assets, and the debtor is free to resume business and acquire property without interference from prior creditors.

CHAPTER 11 REORGANIZATION

debtor in possession

Chapter 11 of the Bankruptcy Code involves the use of the concept of a **debtor in possession.** A debtor in possession is the legal term used by the Code to refer to the retention of the property by the debtor during the pendency of the bankruptcy proceeding. The debtor serves as a fiduciary for the creditors until the conclusion of the matter.

reorganization

The **reorganization** concept of Chapter 11 refers to the preparation of a plan for restructuring the debt of a business to meet with the approval of the court. Chapter 11 allows the debtor to remain in business and to preserve his or her ongoing operations while the debt is resolved, as well as providing relief from the demands of the creditors. If no plan can be developed that is satisfactory to the court, the assets may be liquidated under a Chapter 11 liquidation plan.

CHAPTER 13 ADJUSTMENT OF DEBTS OF AN INDIVIDUAL

Similar to the reorganization plan of Chapter 11 for businesses, the wage earner's petition of Chapter 13 allows the individual with regular income to develop a plan of payment to creditors out of his or her income after filing the petition. A Chapter 13 petition is a voluntary petition only, and may not be initiated by a creditor. Also, Chapter 13 relief is not available to partnerships or corporations. Creditors are paid by the trustee from earned income, allowing the debtor to remain in possession of assets while continuing regular employment.

BANKRUPTCY PROCEDURE

The bankruptcy case begins with the filing of a petition, either voluntary or involuntary, under one of the three chapters discussed. The filing of the petition gives the Bankruptcy Court jurisdiction over the assets of the debtor for liquidation or reorganization. As seen previously, the filing of the petition creates an automatic stay of proceedings in any other matter affecting the assets of the debtor.

The choice of the proper bankruptcy court for the filing of the petition refers to venue. As discussed in prior chapters, venue is the term for the geographical location of the proper court in which to file a matter. In bankruptcy, venue is proper if it is in the district where the debtor resides or has a place of business, or where the principal assets are located.

Following the filing of the petition, the court will notify the list of creditors of the filing. Those wishing to participate in the distribution or plan must file their Proof of Claim. The form must be filed within ninety days of the **first meeting of creditors,** which is the initial hearing scheduled by the court to allow the creditors an opportunity to obtain information concerning the debtor.

first meeting of creditors

The **trustee in bankruptcy** is an impartial person elected by the creditors to administer the estate of the debtor. If a trustee is not elected by the creditors, one will be chosen by the court. The trustee automatically becomes the owner of the debtor's property that is not considered exempt. A significant power of the trustee is the power to void certain transfers made by the debtor before the filing of his or her petition. A **voidable transfer** is one that is made within one year of the filing of the petition with the intent to defraud creditors.

trustee in bankruptcy

voidable transfer

The trustee may also void any transfers that have been made by the debtor within ninety days of the filing of the petition to a creditor who receives more than the creditor would have if listed in the petition. Such a transfer is considered to be a **preferential transfer.** Preferential transfers represent the preference by the debtor of one creditor over another—for example, repayment of a loan made by a parent, who then becomes in need.

preferential transfer

PREPARATION OF DOCUMENTS

The Bankruptcy Code provides the statutory authority for proceedings in Bankruptcy Court. The U.S. Supreme Court and the administrator of the U.S courts have declared the rules for the implementation of the Code through the *Rules of Practice and Procedure in Bankruptcy,* frequently referred to as the Federal Rules of Bankruptcy. These rules determine the information required on the various forms, as well as the format for the document. The rules contain the "Official and Procedural Bankruptcy Forms," which provide the contents and appearance of the forms.

CHECKLIST

The checklist is an indispensable tool for the maintenance of a litigation file and the preparation of any legal document. The type of checklist used depends upon the type of case and the complexity of the issues. Checklists for bankruptcy can be developed in two basic forms:

- a litigation checklist that records the actions to be performed on the case

- a file summary that records the information concerning the client

The litigation checklist is designed to contain an easy reference for the location of information relating to the case. It also serves as a reminder of actions that must be taken and filing deadlines. Each case is unique, and the list must be carefully reviewed for each case. A sample general checklist for the filing of a Chapter 7 petition in bankruptcy is shown in Illustration 17-2.

The file summary checklist is one that will vary greatly from office to office, depending on the preference of the attorneys. Its function is to provide a quick and easy method to locate and obtain information about a client without having to review multiple sources. The file summary checklist for a bankruptcy petition should include the following:

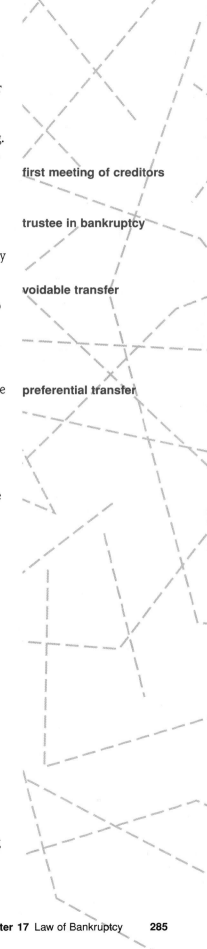

```
Client: _____        File No. _____
_____   Open File
_____   Retention Letter
_____   Client Summary
_____   Obtain Documents
_____   Prepare Petition
_____   Prepare Schedules
_____   Prepare Statement of Financial Affairs
_____   File Petition
          _____   Date
          _____   Case No.
_____   First Meeting of Creditors
_____   Trustee: Name and Address
_____   Hearings on Motions
_____   Discharge
```

Illustration 17-2
Litigation Checklist

- debtor's name and address

- Social Security and/or tax ID number

- prior bankruptcy

- property with a secured interest

- other real property

- personal property

- secured debts

- unsecured debts

- priority claims

- exempt property

- current income sources

No single checklist will cover each case, requiring the development of individualized lists for certain types of cases. Experience will add to the information contained in each checklist.

BANKRUPTCY FORMS

The Official Forms contained in the Rules provide for the content and appearance of each form to be filed in court. In addition to the official forms, each local federal court has its own set of rules that should be consulted before submission of any document.

Caption. Official Form 16A provides the appearance of the caption for any matter filed in the Bankruptcy Court. The caption should include the title of the case, debtor's name, Social Security number, and federal tax identification number, if any. The form is to be used on the petition, the notice of the meeting of creditors, and the order of discharge (see Illustration 17-3).

UNITED STATES BANKRUPTCY COURT
IN THE NORTHERN DISTRICT OF FREMONT

In re: WILLIAM DODGE, a/k/a/

WILL DODGE,   CASE NO.: 123456

    Debtor.   Chapter 7

Social Security No. 123-45-6789
_____/

VOLUNTARY PETITION

Illustration 17-3
Caption

Petition. The initiation of a proceeding in bankruptcy occurs with the filing of a petition that is set forth in Official Form 1. The form is self-explanatory regarding the information that may be taken from the client information checklist. The purpose is to inform the court and the creditors of the nature of the allegations. The petition can be voluntary, pursuant to the dictates of Form 1 (see Illustration 17-4); or the petition can be involuntary, pursuant to Form 5.

Statement of Financial Affairs. Within fifteen days of the filing of a petition in bankruptcy, the debtor must file a **Statement of Financial Affairs.** The Statement of Financial Affairs is a questionnaire designed to provide sufficient information so the court can decide if a discharge should be granted. Official Form 7 is the Statement of Financial Affairs for an individual debtor, providing the debtor's sworn answers to the following areas of inquiry:

- name and residence
- occupation and income
- tax returns and refunds
- financial accounts, certificates of deposit, and safe deposit boxes
- books and records
- property held for another person
- property held by another
- prior bankruptcy
- receiverships, general assignments, and other modes of liquidation
- suits, executions, and attachments
- payment of loans, installment purchases, and other debts
- setoffs
- transfers of property
- repossessions and returns
- losses
- payments and transfers to attorneys

The document is then executed by the debtor with a statement that the answers to the questions are true to the best of his or her knowledge, under penalty of perjury. Appendix F contains Official Form 8, Statement of Financial Affairs.

Schedules. The **schedules** are official forms listing assets and liabilities of the debtor. The schedules consist of multiple forms that enable the debtor to list, in detail, the information sought for the benefit of the court and the creditors. The schedules consist of:

- Summary of Schedules—read as a composite, it forms a general financial statement of the debtor.
- Schedule A—this provides a list of the real property of the debtor.
- Schedule B—this provides a list of the personal property of the debtor.

Statement of Financial Affairs

schedules

United States Bankruptcy Court District of	VOLUNTARY PETITION

IN RE (Name of debtor-If individual, enter Last, First, Middle)	NAME OF JOINT DEBTOR (Spouse) (Last, First, Middle)
ALL OTHER NAMES used by the debtor in the last 6 years (including married, maiden and trade names)	ALL OTHER NAMES used by the joint debtor in the last 6 years (including married, maiden and trade names)
SOC. SEC./TAX I.D. NO. (If more than one, state all)	SOC. SEC./TAX I.D. NO. (If more than one, state all)
STREET ADDRESS OF DEBTOR (No. and street, city, state, zip)	STREET ADDRESS OF JOINT DEBTOR (No. and street, city, state, zip)
COUNTY OF RESIDENCE OR PRINCIPAL PLACE OF BUSINESS	COUNTY OF RESIDENCE OR PRINCIPAL PLACE OF BUSINESS
MAILING ADDRESS OF DEBTOR (If different from street address)	MAILING ADDRESS OF JOINT DEBTOR (If different from street address)

LOCATION OF PRINCIPAL ASSETS OF BUSINESS DEBTOR (If different from addresses listed above)

VENUE (Check one box)

☐ Debtor has been domiciled or has had a residence, principal place of business or principal assets in this District for 180 days immediately preceding the date of this petition or for a longer part of such 180 days than in any other District.

☐ There is a bankruptcy case concerning debtor's affiliate, general partner or partnership pending in this District.

INFORMATION REGARDING DEBTOR (Check applicable boxes)

TYPE OF DEBTOR (Check one box)
☐ Individual
☐ Joint (H&W)
☐ Partnership
☐ Other _____
☐ Corporation Publicly Held
☐ Corporation Not Publicly Held
☐ Municipality

CHAPTER OR SECTION OF BANKRUPTCY CODE UNDER WHICH THE PETITION IS FILED (Check one box)
☐ Chapter 7   ☐ Chapter 11   ☐ Chapter 13
☐ Chapter 9   ☐ Chapter 12   ☐ § 304-Case Ancillary to Foreign Proceeding

SMALL BUSINESS (Chapter 11 only)

NATURE OF DEBT (Check one box)
☐ Non-Business Consumer   ☐ Business - Complete A&B below

☐ Debtor is a small business as defined in 11 U.S.C. § 101.
☐ Debtor is and elects to be considered a small business under 11 U.S.C. § 1121(e). (optional)

A. TYPE OF BUSINESS (Check one box)
☐ Farming   ☐ Transportation   ☐ Commodity Broker
☐ Professional   ☐ Manufacturing/Mining   ☐ Construction
☐ Retail/Wholesale ☐ Stockbroker   ☐ Real Estate
☐ Railroad   ☐ Other Business

FILING FEE (Check one box)
☐ Filing fee attached
☐ Filing fee to be paid in installments. (Applicable to individuals only) Must attach signed application for the court's consideration certifying that the debtor is unable to pay fee except in installments. Rule 1006(b); see page K100-07.

B. BRIEFLY DESCRIBE NATURE OF BUSINESS

NAME AND ADDRESS OF LAW FIRM OR ATTORNEY

Telephone No.

STATISTICAL ADMINISTRATIVE INFORMATION (28 U.S.C. § 604) (Estimates only) (Check applicable boxes)

NAME(S) OF ATTORNEY(S) DESIGNATED TO REPRESENT THE DEBTOR (Print or Type)

☐ Debtor estimates that funds will be available for distribution to unsecured creditors.
☐ Debtor estimates that after any exempt property is excluded and administrative expenses paid, there will be no funds available for distribution to unsecured creditors.

☐ Debtor is not represented by an attorney. Telephone no. of debtor not represented by an attorney:(   )

ESTIMATED NUMBER OF CREDITORS
☐ 1-15   ☐ 16-49   ☐ 50-99   ☐ 100-199   ☐ 200-999   ☐ 1000-over

ESTIMATED ASSETS (in thousands of dollars)
☐ Under 50   ☐ 50-99   ☐ 100-499   ☐ 500-999   ☐ 1000-9999   ☐ 10,000-99,000   ☐ 100,000-over

ESTIMATED LIABILITIES (in thousands of dollars)
☐ Under 50   ☐ 50-99   ☐ 100-499   ☐ 500-999   ☐ 1000-9999   ☐ 10,000-99,000   ☐ 100,000-over

ESTIMATED NUMBER OF EMPLOYEES - CH 11 & 12 ONLY
☐ 0   ☐ 1-19   ☐ 20-99   ☐ 100-999   ☐ 1000-over

ESTIMATED NUMBER OF EQUITY HOLDERS - CH 11 & 12 ONLY
☐ 0   ☐ 1-19   ☐ 20-99   ☐ 100-999   ☐ 1000-over

THIS SPACE FOR COURT USE ONLY

Illustration 17-4
Voluntary Petition

Name of Debtor _____

Case No. _____

FILING OF PLAN

For Chapter 9, 11, 12 and 13 cases only. Check appropriate box.

I A copy of debtor's proposed plan dated _____ is attached.   □ Debtor intends to file a plan within the time allowed by statute, rule, or order of the court.

PRIOR BANKRUPTCY CASE FILED WITHIN LAST 6 YEARS (If more than one, attach additional sheet)

Location Where Filed	Case Number	Date Filed

PENDING BANKRUPTCY CASE FILED BY ANY SPOUSE, PARTNER, OR AFFILIATE OF THIS DEBTOR (If more than one, attach additional sheet)

Name of Debtor	Case Number	Date
Relationship	District	Judge

REQUEST FOR RELIEF

Debtor requests relief in accordance with the chapter of Title 11, United States Code, specified in this petition.

SIGNATURES

ATTORNEY

X _____   _____
Signature   Date

INDIVIDUAL/JOINT DEBTOR(S)	CORPORATE OR PARTNERSHIP DEBTOR
I declare under penalty of perjury that the information provided in this petition is true and correct.	I declare under penalty of perjury that the information provided in this petition is true and correct, and that the filing of the petition on behalf of the debtor has been authorized.
X _____ Signature of Debtor	X _____ Signature of Authorized Individual
_____ Date	_____ Print or Type Name of Authorized Individual
X _____ Signature of Debtor	_____ Title of Individual Authorized by Debtor to File this Petition
_____ Date	_____ Date

EXHIBIT "A" (To be completed if debtor is a corporation requesting relief under Chapter 11.)

□ Exhibit "A" is attached and made a part of this petition.

TO BE COMPLETED BY INDIVIDUAL CHAPTER 7 DEBTOR WITH PRIMARILY CONSUMER DEBTS (SEE P.L. 98-353 § 322)

I am aware that I may proceed under chapter 7, 11, 12, or 13 of Title 11, United States Code. I understand the relief available under each such chapter, and choose to proceed under Chapter 7 of such title.

If I am represented by an attorney, exhibit "B" has been completed.

X _____   _____
Signature of Debtor   Date

X _____   _____
Signature of Joint Debtor   Date

EXHIBIT "B" (To be completed by attorney for individual Chapter 7 debtor(s) with primarily consumer debts.)

I, the attorney for the debtor(s) named in the foregoing petition, declare that I have informed the debtor(s) that (he, she, or they) may proceed under Chapter 7, 11, 12, or 13 of Title 11, United States Code, and have explained the relief available under each such chapter.

X _____   _____
Signature of Attorney   Date

CERTIFICATION AND SIGNATURE OF NON-ATTORNEY BANKRUPTCY PETITION PREPARER (See 11 U.S.C. § 110)

I certify that I am a bankruptcy petition preparer as defined in 11 U.S.C. § 110, that I have prepared this document for compensation, and that I have provided the debtor with a copy of this document.

Printed or Typed Name of Bankruptcy Petition Preparer _____   Social Security Number _____

_____

Names and Social Security Numbers of all other individuals who prepared or assisted in preparing this document:

Address _____   Tel. No. _____

X _____

Signature of Bankruptcy Petition Preparer

If more than one person prepared this document, attach additional signed sheets conforming to the appropriate Official Form for each person.

A bankruptcy petition preparer's failure to comply with the provisions of Title 11 and the Federal Rules of Bankruptcy Procedure may result in fines or imprisonment or both. 11 U.S.C. § 110; 18 U.S.C. § 156.

Illustration 17-4
Voluntary Petition (continued)

- Schedule C—itemizes the property that the debtor claims as exempt; each exempt item should be identified *and* the corresponding statutory provisions allowing the exemption should be cited.

- Schedule D—a list of creditors that hold a secured interest in any property of the debtor is provided, reflecting the debtor's equity in the property.

- Schedule E—this lists those creditors that have a priority claim that is not secured by any property interest; priority of claims is set forth in § 507 of the Code.

- Schedule F—an itemization of the unsecured creditors that do not have any priority claim is provided; failure to list a creditor will mean that there will be no discharge of that debt.

- Schedule G—this presents the debtor's obligations on any contracts or leases, along with any contracts under which the debtor may be owed monies.

- Schedule H—situations in which the debtor is a co-obligor on any debt or obligation are itemized.

- Schedule I—this provides information as to the debtor's current monthly income and his dependency status.

- Schedule J—the debtor's financial picture is completed, with the listing of his or her monthly expenditures.

- Declaration Concerning Debtor's Schedules—the schedules conclude with a statement under threat of perjury that the information contained in the documents is true to the best of the debtor's knowledge.

The actual scheduled forms to be executed by the debtor are contained in Appendix G.

Order Confirming Plan. Proceedings under Chapter 11 of the Bankruptcy Code are the most complex and costly of the bankruptcy proceedings. It is the goal of the debtor to obtain court approval of a plan for reorganization. The reorganization plan must classify the claims of the creditors and provide for their payment. Following a court hearing to confirm the plan's feasibility, the court will issue an Order Confirming Plan. The order will reflect that copies of the complex plan are filed and attached to the Order. The effect of the issuance of the order is to provide the debtor with the equivalent of a discharge of the debts subject to the plan.

Discharge. The ultimate goal of a Chapter 7 Liquidation proceeding is the issuance of a *Discharge of Debtor.* The Discharge is the Court's order relieving the debtor of any obligation for the proven debts that are the subject of the matter. The effect is to vacate any existing judgment against the debtor and to prevent future collection attempts by any creditor on debts subject to the discharge (see Illustration 17-5).

UNITED STATES BANKRUPTCY COURT
_____ DISTRICT OF _____

In re _____ ,
    *[Set forth here all names including married, maiden, and trade
    names used by debtor within last 6 years.]*

                                    Debtor

Social Security No(s). _____ and all
Employer's Tax Identification Nos. *[If any]* _____
_____

Case No. _____

Chapter Seven

DISCHARGE OF DEBTOR

It appearing that a petition commencing a case under Title 11, United States Code, was filed by or against the person named above on _____, and that an order for relief was entered under chapter 7, and that no complaint objecting to the discharge of the debtor was filed within the time fixed by the court [*or* that a complaint objecting to discharge of the debtor was filed and, after due notice and hearing, was not sustained];

IT IS ORDERED that

1. The above-named debtor is released from all dischargeable debts.

2. Any judgment heretofore or hereafter obtained in any court other than this court is null and void as a determination of the personal liability of the debtor with respect to any of the following:

    (a) debts dischargeable under 11 U.S.C. § 523;

    (b) unless heretofore or hereafter determined by order of this court to be nondischargeable, debts alleged to be excepted from discharge under clauses (2), (4) and (6) of 11 U.S.C. § 523(a);

    (c) debts determined by this court to be discharged.

3. All creditors whose debts are discharged by this order and all creditors whose judgments are declared null and void by paragraph 2 above are enjoined from instituting or continuing any action or employing any process or engaging in any act to collect such debts as personal liabilities of the above-named debtor.

Dated: _____

BY THE COURT

_____
United States Bankruptcy Judge

Illustration 17-5
Sample Discharge

SUMMARY

All matters concerning bankruptcy are decided in the Bankruptcy Court, including cases seeking liquidation or reorganization. The bankruptcy laws exist to provide the debtor with relief from an unmanageable debt, while benefiting the creditor with an equitable distribution of the debtor's assets. The proceedings may either be at the election of the debtor in the form of a voluntary bankruptcy, or at the creditor's election with the filing of an involuntary petition.

The preparation of the documents required to process any bankruptcy begins with a detailed client interview and checklist preparation. The pleadings involved in the typical bankruptcy are set forth in the official rules that provide the look and content of each pleading. The pleadings present the debtor's case before the court, and reflect the validity of the creditor's allegations. Once the debts have been proven, the matter is concluded with the discharge, relieving the debtor of the obligation for those debts.

Businesses may be reorganized and continue to operate with a provision for the payment of debts from the business' income. A plan for reorganization must be approved by the Court, allowing the business to pay its obligations over time. With the plan, the debtor will not be harassed by his creditors while the repayment is made.

The bankruptcy system benefits both the creditor and debtor. The debtor receives the protection and relief of the process, while the creditor receives maximum distribution of the debtor's assets.

Chapter Activities

Review Questions

1. Define the bankruptcy system.

2. What is the name of the federal act that is the basis for the bankruptcy law in the United States today?

3. Describe how the debtor benefits from bankruptcy.

4. How does the creditor benefit from bankruptcy?

5. List some types of exempt property.

6. List the debts that are not dischargeable under the Bankruptcy Code.

7. How does a creditor prove a claim before a Bankruptcy Court?

8. Describe the distinction between a voluntary petition and an involuntary petition.

9. How does a Chapter 7 case differ from a Chapter 11?

10. What is the purpose of a discharge?

Computer Activity

Your office has been contacted by Martin "Bub" Brisket, sole owner and proprietor of Bub's Roast & Boast, a local eatery that for years has served the "beef for breakfast bunch." Bub has come on hard times with the national awareness of the high cholesterol content of his stock in trade. Rather than submit to the pressure to serve fat-free yogurt and wheat germ, Bub has decided to pull up stakes and follow Horace Greeley's advice.

Bub owes the following debts:

B. D. Strangle, rent	$15,000
Brown Chow Food Co., supplies	12,000
Fremont Power & Light, utilities	5,000
No. Bell, telephone	2,000
Four Wheel Finance, secured, truck	10,000
Allhart Savings and Loan, unsecured	50,000
Meltdown Master Charge, unsecured	9,000

Other than the furnishings in his double-wide that he rents from his former brother-in-law, and his personal clothing, Bub has no assets. He has approximately $1,200 in equity in his truck and does not want to lose the truck. He plans to move to Montana and obtain a fresh start in the beef business, but cannot make any plans with the creditors breathing down his neck.

A. From the student template retrieve act17.doc. The document is a sample litigation checklist. Key in the necessary information for the filing of a voluntary petition pursuant to Chapter 7. Refer to the illustrations in the chapter for examples.

B. Save this information on the template as chklst.doc.

C. Print one copy for your instructor. Make sure your name appears for identification purposes.

Glossary

abandonment
The act of terminating marital cohabitation without consent or justification.

abatement
The process by which the order of liquidation is decided.

accounting
The maintenance and analysis of financial records.

accounts payable
Obligations to be paid.

accounts receivable
Monies to be received at a later date.

Accredited Legal Secretary (ALS)
A certification obtained by successfully completing a one-day examination covering such topics as written communications comprehension and application, office administration, legal terminology, accounting, ethics, human relations, and applied office procedures; this designation is designed for the apprentice-level legal office assistant.

accrual basis
A bookkeeping system that records legal fees as revenue when they are earned, not actually paid, and expenses at the time incurred, not when an invoice is actually paid.

act
The physical movement engaged in by an accused.

active voice
Where the subject of the sentence is acting.

adjustable rate mortgage
A mortgage that has a variable interest rate tied to an economic index, resulting in the rate moving up or down on a periodic basis.

administrator
The individual responsible for the general administration of the office, including human resources management, accounting, payroll, budget concerns, and marketing.

admission
A statement showing an involvement in the crime.

adultery
A sexual relationship by a married person with someone other than his or her spouse.

affidavit
A sworn statement of facts by the signer acknowledged by a notary.

affirmative defense
Defense to the complaint based on a matter not mentioned in the complaint.

agent
The party receiving the authority from the principal to act for the principal's benefit and subject to his or her direction and control.

age of majority
The age of legal competence.

alibi
An assertion that the defendant was not at the scene at the time the crime was committed.

alimony
The duty of spousal support in the form of an allowance for maintenance.

allegation
An assertion made by a party in a pleading setting out what is to be proven at trial.

alphabetic filing system
A filing system using the last name of the individual client, or the name of the business, for its organization.

alpha-numeric filing system
A filing system using a letter or a series of letters of the alphabet, followed by a series of numbers to designate a particular legal matter.

American Bar Association (ABA)
A voluntary association of attorneys to improve legal services.

amount in controversy
A requirement for jurisdiction in federal courts where the case involves an amount of recovery in excess of $50,000.

annotated law report
A report containing the text of selected cases, along with in-depth discussion on the law of the particular case.

annotation
The in-depth discussion on the law in the form of an essay explaining and commenting on its meaning.

annual report
The statutory report filed with the local secretary of state providing the basic information regarding the corporation and an identification of its officers.

answer
The defendant's responsive pleading stating the grounds for defense.

antenuptial agreement
A contract between prospective spouses in contemplation of marriage.

anti-heart balm statute
An action for a breach of a covenant to marry.

appeal
The right of a superior court to review the correctness of the decision of a lower court on questions of law.

appellant
The party filing the appeal.

appellate brief
A lengthy written legal document submitted to an appellate court to persuade the court that an error has occurred in a lower court.

appellate court
The court to which an appeal is taken.

appellee
The party against whom the appeal was filed.

application software
A computer program that directs the information processing tasks required by the operator.

appreciation
The gain of value of property.

appurtenance
Any structure permanently attached to the land, such as a shed or a fence surrounding an individual's backyard.

arbitration
The submission of the issues to a neutral third person for a binding decision if the procedure is voluntary and non-binding if the procedure is mandatory.

arbitrator
A neutral third party used in an alternative process of dispute resolution.

argument
The advocacy portion of the brief devoted to a discussion of the issues and their legal support.

arraignment
A formal hearing at which the charge is read and the defendant is asked to enter a plea.

arrest
A deprivation of freedom by a legal authority.

arson
The willful burning of a building.

articles of incorporation
A legal instrument filed with the appropriate state agency, which creates the corporate entity.

asset
An item of value owned by the legal office.

associate attorney
An employee of a legal office with no real management role other than some duties delegated by a partner; one who does not share in the profits and losses of the firm.

attestation
The act of witnessing the signing of a written instrument.

attestation clause
A clause stating that the witnesses to the testator's signature have so witnessed the signing.

attorney–client privilege
A rule of evidence that prohibits the disclosure of any confidential communications from the client by an attorney or any person in his office.

attractive nuisance
An enticing condition on the premises that can reasonably be considered to be a source of danger.

authority
The power delegated to one person by another, or by a legal entity such as a corporation, to act on that party's behalf.

authorization
The grant of authority to another to do or obtain something.

bailee
The recipient of the bailment.

bailment
A situation in which possession of personal property is temporarily transferred by the owner to another party for safekeeping until the property is returned or delivered to someone else.

bailor
The owner of the property that is subject to bailment.

balance sheet
A financial statement reflecting the legal office's assets, liabilities, and the owner's equity.

balloon payment mortgage
A mortgage loan requiring periodic payments for a specific length of time with the full principal balance of more than twice the amount of the regular installment payment due on maturity.

bank draft
A type of check issued by a bank upon its funds located in another bank, usually in another city.

bankruptcy
The legal process available to an individual who requires relief from burdensome debt and is seeking relief through court supervision guaranteed by the Bankruptcy Code.

beneficiary
The individual recipient of the trust benefits or property.

bill of particulars
A discovery tool for the criminal defendant to use to obtain information about the prosecution's case by requesting that the information or indictment be made more specific.

binding authority
Lower courts within the same system *must* abide by the legal principles established by the higher courts.

board of directors
The persons appointed by the shareholders to manage the affairs of the business.

breach of contract
Any failure to act or perform in a manner called for by the contract without legal excuse.

breach of duty
A violation of an obligation.

brief
A memorandum of law, providing the court with relevant statutory and case law support for the moving party's position.

burden of proof
The necessity of offering the requisite evidence to prove a fact or guilt.

burglary
The unlawful entry of a building for the purpose of stealing from the premises.

business enterprise
The expenditure of time, labor, skill, technology, management, and capital, in the commencement of an undertaking for profit.

bylaws
The rules and regulations that define the corporate structure and provide the rights and obligations of the officers, directors, and shareholders.

capacity
The level of mental competence required by law to understand the nature of one's acts.

caption
The name of the case consisting of the names of the parties to the case and a designation as plaintiff and defendant.

case law
Written opinions of appellate courts contained in large, multivolume sets of books.

cash basis
Accounting of income and expenses as they are actually received or paid.

cashier's check
A check drawn on a bank's own account.

causation
An act or omission that produces a result.

cause of action
Facts entitling a party to judicial remedy.

central processing unit (CPU)
The main information processing component of the computer that receives input data through the keyboard, stores the data electronically, organizes it, and delivers it through output devices such as the monitor and the printer.

centralized filing system
A system that stores all the office files in one file room or storage area.

certificate of stock
The documentary evidence of an individual's ownership in a corporation.

certified check
A check drawn on the maker's account and certified on its face by the bank that sufficient funds have been set aside to honor the check when presented.

Certified Professional Legal Secretary (PLS)
A certification achieved by an individual completing a two-day examination to test mastery of professional skills, a working knowledge of procedural law, ability to draft correspondence and legal documents, and ability to interact with attorneys, courts, and clients.

check
A written order to a bank to pay to the person named an amount stated and to charge the maker's account.

circuit
The designation for the territories that constitute the United States courts of appeal.

circuit court
The court of original jurisdiction in the state court system.

citation
An abbreviation of the name of the case, including the volume number and reporter series in which it appears, followed by the page number and date of issue.

citators
Multivolume sets of books that provide subsequent history of cases and statutes.

claim
The right of payment, whether or not such right has been reduced to judgment.

class action
A lawsuit maintained by a large group of individuals with the same

characteristic legal rights against a particular defendant.

client trust account
A separate bank account maintained by the legal office for unearned client funds.

codicil
A separate instrument that serves to alter or modify the original will without appearing to be the entire will of the testator.

codified
The rearranging of a chronological order into a subject matter format.

coding
A guide to facilitate referencing information using a letter, number, color, or other symbol to mark items for filing.

collateral attack
A prohibited attack on a prior judgment of another court.

commingling
The mixing of unearned client funds with the funds of the legal office.

communication
The exchange of information and ideas.

community property
All property acquired by the husband and wife during marriage, other than by gift or bequest.

compact laser disc (CD-ROM)
A highly durable optical disk capable of containing large volumes of information, recorded through the use of laser technology.

compensatory damages
The monetary award to compensate for the harm to person or property.

complaint
The initial pleading filed in a lawsuit by the plaintiff to commence an action.

computer
An electronic device to accept and store data, execute a program of instructions, and report the results.

conciseness
The expression of the message in as few words as possible.

conclusion
The section of the brief constituting a summary of the party's position and arguments.

concurrent jurisdiction
Where both the federal government and the state government have jurisdiction over matter.

concurrent ownership
Ownership of real property by two or more individuals.

concurring opinion
A statement of reasoning different than the majority of the judges in the decision.

condition precedent
A specified event that must occur before some right may arise.

confession
A statement confirming the commission of a crime by an accused individual.

confidentiality
An assurance that a client can trust the firm with his or her affairs, and can do so in confidence that those matters will remain private.

conflict of interest
The situation whereby the attorney, or his legal office assistant, has an interest that would interfere with the loyal representation of the interests of the client.

consideration
The element of a contract that forms the inducement to a party to enter into the agreement.

contingency fee
The form of representation by an attorney, whereby no attorney fee is paid unless there has been a recovery in the case.

contract
An agreement that creates legally enforceable obligations binding each party.

contractual capacity
The competency of age and ability to enter into a contract.

conventional mortgage
A security device used by the mortgagor to transfer a lien or defensible title to the mortgagee or lending institution in return for part of the purchase price of the property.

conveyance
A transfer of an interest in real property.

core matters
Issues that are governed by a specific provision of the Bankruptcy Code.

corporate authority
Rights and powers of a corporation separate from its owners.

corporate minute book
The corporate record of the actions of the shareholders and directors of a corporation.

corporation
A legal entity having the same rights and liabilities of citizens.

corpus
The trust property consisting of the property interest owned by the settlor and transferred to the trustee for the benefit of the beneficiary.

counterclaim
A claim against the plaintiff by a defendant to an action.

court order
A written directive by the court determining a step in the proceedings.

court reports
Large, multivolume sets of books containing the written opinions of the appellate courts of a particular jurisdiction.

courts of general jurisdiction
State courts that are empowered to hear cases concerning personal injury, property damage, contracts, domestic relations, and any other general cause of action.

courts of limited jurisdiction
State courts that are permitted to hear only cases of a specific type.

credit
An accounting entry of payment received.

creditor
The one to whom the money is owed.

crime
The term used to refer to an act that is in violation of a law.

criminal complaint
An initial instrument filed with the court charging an individual with a crime.

cross-claim
A claim against another party on the same side of the lawsuit.

cruelty
The intentional infliction of mental and physical harm.

damages
The harm or injury to person or property.

data
Information stored in the computer.

debit
An entry in an account showing money paid out or owed.

debt
A fixed obligation owed by one person to another.

debtor
One who owes money to another.

debtor in possession
The legal term used by the Bankruptcy Code to refer to the retention of the property by the debtor during the pendency of the bankruptcy proceeding.

decentralized filing system
A system that stores office files in various locations throughout the legal office.

deed
A conveyance of real property in writing whereby title is transferred to another.

default divorce
A divorce where no appearance is made by the defendant, so that the plaintiff is granted the dissolution without contest.

default judgment
The defendant's failure to defend a matter.

defendant
The party in a lawsuit against whom an action has been brought.

defense
A term for an assertion of innocence.

deposition
The testimony of a witness taken upon oral examination through the use of question and answer before an officer of the court.

desertion
The act of terminating marital cohabitation without consent or justification.

devise
A specific testamentary gift.

dictionary
A resource book that offers the definition of terms for use in legal argument and reasoning.

digests
A multivolume set of books providing a topical reference to case law.

discharge
The release of the debtor from an obligation.

discovery
The process used to secure the information necessary to prepare for trial.

dissenting opinion
The written opinion of a judge disagreeing with the result reached by the majority of the judges in the decision.

dissolution of marriage
The termination of the legal status of marriage, whereby a man and woman no longer coexist as husband and wife.

dissolution of partnership
The change in the relationship of the partners as a result of one or more partners leaving the partnership.

diversity of citizenship
A requirement for jurisdiction in federal courts where the case involves citizens of different states, or is between citizens of a state and those of a foreign country.

divorce
The termination of the legal status of marriage, whereby a man and woman no longer coexist as husband and wife.

docket control system
A scheduling system to track important dates.

docket number
The number assigned to the case by the court clerk when the appeal is filed.

double-entry bookkeeping
A system of bookkeeping in which each journal entry debit or credit in an account requires a corresponding credit or debit in another account.

duress and necessity
A situation in which the defendant was threatened and had to commit the crime to avoid serious personal injury.

duty
An obligation to do or not do something.

electronic mail (E-mail)
The storing of text messages electronically on a computer for convenient reference at a later time by the user.

embezzlement
The conversion of the property of another by one who has acquired lawful possession with an intent to defraud the owner.

emotional distress
Mental anguish caused by a tortfeasor.

encumbrances
Liens against the property.

encyclopedia
A general, multivolume set providing a research tool for a fundamental understanding of the law.

endorsement
The act of signing the check by the payee.

entrapment
A situation where law enforcement officers encourage the defendant to commit a crime with the intent to make an arrest.

equitable title
The right to profit or benefit from the property.

equity
The owner's interest in the business expressed in dollars and cents.

equity of redemption
The statutory right of the mortgagor who is in default to redeem the mortgage and pay the indebtedness to date.

estate in bankruptcy
Any legal and equitable interest owned by the debtor that is subject to administration.

estate in real property
The nature and extent of ownership that an individual has in the property.

estate planning
The creation of a method for the orderly handling, disposition, and administration of an estate when the owner dies.

ethical standard
An established set of rules defining acceptable conduct and motives.

ethics
An individual's compliance with a professional standard of conduct and behavior.

etiquette
The form and manners considered essential in a professional setting.

executor/executrix
The personal representative of the estate.

exemptions
Property not subject to administration by the court.

ex parte
A hearing by the court attended only by the moving party.

ex parte **divorce**
A divorce where the court did not have jurisdiction over the defendant and only one party is present in court.

expense
The cost of any goods and services used to produce revenue.

expert witness
An individual trained by education and experience in a field beyond the scope of knowledge of the lay person who gives testimony on complicated technical subjects.

express contract
An actual agreement between the parties stated in distinct terms, and it may be either written or oral.

express warranty
An affirmation of fact in writing by the seller as to the quality, fitness, or title to goods.

extortion
The threat of future harm to acquire the property of another.

facsimile machine (fax)
A machine used for the transmission of text and graphic images for their reconstruction and duplication at a receiving location.

false pretense
A false representation made to defraud the victim, causing title to property to pass to another.

fault
Responsible for wrong behavior.

Federal Rules of Civil Procedure
A body of procedural rules governing all civil actions in the federal courts.

felony
A serious crime usually punishable by death or imprisonment for more than one year.

feudal system
The social, political, and economic system that formed the basis of the English common law following the Norman Conquest in 1066.

FHA mortgage
A loan that is insured by the Federal Housing Administration.

fiduciary capacity
The duty to act in good faith with respect to the property of another.

fiduciary duty
The duty to act on another's behalf in good faith and trust.

filing system
The process of the organization, storage, management, preservation, retrieval, and disposal of information in a legal office.

final order
A court order that terminates the action.

finding tools
Legal research aids to locating primary and secondary sources of the law.

first meeting of creditors
The initial hearing scheduled by the court to allow the creditors an opportunity to obtain information concerning the debtor.

fixed rate mortgage
A mortgage in which the interest rate on the loan remains the same for its life.

flat fee
An attorney fee for legal services billed as a fixed amount for a particular service.

floppy disk
A plastic storage diskette used in all computers for saving information in the form of data or software programs.

forbearance
The term for the promise not to do an act.

foreclosure
The legal means available to the mortgagee to require that the property be sold and that the proceeds of the sale be applied to satisfy the debt.

foreign divorce
A divorce obtained in a state other than the current state where enforcement is being sought.

foreseeability
An anticipated result of the specific act or omission.

freehold estate
The right of title in land for an indeterminate period.

general partnership
A contract between two or more individuals to commit their resources to a lawful business enterprise and to share in the profits and losses.

general revocatory clause
A clause showing that it is the testator's intention that this document supersede any previously published will or codicil.

general warranty deed
A deed in which the seller guarantees the title against any defects.

gross income
The amount of revenue received in a given time period before there has been any deduction for expenses.

grounds
Sufficient legal justification for an action.

guardian
A person invested by law with the power to manage the rights and property of another person who cannot manage on his or her own due to a lack of mental capacity or insufficient age.

hard drive
A name for the data storage function of the CPU.

hardware
The physical devices of a computer.

headnote
A summary paragraph on a point of law discussed in the written court opinion.

heirs at law
Individuals entitled to receive a portion of the estate as provided by state laws of intestacy.

holographic will
A will drawn in the testator's own handwriting.

homicide
The act of one human being killing another.

hourly rate fee
An agreed upon rate at which the legal services are billed on an hourly basis to the client.

impleader
The assertion by the defendant that a person not already a party to the action is in fact liable to the defendant for all or part of his or her exposure.

implied contract
A contract that is created by the action of the parties but not reflected in a writing.

implied warranty
A warranty created by the operation of law with respect to fitness for a particular purpose, if the agreement is silent concerning any express warranties made by the seller.

income
Revenue from the generation of fees for providing professional services.

income statement
A detailed financial statement that shows the revenue, expenses, and net income or loss of the legal office over a specific period of time.

incompetent
The lack of mental capacity to appreciate the nature and consequences of acts.

indemnification
The reimbursement or compensation for a loss.

independent contractor
One who has been contracted for a specific purpose and is not controlled by the hiring body.

indexing
A guide to facilitate referencing information using a letter, number, color, or other symbol to treat items.

indictment
The formal accusation of the commission of a crime made in writing by a grand jury, based on evidence presented to it.

information
A formal accusation of the commission of a crime sworn to by a prosecutor to bring a defendant to trial.

***in rem* jurisdiction**
Courts that have power over a particular thing within its geographic borders.

insanity
A defense related to the requirement of *mens rea,* whereby the defendant does not know that the act was wrong, defendant cannot control his actions because of an irresistible impulse, or lacks the capacity to understand the nature of the act.

intangible property
Property that has no physical existence of its own, but stands as representative of something that is tangible and has intrinsic value.

intentional tort
An action in which the tortfeasor's purpose is to injure another.

interlocutory
A court order that decides an intervening matter, but not the ultimate outcome in the case.

interrogatories
A pretrial discovery tool consisting of a set of written questions propounded to a party.

intervention
A procedure through which a person not named as a party wishing to join in the action may move to be added as a party.

intestate
An owner of property who has not provided for its orderly distribution, or has failed to create a valid will at the time of death.

intoxication
An impairment of the defendant's mental or physical abilities because of drugs or alcohol.

invitee
An individual who has been invited on the premises.

involuntary petition
The filing of a petition by a creditor, forcing the debtor into the proceeding.

irrevocable living trust
A trust created and executed during the settlor's lifetime that cannot be revoked by him or her at any time.

issue of fact
A dispute over the existence of a particular fact alleged in a pleading.

issue of law
A dispute in which facts are not in controversy and the matter may be decided by the court through the application of legal principles.

joinder of parties
The addition as parties to an action of all those persons or entities that have the same rights or interests as co-plaintiffs or co-defendants.

joint tenancy
Two or more persons own property and are unified in their ownership based on unity of time, title, interest, and possession.

joint venture
A temporary contractual association of two or more individuals or businesses that agree to share in the responsibilities, profits, and losses of a common enterprise.

joint will
The same instrument comprises the will of two or more persons.

journal
Record of accounting transactions.

judgment
A termination of the lawsuit and the granting of the ultimate relief sought.

judgment creditor
One who has obtained a money judgment against the debtor upon which he can then force collection.

judicial foreclosure
The filing of an action in court to obtain a court order approving the sale of the property to satisfy the debt.

jurisdiction
The power of a court to hear a case.

keyboard
A platform with keys similar to a typewriter, along with alphanumeric keys, function keys, and cursor-moving keys.

key number system
An aid for locating topics in which West Publishing Company assigns a number to each topic and its subtopics, corresponding to the key numbers used in its publications.

kidnapping
The act of taking and detaining a person against the individual's will by force or intimidation.

larceny
The unlawful taking and carrying away of the property of another with the intent to permanently deprive the owner of possession.

Laws of Intestate Succession
A body of statutes determining the manner of the distribution of the deceased's property when there is no valid will concerning that particular property.

ledger
The summary of an account.

legal description
A means of identifying a specific parcel of land within certain boundaries in a uniform manner.

legal issue
A question of law phrased in the best light for the party submitting the brief, and constituting a valuable tool of persuasion.

legal malpractice
The failure of the attorney or legal office assistant to exercise the skill, prudence, and diligence that a client can expect of the ordinary lawyer in such a capacity, causing harm as a result of the failure.

legal office assistant
A highly skilled professional with specialized abilities to assist the attorney and the client.

legal research
The procedure of locating and analyzing the answer to a legal question.

liability
An account representing the debts or obligations of the legal office.

licensee
An individual who has permission to be on the premises.

limited liability company
An unincorporated association.

limited partnership
A form of partnership requiring at least one general partner and one limited partner.

liquidated damages
The sum that a party to a contract agrees to pay if he or she fails to perform as promised.

living trust
A trust created during the settlor's lifetime that becomes operative before his death.

local area network (LAN)
A system to link independent microcomputers to share data, software, and peripheral devices, such as printers, through a common computer server.

long arm statute
A state law used to obtain service on nonresident defendants in situations where there have been certain minimum contacts with that state.

loose-leaf service
A set of binders containing case law, statutes, administrative rules, discussion of the law, and cross-references on a particular area of the law.

mainframe computer
An immensely powerful computer capable of processing a huge volume of information.

majority opinion
The opinion that decides the case and is agreed upon by a majority of the judges of that particular appellate court.

marital property
Any property, whether real or personal, acquired during the marriage.

marriage
The legal status of a man and woman existing as husband and wife and united for life.

master file index
A file index that cross-references between a numeric system and an alphabetic system.

material
An issue of fact necessary to decide the question.

material error
Error that may have influenced the decision of the court in a particular direction.

mediation
The submission of a matter to a neutral third party or panel for a nonbinding decision.

megabyte
The amount of data that can be stored electronically.

memory
Silicon electronic circuitry to hold information in electronically arranged clusters.

mens rea
The mental aspect of the commission of a crime.

microcomputer
The smallest category of computer, known as a *PC,* ranging in size from portable laptop models to standing floor models.

micrographics
A photographic process for duplication of file material for storage on film.

microprocessor chip
The "brain" of the CPU, which is made up of silicon electronic circuitry that performs the mathematical functions of the computer to process information.

migratory divorce
A divorce where the husband and wife travel to another state to obtain a divorce because of the laxity of the laws in that state.

minicomputer
A computer having significantly less memory and capacity than a mainframe, yet can still process a large volume of information.

misdemeanor
An offense of a less serious nature usually punishable by a fine and/or imprisonment for a period less than one year.

misjoinder
A move to be dismissed from the action by a party added by mistake.

Model Rules of Professional Responsibility
A standard of conduct for its licensed professionals, the attorney, adopted by the American Bar Association.

modem
An electronic peripheral device for a computer that allows the computer to exchange information with another computer over telecommunication lines.

modification
A material change in the terms of the agreement.

monitor
A device similar to a television screen for the display of information.

mortgage
A written instrument creating an interest in real property as security for the repayment of a debt.

mortgagee
The borrower in a real estate transaction.

mortgagor
The lender in a real estate transaction.

motion
The petition to the court for an order directing some act.

motion for change of venue
A request to change the location of the trial if the defendant cannot obtain a fair and impartial trial at the location where the case is pending.

motion for more definite statement
A motion for the purpose of gaining sufficient information for an understanding of an allegation in order to admit or deny its correctness.

motion for severance
A request for a separate trial where one or more defendants are charged in the same indictment or information.

motion for summary judgment
The moving party is entitled to judgment as a matter of law where there is no genuine issue as to any material fact.

motion to dismiss
A request made to the court to enter an order that a complaint be dismissed when the defendant believes that the indictment or information is inherently flawed.

motion to suppress
A request made to the court to enter an order to suppress evidence obtained in an unconstitutional manner.

mouse
A pointing device used to move the cursor around the screen of the monitor to perform various functions.

MS-DOS
Microsoft Disk Operating System manufactured by Microsoft Corporation; the most widely used operating system for microcomputers.

mutual will
An occurrence in which two persons create their respective wills with provisions that favor each other.

National Association of Legal Secretaries (NALS)
The largest professional organization for the legal office assistant.

National Reporter System
Court reports published by West Publishing Company presenting the cases in chronological order and arranged by jurisdiction in sets.

negligence
The failure to use reasonable care to avoid injury to another.

no-fault
An acknowledgment that the bonds and ends of matrimony no longer exist without any of the fault grounds existing.

noncore matters
Issues that are not governed by a specific section of the Bankruptcy Code, but are related to the debtor and his estate.

nondischargeable debts
Debts from which there is no discharge under the Bankruptcy Code.

non-freehold estate
Possession of real property without title or absolute right to dispose of it.

non-marital property
Property acquired solely by one spouse as through a gift or bequest.

notice
The method and necessity of the conveyance of any information called for by the terms of the contract.

notice of appeal
A formal request for a hearing before the appellate court.

notice of hearing
Notification to the opposing party of time and place of the hearing and of the nature and grounds for the motion.

numeric filing system
A filing system using an office-assigned case number for each case, resulting in the files being arranged chronologically.

nuncupative will
A will that is entirely oral.

offer
A proposal demonstrating a willingness to enter into an agreement and creating a power of acceptance in the person to whom the offer is conveyed.

offeree
The person to whom the power of acceptance is given in order for the contract to exist.

offeror
The person making the offer.

officers
The persons charged with carrying out the wishes of the board of directors for the day-to-day management of the business.

official court reports
The published reports of the written opinions of cases that are authorized by the state or federal government.

official documents
Documents that are kept in the performance of an official's authorized duties.

omission
The failure to act.

operating system software
The computer program that instructs the computer hardware on how to communicate within itself.

opinion
The written statement on the case, along with a discussion of the law and reasoning upon which the decision is based.

oral argument
A session before the appellate court in which each side presents the legal arguments in support of the client's position to the panel of appellate judges.

original jurisdiction
The district court in which a lawsuit was started and the trial took place.

overhead
The costs involved in the administration of the legal office.

partner
The attorney that has an ownership interest in the legal office, shares in the profits and losses of the firm, and has a management role.

partnership
A form of private legal office where two or more attorneys own all of the assets of the law firm, organized as a partnership under the laws of the state in which it practices.

party
The person or legal entity having an interest in the subject matter of the contract and legally bound by his or her promise.

passive voice
Where the subject of the sentence is acted upon.

periodicals
Numerous magazines are available for any area of practice, enabling the practicing attorney to remain current on changes in the law.

personal jurisdiction
The authority of a court over a person, sometimes called *in personam* jurisdiction.

personal property
Property that is not considered real property.

personal representative
The individual named in the will to carry out the testator's wishes and enforce the provisions of the will.

persuasive authority
The reliance by a court on the decisions of another court on the same legal issue, but not one that it is bound to follow.

petition
A legal pleading filed to begin the bankruptcy proceedings.

plaintiff
The party to a lawsuit that commences the action.

plea
The formal response of the defendant to the accusation.

pleading
A document filed with the court containing the claims of a party with the purpose of giving notice of the issues to be presented at trial.

pocket supplements
A small pamphlet placed inside the back cover of a hardbound volume, containing updated information on specific new law addressing subjects covered in the volume.

posting
The process of recording information from the journal to each ledger.

power of sale foreclosure
An out-of-court sale based on a provision in the mortgage

document allowing for the sale without court supervision.

praecipe
An order from the clerk of the court to a party to show in court why something should or should not occur.

prayer for relief
A request of the court for judicial relief or damages.

preferential transfer
Transfers made by the debtor within ninety days of the filing of the petition to a creditor who receives more than the creditor would have if listed in the petition.

preliminary hearing
A hearing in which the court determines if there is probable cause to formally accuse the defendant of a crime.

prepaid legal service fee
A plan that has been purchased by the individual client, an employer, or the client's labor union, to provide legal services as a fringe benefit.

primary sources
Sources of the law that are considered binding on the court.

principal
The party granting authority to another to act for his or her benefit and subject to his or her direction and control.

printer
A machine used to produce the information onto paper, known as a "hard copy."

priority claim
A creditor with a preference granted by some statutory authority.

private branch exchange (PBX)
A computerized telecommunications system.

private express trust
A trust created solely by operation of law to correct some inequity.

privity of contract
The relationship between the promisor and promisee of a contract.

probate
A court procedure involving the collection of the decedent's assets, payment of debts, and the distribution to heirs.

professional
An individual employed in a capacity requiring a high level of training and competence.

professional corporation
A form of private legal office where two or more attorneys own all of the assets of the law firm, organized as a corporation under the laws of the state in which it practices.

profit
Gross income less expenses.

promisee
The party to whom the promise which is the subject matter of the contract is made.

promisor
The party making a promise that is the subject matter of the contract.

promissory note
A promise in writing to pay a certain sum of money at a time stated, or on demand, to a person or to his order.

proof of claim
A legal document submitted under oath, which sets forth the amount owed and the details forming the basis for the claim.

proof of service
A written indication by the process server that he or she has made service as prescribed upon the defendant.

prosecutor
An attorney representing the interests of the public in the criminal case.

protective order
A court order to protect information that is not privileged, but that would cause annoyance, embarrassment, oppression, undue burden, or expense.

proximate cause
The act or omission that is the foreseeable cause of the injury.

public records
Records required by law to be kept by a county clerk or other official.

punitive damages
The monetary award devised to make an example or punish the tortfeasor.

purchase money mortgage
A mortgage in which the parties to the transaction are private parties, as opposed to the involvement of a commercial lending institution.

quitclaim deed
A covenant by the seller to release any claim that the seller may have had in the property.

rape
Sexual intercourse by force or by putting the victim in fear or in circumstances under which there can be no resistance.

real property
Land and whatever is built upon it, or growing on or affixed to it.

reasonable care
The responsibility to act or not act sensibly under the circumstances to avoid injury.

reasonable person standard
The measure of whether an act or omission is reasonable, based on the behavior of an imaginary reasonable person.

receiving stolen property
Knowingly receiving property that has been stolen with the intent to deprive the owner of possession.

reconcile
To make sure that the bank's records for an account agree with the legal office's records.

record below
The record of the case made at the time of trial, consisting of case docket, transcripts of the proceedings, exhibits, pleadings, motions, and briefs.

relief
The request by the proponent of an argument that the court hold in a certain manner on behalf of that party.

reorganization
The preparation of a plan for restructuring the debt of a business to meet with the approval of the court.

request for production
The request of a party for documents and other things that are relevant to the subject matter and are not privileged.

residuary
The remainder of the testator's estate not subject to a specific devise.

retainer fee
A fee paid by the client to the attorney for legal services already performed, or to be performed in the future.

revenue
Income from legal fees.

revocable living trust
A trust created by a settlor during his lifetime that reserves the right of revocation of the trust.

right of survivorship
At the moment of death of one joint owner, property passes automatically to the remaining joint owner.

robbery
The unlawful taking and carrying away of property from a person by another who uses threat or force with intent to steal.

rules of court
The duties and power of each court.

Satisfaction of Mortgage
A discharge signed by the mortgagee indicating that the debt has been paid and that all terms and conditions of the mortgage have been satisfied.

scanner
A computer hardware peripheral device that "reads" documents, photographs, or other written material, reducing the image to electronic data.

schedules
Official forms listing assets and liabilities of the debtor.

scope of discovery
The depth and breadth of inquiry, permitting any matter relevant to the subject and not subject to privilege.

seal
An impression made upon the original copy of an agreement to authenticate an act.

search warrant
A court order allowing a law enforcement officer to search for evidence.

secondary sources
Sources of the law that, for legal research purposes, discuss and analyze the law.

secured claim
A claim that is represented by a security interest in property.

self-defense
The use of force to avoid harm to one's self.

separation agreement
A contract between a husband and wife establishing their respective rights and obligations while they are separated.

service of process
Delivery of the summons and complaint to the defendant.

settlor
The owner of the property that has been placed in a trust.

severability
The terms of a contract are divisible.

share
The unit into which the ownership of the business is divided.

shared parental responsibility
Each minor child has frequent contact with both parents, and those parents share the responsibilities of child-raising.

shareholders
The owners of the business.

shepardizing
The use of *Shepard's Citations* to find out the subsequent treatment of cases, statutes, court rules, and other sources of the law.

slip law
In loose-leaf or pamphlet form, the first publication of a law as it is enacted.

small claims court
A court of limited jurisdiction where the value of the matter at issue is not to exceed a maximum dollar amount, i.e. $1500.

sodomy
Statutorily defined unnatural sexual conduct.

software
An electronic set of instructions known as a *computer program*.

sole practitioner
The most commonly seen type of private legal office in which one individual owns all of the assets of the business, and is its sole licensed attorney.

sole proprietorship
A business enterprise in which one person owns the assets, is liable for the debts, and is entitled to the profits of the business.

special damages
Actual damages flowing from an act or breach due to special circumstances.

special warranty deed
A deed is used in which the seller only covenants to defend the title against persons making a claim or demand through the seller.

stare decisis
Legal doctrine in which a court will stand by the precedent set down by another court on a similar legal question.

Statement of Financial Affairs
A questionnaire designed to provide sufficient information to the Court to decide if a discharge should be granted.

statute
The formal written law enacted by Congress or a state's legislature.

statute of limitation
A law establishing the time limitation to the right of filing an action.

Statutes at Large
A compilation of the session's laws arranged chronologically.

statutory law
Large, multivolume sets containing the statutory codes of the state in which the firm is located and the United States.

statutory rape
Sexual intercourse with a female under the age of consent.

statutory redemption
The allowance by statute of the mortgagor to redeem the mortgaged property after the foreclosure sale.

stay of proceedings
No further action may be taken in any other court involving this particular bankrupt person.

stock
The capital or principal fund of a corporation formed by the contributions of subscribers or the sale of shares.

stock subscription agreement
The agreement to commit to the purchase of a set number of shares of stock of the new corporation at a stated price.

stock transfer ledger
A record of the identity of the shareholders.

strict liability
Responsibility for actions regardless of intention or fault.

subject matter jurisdiction
The power of a court over a particular type of cause of action and the relief sought.

subpoena
An order to appear at a certain time and place.

subpoena duces tecum
An order to produce documents or records at a certain time and place.

subrogation
The substitution of one person in the place of another so that the one substituted has the rights of the other in relation to the debt or claim.

substantive law
That part of the law that establishes rights, duties, and obligations.

substitution of parties
A motion to provide for the maintenance of an action after the original plaintiff is no longer available.

survey
An evaluation of real property to determine its boundaries and physical limits.

survival statutes
Amendment of the pleadings where the original plaintiff is no longer available to carry on the action, yet the cause of action remains alive.

syllabus
A synopsis of the case prepared by the publisher of the opinion consisting of a brief summary of the case including its facts, its history through the court system, and the decision of the court.

T account
A graphical means of displaying the entries to an account and its current status.

tangible property
Property that has some form or physical nature and that may be felt or touched.

telecommunications
A term applied to the sending of any information by voice, data, or image signal over long distances through communication technology.

telex machine
A form of electronic teletypewriter used to electronically transmit messages over telephone lines.

tenancy by the entirety
A form of concurrent ownership that occurs between a husband and wife.

tenancy in common
Each concurrent owner of the property holds an undivided interest in the whole property.

tenancy in partnership
The interest in partnership property held by each owner.

tenancy in severalty
Ownership of real property by one person.

terminal
A monitor and a keyboard with no internal computing capability.

testamentary trust
A trust created by a will, and executed with the statutory formalities required by state law.

testate
An owner of property having left a valid will providing for the distribution of an estate at the time of death.

testator
The maker of the will.

testimonium clause
A clause stating that the testator is freely signing the will as the last will and testament and is requesting that the witnesses do similarly.

theft
The unlawful taking of the property of another.

thesaurus
A resource book that offers the legal researcher alternative terminology for legal research in the form of synonyms and antonyms.

timekeeping
The tracking of the time spent in the delivery of legal services on behalf of a client.

timesheet
A written record of all time spent by a legal office staff employee in the representation of a client's interests.

title
(1) Subject matter headings; (2) The formal right of ownership of real property.

toll
Condition in which the statutory period for limitation scheduled to expire on a weekend or holiday does not expire until the next business day.

tone
The attitude of the writer as expressed through the written word.

tort
A wrongful act resulting in injury to a person or property.

tortfeasor
An individual that performs the wrongful act resulting in injury.

transcript
The official daily record of the proceedings before the court.

treatise
A single or multivolume work on one specific area of the law providing a learned analysis and discussion of all aspects of the particular topic.

trespasser
An individual who enters another's property without consent.

trial court
The court in which a lawsuit is commenced.

trust
A separate legal entity to hold property for the benefit of another.

trustee
The person that holds legal title to property for the benefit of another person.

trustee in bankruptcy
An impartial person elected by the creditors to administer the estate of the debtor.

U.S. Code
Federal statutes arranged by subject into fifty titles, or subjects, which are accessed by a general index.

ultimate issue
The question that must be finally answered to support a cause of action.

unauthorized practice of law
The furnishing of advice on the law as it applies to a particular case or situation.

unofficial court reports
In most jurisdictions, a private publisher will offer a version of the actual written opinions of the court.

unsecured claim
A claim that is unrepresented by a security interest in property without any statutory priority.

VA mortgage
A loan that is insured by the Veterans' Administration.

venue
The geographic location of a court, referring to the particular county, or geographical area, in which a court may hear a case.

vicarious liability
The liability of one person for the wrongful conduct of another subordinate individual.

voice mail
A system that stores and delivers voice messages.

voidable contract
A contract that is valid, yet may be declared invalid at the option of a party to the agreement.

voidable transfer
A transfer that is made within one year of the filing of the petition with the intent to defraud creditors.

voluntary petition
The filing of the petition by a debtor under one of the provisions of the Bankruptcy Code.

warranty
A representation made by the seller as to the quality, fitness, or title to goods assuring the purchaser that certain facts are as represented.

wide area telecommunication service (WATS)
A flat monthly rate for a line that can be used as often as needed to reduce the cost of long-distance calling.

will
An instrument that declares the intended distribution of one's property at death.

will contest
An action in court to challenge the validity of a will.

Windows
A graphical operating system rather than text-based, using icons, dialog boxes, and a mouse to communicate with the hardware and perform operations.

work product
Any notes, papers, or memorandum of the attorney in preparation for litigation.

writ of certiorari
An order of the Supreme Court agreeing to hear a case.

Appendix A

INTERROGATORIES

IN THE CIRCUIT COURT
FOR THE COUNTY OF ORANGE

BELLE BLISS,

    Plaintiff,

v.   CASE NO.: 34567

THE THIRSTY TURTLE,

    Defendant.

_____/

INTERROGATORIES TO PLAINTIFF

Defendant, THE THIRSTY TURTLE, through his undersigned attorney, propounds the following interrogatories to Plaintiff pursuant to court rules to be answered within thirty (30) days from the date hereof.

As used herein, "person" means the full name, present or last-known residence address. Any reference to the singular person, place, thing, or entity, including but not limited to any partnership, corporation, firm, proprietorship, association, or governmental body, shall include the plural, as well as the singular, and the feminine as well as the masculine or neuter.

The term "accident" means that certain accident between the automobiles of Plaintiff and Defendant.

If answering for another person or entity, answer with respect to that person or entity, unless otherwise stated.

1. What is the name and address of the person answering these interrogatories, and, if applicable, the person's official position or relationship with the party to whom the interrogatories are directed?

2. List the names, business addresses, dates of employment, and rates of pay regarding all employers, including self-employment, for whom you have worked in the past ten (10) years.

Page 1 of 6--Interrogatories to Plaintiff

3. List all former names and when you were known by those names. State all addresses where you have lived for the past ten (10) years, the dates you lived at each address, your Social Security number, your date of birth, and, if you are or have ever been married, the name of your spouse or spouses.

4. Do you wear glasses, contact lenses, or hearing aids? If so, who prescribed them; when were they prescribed; when were your eyes or ears last examined; and what is the name and address of the examiner?

5. Have you ever been convicted of a crime, other than any juvenile adjudication, where the law under which you were convicted was punishable by death or imprisonment in excess of one year, or that involved dishonesty or a false statement regardless of the punishment? If so, state as to each conviction the specific crime, the date, and the place of conviction.

6. Were you suffering from physical infirmity, disability, or sickness at the time of the accident described in the complaint? If so, what was the nature of the infirmity, disability, or sickness?

7. Did you consume any alcoholic beverages or take any drugs or medications within twelve hours before the time of the incident described in the complaint? If so, state the type and amount of alcoholic beverages, drugs, or medication that were consumed and when and where you consumed them.

8. Describe in detail how the incident described in the Complaint happened, including all actions taken by you to prevent the accident.

9. Describe in detail each act or omission on the part of any party to this lawsuit that you contend constituted negligence that was a contributing legal source of the incident in question.

10. Were you charged with any violation of law (including any regulations or ordinances) arising from the incident described in the

Page 2 of 6--Interrogatories to Plaintiff

complaint? If so, what was the nature of the charge, what plea, or answer, if any, did you enter to the charge; what court or agency heard the charge; was any written report prepared by anyone regarding this charge; and, if so, what is the name and address of the person or entity that prepared the report? Do you have a copy of the report; and was the testimony at any trial, hearing, or other proceeding on the charge recorded in any manner, and, if so, what was the name and address of the person who recorded the testimony?

11. Describe each injury for which you are claiming damages in this case, specifying the part of your body that was injured, the nature of the injury, and, as to any injuries you contend are permanent, the effects on you that you claim are permanent.

12. List each item of expense or damage, other than loss of income or earning capacity, that you claim to have incurred as a result of the incident described in the complaint, giving for each item: the date incurred, the name and business address to whom each was paid or is owed, and the goods or services for which each was incurred.

13. Do you contend that you have lost any income, benefits, or earning capacity in the past or future as a result of the incident described in the complaint? If so, state the nature of the income, benefits, or earning capacity, and the amount and the method that you used in computing the amount.

14. Has anything been paid or is anything payable from any third party for the damages listed in your answers to these interrogatories? If so, state the amounts paid or payable, the name and business address of the person or entity who paid or owes said amounts, and which of those third parties have or claim a right of subrogation.

Page 3 of 6--Interrogatories to Plaintiff

15. List the names and business addresses of each physician who has treated or examined you, and each medical facility where you have received any treatment or examination of the injuries for which you seek damages in this case; and state as to each the date of treatment or examination and the injury or condition for which you were examined or treated.

16. List the names and business addresses of all other physicians, medical facilities, or other health care providers by whom or at which you have been examined or treated in the past ten (10) years; and state as to each the dates of examination or treatment and the condition or injury for which you were examined or treated.

17. List the names and addresses of all persons who are believed or known by you, your agents, or your attorneys to have any knowledge concerning any of the issues in this lawsuit; and specify the subject matter about which the witness has knowledge.

18. Have you heard or do you know about any statement or remark made by or on behalf of any party to this lawsuit, other than yourself, concerning any issue in this lawsuit? If so, state the name and address of each person who made the statement or statements, the name and address of each person who heard it, and the date, time, place, and substance of each statement.

19. State the name and address of every person known to you, your agents, or attorneys, who has knowledge about, or possession, custody, or control of any model, plat, map, drawing, motion picture, videotape, or photograph pertaining to any fact or issue involved in this controversy; and describe as to each, what such person has, the name and address of the person who took or prepared it, and the date it was taken or prepared.

Page 4 of 6--Interrogatories to Plaintiff

20. Do you intend to call any expert witnesses at the trial of this case? If so, state as to each such witness the name and business address of the witness, the witness's qualifications as an expert, the subject matter upon which the witness is expected to testify, and a summary of the grounds for each opinion.

21. Have you made an agreement with anyone that would limit that party's liability to anyone for any of the damages sued upon in this case? If so, state whether you were plaintiff or defendant, the nature of the action, and the date and court in which such suit was filed.

_____
BELLE BLISS

BEFORE ME, the undersigned authority, personally appeared BELLE BLISS, known to me and known by me to be the plaintiff in the above-mentioned lawsuit and who executed the foregoing Answers to Interrogatories, under oath, stated that she is the person who executed the same and that according to her best knowledge and belief the answers are true and correct. BELLE BLISS was under oath.

Form of Identification _____.
Sworn to and subscribed before me, this _____ day of _____, 19__.

_____

Printed name _____

Notary Public, state of Fremont at Large
My Commission expires:

Page 5 of 6--Interrogatories to Plaintiff

I HEREBY CERTIFY that the original and one copy of the foregoing Interrogatories to Plaintiff were furnished to WILL PURVALE, Attorney for Plaintiff, One Harmony Drive, Orange, Georgia, 45090-6540, this _____ day of _____, 19___, by U.S. Mail.

_____
BARNWELL BARNETT
Attorney for Defendant
1234 S. Drainage St.
Orange, Georgia 45091-7689

I HEREBY CERTIFY that the original Interrogatories with answers were furnished to BARNWELL BARNETT, Attorney for Defendant, 1234 S. Drainage St., Orange, Georgia 45091-7689, this _____ day of _____, 19___, by U.S. Mail.

_____
WILL PURVALE
Attorney for Plaintiff
One Harmony Drive
Orange, Georgia 45090-6540

Page 6 of 6--Interrogatories to Plaintiff

Appendix B

STATE STATUTORY SOURCES

State	Official	Unofficial
Alabama	*Code of Alabama*	
Alaska	*Alaska Statutes*	
Arizona	*Arizona Revised Statutes Annotated*	
Arkansas	*Arkansas Code*	
California	*West's Annotated California Code* *Deering's Annotated and Unannotated California Code*	
Colorado	*Colorado Revised Statutes* *West's Colorado Revised Statutes Annotated*	
Connecticut	*General Statutes of Connecticut*	*Connecticut General Statutes Annotated (West)*
Delaware	*Delaware Code Annotated*	
District of Columbia	*District of Columbia Code Annotated*	
Florida	*Florida Statutes*	*Florida Statutes Annotated (West)* *Florida Statutes Annotated (Harrison)*
Georgia	*Official Code of Georgia Annotated (Michie)*	*Code of Georgia Annotated (Harrison)*
Hawaii	*Hawaii Revised Statutes*	
Idaho	*Idaho Code*	
Illinois	*Illinois Revised Statutes*	*Smith-Hurd Illinois Annotated Statutes*
Indiana	*Indiana Code*	*Burns Indiana Statutes Annotated* *West's Annotated Indiana Code*
Iowa	*Code of Iowa*	*Iowa Code Annotated*
Kansas	*Kansas Statutes Annotated* *Vernon's Kansas Statutes Annotated*	
Kentucky	*Baldwin's Official Edition, Kentucky Revised Statutes Annotated* *Kentucky Revised Statutes Annotated, Official Edition (Michie/Bobbs-Merrill)*	
Louisiana	*West's Louisiana Revised Statutes Annotated* *West's Louisiana Code of Evidence Annotated* *West's Louisiana Code of Juvenile Procedure Annotated*	

State	Official	Unofficial
Maine	*Maine Revised Statutes Annotated (West)*	
Maryland	*Annotated Code of Maryland*	*Annotated Code of Maryland (1957)*
Massachusetts	*General Laws of the Commonwealth of Massachusetts (Mass./Law. Co-op.)*	*Massachusetts General Laws Annotated (West)* *Annotated Laws of Massachusetts (Law. Co-op.)*
Michigan	*Michigan Compiled Laws*	*Michigan Compiled Laws Annotated (West)* *Michigan Statutes Annotated (Callaghan)*
Minnesota	*Minnesota Statutes*	*Minnesota Statutes Annotated (West)*
Mississippi	*Mississippi Code Annotated*	
Missouri	*Missouri Revised Statutes*	*Vernon's Annotated Missouri Statutes*
Montana	*Montana Code Annotated*	
Nebraska	*Revised Statutes of Nebraska*	
Nevada	*Nevada Revised Statutes*	*Nevada Revised Statutes Annotated (Michie)*
New Hampshire	*New Hampshire Revised Statutes Annotated*	
New Jersey	*New Jersey Revised Statutes*	*New Jersey Statutes Annotated (West)*
New Mexico	*New Mexico Statutes Annotated (Michie)*	
New York	*McKinney's Consolidated Laws of New York Annotated* *Consolidated Laws Service*	
North Carolina	*General Statutes of North Carolina*	
North Dakota	*North Dakota Century Code*	
Ohio	*Ohio Revised Code Annotated (Anderson)* *Ohio Revised Code Annotated (Baldwin)*	
Oklahoma	*Oklahoma Statutes*	*Oklahoma Statutes Annotated (West)*
Oregon	*Oregon Revised Statutes*	
Pennsylvania	*Pennsylvania Consolidated Statutes* *Purdon's Pennsylvania Consolidated Statutes Annotated*	
Rhode Island	*General Laws of Rhode Island*	
South Carolina	*Code of Laws of South Carolina 1976 Annotated (Law. Co-op.)*	
South Dakota	*South Dakota Codified Laws Annotated*	
Tennessee	*Tennessee Code Annotated*	
Texas	*Vernon's Texas Codes Annotated*	
Utah	*Utah Code Annotated*	

State	Official	Unofficial
Vermont	*Vermont Statutes Annotated*	
Virginia	*Code of Virginia Annotated*	
Washington	*Revised Code of Washington*	*Revised Code of Washington Annotated*
West Virginia	*West Virginia Code*	
Wisconsin	*Wisconsin Statutes*	*West's Wisconsin Statutes Annotated*
Wyoming	*Wyoming Statutes*	

Appendix C

ANTENUPTIAL AGREEMENT

AGREEMENT made as of this 14th day of June, 1999, between WINSTON P. BLANSFORD, III ("WINSTON"), residing at 1590 West Denton Street, Nelton, New York 10079, and ARCADIA HOLLOWELL ("ARCADIA"), residing at 3898 Georgetown Drive, Geneva, New York 10076.

WITNESSETH:

WHEREAS, each of the parties has known the other for a period of time, is fully satisfied with the disclosure of the financial circumstances of the other, and desires to make an agreement regarding his and her property rights in consideration of the marriage to each other, and

WHEREAS, each party acknowledges that the other may hereafter acquire by gift and inheritance, as well as through professional endeavor and from other sources, assets and income of values, and

WHEREAS, each of the parties has assets and earnings, or earnings potential, sufficient to provide for his or her own maintenance and support in a proper and acceptable standard of living without the necessity of financial contributions by the other, and each of the parties is aware of the hazards and risks of the continuance of earnings and the changes; in assets and liabilities of the other and of the possibility of substantially changed financial circumstances of the other with the result that the earnings and/or net worth of one party is or may be substantially different from those of the other party, and

WHEREAS, except as otherwise herein set forth, each of the parties desires to own, hold, acquire, and dispose of property now and in the future and subsequent to their marriage to each other with the same freedom as though unmarried and to dispose of said property during their respective

Page 1 of 8--Antenuptial Agreement

lifetimes or upon death or upon any other termination of the marriage without restriction or limitation in accordance with his and her own desires, and

WHEREAS, except as otherwise herein set forth, it is the intention of each of the parties by entering into this agreement to determine unilaterally what property, now and in the future, shall be his or her own separate property and that all of the property of each, however acquired or held, shall be free from any consideration as marital property, community property, quasi-community property or any other form of marital or community property, as those terms are used and understood in any jurisdiction, including but not limited to the state of New York.

NOW, THEREFORE, in consideration of the marriage of each party to the other and the mutual promises and covenants herein, the parties have mutually agreed as follows:

1. *Present property.* All of the property, real, personal, and mixed, which each party has previously acquired and now holds in his or her name or possession, shall be and continue to remain the sole and separate property of that person, together with all future appreciation, increases, and other changes in value of that property and irrespective of the contributions (if any) that either party might have made or may hereafter make to said property or to the marriage, directly or indirectly.

2. *Future property.* All of the property, real, personal, or mixed, which each party may hereafter acquire in his or her own name or possession shall be and remain the sole and separate property of that person, together with all future appreciation, increases, and other changes in value of that property and irrespective of the contributions (if any) that either party

Page 2 of 8--Antenuptial Agreement

may make to said property or to the marriage, directly or indirectly. Notwithstanding the foregoing, any property that is a gift from one party to the other shall remain the sole and separate property of the donee of the gift; and all wedding presents given to both parties shall be deemed jointly owned by the parties wherein each shall hold an undivided one-half interest.

3. *Joint property.* Any property, real, personal, or mixed, which shall now or hereafter be held in the joint names of the parties shall be owned in accordance with the kind of joint ownership as title is held, and if there is no other designation, shall be held equally by the parties with such survivorship rights (if any) as may be specifically designated by the title ownership or as may be implied or be derived by operation of law other than the operation of the so-called equitable distribution law or community property or any similar law of any jurisdiction involving marital property, community property, quasi-community property, or any other form of marital or community property.

4. *Life insurance.* From and after the marriage of the parties, BLANSFORD shall maintain at his own expense a policy or policies of life insurance on his life, having death benefits payable in the sum or not less than Two Hundred Fifty Thousand Dollars ($250,000) for the benefit of HOLLOWELL until the earlier occurrence of the death of either party or the remarriage of HOLLOWELL (as "remarriage" is hereinafter defined), and he will not encumber said insurance whereby the death benefits that are actually payable shall be less than Two Hundred Fifty Thousand Dollars ($250,000). BLANSFORD shall furnish proof of his compliance with this paragraph upon the reasonable request of HOLLOWELL, but not more often than annually; and HOLLOWELL, in addition, is authorized to obtain direct confirmation from any

Page 3 of 8--Antenuptial Agreement

insurance carrier or employer through which said policy or policies are issued or administered.

5. *Estate rights*. Except as otherwise herein set forth, each party hereby releases, waives, and relinquishes any right or claim of any nature whatsoever in the property of the other or otherwise, now or hereafter acquired, and, without limitation, expressly forever waives any right or claim that he or she may have or hereafter acquire, whether as the spouse of the other or otherwise, under the present or future laws of any jurisdiction: (a) to share in the estate of the other party upon the death of the other party; and (b) to act as executor or administrator of the estate of the other or as trustee, personal representative, or in any fiduciary capacity with respect to the estate of the other. All rights that either party may acquire in the other's estate by virtue of the marriage, including but not limited to rights of set-off in New York, all distributive shares in New York, and all rights of election in New York, as such laws may now exist or hereafter be changed, and any similar or other provision of law in this or any other jurisdiction, are hereby waived by each party.

6. *Wills*. Nothing in this agreement shall prevent or limit either party from hereafter making provisions for the other by Last Will and Testament: (a) to inherit from the estate of the other; and/or (b) to serve in any fiduciary capacity, in which event the provisions thus made in said Last Will and Testament shall control.

7. *Primary residence*. In the event that BLANSFORD should predecease HOLLOWELL during the time when they are married to each other (as "married" is hereinafter defined), HOLLOWELL shall have the right to continue to reside in their primary residence until the occurrence of her remarriage;

Page 4 of 8--Antenuptial Agreement

provided, however, that HOLLOWELL shall pay all expenses of every kind and nature in connection with said residence (including but not limited to all repairs, whether ordinary, extraordinary, structural, or otherwise), except only for the payment of real estate taxes and, if the primary residence is a condominium or cooperative apartment, the maintenance or common charges, as the case may be, which real estate taxes and maintenance charges or common charges, as applicable, shall be paid for by BLANSFORD'S estate as an obligation of the estate. If the primary residence is rented and occupied by the parties under a lease (not a proprietary lease of a cooperative apartment), HOLLOWELL shall have the right to cause said lease to be transferred to her sole name, including any rent security deposited under said lease, without payment to BLANSFORD'S estate, provided that said request is made in writing to BLANSFORD'S estate representatives within ninety (90) days after his death. This paragraph shall apply only to the primary residence of the parties and not to any other residence which they or either of them may own at the time of BLANSFORD'S death.

8. *Support.*

(a) In the event that the parties shall cease to be married for any reason other than BLANSFORD'S death (as "married" is hereinafter defined), BLANSFORD, or his estate, shall pay to HOLLOWELL as and for her support and maintenance the sum of Five Hundred Dollars ($500) per week, commencing as of the first Friday after the parties shall cease to be married (by reason of death or otherwise) and continuing on each successive Friday thereafter. Said payments shall continue for one week for each full week that the parties are married, but in no event shall said payments continue for a period of more than 260 weeks, whereby said payments shall automatically and without further

Page 5 of 8--Antenuptial Agreement

notice cease. By way of example, if the parties are married for 210 full weeks, a total of 210 weekly payments shall be made; if they are married for $20\frac{1}{2}$ weeks, 20 weekly payments shall be made. Notwithstanding the foregoing, all of said weekly payments shall sooner cease upon the earliest happening of: (i) the death of HOLLOWELL; (ii) the remarriage of HOLLOWELL; or (iii) the fifth anniversary date after the date when payments are required to be commenced. This paragraph shall not be construed as an indication of any financial need on the part of HOLLOWELL, but rather an expression by BLANSFORD of his desire to make a contribution to the future life of HOLLOWELL under the circumstances and provisions herein set forth.

(b) In the event that BLANSFORD shall die while the parties are married to each other (as "marriage" as hereunder defined), BLANSFORD'S estate shall pay to HOLLOWELL as and for her support and maintenance the sum of Five Hundred Dollars ($500) per week, commencing as of the first Friday after his death and continuing on each successive Friday thereafter until the earliest happening of: (i) the death of HOLLOWELL; or (ii) the remarriage of HOLLOWELL; or (iii) the fifth anniversary date after the date when payments are required to be commenced.

9. *Definitions.* The following definitions shall apply to the respective expressions whenever used in this agreement:

(a) "Remarriage" as used everywhere in this agreement shall be deemed a remarriage of HOLLOWELL, regardless of whether said remarriage shall be void or voidable or terminated by divorce or annulment or otherwise and shall also be deemed to include circumstance whereby HOLLOWELL shall live with an unrelated person in a husband-wife relationship (irrespective of whether or not they hold themselves out as such) for a continuous period of

Page 6 of 8--Antenuptial Agreement

sixty (60) days or for a period or periods of time aggregating one hundred twenty (120) days or more on a noncontinuous, or interrupted, basis in any eighteen (18) month period.

(b) The time during which the parties are "married," or the period of the "marriage" of the parties, as used everywhere in this agreement, shall constitute the period of time commencing with the ceremonial marriage of the parties to each other and continuing until the earliest happening of any of the following events: (i) the commencement of a matrimonial action (as "matrimonial action" is currently defined by the state of New York or any similar action or proceeding in any other jurisdiction; (ii) the divorce or legal separation (by decree or judgment or by agreement) of the parties; or (iii) the physical separation of the parties wherein either or both of the parties have commenced to live separate and apart from the other with the intent not thereafter to live together, regardless of whether that intent is expressed in writing, orally, or otherwise; or (iv) the death of either party.

10. *Disclosure.* Each party has been apprised of the right to obtain further disclosure of the financial circumstances of the other party and is satisfied with the disclosure made. Each party expressly waives the right to any further financial disclosure and acknowledges that said waiver is made with the full benefit of legal counsel and knowledge of the legal consequences thereof, and that neither party properly cannot, and shall not, subsequently assert that this agreement should be impaired or invalidated by reason of any lack of financial disclosure or lack of understanding or of fraud, duress, or coercion. Without limiting the generality of the foregoing. BLANSFORD represents that his present net worth is in excess of Two Hundred Fifty Thousand Dollars ($250,000) and that his annual income is in excess of Sixty-

Page 7 of 8--Antenuptial Agreement

Three Thousand Dollars ($63,000), which representation admittedly is not all-inclusive and which is not intended to be relied upon by either party.

11. *General provisions.* This Agreement shall be construed as an agreement made and to be performed in the state of New York and cannot be changed, or any of its terms waived, except by a writing signed and acknowledged by both parties. Each party hereby consents to the personal jurisdiction of the state of New York in the event of any dispute or question regarding this Agreement. Each party acknowledges receipt of fully executed copy of this Agreement, has had an opportunity to read it, and understands the same after consultation with independent counsel and is fully satisfied with the disclosure made of all of the financial circumstances of the other party. The paragraph captions in this Agreement are for the purpose of convenience only and are not a part of this agreement.

12. Each party has been separately represented by an attorney of his or her own choice. HOLLOWELL has been represented by Lane & Price, P.A., 496 Churchill Road, New York, New York 10024, and BLANSFORD has been represented by Kleinig & Stein, P.A., 389 Washington, New York, New York 10024 in connection with the negotiation, making, and execution of this agreement.

IN WITNESS WHEREOF the parties, for themselves, their heirs, next-of-kin, representatives, and assigns have executed these presents prior to their marriage to each other on the day and year first above written.

_____

ARCADIA HOLLOWELL

_____

WINSTON P. BLANSFORD, III

Page 8 of 8--Antenuptial Agreement

Appendix D

PARTNERSHIP AGREEMENT

KING, QUEEN & SQUIRE
PARTNERSHIP AGREEMENT

Agreement made November 30, 1999, between REX KING, of 1044 Hastings, city of Orange, county of York, state of Wyoming; COURTNEY QUEEN, of 1215 Bayeaux Street, city of Orange, county of York, state of Wyoming; and MARSHALL SQUIRE, of 1100 Norman Drive, city of Orange, county of York, state of Wyoming; herein referred to as Partners.

RECITALS

1. Partners desire to join together for the pursuit of common business goals.

2. Partners have considered various forms of joint business enterprises for their business activities.

3. Partners desire to enter into a partnership agreement as the most advantageous business form for their mutual purposes.

In consideration of the mutual promises contained herein, partners agree as follows:

ARTICLE I

NAME, PURPOSE, AND DOMICILE

The name of the partnership shall be KING, QUEEN & SQUIRE. The partnership may engage in any and all activities as may be necessary, incidental, or convenient to carry out the business of providing paralegal services. The principal place of business shall be at 10 Court Street, city of Orange, county of York, state of Wyoming, unless relocated by majority consent of partners.

Page 1 of 10--Partnership Agreement

ARTICLE II

DURATION OF AGREEMENT

The term of this agreement shall be for twenty (20) years, commencing on November 30, 1999, and terminating on November 30, 2019, unless sooner terminated by mutual consent of the parties or by operation of the provisions of this agreement.

ARTICLE III

CLASSIFICATION AND PERFORMANCE BY PARTNERS

1. Partners shall be classified as active partners, advisory partners, or estate partners.

An active partner may voluntarily become an advisory partner, may be required to become one irrespective of age, and shall automatically become one after attaining the age of sixty-five (65) years, and in each case shall continue as such for two (2) years unless he sooner withdraws or dies.

If an active partner dies, his estate will become an estate partner for two (2) years. If an advisory partner dies within one (1) year of having become an advisory partner, his estate will become an estate partner for the balance of the two-year period.

Only active partners shall have a vote in any partnership matter.

At the time of the taking effect of this partnership agreement, all the partners shall be active partners.

2. An active partner, after attaining the age of sixty-five (65) years, or prior thereto if the executive committee with the approval of two-thirds of all the other active partners determines that the reason for the change in status is bad health, may become an advisory partner at the end of any calendar month upon giving one (1) calendar month's prior notice in

Page 2 of 10--Partnership Agreement

writing of his intention so to do. Such notice shall be deemed to be sufficient if sent by registered mail addressed to the partnership at its principal office at 10 Court Street, Orange, Wyoming 00001 not less than one (1) calendar month prior to the date when such change is to become effective.

3. Any active partner may at any age be required to become an advisory partner at any time if the executive committee with the approval of two-thirds of the other active partners shall decide that such change is for any reason in best interests of the partnership, provided notice thereof shall be given in writing to such partner. Such notice shall be signed by the chairman of the executive committee or, in the event of his being unable to sign at such time, by another member of such executive committee, and shall be served personally upon such partner required to change his status, or mailed by registered mail to his last known address, and thereupon such change shall become effective as of the date specified in such notice.

4. Every active partner shall automatically and without further act become an advisory partner at the end of the fiscal year in which his sixty-fifth (65th) birthday occurs.

5. In the event that an active partner becomes an advisory partner or dies, he or his estate shall be entitled to payments to be agreed upon.

Each active partner shall apply all of his experience, training, and ability in discharging his assigned functions in the partnership and in the performance of all work that may be necessary or advantageous to further the business interests of the partnership.

Page 3 of 10--Partnership Agreement

ARTICLE IV

CONTRIBUTION

Each partner shall contribute Ten Thousand Dollars ($10,000) on or before November 30, 1999, to be used by the partnership to establish its capital position. Any additional contribution required of partners shall only be determined and established in accordance with Article XIX herein.

ARTICLE V

BUSINESS EXPENSES

The rent of the buildings where the partnership business shall be carried on, and the cost of repairs and alterations, all rates, taxes, payments for insurance, and other expenses in respect to the buildings used by the partnership, and the wages for all persons employed by the partnership, are all to become payable on the account of the partnership. All losses incurred shall be paid out of the capital of the partnership business, or, if both shall be deficient, by the partners on a pro rata basis, in proportion to their original contributions, as provided in Article XIX.

ARTICLE VI

AUTHORITY

No partner shall buy any goods or articles or enter into any contract exceeding the value of One Hundred Dollars ($100.00) without the prior consent in writing of the other partners. If any partner exceeds this authority, the other partners shall have the option to take the goods or accept the contract on account of the partnership or to let the goods remain the sole property of the partner who shall have obligated himself.

Page 4 of 10--Partnership Agreement

ARTICLE VII

SEPARATE DEBTS

No partner shall enter into any bond or become surety, security, bail or cosigner for any person, partnership or corporation, or knowingly condone anything whereby the partnership property may be attached or taken in execution, without the written consent of the other partners.

Each partner shall punctually pay his separate debts and indemnify the other partners and the capital and property of the partnership against his separate debts and all expenses relating thereto.

ARTICLE VIII

BOOKS AND RECORDS

Books of accounts shall be maintained by the partners, and proper entries made therein of all sales, purchases, receipts, payments, transactions, and property of the partnership, and the books of accounts and all records of the partnership shall be retained at the principal place of business as specified in Article I herein. Each partner shall have free access at all times to all books and records maintained relative to the partnership business.

ARTICLE IX

ACCOUNTING

The fiscal year of the partnership shall be from January 1 to December 31 of each year. On the 31st day of January, commencing in 2001, and on the 31st day of January in each succeeding year, a general accounting shall be made and taken by the partners of all sales, purchases, receipts, payments, and transactions of the partnership during the preceding fiscal year, and of all the capital property and current liabilities of the partnership. The

Page 5 of 10--Partnership Agreement

general accounting shall be written in the partnership account books and signed in each book by each partner immediately after it is completed. After the signature of each partner is entered, each partner shall keep one of the books and shall be bound by every account, except that if any manifest error is found therein by any partner and shown to the other partners within one (1) month after the error shall have been noted by all of them, the error shall be rectified.

ARTICLE X

DIVISION OF PROFITS AND LOSSES

Each partner shall be entitled to thirty-three and one-third percent ($33^{1}/_{3}\%$) of the net profits of the business, and all losses occurring in the course of the business shall be borne in the same proportion, unless the losses are occasioned by the wilful neglect or default, and not the mere mistake or error, of any of the partners, in which case the loss so incurred shall be made good by the partner through whose neglect or default the losses shall arise. Distribution of profits shall be made on the 31st day of January each year.

ARTICLE XI

ADVANCE DRAWS

Each partner shall be at liberty to draw out of the business in anticipation of the expected profits any sums that may be mutually agreed on, and the sums are to be drawn only after there has been entered in the books of the partnership the terms of agreement, giving the date, the amount to be drawn by the respective partners, the time at which the sums shall be drawn, and any other conditions or matters mutually agreed on. The signatures of each partner shall be affixed thereon. The total sum of the

Page 6 of 10--Partnership Agreement

advanced draw for each partner shall be deducted from the sum that partner is entitled to under the distribution of profits as provided for in Article X of this agreement.

ARTICLE XII

SALARY

No partner shall receive any salary from the partnership, and the only compensation to be paid shall be as provided in Articles X and XI herein.

ARTICLE XIII

RETIREMENT

In the event any partner shall desire to retire from the partnership, he shall give three (3) months' notice in writing to the other partners, and the continuing partners shall pay to the retiring partner at the termination of the three (3) months' notice the value of the interest of the retiring partner in the partnership. The value shall be determined by a closing of the books and a rendition of the appropriate profit and loss, trial balance, and balance sheet statements. All disputes arising therefrom shall be determined as provided in Article XX.

ARTICLE XIV

RIGHTS OF CONTINUING PARTNERS

On the retirement of any partner, the continuing partners shall be at liberty, if they so desire, to retain all trade names designating the firm name used, and each of the partners shall sign and execute any assignments, instruments, or papers that shall be reasonably required for effectuating an amicable retirement.

Page 7 of 10--Partnership Agreement

ARTICLE XV

DEATH OF PARTNER

In the event of the death of one partner, the legal representative of the deceased partner shall remain as a partner in the firm, except that the exercising of the right on the part of the representative of the deceased partner shall not continue for a period in excess of three (3) months, even though under the terms hereof a greater period of time is provided before the termination of this agreement. The original rights of the partners herein shall accrue to their heirs, executors, or assigns.

ARTICLE XVI

EMPLOYEE MANAGEMENT

No partner shall hire or dismiss any person in the employment of the partnership without the consent of the other partners, except in cases of gross misconduct by the employee.

ARTICLE XVII

RELEASE OF DEBTS

No partner shall compound, release, or discharge any debt that shall be due or owing to the partnership, without receiving the full amount thereof, unless that partner obtains the prior written consent of the other partners to the discharge of the indebtedness.

ARTICLE XVIII

COVENANT AGAINST REVEALING TRADE SECRETS

No partner shall, during the continuance of the partnership or for five (5) years after its determination by any means, divulge to any person not a member of the firm any trade secret or special information employed in or conducive to the partnership business and, which may come to his knowledge

Page 8 of 10--Partnership Agreement

in the course of this partnership, without the consent in writing of the other partners, or of the other partners' heirs, administrators, or assigns.

ARTICLE XIX

ADDITIONAL CONTRIBUTIONS

The partners shall not have to contribute any additional capital to the partnership to that required under Article IV herein, except as follows: (1) each partner shall be required to contribute a proportionate share in additional contributions if the fiscal year closes with an insufficiency in the capital account or profits of the partnership to meet current expenses, or (2) the capital account falls below Thirty Thousand Dollars ($30,000) for a period of six (6) months.

ARTICLE XX

ARBITRATION

If any difference shall arise between or among the partners as to their rights or liabilities under this agreement, or under any instrument made in furtherance of the partnership business, the difference shall be determined and the instrument shall be settled by LANCE L. KNIGHT, acting as arbitrator, and the decision shall be final as to the contents and interpretations of the instrument and as to the proper mode of carrying the provision into effect.

ARTICLE XXI

ADDITIONS, ALTERATIONS, OR MODIFICATIONS

Where it shall appear to the partners that this agreement, or any terms and conditions contained herein, are in any way ineffective or deficient, or not expressed as originally intended, and any alteration or addition shall be deemed necessary, the partners will enter into, execute, and perform all

Page 9 of 10--Partnership Agreement

further deeds and instruments as their counsel shall advise. Any addition, alteration, or modification shall be in writing, and no oral agreement shall be effective.

IN WITNESS WHEREOF, the parties have executed this agreement at Orange, Wyoming, the day and year first above written.

_____
REX KING

_____
COURTNEY QUEEN

_____
MARSHALL SQUIRE

Page 10 of 10--Partnership Agreement

Appendix E

MORTGAGE

MORTGAGE

This Mortgage is made 20th day of February, 1999, between VIRGINIA RAIL, of 1122 North Tern Blvd., city of Osceola, county of Jay, state of Michigan, herein referred to as Mortgagor, and BLACK VULTURE SAVINGS AND LOAN COMPANY, of 1400 East Wren Avenue, City of Osceola, County of Jay, State of Michigan, herein referred to as Mortgagee.

Mortgagor, by a note dated February 20, 1999, is indebted to Mortgagee in the sum of Sixty-five Thousand Dollars ($65,000), with interest from date at the rate of nine percent (9%) per annum on the unpaid balance until paid, principal and interest to be paid at the office of Mortgagee, or at such other place as the holder may designate in writing, delivered or mailed to Mortgagor, in two hundred (200) monthly installments of Five Hundred Sixty Dollars ($560), beginning April 1, 1999, and continuing on the first day of each month thereafter until the indebtedness is fully paid; except that, if not paid sooner, the final payment thereof shall be due and payable on February 1, 1999. The terms of such note are incorporated herein by reference.

Mortgagor, in consideration of the above-stated obligation, hereby mortgages to Mortgagee all of the following described property in the county of Jay, State of Michigan, known as 1122 North Tern Boulevard, described as Lot 84, Block B, Indigo Bunting Preserve, as recorded, together with the appurtenances and all the estate and rights of the Mortgagor in and to such premises.

Mortgagor covenants and agrees as follows:

I.

PAYMENT

Mortgagor shall pay the indebtedness as herein before provided.

Page 1 of 7--Mortgage

II.

WARRANTY

Mortgagor warrants that she is lawfully seised of an indefeasible estate in fee in the premises.

III.

INSURANCE

Mortgagor shall keep the buildings on the premises insured for loss by fire for Mortgagee's benefit; Mortgagor shall assign and deliver the policies to Mortgagee; and Mortgagor shall reimburse Mortgagee for any insurance premiums paid by Mortgagee on Mortgagor's default in so insuring the buildings or in so assigning and delivering the policies.

IV.

TAXES AND ASSESSMENTS

Mortgagor shall pay all taxes and assessments. In default thereof, Mortgagee may pay such taxes and assessments and Mortgagor shall reimburse Mortgagee therefor.

V.

REMOVAL

No building on the premises shall be removed or demolished without Mortgagee's consent.

VI.

ACCELERATION

The full amount of the principal sum and interest shall become due at the option of Mortgagee: After default in the payment of any installment of principal or of interest for thirty (30) days; or after default in the payment of any tax or assessment for thirty (30) days after notice and

Page 2 of 7--Mortgage

demand; or after default after notice and demand either in assigning and delivering the policies insuring the buildings against loss by fire or reimbursing Mortgagee for premiums paid on such insurance, as provided above; or after failure to furnish a statement of the amount due on the Mortgage and of any offsets and/or defenses existing against the mortgaged debt, after such has been requested as provided below.

VII.

RECEIVER

The holder of this mortgage, in any action to foreclose it, shall be entitled to the appointment of a receiver.

VIII.

AMOUNT DUE

Mortgagor, within thirty (30) days when requested in person, or within thirty (30) days when requested by mail, shall furnish to Mortgagee a duly acknowledged written statement of the amount due on the mortgage and whether any offsets and/or defenses exist against the mortgaged debt.

IX.

SALE

In case of a foreclosure sale, the premises, or so much thereof as may be affected by this Mortgage, may be sold in one parcel.

X.

ASSIGNMENT

Mortgagor hereby assigns to Mortgagee the rents, issues, and profits of the premises as further security for the payment of the obligations secured hereby, and grants to Mortgagee the right to enter on the premises to collect the same, to let the premises or any part thereof, and to apply the

Page 3 of 7--Mortgage

monies received therefrom, after payment of all necessary charges and expenses, to the obligations secured by this Mortgage, on default under any of the covenants, conditions, or agreements contained herein. In the event of any such default, Mortgagor shall pay to Mortgagee or to any receiver appointed to collect the rents, issues, and profits of the premises, the fair and reasonable rental value for the use and occupation of the premises, or of such part thereof as may be in Mortgagor's possession; and on default in payment of such rental, to vacate and surrender possession of the premises, or that portion thereof occupied by Mortgagor, to Mortgagee or the receiver appointed to collect the same.

XI.

EXPENSES

If any action or proceeding is commenced, except an action to foreclose this Mortgage or to collect the debt secured hereby, in which it is necessary to defend or assert the lien of this Mortgage, whether or not the Mortgagee is made or becomes a party to any such action or proceeding, all of Mortgagee's expenses incurred in any such action or proceeding to prosecute or defend the rights and lien created by this montage, including reasonable counsel fees, shall be paid by Mortgagor, and if not so paid promptly on request, shall be added to the debts secured hereby and become a lien on the mortgaged premises, and shall be;

On payment of the purchase price as herein provided, or deemed to be fully secured by this Mortgage and to be prior and paramount to any right, title, interest or claim to or on the premises accruing or attaching subsequent to the lien of this Mortgage, and shall bear interest at the rate provided for the obligations secured hereby. This covenant shall not govern

Page 4 of 7--Mortgage

or affect any action or proceeding to foreclose this Mortgage or to recover or to collect the debt secured hereby, which action or proceeding shall be governed by the provisions of the law respecting the recovery of costs, disbursements, and allowances in foreclosure actions.

XII.

CONDEMNATION

If the premises or any part thereof shall be condemned and taken under the power of eminent domain, or if any award for any change of grade of streets affecting the premises shall be made, all damages and awards for the property so taken or damaged shall be paid to the holder of this Mortgage, up to the amount then unpaid on the indebtedness hereby secured, without regard to whether or not the balance remaining unpaid on the indebtedness may then be due and payable; and the amount so paid shall be credited against the indebtedness and, if it is insufficient to pay the entire amount thereof, it may, at the option of the holder of this Mortgage, be applied to the last maturing installments. The balance of such damages and awards, if any, shall be paid to mortgagor. Mortgagee and subsequent holders of this Mortgage are hereby given full power, right, and authority to receive and receipt for all such damages and awards.

XIII.

BANKRUPTCY

If Mortgagor or any obligor on the note secured hereby: (1) files a Voluntary Petition in Bankruptcy under the Bankruptcy Act of the United States, or (2) is adjudicated a bankrupt under such act, or (3) is the subject of a petition filed in federal or state court for the appointment of a trustee or receiver in bankruptcy or insolvency, or (4) makes a general

Page 5 of 7--Mortgage

assignment for the benefit of creditors, then and on the occurrence of any of such conditions, at the option of Mortgagee, the entire balance of the principal sum secured hereby, together with all accrued interest thereon, shall become immediately due and payable.

XIV.

WASTE

Mortgagor shall not commit, suffer, or permit any waste, impairment, or deterioration of the premises or of any improvement thereon, and shall maintain the premises and all improvements thereon in good condition and repair. If Mortgagor fails or neglects to make any necessary repair or replacement in any improvement for thirty (30) days after notice to do so from Mortgagee, Mortgagee may effect such repair or replacement and the cost thereof shall be added to the debt secured hereby, shall bear interest at the rate provided in the note secured hereby, and shall be covered by this Mortgage and the lien hereof.

XV.

COMPLIANCE

Mortgagor shall comply with all statutes, ordinances, and governmental requirements that affect the premises. If Mortgagor neglects or refuses to so comply and such failure or refusal continues for three (3) months, then, at Mortgagee's option, the entire balance of the principal sum secured hereby, together with all accrued interest, shall become immediately due and payable.

Wherever the sense of this Mortgage so requires, the word "Mortgagor" shall be construed as if it read "Mortgagors" and the word "Mortgagee" shall be construed as if it read "Mortgagees." The word "holder" shall include any

Page 6 of 7--Mortgage

payee of the indebtedness hereby secured or any transferee thereof, whether by operation of law or otherwise. Unless otherwise provided, any notice and demand or request specified in this Mortgage may be made in writing and may be served in person or by mail.

IN WITNESS WHEREOF, this Mortgage has been duly executed by Mortgagor the day and year first written above.

_____
VIRGINIA RAIL

(Acknowledgment)

This instrument was prepared by:

Page 7 of 7--Mortgage

Appendix F

STATEMENT OF FINANCIAL AFFAIRS

UNITED STATES BANKRUPTCY COURT
_____DISTRICT OF_____

In re: _____,   Case No. _____
          Debtor   (if known)

STATEMENT OF FINANCIAL AFFAIRS

This statement is to be completed by every debtor. Spouses filing a joint petition may file a single statement on which the information for both spouses is combined. If the case is filed under Chapter 12 or Chapter 13, a married debtor must furnish information for both spouses whether or not a joint petition is filed, unless the spouses are separated and a joint petition is not filed. An individual debtor engaged in business as a sole proprietor, partner, family farmer, or self-employed professional should provide the information requested on this statement concerning all such activities as well as the individual's personal affairs.

Questions 1-15 are to be completed by all debtors. Debtors that are or have been in business, as defined below, also must complete Questions 16-21. **Each question must be answered. If the answer to any question is "None," or the question is not applicable, mark the box labeled "None."** If additional space is needed for the answer to any question, use and attach a separate sheet properly identified with the case name, case number (if known), and the number of the question.

DEFINITIONS

In business - A debtor is "in business" for the purpose of this form if the debtor is a corporation or partnership. An individual debtor is "in business" for the purpose of this form if the debtor is or has been, within the two years immediately preceding the filing of this bankruptcy case, any of the following: an officer, director, managing executive, or person in control of a corporation; a partner, other than a limited partner, of a partnership; a sole proprietor or self-employed.

Insider - The term "insider" includes but is not limited to: relatives of the debtor; general partners of the debtor and their relatives; corporations of which the debtor is an officer, director, or person in control; officers, directors, and any person in control of a corporate debtor and their relatives; affiliates of the debtor and insiders of such affiliates; any managing agent of the debtor. 11 U.S.C.§ 101(30).

_____

1. Income from employment or operation of business

None ☐   State the gross amount of income the debtor has received from employment, trade, or profession, or from operation of the debtor's business from the beginning of this calendar year to the date this case was commenced. State also the gross amounts received during the two years immediately preceding this calendar year. (A debtor that maintains, or has maintained, financial records on the basis of a fiscal rather than a calendar year may report fiscal year income. Identify the beginning and ending dates of the debtor's fiscal year.) If a joint petition is filed, state income for each spouse separately. (Married debtors filing under Chapter 12 or Chapter 13 must state income of both spouses whether or not a joint petition is filed, unless the spouses are separated and a joint petition is not filed.)

Amount   Source (if more than one)

2. Income other than from employment or operation of business

None ☐ State the amount of income received by the debtor other than from employment, trade, profession, or operation of the debtor's business during the **two years** immediately preceding the commencement of this case. Give particulars. If a joint petition is filed, state income for each spouse separately. (Married debtors filing under Chapter 12 or Chapter 13 must state income for each spouse whether or not a joint petition is filed, unless the spouses are separated and a joint petition is not filed.)

Amount   Source

3. Payments to creditors

None ☐ **a.** List all payments on loans, installment purchases of goods or services, and other debts, aggregating more than $600 to any creditor, made within **90 days** immediately preceding the commencement of this case. (Married debtors filing under Chapter 12 or Chapter 13 must include payments by either or both spouses whether or not a joint petition is filed, unless the spouses are separated and a joint petition is not filed.)

Names and addresses of creditors	Dates of payments	Amount paid	Amount still owing

None ☐ **b.** List all payments made within **one year** immediately preceding the commencement of this case to or for the benefit of creditors who are or were insiders. (Married debtors filing under Chapter 12 or Chapter 13 must include payments by either or both spouses whether or not a joint petition is filed, unless the spouses are separated and a joint petition is not filed.)

Name and address of creditor and relationship of debtor	Date of payment	Amount paid	Amount still owing

4. Suits, executions, garnishments and attachments

None ☐ **a.** List all suits to which the debtor is or was a party within **one year** immediately preceding the filing of this case. (Married debtors filing under Chapter 12 or Chapter 13 must include information concerning either or both spouses whether or not a joint petition is filed, unless the spouses are separated and a joint petition is not filed.)

Caption of suit and case number	Nature of proceeding	Court and location	Status or disposition

None **b.** Describe all property that has been attached, garnished or seized under any legal or equitable process within **one year** immediately preceding the commencement of this case. (Married debtors filing under Chapter 12 or Chapter 13 must include information concerning property of either or both spouses whether or not a joint petition is filed, unless the spouses are separated and a joint petition is not filed.)

Name and address of person for whose benefit property was seized	Date of seizure	Description and value of property

5. Repossessions, foreclosures and returns

None List all property that has been repossessed by a creditor, sold at a foreclosure sale, transferred through a deed in lieu of foreclosure or returned to the seller within **one year** immediately preceding the commencement of this case. (Married debtors filing under Chapter 12 or Chapter 13 must include information concerning property of either or both spouses whether or not a joint petition is filed, unless the spouses are separated and a joint petition is not filed.)

Name and address of creditor or seller	Date of repossession, foreclosure sale, transfer or return	Description and value of property

6. Assignments and receiverships

None **a.** Describe any assignment of property for the benefit of creditors made within **120 days** immediately preceding the commencement of this case. (Married debtors filing under Chapter 12 or Chapter 13 must include any assignment by either or both spouses whether or not a joint petition is filed, unless the spouses are separated and a joint petition is not filed.)

Name and address of assignee	Date of assignment	Terms of assignment or settlement

None **b.** List all property which has been in the hands of a custodian, receiver, or court-appointed official within **one year** immediately preceding the commencement of this case. (Married debtors filing under Chapter 12 or Chapter 13 must include information concerning property of either or both spouses whether or not a joint petition is filed, unless the spouses are separated and a joint petition is not filed.)

Name and address of custodian	Name and location of court	Case title and number	Date of order	Description and value of property

7. Gifts

None List all gifts or charitable contributions made within **one year** immediately preceding the commencement of this case except ordinary and usual gifts to family members aggregating less than $200 in value per individual family member, and charitable contributions aggregating less than $100 per recipient. (Married debtors filing under Chapter 12 or Chapter 13 must include gifts or contributions by either or both spouses whether or not a joint petition is filed, unless the spouses are separated and a joint petition is not filed.)

Name and address of person or organization	Relationship to debtor, if any	Date of gift	Description and value of gift

8. Losses

None List all losses from fire, theft, other casualty or gambling within **one year** immediately preceding the commencement of this case **or since the commencement of this case.** (Married debtors filing under Chapter 12 or Chapter 13 must include losses by either or both spouses whether or not a joint petition is filed, unless the spouses are separated and a joint petition is not filed.)

Description and value of property	Description of circumstances and, if loss was covered in whole or in part by insurance, give particulars	Date of loss

9. Payments related to debt counseling or bankruptcy

None List all payments made or property transferred by or on behalf of the debtor to any persons, including attorneys, for consultation concerning debt consolidation, relief under the bankruptcy law or preparation of a petition in bankruptcy within **one year** immediately preceding the commencement of this case.

Name and address of payee	Date of payment	Name of payor if other than debtor	Amount of money or description and value of property

10. Other transfers

None **a.** List all other property, other than property transferred in the ordinary course of the business or financial affairs of the debtor, transferred either absolutely or as security within **one year** immediately preceding the commencement of this case. (Married debtors filing under Chapter 12 or Chapter 13 must include transfers by either or both spouses whether or not a joint petition is filed, unless the spouses are separated and a joint petition is not filed.)

Name and address of transferee	Relationship to debtor	Transfer date	Property transferred and value received

11. Closed financial accounts

None List all financial accounts and instruments held in the name of the debtor or for the benefit of the debtor that were closed, sold, or otherwise transferred within **one year** immediately preceding the commencement of this case. Include checking, savings, or other financial accounts, certificates of deposit, or other instruments; shares and share accounts held in banks, credit unions, pension funds, cooperatives, associations, brokerage houses and other financial institutions. (Married debtors filing under Chapter 12 or Chapter 13 must include information concerning accounts or instruments held by or for either or both spouses whether or not a joint petition is filed, unless the spouses are separated and a joint petition is not filed.)

Name and address of institution	Type and number of account and final balance	Amount and rate of sale or closing

12. Safe deposit boxes

None List each safe deposit or other box or depository in which the debtor has or had securities, cash, or other valuables within **one year** immediately preceding the commencement of this case. (Married debtors filing under Chapter 12 or Chapter 13 must include boxes or depositories of either or both spouses whether or not a joint petition is filed, unless the spouses are separated and a joint petition is not filed.)

Name and address of bank or other depository	Name and addresses of those with access to box or depository	Description of contents	Date of transfer or surrender, if any

13. Setoffs

None ☐ List all setoffs made by any creditor, including a bank, against a debt or deposit of the debtor within **90 days** preceding the commencement of this case. (Married debtors filing under Chapter 12 or Chapter 13 must include information concerning either or both spouses whether or not a joint petition is filed, unless the spouses are separated and a joint petition is not filed.)

Name and address of creditor	Date of setoff	Amount of setoff

14. Property held for another person

None ☐ List all property owned by another person that the debtor holds or controls.

Name and address of owner	Description and value of property	Location of property

15. Prior address of debtor

None ☐ If the debtor has moved within the **two years** immediately preceding the commencement of this case, list all premises which the debtor occupied during that period and vacated prior to the commencement of this case. If a joint petition is filed, report also any separate address of either spouse.

Address	Name used	Dates of occupancy

The following questions are to be completed by every debtor that is a corporation or partnership and by any individual debtor who is or has been, within the **two years** immediately preceding the commencement of this case, any of the following: an officer, director, managing executive, or owner of more than 5 percent of the voting securities of a corporation; a partner, other than a limited partner, of a partnership; a sole proprietor or otherwise self-employed.

*(An individual or joint debtor should complete this portion of the statement **only** if the debtor is or has been in business, as defined above, within the **two years** immediately preceding the commencement of this case.)*

16. **Nature, location and name of business**

None **a.** If the debtor is an individual, list the names and addresses of all businesses in which the debtor
☐ was an officer, director, partner, or managing executive of a corporation, partnership, sole proprietorship, or was a self-employed professional within the **two years** immediately preceding the commencement of this case, or in which the debtor owned 5 percent or more of the voting or equity securities within the **two years** immediately preceding the commencement of this case.

b. If the debtor is a partnership, list the names and addresses of all businesses in which the debtor was a partner or owned 5 percent or more of the voting securities within the **two years** immediately preceding the commencement of this case.

c. If the debtor is a corporation, list the names and addresses of all businesses in which the debtor was a partner or owned 5 percent or more of the voting securities within the **two years** immediately preceding the commencement of this case.

Name	Address	Nature of business	Beginning and ending Dates of operation

17. **Books, records and financial statements**

None **a.** List all bookkeepers and accountants who within the **six years** immediately preceding the filing
☐ of this bankruptcy case kept or supervised the keeping of books of account and records of the debtor.

Name	Address	Dates services rendered

None **b.** List all firms or individuals who within the **two years** immediately preceding the filing of this
☐ bankruptcy case have audited the books of account and records, or prepared a financial statement of the debtor.

Name	Address	Dates services rendered

None ☐ **c.** List all firms or individuals who at the time of the commencement of this case were in possession of the books of account and records of the debtor. If any of the books of account and records are not available, please explain.

Name   Address

None ☐ **d.** List all financial institutions, creditors and other parties, including mercantile and trade agencies, to whom a financial statement was issued within the **two years** immediately preceding the commencement of this case by the debtor.

Name   Address   Date issued

18. Inventories

None ☐ **a.** List the dates of the **last two** inventories taken of your property, the name of the person who supervised the taking of each inventory, and the dollar amount and basis of each inventory.

Date of inventory   Inventory supervisor   Dollar amount of inventory
                                                             (Specify cost, market or other basis)

None ☐ **b.** List the name and address of the person having possession of the records of each of the **two** inventories reported in a., above.

Date of inventory   Name and addresses of custodian
                                           of inventory records

19. Current partners, officers, directors and shareholders

None ☐ **a.** If the debtor is a partnership, list the nature and percentage of partnership interest of each member of the partnership.

Name and address   Nature of interest   Percentage of interest

None b. If the debtor is a corporation, list all officers and directors of the corporation, and each stockholder who directly or indirectly owns, controls, or holds 5 percent or more of the voting securities of the corporation.

☐

Name and address	Title	Nature and percentage of stock ownership

20. Former partners, officers, directors and shareholders

None a. If the debtor is a partnership, list each member who withdrew from the partnership within **one year** immediately preceding the commencement of this case.

☐

Name	Address	Date of withdrawal

None b. If the debtor is a corporation, list all officers or directors whose relationship with the corporation terminated within **one year** immediately preceding the commencement of this case.

☐

Name and address	Title	Date of termination

21. Withdrawals from a partnership or distributions by a corporation

None If the debtor is a partnership or corporation, list all withdrawals or distributions credited or given to an insider, including compensation in any form, bonuses, loans, stock redemptions, options exercised and any other perquisite during **one year** immediately preceding the commencement of this case.

☐

Name and address of recipient	Relationship to debtor	Date and purpose of withdrawal	Amount of money or description and value of property

[If completed by an individual or individual and spouse]

I declare under penalty of perjury that I have read the answers contained in the foregoing statement of financial affairs and any attachments thereto and that they are true and correct.

Date _____   Signature _____
                                  of Debtor

Date _____   Signature _____
                                  of Joint Debtor
                                  (if any)

CERTIFICATION AND SIGNATURE OF NON-ATTORNEY BANKRUPTCY PETITION PREPARER (See 11 U.S.C. § 110)

I certify that I am a bankruptcy petition preparer as defined in 11 U.S.C. § 110, that I prepared this document for compensation, and that I have provided the debtor with a copy of this document.

_____
Printed or Typed Name of Bankruptcy Petition Preparer

Names and Social Security Numbers of all other individuals who prepared or assisted in preparing this document.

If more than one person prepared this document, attach additional signed sheets conforming to the appropriate Official Form for each person.

_____
Social Security Number

_____

_____
Address

X_____
Signature of Bankruptcy Petition Preparer   Date

A bankruptcy petition preparer's failure to comply with the provisions of Title 11 and the Federal Rules of Bankruptcy Procedure may result in fines or imprisonment or both. 11 U.S.C. § 110; 18 U.S.C. § 156.

[If completed on behalf of a partnership or corporation]

I declare under penalty of perjury that I have read the answers contained in the foregoing statement of financial affairs and any attachments thereto and that they are true and correct to the best of my knowledge, information and belief.

Date _____   Signature _____

_____
Print Name and Title

[An individual signing on behalf of a partnership or corporation must indicate position or relationship to debtor.]

_____ continuation sheets attached

Penalty for making a false statement: Fine of up to $500,000 or imprisonment for up to 5 years, or both. 18 U.S.C. § 152 and 3571.

Appendix G

SCHEDULES

United States Bankruptcy Court

_____ DISTRICT OF _____

In re_____,   Case No._____
                    Debtor   (If known)

SUMMARY OF SCHEDULES

Indicate as to each schedule whether that schedule is attached and state the number of pages in each. Report the totals from Schedules A,B,D,E,F,I, and J in the boxes provided. Add the amounts from Schedules A and B to determine the total amount of the debtor's assets. Add the amounts from Schedules D,E, and F to determine the total amount of the debtor's liabilities.

NAME OF SCHEDULE	ATTACHED (YES/NO)	NO. OF SHEETS	AMOUNTS SCHEDULED		
			ASSETS	LIABILITIES	OTHER
A - Real Property			$		
B - Personal Property			$		
C - Property Claimed as Exempt					
D - Creditors Holding Secured Claims				$	
E - Creditors Holding Unsecured Priority Claims				$	
F - Creditors Holding Unsecured Non Priority Claims				$	
G - Executory Contracts and Unexpired Leases					
H - Codebtors					
I - Current Income of Individual Debtor(s)					$
J. - Current Expenditures of Individual Debtor(s)					$
Total Number of Sheets of ALL Schedules ->					
Total Assets ->			$		
Total Liabilities ->				$	

In re_____   Case No._____
            Debtor   (If known)

SCHEDULE A - REAL PROPERTY

Except as directed below, list all real property in which the debtor has any legal, equitable, or future interest, including all property owned as a co-tenant, community property, or in which the debtor has a life estate. Include any property in which the debtor holds rights and powers exercisable for the debtor's own benefit. If the debtor is married, state whether husband, wife, or both own the property by placing an "H," "W," "J," or "C" in the column labeled "Husband, Wife, Joint, Or Community." If the debtor holds no interest in real property, write "None" under "Description and Location of Property."

Do not include interests in executory contracts and unexpired leases on this schedule. List them in Schedule G - Executory Contracts and Unexpired Leases.

If an entity claims to have a lien or hold a secured interest in any property, state the amount of the secured claim. See Schedule D. If no entity claims to hold a secured interest in the property, write "None" in the column labeled "Amount of Secured Claim."

If the debtor is an individual or if a joint petition is filed, state the amount of any exemption claimed in the property only in Schedule C - Property Claimed as Exempt.

DESCRIPTION AND LOCATION OF PROPERTY	NATURE OF DEBTOR'S INTEREST IN PROPERTY	HUSBAND,WIFE,JOINT OR COMMUNITY	CURRENT MARKET VALUE OF DEBTOR'S INTEREST IN PROPERTY, WITHOUT DEDUCTING ANY SECURED CLAIM OR EXEMPTION	AMOUNT OF SECURED CLAIM

Total -> | $

(Report also on Summary of Schedules.)

In re_____, Case No._____
                    Debtor   (If known)

SCHEDULE B - PERSONAL PROPERTY

Except as directed below, list all personal property of the debtor of whatever kind. If the debtor has no property in one or more of the categories, place an "X" in the appropriate position in the column labeled "None." If additional space is needed in any category, attach a separate sheet properly identified with the case name, and the number of the category. If the debtor is married, state whether husband, wife, or both own the property by placing an "H," "W," "J," or "C" in the column labeled "Husband, Wife, Joint, or Community." If the debtor is an individual or a joint petition is filed, state the amount of any exemptions claimed only in Schedule C - Property Claimed as Exempt.

Do not list interests in executory contracts and unexpired leases on this schedule. List them in Schedule G - Executory Contracts and Unexpired Leases.

If the property is being held for the debtor by someone else, state that person's name and address under "Description and Location of Property."

TYPE OF PROPERTY	NONE	DESCRIPTION AND LOCATION OF PROPERTY	HUSBAND, WIFE, JOINT OR COMMUNITY	CURRENT MARKET VALUE OF DEBTOR'S INTEREST IN PROPERTY, WITHOUT DEDUCTING ANY SECURED CLAIM OR EXEMPTION
1. Cash on hand.				
2. Checking, savings or other financial accounts, certificates of deposit, or shares in banks, savings and loan, thrift, building and loan, and homestead associations, or credit unions, brokerage houses, or cooperatives.				
3. Security deposits with public utilities, telephone companies, landlords, and others.				
4. Household goods and furnishings, including audio, video, and computer equipment.				
5. Books; pictures and other art objects; antiques; stamp, coin, record, tape, compact disc, and other collections or collectibles.				
6. Wearing apparel.				
7. Furs and jewelry.				
8. Firearms and sports, photographic, and other hobby equipment.				
9. Interests in insurance policies. Name insurance company of each policy and itemize surrender or refund value of each.				
10. Annuities. Itemize and name each issuer.				

In re_____, Case No._____
Debtor (If known)

SCHEDULE B - PERSONAL PROPERTY
(Continuation Sheet)

TYPE OF PROPERTY	NONE	DESCRIPTION AND LOCATION OF PROPERTY	HUSBAND,WIFE,JOINT OR COMMUNITY	CURRENT MARKET VALUE OF DEBTOR'S INTEREST IN PROPERTY, WITHOUT DEDUCTING ANY SECURED CLAIM OR EXEMPTION
11. Interests in IRA, ERISA, Keogh, or other pension or profit sharing Plans. Itemize.				
12. Stock and interests in incorporated and unincorporated businesses. Itemize.				
13. Interests in partnerships or joint ventures. Itemize.				
14. Government and corporate bonds and other negotiable and nonnegotiable instruments.				
15. Accounts Receivable.				
16. Alimony, maintenance, support, and property settlements to which the debtor is or may be entitled. Give particulars.				
17. Other liquidated debts owing debtor including tax refunds. Give particulars.				
18. Equitable or future interests, life estates, and rights or powers exercisable for the benefit of the debtor other than those listed in Schedule of Real Property.				
19. Contingent and non-contingent interests in estate of a decedent, death benefit plan, life insurance policy, or trust.				
20. Other contingent and unliquidated claims of every nature, including tax refunds, counterclaims of the debtor, and rights to setoff claims. Give estimated value of each.				
21. Patents, copyrights, and other intellectual property. Give particulars.				
22. Licenses, franchises, and other general intangibles. Give particulars.				

In re_____ ,   Case No._____
                 Debtor   (If known)

SCHEDULE B - PERSONAL PROPERTY
(Continuation Sheet)

TYPE OF PROPERTY	NONE	DESCRIPTION AND LOCATION OF PROPERTY	HUSBAND, WIFE, JOINT OR COMMUNITY	CURRENT MARKET VALUE OF DEBTOR'S INTEREST IN PROPERTY, WITHOUT DEDUCTING ANY SECURED CLAIM OR EXEMPTION
23. Automobiles, trucks, trailers, and other vehicles and accessories.				
24. Boats, motors, and accessories.				
25. Aircraft and accessories.				
26. Office equipment, furnishings, and supplies.				
27. Machinery, fixtures, equipment, and supplies used in business.				
28. Inventory.				
29. Animals.				
30. Crops - growing or harvested. Give particulars.				
31. Farming equipment and implements.				
32. Farm supplies, chemicals, and feed.				
33. Other personal property of any kind not already listed. Itemize.				

_____ continuation sheets attached   **Total** -> $ _____

(Include amounts from any continuation sheets attached. Report total also on Summary of Schedules.)

In re_____, Case No._____
                Debtor   (If known)

SCHEDULE C - PROPERTY CLAIMED AS EXEMPT

Debtor elects the exemptions to which debtor is entitled under:

(Check one box)

☐ 11 U.S.C. § 522(b)(1): Exemptions provided in 11 U.S.C. § 522(d). **Note: These exemptions are available only in certain states.**

☐ 11 U.S.C. § 522(b)(2): Exemptions available under applicable nonbankruptcy federal laws, state or local law where the debtor's domicile has been located for the 180 days immediately preceding the filing of the petition, or for a longer portion of the 180-day period than in any other place, and the debtor's interest as a tenant by the entirety or joint tenant to the extent the interest is exempt from process under applicable nonbankruptcy law.

DESCRIPTION OF PROPERTY	SPECIFY LAW PROVIDING EACH EXEMPTION	VALUE OF CLAIMED EXEMPTION	CURRENT MARKET VALUE OF PROPERTY WITHOUT DEDUCTING EXEMPTION

In re_____, Case No._____
                    Debtor   (If known)

SCHEDULE D - CREDITORS HOLDING SECURED CLAIMS

State the name, mailing address, including zip code, and account number, if any, of all entities holding claims secured by property of the debtor as of the date of filing of the petition. List creditors holding all types of secured interests such as judgment liens, garnishments, statutory liens, mortgages, deeds of trust, and other security interests. List creditors in alphabetical order to the extent practicable. If all secured creditors will not fit on this page, use the continuation sheet provided.

If any entity other than a spouse in a joint case may be jointly liable on a claim, place an "X" in the column labeled "Codebtor," include the entity on the appropriate schedule of creditors, and complete Schedule H - Codebtors. If a joint petition is filed, state whether husband, wife, both of them, or the marital community may be liable on each claim by placing an"H," "W," "J," or "C" in the column labeled "Husband, Wife, Joint, or Community."

If the claim is contingent, place an"X" in the column labeled "Contingent." If the claim is unliquidated, place an "X" in the column labeled "Unliquidated." If the claim is disputed, place an "X" in the column labeled "Disputed." (You may need to place an "X" in more than one of these three columns.)

Report the total of all claims listed on this schedule in the box labeled "Total" on the last sheet of the completed schedule. Report this total also on the Summary of Schedules.

☐ Check this box if debtor has no creditors holding secured claims to report on this Schedule D.

CREDITOR'S NAME AND MAILING ADDRESS INCLUDING ZIP CODE	CODEBTOR	HUSBAND,WIFE,JOINT OR COMMUNITY	DATE CLAIM WAS INCURRED, NATURE OF LIEN, AND DESCRIPTION AND MARKET VALUE OF PROPERTY SUBJECT TO LIEN	CONTINGENT	UNLIQUIDATED	DISPUTED	AMOUNT OF CLAIM WITHOUT DEDUCTING VALUE OF COLLATERAL	UNSECURED PORTION, IF ANY
ACCOUNT NO.								
			VALUE $					
ACCOUNT NO.								
			VALUE $					
ACCOUNT NO.								
			VALUE $					
ACCOUNT NO.								
			VALUE $					

_____ continuation sheets attached

Subtotal -> $_____
(Total of this page)

Total -> $_____
(Use only on last page)

(Report total also on Summary of Schedules)

In re_____, Case No._____
         Debtor   (If known)

SCHEDULE D - CREDITORS HOLDING SECURED CLAIMS
(Continuation Sheet)

CREDITOR'S NAME AND MAILING ADDRESS INCLUDING ZIP CODE	CODEBTOR	HUSBAND, WIFE, JOINT OR COMMUNITY	DATE CLAIM WAS INCURRED, NATURE OF LIEN, AND DESCRIPTION AND MARKET VALUE OF PROPERTY SUBJECT TO LIEN	CONTINGENT	UNLIQUIDATED	DISPUTED	AMOUNT OF CLAIM WITHOUT DEDUCTING VALUE OF COLLATERAL	UNSECURED PORTION, IF ANY
ACCOUNT NO.								
			VALUE $					
ACCOUNT NO.								
			VALUE $					
ACCOUNT NO.								
			VALUE $					
ACCOUNT NO.								
			VALUE $					
ACCOUNT NO.								
			VALUE $					

Sheet no.____of____continuation sheets attached to Schedule of Creditors
Holding Secured Claims

Subtotal -> $_____
(Total of this page)

Total -> $_____
(Use only on last page)

(Report total also on Summary of Schedules)

In re: _____,   Case No._____
               Debtor(s)   (if known)

SCHEDULE E - CREDITORS HOLDING UNSECURED PRIORITY CLAIMS

☐ Check this box if debtor has no creditors holding unsecured claims to report on this Schedule E.

TYPE OF PRIORITY CLAIMS (Check the appropriate box(es) below if claims in that category are listed on the attached sheets)

☐ **Extensions of credit in an involuntary case**   Claims arising in the ordinary course of the debtor's business or financial affairs after the commencement of the case but before the earlier of the appointment of a trustee or the order for relief. 11 U.S.C. §507 (a)(2).

☐ **Wages, salaries, and commissions**   Wages, salaries, and commissions, including vacation, severance, and sick leave pay owing to employees, and commissions owing to qualifying independent sales representatives up to $4,000* per person, earned within 90 days immediately preceding the filing of the original petition or the cessation of business, whichever occurred first, to the extent provided in 11 U.S.C. §507 (a)(3).

☐ **Contributions to employee benefit plans**   Money owed to employee benefit plans for services rendered within 180 days immediately preceding the filing of the original petition or the cessation of business, whichever occurred first, to the extent provided in 11 U.S.C. §507 (a)(4).

☐ **Certain farmers and fishermen**   Claims of certain farmers and fishermen, up to $4,000* per farmer or fisherman, against the debtor, as provided in 11 U.S.C. § 507 (a)(5).

☐ **Deposits by individuals**   Claims of individuals up to $1,800* for deposits for the purchase, lease, or rental of property or services for personal, family, or household use that were not delivered or provided. 11 U.S.C. §507 (a)(6).

☐ **Alimony, Maintenance, or Support**   Claims of a spouse, former spouse, or child of the debtor for alimony, maintenance, or support, to the extent provided in 11 U.S.C. §507 (a)(7).

☐ **Taxes and Certain Other Debts Owed to Governmental Units**   Taxes, customs duties, and penalties owing to federal, state, and local governmental units as set forth in 11 U.S.C. §507 (a)(8).

☐ **Commitments to Maintain the Capital of an Insured Depository Institution**   Claims based on commitments to the FDIC, RTC, Director of the Office of Thrift Supervision, Comptroller of the Currency, or Board of Governors of the Federal Reserve System, or their predecessors or successors, to maintain the capital of an insured depository institution. 11 U.S.C. §507 (a)(9).

● Amounts are subject to adjustment on April 1, 1998, and every three years thereafter with respect to cases commenced on or after the date of adjustment.

CREDITOR'S NAME AND MAILING ADDRESS INCLUDING ZIP CODE	CO DEBTOR	H W J C	DATE CLAIM WAS INCURRED AND CONSIDERATION FOR CLAIM	C U D •	TOTAL AMOUNT OF CLAIM	AMOUNT ENTITLED TO PRIORITY
A/C#						
A/C#						
A/C#						
A/C#						
A/C#						

_____ Continuation sheets attached.

Subtotal -> (Total of this page) $ _____

Total -> (use only on last page of the completed Schedule E) $ _____

(Report total also on Summary of Schedules)

*If contingent, enter C; if unliquidated, enter U; if disputed, enter D.

In re_____,   Case No._____
                    Debtor   (If Known)

SCHEDULE F - CREDITORS HOLDING UNSECURED NONPRIORITY CLAIMS

State the name, mailing address, including zip code, and account number, if any, of all entities holding unsecured claims without priority against the debtor or the property of the debtor, as of the date of filing of the petition. Do not include claims listed in Schedules D and E. If all creditors will not fit on this page, use the continuation sheet provided.

If any entity other than a spouse in a joint case may be jointly liable on a claim, place an "X" in the column labeled "Codebtor," include the entity on the appropriate schedule of creditors, and complete Schedule H - Codebtors. If a joint petition is filed, state whether husband, wife, both of them, or the marital community may be liable on each claim by placing an "H," "W," "J," or "C" in the column labeled "Husband, Wife, Joint, or Community."

If the claim is contingent, place an "X" in the column labeled "Contigent." If the claim is unliquidated, place an "X" in the column labeled "Unliquidated." If the claim is disputed, place an "X" in the column labeled "Disputed." (You may need to place an "X" in more than one of these three columns.)

Report total of all claims listed on this schedule in the box labeled "Total" on the last sheet of the completed schedule. Report this total also on the Summary of Schedules.

☐ Check this box if debtor has no creditors holding unsecured nonpriority claims to report on this Schedule F.

CREDITOR'S NAME AND MAILING ADDRESS INCLUDING ZIP CODE	CODEBTOR	HUSBAND, WIFE, JOINT OR COMMUNITY	DATE CLAIM WAS INCURRED AND CONSIDERATION FOR CLAIM. IF CLAIM IS SUBJECT TO SETOFF, SO STATE	CONTINGENT	UNLIQUIDATED	DISPUTED	AMOUNT OF CLAIM
ACCOUNT NO.							
ACCOUNT NO.							
ACCOUNT NO.							
ACCOUNT NO.							

_____ Continuation sheets attached

Subtotal - > (Total of this page) $

Total - > $
(Use only on last page of the completed Schedule F)

(Report total also on Summary of Schedules)

In re _____, Case No. _____
     (Debtor)   (If known)

SCHEDULE F - CREDITORS HOLDING UNSECURED NONPRIORITY CLAIMS
(Continuation Sheet)

CREDITOR'S NAME AND MAILING ADDRESS INCLUDING ZIP CODE	CODEBTOR	HUSBAND,WIFE,JOINT OR COMMUNITY	DATE CLAIM WAS INCURRED AND CONSIDERATION FOR CLAIM. IF CLAIM IS SUBJECT TO SETOFF, SO STATE	CONTINGENT	UNLIQUIDATED	DISPUTED	AMOUNT OF CLAIM
ACCOUNT NO.							
ACCOUNT NO.							
ACCOUNT NO.							
ACCOUNT NO.							
ACCOUNT NO.							

Sheet no. _____ of _____ sheets attached to Schedule of Creditors Holding Unsecured Nonpriority Claims

Subtotal - > $ _____
(Total of this page)

Total - > $ _____
(Use only on last page of the completed Schedule F)

(Report total also on Summary of Schedule)

In re_____, Case No._____
Debtor   (If known)

SCHEDULE G. EXECUTORY CONTRACTS AND UNEXPIRED LEASES

Describe all executory contracts of any nature and all unexpired leases of real or personal property. Include any timeshare interests.

State nature of debtor's interest in contract, i.e., "Purchaser," "Agent," etc. State whether debtor is the lessor or lessee of a lease.

Provide the names and complete mailing addresses of all other parties to each lease or contract described.

NOTE: A party listed on this schedule will not receive notice of the filing of this case unless the party is also scheduled in the appropriate schedule of creditors.

☐ Check this box if debtor has no executory contracts or unexpired leases.

NAME AND MAILING ADDRESS, INCLUDING ZIP CODE, OF OTHER PARTIES TO LEASE OR CONTRACT.	DESCRIPTION OF CONTRACT OR LEASE AND NATURE OF DEBTOR'S INTEREST. STATE WHETHER LEASE IS FOR NONRESIDENTIAL REAL PROPERTY. STATE CONTRACT NUMBER OF ANY GOVERNMENT CONTRACT.

In re_____,   Case No._____
          Debtor   (If known)

SCHEDULE H - CODEBTORS

Provide the information requested concerning any person or entity, other than a spouse in a joint case, that is also liable on any debts listed by debtor in the schedules of creditors. Include all guarantors and co-signers. In community property states, a married debtor not filing a joint case should report the name and address of the nondebtor spouse on this schedule. Include all names used by the nondebtor spouse during the six years immediately preceding the commencement of this case.

☐ Check this box if debtor has no codebtors.

NAME AND ADDRESS OF CODEBTOR	NAME AND ADDRESS OF CREDITOR

In re_____,   Case No._____
                    Debtor   (If known)

SCHEDULE I - CURRENT INCOME OF INDIVIDUAL DEBTOR(S)

The column labeled "Spouse" must be completed in all cases filed by joint debtors and by a married debtor in a chapter 12 or 13 case whether or not a joint petition is filed, unless the spouses are separated and a joint petition is not filed.

Debtor's Marital Status:	DEPENDENTS OF DEBTOR AND SPOUSE		
	NAMES	AGE	RELATIONSHIP

Employment:	DEBTOR	SPOUSE
Occupation		
Name of Employer		
How long employed		
Address of Employer		

Income: (Estimate of average monthly income)   DEBTOR   SPOUSE
Current monthly gross wages, salary, and commissions
    (prorate if not paid monthly.) $_____ $_____
Estimated monthly overtime $_____ $_____

SUBTOTAL $_____ $_____

    LESS PAYROLL DEDUCTIONS
    a. Payroll taxes and social security $_____ $_____
    b. Insurance $_____ $_____
    c. Union dues $_____ $_____
    d. Other(Specify:_____) $_____ $_____

    SUBTOTAL OF PAYROLL DEDUCTIONS $_____ $_____

TOTAL NET MONTHLY TAKE HOME PAY $_____ $_____

Regular income from operation of business or profession or farm $_____ $_____
(attach detailed statement)
Income from real property $_____ $_____
Interest and dividends $_____ $_____
Alimony, maintenance or support payments payable to the debtor for the
debtor's use or that of dependents listed above. $_____ $_____
Social security or other government assistance
(Specify)_____ $_____ $_____
Pension or retirement income $_____ $_____
Other monthly income $_____ $_____
(Specify)_____ $_____ $_____
_____ $_____ $_____

TOTAL MONTHLY INCOME $_____ $_____

TOTAL COMBINED MONTHLY INCOME $_____   (Report also on Summary of Schedules)

Describe any increase or decrease of more than 10% in any of the above categories anticipated to occur within the year following the filing of this document:

In re _____, Case No. _____
                     Debtor   (If known)

SCHEDULE J- CURRENT EXPENDITURES OF INDIVIDUAL DEBTOR(S)

Complete this schedule by estimating the average monthly expenses of the debtor and the debtor's family. Prorate any payments made bi-weekly, quarterly, semi-annually, or annually to show monthly rate.

☐ Check this box if a joint petition is filed and debtor's spouse maintains a separate household. Complete a separate schedule of expenditures labeled "Spouse."

Rent or home mortgage payment (include lot rented for mobile home) $_____
Are real estate taxes included?   Yes _____   No _____
Is property insurance included?   Yes _____   No _____
Utilities Electricity and heating fuel $_____
           Water and sewer $_____
           Telephone $_____
           Other _____ $_____
Home maintenance (repairs and upkeep) $_____
Food $_____
Clothing $_____
Laundry and dry cleaning $_____
Medical and dental expenses $_____
Transportation (not including car payment) $_____
Recreation, clubs and entertainment, newspapers, magazines, etc. $_____
Charitable contributions $_____
Insurance (not deducted from wages or included in home mortgage payments)
           Homeowner's or renter's $_____
           Life $_____
           Health $_____
           Auto $_____
           Other _____ $_____
Taxes (not deducted from wages or included in home mortgage payments)
(Specify)_____ $_____
Installment payments: (in Chapter 12 and 13 cases, do not list payments to be included in the plan)
           Auto $_____
           Other_____ $_____
           Other_____ $_____
Alimony, maintenance, and support paid to others $_____
Payments for support of additional dependents not living at your home $_____
Regular expenses from operation of business, profession, or farm (attach detailed statement) $_____
Other_____ $_____

TOTAL MONTHLY EXPENSES (Report also on Summary of Schedules) $_____

[FOR CHAPTER 12 AND 13 DEBTORS ONLY]
Provide the information requested below, including whether plan payments are to be made bi-weekly, monthly, annually, or at some other regular interval.

A. Total projected monthly income $_____
B. Total projected monthly expenses $_____
C. Excess income (A minus B) $_____
D. Total amount to be paid into plan each _____ $_____
                                                    (interval)

In re _____, Case No. _____
                  Debtor   (If known)

DECLARATION CONCERNING DEBTOR'S SCHEDULES

DECLARATION UNDER PENALTY OF PERJURY BY INDIVIDUAL DEBTOR

I declare under penalty of perjury that I have read the foregoing summary and schedules, consisting of _____ sheets and that they are true and correct to the best of my knowledge, information, and belief.   (Total shown on summary page plus 1)

Date _____   Signature: _____
                                                                                    Debtor

Date _____   Signature: _____
                                                                           (Joint Debtor, if any)
                                                                   (If joint case, both spouses must sign.)

CERTIFICATION AND SIGNATURE OF NON-ATTORNEY BANKRUPTCY PETITION PREPARER (See 11 U.S.C. § 110)

I certify that I am a bankruptcy petition preparer as defined in 11 U.S.C. § 110, that I have prepared this document for compensation, and that I have provided the debtor with a copy of this document.

_____   _____
Printed or Typed Name of Bankruptcy Petition Preparer   Social Security Number

_____

_____
Address

Names and Social Security Numbers of all other individuals who prepared or assisted in preparing this document:

If more than one person prepared this document, attach additional signed sheets conforming to the appropriate Official Form for each person.

X_____   _____
  Signature of Bankruptcy Petition Preparer   Date

A bankruptcy petition preparer's failure to comply with the provisions of Title 11 and the Federal Rules of Bankruptcy Procedure may result in fines or imprisonment or both. 11 U.S.C. § 110; 18 U.S.C. § 156.

DECLARATION UNDER PENALTY OF PERJURY ON BEHALF OF CORPORATION OR PARTNERSHIP

I, the _____ [president or other officer or an authorized agent of the corporation or a member or an authorized agent of the partnership] of the _____ [corporation or partnership] named as debtor in this case, declare under penalty of perjury that I have read the foregoing summary and schedules, consisting of _____ sheets (total shown on summary page plus 1), and that they are true and correct to the best of my knowledge, information, and belief.

Date _____

                                                              Signature: _____

                                                                           _____
                                                                           [Print or type name of individual signing on behalf of debtor.]

[An individual signing on behalf of a partnership or corporation must indicate position or relationship to debtor.]
_____

Penalty for making a false statement or concealing property: Fine of up to $500,000 or imprisonment for up to 5 years or both. 18 U.S.C. § 152 and 3571.

Index